PETERSON'S

1999

Christian Colleges & Universities

Top Schools Serious About Scholarship, Faith, and Service

The Official Guide to Member Schools of the Coalition for Christian Colleges & Universities

PETERSON'S
Princeton, New Jersey

About Peterson's

Peterson's is the country's largest educational information/ communications company, providing the academic, consumer, and professional communities with books, software, and online services in support of lifelong education access and career choice. Well-known references include Peterson's annual guides to private schools, summer programs, colleges and universities, graduate and professional programs, financial aid, international study, adult learning, and career guidance. Peterson's Web site at petersons.com is the only comprehensive—and most heavily traveled—education resource on the Internet. The site carries all of Peterson's fully searchable major databases and includes financial aid sources, test-prep help, job postings, direct inquiry and application features, and specially created Virtual Campuses for every accredited academic institution and summer program in the U.S. and Canada that offers in-depth narratives, announcements, and multimedia features.

Visit Peterson's on the Internet at http://www.petersons.com

ISSN 1521-9070
ISBN 0-7689-0050-6

Printed in the United States of America

10 9 8 7 6 5 4 3 2 1

Contents

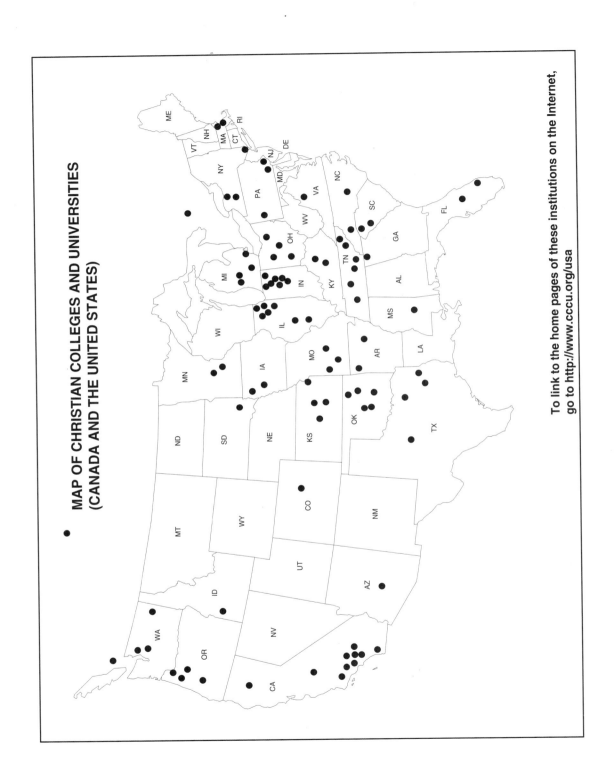

MAP OF CHRISTIAN COLLEGES AND UNIVERSITIES (CANADA AND THE UNITED STATES)

To link to the home pages of these institutions on the Internet, go to http://www.cccu.org/usa

iv

Institutions of the Coalition for Christian Colleges & Universities

Religious Affiliations

ASSEMBLIES OF GOD
Evangel University
Northwest College
Southern California College

BAPTIST DENOMINATIONS

American Baptist
Eastern College
Judson College
University of Sioux Falls

Baptist General Conference
Bethel College (MN)

General Association of Regular Baptist Churches
Cedarville College
Cornerstone College
Western Baptist College

Southern Baptist
California Baptist University
Campbell University
Campbellsville University
Dallas Baptist University
East Texas Baptist University
Grand Canyon University
Oklahoma Baptist University
Southwest Baptist University
Union University
Williams Baptist College

BRETHREN IN CHRIST
Messiah College

CHRISTIAN & MISSIONARY ALLIANCE
Nyack College
Simpson College

CHRISTIAN CHURCH/CHURCH OF CHRIST
Milligan College

CHURCH OF CHRIST
Abilene Christian University
Oklahoma Christian University

CHRISTIAN CHURCH (DISCIPLES OF CHRIST) AND
CHRISTIAN CHURCHES/CHURCHES OF
   CHRIST
Hope International University
Northwest Christian College

CHURCH OF GOD/ANDERSON
Anderson University
Warner Pacific College
Warner Southern College

CHURCH OF GOD/CLEVELAND
Lee University

CHURCH OF THE NAZARENE
Eastern Nazarene College
MidAmerica Nazarene University
Mount Vernon Nazarene College
Northwest Nazarene College
Olivet Nazarene University
Point Loma Nazarene University
Southern Nazarene University
Trevecca Nazarene University

CHURCH OF THE UNITED BRETHREN IN CHRIST

Huntingon College

EVANGELICAL COVENANT

North Park University

EVANGELICAL FREE CHURCH OF AMERICA

Trinity International University

EVANGELICAL FREE CHURCH

Trinity Western University

FELLOWSHIP OF GRACE BRETHREN CHURCHES

Grace College

FRIENDS DENOMINATIONS

Evangelical Friends Church, Eastern Region
Malone College

Friends
George Fox University

FREE METHODIST

Greenville College
Roberts Wesleyan College
Seattle Pacific University
Spring Arbor College

FUNDAMENTAL NONDENOMINATIONAL

The Master's College

MENNONITE DENOMINATIONS

General Conference Mennonite Church
Bethel College (KS)

Mennonite Brethren Church
Fresno Pacific University
Tabor College

Mennonite Church
Bluffton College

Eastern Mennonite University
Goshen College

MISSIONARY CHURCH

Bethel College (IN)

PRESBYTERIAN DENOMINATIONS

Associate Reformed Presbyterian
Erskine College

Presbyterian Church (USA)
Belhaven College
College of the Ozarks
King College
Montreat College
Sterling College
Whitworth College

Presbyterian Church in America
Covenant College

Reformed Presbyterian Church
Geneva College

REFORMED DENOMINATIONS

Christian Reformed Church
Calvin College
Dordt College

Reformed Church in America
Northwestern College (IA)

WESLEYAN CHURCH

Bartlesville Wesleyan College
Houghton College
Indiana Wesleyan University
Southern Wesleyan University

INTERDENOMINATIONAL/ NONDENOMINATIONAL

Asbury College
Azusa Pacific University
Biola University
Bryan College
Colorado Christian University

Gordon College
John Brown University
The King's University College
LeTourneau University
Northwestern College (MN)
Oral Roberts University
Palm Beach Atlantic College

Redeemer College
Taylor University
Trinity Christian College
Westmont College
Wheaton College
William Tyndale College

Education is More Than the Exchange of Knowledge

■ Choosing a college is one of life's most important decisions. It represents not only a significant financial investment, but also influences so much of who we become in all areas of life—our philosophy, values, intellectual and emotional preparedness for careers, long-term friendships, and a commitment to serving others.

The array of choices is overwhelming, even for students and families desiring a "Christian" college education. For example, some colleges are church-related only in the sense of being historically linked to a particular denomination. Then there are all the choices among locations, academic offerings, available financial aid, and more.

Of the 3,500 colleges and universities in the United States, only 650 maintain some tie to a specific church denomination or religious tradition. Among these, a smaller number are referred to as "Christ-centered." Ninety of these colleges and universities are members of the Coalition for Christian Colleges & Universities, an association of regionally accreditd four-year colleges and universities rooted in the liberal arts and professional studies. These are the institutions featured in this guide.

On the surface, most small colleges look a lot alike. They promise a strong academic program, varied co-curricular offerings, a pleasant campus, and a friendly faculty. What sets Christ-centered colleges apart is the way in which faith, learning, and life come together.

Faculty members play a key role in making Christian colleges and universities truly Christ-centered. Faculty members at Christian colleges are hired for their mature faith as well as their academic credentials. Classroom instruction is first-rate. Professors are not afraid to pose tough questions and challenge young scholars to think deeply about their faith. These professors are willing to reveal their own imperfections as humans and recognize the complexity even for Christians, freeing students to ask honest questions about anything. For many students, faculty members become much more than teachers— they are role models, mentors, and lifelong friends.

Academically

- Find all the advantages expected from a smaller, private college.
- Choose from more than 250 majors and 90 graduate programs.
- Be taught by real professors, not graduate students.
- Be sought after by graduate programs.
- Interact with challenging classmates.
- Expand your world through study-abroad experiences.

Spiritually

- Be strengthened and encouraged to live a vibrant Christian faith, equipping you to face life's challenges.
- Work with professors committed to their faith.

- Learn to witness God's hand in all subjects—from accounting to history to dance.
- Broaden your faith through student-led worship services, prayer, and Bible study groups.

Personally

- Be challenged to think critically
- Live in a community that values your character development as much as knowledge development.
- Actively seek out your gifts and God's purpose for your life.
- Take on leadership responsibilities through on-campus activities and outreach ministries.

Relationally

- Receive one-on-one attention from professors.

- Meet friends who share your views, understand what makes you tick, challenge you.
- Be matched to mentors in your academic field.

Professionally

- Be in demand. Major employers seek out CCCU graduates because of their competence and values.
- Stand beside alumni who are national leaders in medicine, science, business, law, religion, education, and many other fields.
- Build a powerful resume through excellent internships with recognized companies.
- Get connected through campus career centers.
- Be involved in a wide array of clubs and student-run organizations.

One Perspective: The Benefits of Christian Higher Education

by James C. Dobson, Ph.D.

■ You have much to think about and many education options. As you consider the array of choices before you, you should include one or more Christian colleges and universities—for the range and depth of their academic quality, their reasonable costs, and for their adherence to traditional Christian principles.

In an age in which higher education is increasingly dominated by "political correctness" and moral relativism, the real question is why you would want to attend any other kind of college.

Christian colleges are wonderful places to live and study—great places to learn, to grow, to prepare for graduate school or a career and to enrich your faith. And we should thank God that He works through them to nurture new generations of students to become responsible, mature, productive Christian members of our society.

———————

James C. Dobson is president of Focus on the Family in Colorado Springs, Colorado. Focus on the Family is a 21-year old, nonprofit organization dedicated to strengthening the home. The ministry produces several radio programs and magazines, as well as family-oriented books, films, videos, and audiocassettes, all from a Christian perspective.

(Reprinted with permission from Christian Colleges & Universities, an edition of Private Colleges & Universities, Carnegie Communications, Inc.)

Principles for Financing a Christian College Education

by Larry Burkett

■ The lasting value of a Christian education makes it one of the most important investments a parent can make. After all, who can put a price tag on your young adult's character being influenced by a biblical worldview? And how do you measure parents' peace of mind as their sons or daughters leave home for the first time, headed for the campus of a Christian college?

Since the cost of a college education—Christian or secular—has risen rapidly over the past decade, a more conscientious effort toward both savings and financial planning is required to help students through college. But meeting the challenge is not impossible, and it's never too late to start. You may find it helpful to have frank conversations with your student regarding mutual sacrifices that can be made in order to make ends meet. Of course, one of the greatest contributions the student can make is maintaining good grades in high school that could translate into scholarships or grants.

Over the years, I have had the opportunity to visit with hundreds of parents about financing their son or daughter's education. From those experiences, the following are principles that you may find helpful.

1. Explore possible support from your extended family, your home church, scholarships and grants, part-time work, co-op programs, and summer employment. Grandparents may desire to contribute to this critical period of their grandchildren's training.

2. Teach your child to live on a budget. A budget will help him or her track monthly expenses, plan for future bills, and limit excessive spending.

3. Contact the schools' financial aid officer early in the admissions process. Resources available today may evaporate by next month.

4. Investigate cost-reducing steps such as living at home and commuting to class, purchasing used textbooks, and preparing meals instead of eating out. If your son or daughter lives on campus, he or she may consider riding a bike instead of driving a car.

5. Make borrowing a last resort, not the first choice. Many college graduates find themselves disqualified from Christian ministry opportunities because of indebtedness, which also can burden a person when entering the workplace.

When it comes to the wisdom of investing in a Christian education, the apostle Paul said it succinctly in Galatians 6:7: "For whatever a man sows, this he will also reap." Providing a Christian education for your son or daughter will yield eternal dividends that cannot be measured in earthly terms.

Dr. Larry Burkett is president and founder of Christian Financial Concepts. Dr. Burkett has published 47 books on finances. His daily radio broadcasts, "Money Matters" and "How to Manage Your Money," are carried on over 1,000 outlets worldwide.

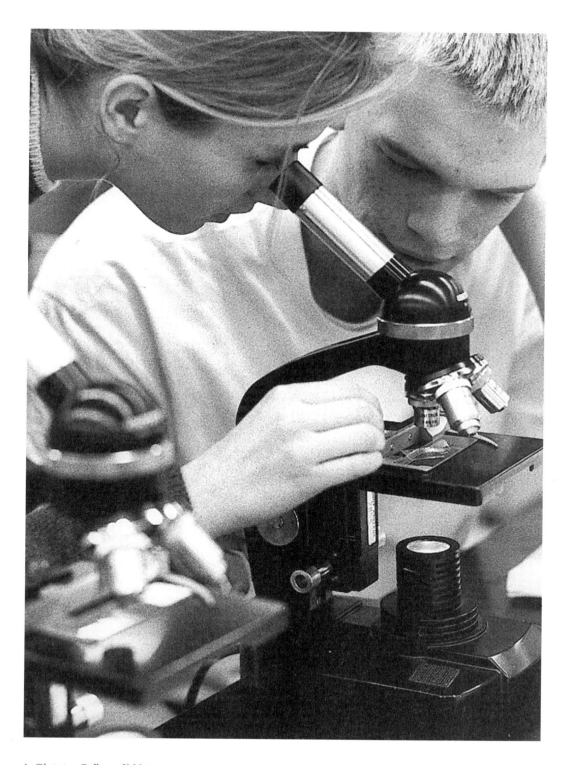

What is the Return to Expect from Your Investment?

Any private college is a big investment. However, many thousands of families have found a Christian college education well worth the price. Parents and alumni alike agree that it is impossible to place a dollar value on the lifelong benefits of a Christ-centered undergraduate experience.

It is no accident that most graduates of Christian colleges have little trouble finding a first job or gaining admittance to graduate or professional schools. These colleges and universities work hard at providing students with a broad array of resources and at helping alumni succeed in life after college. The individual stories of Christian college alumni illustrates their faithfulness to the cause of Christ. Evangelist Billy Graham; president of Youth for Christ/USA Roger Cross; former NFL running back Christian Okoye; U.S. Senator Dan Coates; and award-winning author of books for young people Katherine Paterson are all graduates of Christian colleges and universities. Their lives stand as a testimony to the lifelong impact and value of a Christian college education.

To assist families in meeting educational costs, most Christian colleges and universities provide generous aid packages to financially and/or academically qualified students. At many Christian colleges about two thirds of all students receive some form of institutional aid. Financial aid officers are eager to work with families to structure financial aid packages to meet individual situations. At some colleges, more aid is available for students who apply and are accepted early, so an early conversation with an admissions officer is wise. A majority of students receive a financial aid package of grants, work study and loans that each college determines for its students. Students may also be able to graduate in less time at a private Christian college than at other public universities. This will mean fewer years of tuition, room and board and an earlier transition into the job market or graduate studies.

We hope this guide helps you narrow your options to several Christian colleges and universities from which you can request additional information. You will find their admissions offices to be friendly and anxious to be of service to you. Nothing will help you make a better decision than visiting campus. When you are on campus, spend time visiting with students and professors to get a feel for what life is like at the college. Through the Internet you can learn more about Christian colleges at http://www.christiancolleges.org.

Understanding Cost and Financing a Christian College Education

by Ron Blue

■ If you are serious about attending a Christian college or university, you are probably already aware that your education is apt to cost significantly more than it would at a public state-supported school. What you may not know is that, in general, a Christian college costs less than the average private school, according to statistics provided annually to the federal government.

But actual numbers can become somewhat staggering when you stop to consider the total cost of going to college—public or private. These days, some experts tell young parents to set aside upwards of $500 per month to prepare for a toddler's future education! Gone are the days when you could realistically expect to totally "work your way" through school. Today, almost everyone has to borrow at least a little money by the time they finish their fourth year.

For most Christians, this prospect is unpleasant. For some it may even be unthinkable. Yet the Bible does not prohibit borrowing; rather, Scripture discourages it by pointing out the dangers associated with going into debt (see, for example, Proverbs 22:7). While we must keep these admonitions in mind, we must also recognize that there are some cases in which borrowing may make sense. One common example is purchasing a home. Another is financing a college education.

As I've counseled clients over the years about borrowing, I have asked them to keep two principles in mind. First, do not go into debt without a carefully considered repayment plan. Borrowing itself is not a sin—but as Psalm 37:21 warns, "The wicked borrow and do not repay." Instead of presuming on the future, parents and students must get together and map out a strategy whereby a college loan will be repaid on time.

Second, go into debt only when the return outweighs the cost. Borrowing money to pay for college is not like borrowing money to buy a car. A new car may make you feel good, but it does not add value to your life. By contrast, a college education increases your career options and your earning power. Whether from savings, earnings or borrowing, you will find the benefit and value you get from attending a Christian college or university will be well worth the cost.

Ron Blue is managing partner of Ronald Blue & Co. He is the author of six books on personal finance, including Master Your Money, *a best-seller first published in 1986 and now in its twenty-first printing,* The Master Your Money Workbook, *and* Taming the Money Monster. *He has appeared on numerous radio and television programs, including* Prime Time America *and* Moody Radio Open Line.

A World of Opportunity

■ The heart of the book is detailed profiles of the ninety-three member institutions of the Coalition for Christian Colleges & Universities, containing data supplied by each of them. Each one provides information on things like enrollment, academic offerings, costs, athletic programs, admission procedures, and financial aid. Familiarizing yourself with the format of the profiles will help you review them and compare schools easily.

A special note from each school appears at the beginning of each profile. These notes include information about the school's mission, special programs and curricular emphases, and campus life.

Off-Campus Opportunities Available to All Students

The Coalition makes available seven student programs around the world. These specialized programs are open to application from all students of member institutions. These programs provide opportunities for off-campus study in China, Washington, D.C., Costa Rica, Hollywood, Egypt, Russia and an honors program at the University of Oxford in England. The Coalition also offers summer programs at the University of Oxford and a journalism institute in Washington, DC. These programs allow you to make the world your classroom!

Christian College and University Graduates...

- gain a solid biblical foundation through coursework and community life.
- attend leading graduate schools.
- have developed marketable skills for the world of work.
- are prepared for life after college through valuable networks of professors and alumni.
- are involved in their communities through volunteer service.

How To Use This Book

It is likely you are reading this book because you are a student or care about a student who is thinking seriously about going to college and wondering how to select a school that will best allow you to get everything you want out of your college years. If you believe that a college with an active Christian orientation might be what you're looking for, this book can help you by providing information on ninety-three colleges and universities that combine academically challenging programs in the liberal arts and sciences with a Christ-centered campus life.

The Introduction: Choose a Christian College

The introductory essays can help you determine whether a Christian college or university is the best choice for you. It provides a rich overview of what you can expect from a Christian liberal arts institution, compared to other approaches to higher education.

The College Profiles

The heart of the book is detailed profiles of the ninety-three member campuses of the Coalition for Christian Colleges & Universities, each containing data supplied by the colleges and universities themselves. The profiles provide information on things like enrollment, academic offerings, costs, athletic programs, admission procedures, international admissions, and financial aid. Familiarizing yourself with the format of the profiles will help you review them and compare schools easily.

Programs Sponsored by the Coalition for Christian Colleges & Universities

The Coalition makes available seven semester-long student programs. These programs provide opportunities for off-campus study in Washington, D.C., Costa Rica, Hollywood, Egypt, Russia, the University of Oxford, and China. The Coalition also offers summer programs at the University of Oxford in England and a journalism institute in Washington, D.C. Consider these programs when choosing a college since they can not only round out your studies but also provide a rich setting for personal growth.

The Indexes

We've provided indexes at the back of the book to assist you in picking out the profiles you wish to review, based on three criteria: academic majors, intercollegiate athletics, and graduate programs. In addition, to make it easy to pick out the schools that are in a particular geographical area, we've provided a geographical listing and map, which appear at the front of the book immediately following the contents page.

About the Coalition for Christian Colleges & Universities

The Coalition for Christian Colleges & Universities, a Washington, D.C.-based association of ninety-three colleges and universities of the liberal arts and sciences, is North America's primary organization devoted specifically to serving and strengthening Christian higher education. Coalition institutions meet eight criteria for membership: an institutional commitment to the centrality of Jesus Christ to all campus life, integration of biblical faith with academics and student life, hiring practices that require a personal Christian commitment from each full-time faculty member and administrator, accreditation and primary orientation as a four-year liberal arts college, fund-raising activities consistent with the standards set by the Evangelical Council for Financial Accountability, a commitment to participating Coalition programs, cooperation

Sample Profile

Special Note from the College
In a brief statement, each institution presents key information about itself that prospective students should know.

Academics
Tells the types and level of degrees, special programs, most popular majors, number of faculty, percent with terminal degrees, and student-faculty ratio.

Campus Resources
Provides details about campus computerization and library resources.

The Statistical Snapshot
Provides a quick reference portrait of the school in numbers and percentages related to admission difficulty, aspects of the freshman class and student body, costs, financial aid, and outcomes for graduates.

GENEVA COLLEGE
Beaver Falls, Pennsylvania   http://www.geneva.edu/

Founded in 1848, Geneva College is one of the oldest evangelical Christian colleges in the nation, the second oldest in the Coalition of Christian Colleges & Universities. It offers an education that articulates the implications of Christ's sovereignty over all his creation. Geneva is one of 14 model sites chosen for the Coalition Racial and Ethnic Diversity Project. Students of color are encouraged to explore educational opportunities at Geneva. Majors include engineering, speech pathology, and cardiovascular technology. Through a cooperative program, students can combine degrees in aviation, air traffic control, or aerospace management with our business degree. All students complete a core program, which integrates courses in history, music, art, literature, and culture with biblical Christianity. Cocurricular activities include intercollegiate programs in all major sports, theater, choir, an FM radio station, and marching and concert bands. Although Geneva seeks students with a biblical world and life view, all students are welcome.

Academics
Geneva offers a Christian liberal arts and sciences curriculum and core academic program; a few graduate courses are open to undergraduates. It awards associate, bachelor's, and master's **degrees**. Challenging opportunities include advanced placement, accelerated degree programs, student-designed majors, tutorials, freshman honors college, an honors program, double majors, independent study, and a senior project. **Special programs** include cooperative education, internships, summer session for credit, off-campus study, and study-abroad.

The most popular **majors** include elementary education, business administration, and biology. A complete listing of majors at Geneva appears in the Majors Index beginning on page .

The **faculty** at Geneva has 60 full-time undergraduate teachers, 72% with terminal degrees. The student-faculty ratio is 18:1, and the average **class size** in required courses is 35.

Campus Resources
Students are not required to have a computer. 150 **computers** available in the computer center, computer labs, classrooms, the library, and the student center provide access to on-campus e-mail addresses, off-campus e-mail addresses, and the Internet. Staffed computer lab on campus provides training in the use of computers, software, and the Internet.

The 5 **libraries** have 158,045 books and 855 subscriptions.

Career Services
The career planning and placement office has 3 full-time staff members. Services include job fairs, resume preparation, interview workshops, resume referral, career/interest testing, career counseling, careers library, job bank (available online), and job interviews.

Campus Life
There are 25 active organizations on campus, including a drama/theater group and student-run newspaper and radio station. 80% of students participate in student government elections. No national or local **fraternities** or **sororities**. Student **safety services** include late night transport/escort service, 24-hour emergency telephone alarm devices, 24-hour patrols by trained security personnel, and electronically operated dormitory entrances.

Geneva is a member of the NAIA and NCCAA. **Intercollegiate sports** (some offering scholarships) include baseball (m), basketball (m,w), cross-country running (m,w), football (m), soccer (m,w), softball (w), tennis (m,w), track and field (m,w), volleyball (m,w).

International Students
For fall 1997, 63 international students applied, 32 were accepted, and 25 enrolled. Students can start in fall, spring, and summer. The **admissions test** required for entrance is TOEFL (minimum score: 550); recommended is SAT I or ACT. Application deadline is rolling. On-campus **housing** is guaranteed, also available during summer. Services include an international student adviser on campus.

Applying
Geneva requires an essay, SAT I or ACT, a high school transcript, recommendations, 4 years of high school English, 2 years of high school math, 1 year of high school science, 2 years of high school foreign language, 3 years of high school social studies, 4 years of high school academic electives, and a minimum high school GPA of 2.0, and in some cases an interview. It recommends a minimum high school GPA of 3.0. Application deadline: rolling admissions; 4/15 priority date for financial aid. Early and deferred entrance are possible. **Contact:** Mr. David Layton, Director of Admissions, 3200 College Avenue, Beaver Falls, PA 15010-3599, 724-847-6500 or toll-free 800-847-8255 (out-of-state); fax 724-847-6776; e-mail admissions@geneva.edu.

GETTING IN LAST YEAR	From 36 states and territories,	Average percent of need met 75%
875 applied	15 other countries	Average amount received per student $9000
54% were accepted	80% from Pennsylvania	
13% from top tenth of their h.s. class	53.2% women, 46.9% men	**AFTER FRESHMAN YEAR**
21% had SAT verbal scores over 600	2.3% international students	78% returned for sophomore year
22% had SAT math scores over 600		
65% had ACT scores over 24	**COSTS AND FINANCIAL INFORMATION**	**AFTER GRADUATION**
1 National Merit Scholars	1997–98 tuition and fees $11,534	15% pursued further study (6% arts and
5 valedictorians	1997–98 room and board $4750	sciences, 4% medicine, 3% education)
		74% had job offers within 6 months
THE STUDENT BODY		35 organizations recruited on campus
Total 1,956, of whom 1,763		
are undergraduates		

Career Services
Tells the extent of and kinds of career planning and placement help available to students and graduates.

Campus Life
Provides a picture of extracurricular life, student participation in student participation in student government, campus safety services, and intercollegiate athletic programs.

International Students
This tells the number of international students who applied, were accepted, and enrolled. Standardized tests and required scores, application deadline dates, the availability of housing and presence of special student services are noted.

Applying
This section shows all basic application requirements, deadlines for admission and financial aid applications, and the appropriate admissions contact name, postal address, phone, fax, and e-mail information.

with and support of other Coalition colleges, and responsible financial operation. The Coalition also includes a growing number of nonmember affiliates. Affiliate institutions may include institutions that do not meet member curriculum or hiring criteria, are not primarily four-year undergraduate colleges, or are outside North America.

To conduct searches on the 93 member institutions go to http://www.christiancolleges. org. For information on the Coalition for Christian Colleges & Universities at 329 Eighth Street NE, Washington, D.C., 20002; telephone 202-546-8713; e-mail coalition@cccu.org. Visit the Coalition Web site at http://www. christiancolleges.org.

Coalition for Christian Colleges & Universities College Profiles and Special Notes

■ This section contains detailed factual profiles of the member campuses of the Coalition for Christian Colleges & Universities, covering such items as background facts, enrollment figures, number of faculty members, academic programs, majors, expenses, financial aid, campus life, athletics, admission procedures, and whom to contact for more information. In addition, there is a special note from each college describing the institution's distinctive features.

The data in each of these profiles, collected from fall 1997 to spring 1998, come primarily from Peterson's Annual Survey of Undergraduate Institutions, which was sent to deans or admission officers at each institution.

ABILENE CHRISTIAN UNIVERSITY

Abilene, Texas

http://www.acu.edu/

Abilene Christian University emphasizes high quality academics in a distinctively Christian environment. Christian education at ACU is a total integration of faith and hands-on learning represented in every facet of campus life. Located about 180 miles west of Dallas, it is one of the largest private universities in the Southwest. The university offers 117 bachelor programs through its three colleges, Arts and Sciences, Biblical Studies, and Business Administration, and the School of Nursing. As a teaching institution, ACU emphasizes a dynamic personal relationship between professors and their students. Qualified faculty members teach underclassmen, and when professors do research, undergraduates work with them. On ACU's state-of-the-art campus, each student has many opportunities to become technologically proficient with easy access to about 400 computers during daytime and evening hours. Students have access to e-mail and the Internet through ACU's network and multiple labs on campus.

Academics

ACU offers an interdisciplinary curriculum and core academic program; fewer than half of graduate courses are open to undergraduates. It awards associate, bachelor's, master's, doctoral, and first professional **degrees**. Challenging opportunities include advanced placement, accelerated degree programs, student-designed majors, tutorials, freshman honors college, an honors program, double majors, independent study, and a senior project. **Special programs** include cooperative education, internships, summer session for credit, off-campus study, and study-abroad.

The most popular **majors** include biology, elementary education, and accounting. A complete listing of majors at ACU appears in the Majors Index beginning on page 141.

The **faculty** at ACU has 189 full-time graduate and undergraduate teachers, 76% with terminal degrees. The student-faculty ratio is 18:1, and the average **class size** in required courses is 30.

Campus Resources

Students are not required to have a computer. Purchase and/or lease options are available. Student rooms are linked to a campus network. 500 **computers** available in the computer center, computer labs, the learning resource center, learning labs, classrooms, the library, and dormitories provide access to on-campus e-mail addresses, off-campus e-mail addresses, and the Internet. Staffed computer labs on campus (open 24 hours a day) provide training in the use of computers, software, and the Internet.

The **library** has 471,699 books and 2,317 subscriptions.

Career Services

The career planning and placement office has 2 full-time, 1 part-time staff members. Services include job fairs, resume preparation, resume referral, career counseling, careers library, job bank, and job interviews.

Campus Life

There are 96 active organizations on campus, including a drama/theater group and student-run newspaper and radio station. 25% of students participate in student government elections. 21% of eligible men and 22% of eligible women are members of 16 local **social clubs.** Student **safety services** include late night transport/escort service, 24-hour emergency telephone alarm devices, and 24-hour patrols by trained security personnel.

ACU is a member of the NCAA (Division II). **Intercollegiate sports** (some offering scholarships) include baseball (m), basketball (m,w), cross-country running (m,w), football (m), golf (m), soccer (m,w), softball (w), tennis (m,w), track and field (m,w), volleyball (w).

International Students

For fall 1997, 200 international students applied, 114 were accepted, and 64 enrolled. Students can start in fall, spring, and summer. The **admissions test** required for entrance is TOEFL (minimum score: 525; minimum score for ESL admission: 400); recommended is SAT I or ACT. Application deadline is rolling. On-campus **housing** is guaranteed, also available during summer. Services include an international student adviser on campus.

Applying

ACU requires SAT I or ACT, a high school transcript, and 2 recommendations. It recommends an interview, 3 years of high school math and science, 2 years of high school foreign language, and a minimum high school GPA of 2.0. Application deadline: rolling admissions; 3/1 priority date for financial aid. **Contact:** Mr. Tim Johnston, Director of Admissions, ACU Box 29000, Abilene, TX 79699-9000, 915-674-2650 or toll-free 800-460-6228; e-mail info@admissions.acu.edu.

GETTING IN LAST YEAR
2,253 applied
89% were accepted
49% enrolled (978)
23% from top tenth of their h.s. class
30% had SAT verbal scores over 600
30% had SAT math scores over 600
43% had ACT scores over 24
12 National Merit Scholars
30 valedictorians

THE STUDENT BODY
Total 4,507, of whom 3,909
  are undergraduates

From 47 states and territories,
  57 other countries
73% from Texas
53.9% women, 46.1% men
4.8% international students

COSTS AND FINANCIAL INFORMATION
1997–98 tuition and fees $9180
1997–98 room and board $3810

Average percent of need met 68%
Average amount received per student $7448

AFTER FRESHMAN YEAR
72% returned for sophomore year
26% got a degree in 4 years
20% got a degree in 5 years
5% got a degree in 6 years

AFTER GRADUATION
25% pursued further study
75% had job offers within 6 months
130 organizations recruited on campus

ANDERSON UNIVERSITY

Anderson, Indiana

http://www.anderson.edu/

Anderson University is a community of Christian higher education where high-quality learning and Christian service come alive. Believing that scholarship and scholars should serve a purpose, Anderson University is a mission-minded school that offers students a strong liberal arts foundation on which to build career credentials. Business, computer science, education, music, religious studies, social work, and sociology are among the most popular of the 60 majors and programs offered. The Tri-S program (study, serve, and share) is probably most representative of the spirit of the University. Through this program, more than 500 students volunteer each year for 50 different cross-cultural work projects throughout the world. Bill and Gloria Gaither and Sandi Patti are a few of the nearly 25,000 loyal alumni who make up the University's international alumni association and whose strength is not only in their numbers but also in their belief.

Academics

Anderson University offers a liberal arts curriculum and core academic program. It awards associate, bachelor's, master's, doctoral, and first professional **degrees**. Challenging opportunities include advanced placement, accelerated degree programs, student-designed majors, tutorials, and a senior project. **Special programs** include cooperative education, internships, summer session for credit, off-campus study, and study-abroad.

The most popular **majors** include music, education, and business. A complete listing of majors at Anderson University appears in the Majors Index beginning on page 141. The **faculty** at Anderson University has 135 full-time graduate and undergraduate teachers, 75% with terminal degrees. The student-faculty ratio is 13:1, and the average **class size** in required courses is 27.

Campus Resources

Students are not required to have a computer. Student rooms are linked to a campus network. 130 **computers** available in the computer center, computer labs, the learning resource center, instructional materials center, classrooms, the library, and dormitories provide access to microcomputer software, on-campus e-mail addresses, off-campus e-mail addresses, and the Internet. Staffed computer lab on campus.

The **library** has 219,288 books and 958 subscriptions.

Career Services

The career planning and placement office has 3 full-time staff members. Services include job fairs, resume preparation, career/interest testing, career counseling, careers library, and job interviews.

Campus Life

There are 15 active organizations on campus, including a drama/theater group and student-run newspaper and radio station. 60% of students participate in student government elections. No national or local **fraternities** or **sororities**. Student **safety services** include 24-hour crimeline, late-night transport/escort service, 24-hour emergency telephone alarm devices, 24-hour patrols by trained security personnel, and student patrols.

Anderson University is a member of the NCAA (Division III). **Intercollegiate sports** include baseball (m), basketball (m,w), cross-country running (m,w), football (m), golf (m,w), soccer (m,w), softball (w), tennis (m,w), track and field (m,w), volleyball (w).

International Students

For fall 1997, 23 international students applied, 9 were accepted, and 6 enrolled. The **admissions test** required for entrance is TOEFL (minimum score: 550). Application deadline is 1/1. On-campus **housing** is guaranteed, also available during summer. Services include an international student adviser on campus.

Applying

Anderson University requires SAT I or ACT, a high school transcript, 2 recommendations, lifestyle statement, 4 years of high school English, 3 years of high school math, 2 years of high school science, 2 years of high school social studies, 2 years of high school history, and a minimum high school GPA of 2.0, and in some cases an interview. It recommends an essay, 3 years of high school science, 2 years of high school foreign language, and 3 years of high school social studies. Application deadline: 8/25; 3/1 priority date for financial aid. Early and deferred entrance are possible. **Contact:** Mr. Jim King, Director of Admissions, 1100 East Fifth Street, Anderson, IN 46012-3495, 765-641-4080 or toll-free 800-428-6414; fax 765-641-4091; e-mail info@anderson.edu.

GETTING IN LAST YEAR
1,373 applied
77% were accepted
44% enrolled (467)
25% from top tenth of their h.s. class
25% had SAT verbal scores over 600
27% had SAT math scores over 600
51% had ACT scores over 24
14 valedictorians

THE STUDENT BODY
Total 2,165, of whom 1,929
    are undergraduates

From 43 states and territories,
    14 other countries
63% from Indiana
59.7% women, 40.3% men
1.1% international students

COSTS AND FINANCIAL INFORMATION
1998–99 tuition and fees $13,360
1998–99 room and board $4330
Average percent of need met 95%

Average amount received per student $12,500

AFTER FRESHMAN YEAR
72% returned for sophomore year
27% got a degree in 4 years
15% got a degree in 5 years
3% got a degree in 6 years

AFTER GRADUATION
21% pursued further study
46 organizations recruited on campus

ASBURY COLLEGE
Wilmore, Kentucky

http://www.asbury.edu/

At Asbury College, students join in a century-long tradition of personal, spiritual, and professional excellence. Ranked seventh among liberal arts colleges in the South by *U.S. News & World Report* for 1999, Asbury offers programs ranging from accounting and broadcast communication to education and psychology. A leadership program complements outstanding academics and enables students to realize their full potential. Students come from approximately 43 states and 16 countries and live on a campus that features stately white columns and central Kentucky's rolling landscape. Lexington's educational, commercial, and cultural resources are within a 20-minute commute of Wilmore's relaxed, tree-lined streets.

Academics
Asbury College offers a Christian liberal arts curriculum and core academic program. It awards bachelor's **degrees**. Challenging opportunities include advanced placement, tutorials, double majors, and a senior project. **Special programs** include internships, summer session for credit, study-abroad, and Army and Air Force ROTC. A complete listing of majors at Asbury College appears in the Majors Index beginning on page 141.

The **faculty** at Asbury College has 85 full-time teachers, 75% with terminal degrees. The student-faculty ratio is 14:1, and the average **class size** in required courses is 30.

Campus Resources
Students are not required to have a computer. Student rooms are linked to a campus network. 290 **computers** available in the computer center, computer labs, the learning resource center, the library, and student rooms provide access to on-campus e-mail addresses, off-campus e-mail addresses, and the Internet. Staffed computer lab on campus provides training in the use of computers, software, and the Internet.

The **library** has 140,700 books and 620 subscriptions.

Career Services
The career planning and placement office has 1 full-time staff member. Services include job fairs, resume preparation, interview workshops, resume referral, career/interest testing, career counseling, careers library, job bank (available on line), and job interviews.

Campus Life
There are 30 active organizations on campus, including a drama/theater group and student-run newspaper and radio station. 40% of students participate in student government elections. No national or local **fraternities** or **sororities**. Student **safety services** include late-night security personnel, late-night transport/escort service, 24-hour emergency telephone alarm devices, and electronically operated dormitory entrances.

Asbury College is a member of the NAIA and NCCAA. **Intercollegiate sports** include baseball (m), basketball (m,w), cross-country running (m,w), soccer (m), softball (w), swimming and diving (m,w), tennis (m,w), volleyball (w).

International Students
For fall 1997, 32 international students applied, 20 were accepted, and 14 enrolled. Students can start in fall, spring, and summer. The **admissions test** required for entrance is TOEFL (minimum score: 550; minimum score for ESL admission: 550); recommended is ELS. Application deadline is 2/1. On-campus **housing** available during summer. Services include an international student adviser on campus.

Applying
Asbury College requires SAT I or ACT, a high school transcript, 3 recommendations, and a minimum high school GPA of 2.5, and in some cases an essay and an interview. It recommends SAT I, SAT II Subject Tests, 4 years of high school English, 3 years of high school math, 2 years of high school science, 2 years of high school foreign language, 1 year of high school social studies, 1 year of high school history, and 7 years of high school academic electives. Application deadline: rolling admissions; 3/1 priority date for financial aid. Early and deferred entrance are possible. **Contact:** Mr. Stan F. Wiggam, Dean of Admissions, 1 Macklem Drive, Wilmore, KY 40390, 606-858-3511 ext. 2142 or toll-free 800-888-1818; fax 606-858-3921; e-mail admissions@asbury.edu.

GETTING IN LAST YEAR
864 applied
89% were accepted
51% enrolled (395)
32% from top tenth of their h.s. class
34% had SAT verbal scores over 600
31% had SAT math scores over 600
52% had ACT scores over 24

THE STUDENT BODY
1,258 undergraduates

From 43 states and territories,
16 other countries
21% from Kentucky
57.6% women, 42.4% men
2% international students

COSTS AND FINANCIAL INFORMATION
1998–99 tuition and fees $12,020
1998–99 room and board $3390

Average percent of need met 87%
Average amount received per student $9630

AFTER FRESHMAN YEAR
73.4% returned for sophomore year
31% got a degree in 4 years
18% got a degree in 5 years
4% got a degree in 6 years

AZUSA PACIFIC UNIVERSITY

Azusa, California

http://www.apu.edu/

At APU, students participate in exceptional academic programs in 40 fields, dynamic leadership and music projects, innovative service opportunities, and on strong athletic teams. They train alongside Olympic athletes; gain acceptance to America's most prestigious graduate schools (Harvard, Stanford, Georgetown); participate in Bridges, a San Francisco outreach to homeless people and AIDS patients, and Walk-About, an intense, nine-day wilderness excursion that hones leadership skills and deepens faith; and minister in Haiti, Guatemala, Laos, Mexico, Romania, and Russia. Whether in the classroom, in athletics, or on the mission field, Azusa Pacific students learn that serving others is the cornerstone of effective leadership.

Academics

APU offers a core academic program. It awards bachelor's, master's, and doctoral **degrees**. Challenging opportunities include advanced placement, accelerated degree programs, an honors program, and a senior project. **Special programs** include cooperative education, internships, summer session for credit, study-abroad, and Army ROTC.

The most popular **majors** include liberal arts and studies, business administration, and nursing. A complete listing of majors at APU appears in the Majors Index beginning on page 141.

The **faculty** at APU has 190 full-time graduate and undergraduate teachers, 59% with terminal degrees. The student-faculty ratio is 15:1.

Campus Resources

Students are not required to have a computer. Purchase and/or lease options are available. 350 **computers** available in the computer center and the library provide access to the Internet. Staffed computer lab on campus provides training in the use of computers and software.

The 3 **libraries** have 147,377 books and 1,411 subscriptions.

Career Services

The career planning and placement office has 3 full-time, 3 part-time staff members. Services include job fairs, resume preparation, career counseling, careers library, and job interviews.

Campus Life

There are 14 active organizations on campus, including a drama/theater group and student-run newspaper. No national or local **fraternities** or **sororities**. Student **safety services** include late-night transport/escort service, 24-hour emergency telephone alarm devices, 24-hour patrols by trained security personnel, student patrols, and electronically operated dormitory entrances.

APU is a member of the NAIA. **Intercollegiate sports** (some offering scholarships) include baseball (m), basketball (m,w), cross-country running (m,w), football (m), golf (m), soccer (m,w), softball (w), tennis (m), track and field (m,w), volleyball (m,w).

International Students

For fall 1997, 121 international students applied, 50 were accepted, and 32 enrolled. Students can start in fall, spring, and summer. The **admissions test** required for entrance is TOEFL (minimum score: 550). Application deadline is 7/15. On-campus **housing** is guaranteed, also available during summer. Services include an international student adviser on campus.

Applying

APU requires an essay, SAT I or ACT, a high school transcript, and 2 recommendations, and in some cases an interview. Application deadline: 7/15; 8/1 for financial aid, with a 3/2 priority date. Deferred entrance is possible. **Contact:** Mrs. Deana Porterfield, Dean of Admissions, 901 East Alosta Avenue, PO Box 7000, Azusa, CA 91702-7000, 626-812-3016 or toll-free 800-TALK-APU; e-mail admissions@apu.edu.

GETTING IN LAST YEAR
1,941 applied
85% were accepted
34% enrolled (565)

THE STUDENT BODY
Total 5,069, of whom 2,595 are undergraduates

From 25 states and territories, 32 other countries
63.3% women, 36.7% men
4.8% international students

COSTS AND FINANCIAL INFORMATION
1997–98 tuition and fees $13,947
1997–98 room and board $4482

AFTER FRESHMAN YEAR
74% returned for sophomore year

AFTER GRADUATION
150 organizations recruited on campus

BARTLESVILLE WESLEYAN COLLEGE

Bartlesville, Oklahoma

http://www.bwc.edu/

Bartlesville Wesleyan College is a distinctive Christian college. The campus community strongly believes in providing a Christ-centered educational experience that will produce lifelong results. It is located in the south-central part of the United States, 45 miles north of suburban Tulsa. Bartlesville is a cosmopolitan city of 40,000 and is the world headquarters for Phillips Petroleum Company. Local cultural opportunities include a choral society, a civic ballet, a theater guild, a symphony orchestra, and an annual International OK Mozart festival. The focal point of the 27-acre campus is an elegant 60-year-old, 32-room, Spanish-style mansion overlooking a beautiful lake.

Academics

BWC offers a liberal arts curriculum and core academic program. It awards associate and bachelor's **degrees**. Challenging opportunities include advanced placement, student-designed majors, independent study, and a senior project. **Special programs** include internships, summer session for credit, off-campus study, and study-abroad.

The most popular **majors** include business administration, education, and behavioral sciences. A complete listing of majors at BWC appears in the Majors Index beginning on page 141.

The **faculty** at BWC has 34 full-time teachers, 44% with terminal degrees. The student-faculty ratio is 14:1.

Campus Resources

Students are not required to have a computer. Purchase and/or lease options are available. Student rooms are linked to a campus network. 30 **computers** available in the computer center, computer labs, the learning resource center, and the library provide access to on-campus e-mail addresses, off-campus e-mail addresses, and the Internet. Staffed computer lab on campus provides training in the use of computers, software, and the Internet.

The **library** has 124,722 books and 300 subscriptions.

Career Services

The career planning and placement office has 2 full-time, 3 part-time staff members. Services include resume preparation, career counseling, careers library, and job bank.

Campus Life

There are 10 active organizations on campus, including a drama/theater group and student-run newspaper. 80% of students participate in student government elections. No national or local **fraternities** or **sororities**. Student **safety services** include 24-hour emergency telephone alarm devices, 24-hour patrols by trained security personnel, and electronically operated dormitory entrances.

BWC is a member of the NAIA and NCCAA. **Intercollegiate sports** (some offering scholarships) include baseball (m), basketball (m,w), golf (m), soccer (m,w), softball (w), volleyball (w).

International Students

For fall 1997, 20 international students applied, 20 were accepted, and 14 enrolled. Students can start in fall, spring, and summer. The **admissions test** required for entrance is TOEFL (minimum score: 550; minimum score for ESL admission: 500); recommended is SAT I or ACT. Application deadline is 7/1. On-campus **housing** is guaranteed, also available during summer. Services include an international student adviser on campus.

Applying

BWC requires SAT I or ACT, a high school transcript, recommendations, 4 years of high school English, 2 years of high school math, 1 year of high school science, 2 years of high school history, and 6 years of high school academic electives. It recommends a minimum high school GPA of 2.0. Application deadline: rolling admissions. Early and deferred entrance are possible. **Contact:** Mr. Marty Carver, Enrollment Services Administrator, 2201 Silver Lake Road, Bartlesville, OK 74006-6299, 918-335-6219 or toll-free 800-GO-TO-BWC (in-state); fax 918-335-6229; e-mail admissions@bwc.edu.

GETTING IN LAST YEAR
30% from top tenth of their h.s. class
32% had SAT verbal scores over 600
19% had SAT math scores over 600
38% had ACT scores over 24
1 National Merit Scholars

THE STUDENT BODY
570 undergraduates

From 28 states and territories,
   12 other countries
54% from Oklahoma
64.6% women, 35.4% men
6.1% international students

COSTS AND FINANCIAL INFORMATION
1998–99 tuition and fees $8700
1998–99 room and board $3800

Average percent of need met 82%
Average amount received per student $14,100

AFTER FRESHMAN YEAR
70% returned for sophomore year

AFTER GRADUATION
10% pursued further study (6% theology, 2% arts and sciences, 1% business)

BELHAVEN COLLEGE
Jackson, Mississippi

Founded in 1883, Belhaven College is a four-year, coeducational Christian liberal arts college, serving students from across the state, the South, and the nation. The 42-acre campus features traditional Southern architecture and landscaping and is located within the historic Belhaven residential neighborhood of Jackson, Mississippi, the state's political, economic, and educational capital. The stated mission of Belhaven College is to prepare men and women to serve Christ Jesus in their lives, their careers, and in the world of ideas. To that end, the college offers an academic program that unifies faith and learning, and integrates the rigor of scholarship with the passion of Christian ministry.

Academics
Belhaven offers a core academic program. It awards bachelor's and master's **degrees**. Challenging opportunities include advanced placement, accelerated degree programs, tutorials, an honors program, double majors, independent study, and a senior project. **Special programs** include internships, summer session for credit, off-campus study, and study-abroad.

The most popular **majors** include business administration, computer science, education, and psychology. A complete listing of majors at Belhaven appears in the Majors Index beginning on page 141.

The **faculty** at Belhaven has 40 full-time graduate and undergraduate teachers, 90% with terminal degrees. The student-faculty ratio is 14:1, and the average **class size** in required courses is 22.

Campus Resources
Students are not required to have a computer. Purchase and/or lease options are available. 54 **computers** available in computer labs, career center, art department, dormitories, student rooms, and the library provide access to the Internet. Staffed computer lab on campus provides training in the use of computers, software, and the Internet.

The **library** has 97,208 books and 495 subscriptions.

Career Services
The career planning and placement office has 1 full-time, 1 part-time staff members. Services include job fairs, resume preparation, resume referral, career/interest testing, career counseling, careers library, job bank, and job interviews.

Campus Life
There are 24 active organizations on campus, including a drama/theater group and student-run newspaper. 29% of students participate in student government elections. 1% of eligible women are members of 1 local **sorority**. Student **safety services** include late-night transport/escort service, 24-hour emergency telephone alarm devices, 24-hour patrols by trained security personnel, and electronically operated dormitory entrances.

Belhaven is a member of the NAIA. **Intercollegiate sports** (all offering scholarships) include baseball (m), basketball (m,w), cross-country running (m,w), football (m), golf (m,w), soccer (m,w), softball (w), tennis (m,w), volleyball (w).

International Students
Students can start in fall, winter, spring, and summer. The **admissions tests** required for entrance are SAT I or ACT, TOEFL (minimum score: 500). Application deadline is rolling. On-campus **housing** is guaranteed, also available during summer.

Applying
Belhaven requires SAT I (930-960) or ACT (20), a high school transcript, 1 academic reference, a minimum high school GPA of 2.0, and 16 high school units to include: 4 units of English, 2 units of math, 1 unit of history, 1 unit of natural science, and 8 units of academic electives. Two units of high school foreign language are recommended. In some cases an essay and an interview are recommended. Application deadline: rolling admissions; 4/1 priority date for financial aid. Early and deferred entrance are possible. **Contact:** Ms. Lisa Greer, Director of Admissions, 1500 Peachtree Street, Jackson, MS 39202-1789, 601-968-5940 or toll-free 800-960-5940; fax 601-968-9998; e-mail admissions@belhaven.edu.

GETTING IN LAST YEAR
455 applied
90% were accepted
21% enrolled (88)

THE STUDENT BODY
Total 1,317, of whom 1,217
  are undergraduates
From 21 states and territories

85% from Mississippi
62.5% women, 37.5% men
.6% international students

COSTS AND FINANCIAL INFORMATION
1998–99 tuition and fees $9870
1998–99 room and board $3660
Average percent of need met 78%
Average amount received per student $8740

AFTER FRESHMAN YEAR
77% returned for sophomore year
17% got a degree in 4 years
4% got a degree in 5 years
2% got a degree in 6 years

AFTER GRADUATION
72% had job offers within 6 months
26 organizations recruited on campus

BETHEL COLLEGE
Mishawaka, Indiana

http://www.bethel-in.edu/

Bethel College is located in northern Indiana on a beautiful 60-acre wooded campus. Bethel is the College of the Missionary Church, an evangelical denomination with roots in Methodist and Mennonite traditions. Since its founding in 1947, the hallmark of the College has been an emphasis on excellent teaching and warm student-faculty relationships. Bethel College has a challenging and participatory environment: students work hard in the classroom, on the athletic field, in performance, and in ministry opportunities. Bethel is a college with a deep Christian commitment. There is an open and joyful emphasis on the Christian life. Chapel meets 3 times a week and is the center of the campus culture. "With Christ at the helm" is more than a motto—it is the purpose and intent of living and studying together.

Academics
Bethel offers a liberal arts curriculum and core academic program; a few graduate courses are open to undergraduates. It awards associate, bachelor's, and master's **degrees**. Challenging opportunities include advanced placement, accelerated degree programs, freshman honors college, an honors program, independent study, and a senior project. **Special programs** include internships, summer session for credit, off-campus study, study-abroad, and Air Force and Army ROTC.

The most popular **majors** include elementary education, nursing, and business. A complete listing of majors at Bethel appears in the Majors Index beginning on page 141.

The **faculty** at Bethel has 64 full-time undergraduate teachers, 70% with terminal degrees. The student-faculty ratio is 18:1, and the average **class size** in required courses is 30.

Campus Resources
Students are not required to have a computer. 50 **computers** available in the computer center, education resource center, and the library provide access to on-campus e-mail addresses, off-campus e-mail addresses, and the Internet. Staffed computer lab on campus provides training in the use of computers and software.

The **library** has 90,000 books and 4,000 subscriptions.

Career Services
The career planning and placement office has 1 full-time, 1 part-time staff members. Services include job fairs, resume preparation, resume referral, career counseling, careers library, job bank, and job interviews.

Campus Life
There are 23 active organizations on campus, including a drama/theater group and student-run newspaper and radio station. 40% of students participate in student government elections. No national or local **fraternities** or **sororities**. Student **safety services** include 24-hour patrols by trained security personnel, student patrols, and electronically operated dormitory entrances.

Bethel is a member of the NAIA and NCCAA. **Intercollegiate sports** (some offering scholarships) include baseball (m), basketball (m,w), cross-country running (m,w), golf (m), soccer (m,w), softball (w), tennis (m,w), track and field (m,w), volleyball (w).

International Students
For fall 1997, 24 international students applied, 15 were accepted, and 8 enrolled. Students can start in fall and spring. The **admissions test** required for entrance is TOEFL (minimum score: 540). Application deadline is 7/1. Services include an international student adviser on campus.

Applying
Bethel requires SAT I or ACT, a high school transcript, and 1 recommendation, and in some cases an essay. It recommends an interview, 4 years of high school English, 3 years of high school math and science, 2 years of high school foreign language, 2 years of high school social studies, 1 year of high school history, 2 years of high school academic electives, and a minimum high school GPA of 2.3. Application deadline: 8/1; 3/11 priority date for financial aid. Early and deferred entrance are possible.
Contact: Mr. Steve Matteson, Dean of Admissions, 1001 West McKinley Avenue, Mishawaka, IN 46545-5591, 219-257-3339 ext. 319 or toll-free 800-422-4101; fax 219-257-3326; e-mail admissions@bethel-in.edu.

GETTING IN LAST YEAR
467 applied
85% were accepted
58% enrolled (233)
24% from top tenth of their h.s. class
21% had SAT verbal scores over 600
27% had SAT math scores over 600
42% had ACT scores over 24
7 valedictorians

THE STUDENT BODY
Total 1,526, of whom 1,443 are undergraduates

From 27 states and territories, 13 other countries
78% from Indiana
66.6% women, 33.4% men
2.4% international students

COSTS AND FINANCIAL INFORMATION
1998–99 tuition and fees $11,850
1998–99 room and board $3750

Average percent of need met 80%
Average amount received per student $4100

AFTER FRESHMAN YEAR
78% returned for sophomore year

AFTER GRADUATION
10% pursued further study (4% business, 3% theology, 2% arts and sciences)
82% had job offers within 6 months
34 organizations recruited on campus

BETHEL COLLEGE

North Newton, Kansas

http://www.bethelks.edu/

Bethel College offers a high-quality educational environment unique in Kansas and rare throughout the nation. Bethel rests within a secure Mennonite tradition of religios and community values, yet opens the way for individual intellectual and spiritual discovery by stimulation inquiry, fostering discussion, and expecting excellence. The college welcomes into its small circle students of every religious and ethnic heritage, and nurtures their growth as whole persons. Bethel College opens doors by cultivating a global perspective, opportunities for far-ranging service and travel, and clear paths to professional careers, advanced study and a life rich in possibility.

Academics
Bethel offers a liberal arts curriculum and core academic program. It awards bachelor's **degrees**. Challenging opportunities include advanced placement, accelerated degree programs, student-designed majors, tutorials, double majors, independent study, and a senior project. **Special programs** include internships, summer session for credit, off-campus study, and study-abroad.

The most popular **majors** include nursing, education, and business administration. A complete listing of majors at Bethel appears in the Majors Index beginning on page 141.

The **faculty** at Bethel has 50 full-time teachers, 82% with terminal degrees. The student-faculty ratio is 12:1, and the average **class size** in required courses is 16.

Campus Resources
Students are not required to have a computer. 38 **computers** available in the computer center, computer labs, classrooms, and the library provide access to on-campus e-mail addresses, off-campus e-mail addresses, and the Internet. Staffed computer lab on campus provides training in the use of computers, software, and the Internet.

The 2 **libraries** have 127,300 books and 787 subscriptions.

Career Services
The career planning and placement office has 1 full-time staff member. Services include job fairs, resume preparation, interview workshops, resume referral, career/interest testing, career counseling, careers library, job bank, and job interviews.

Campus Life
There are 30 active organizations on campus, including a drama/theater group and student-run newspaper and radio station. 75% of students participate in student government elections. No national or local **fraternities** or **sororities**. Student **safety services** include community police patrols, late-night transport/escort service, 24-hour emergency telephone alarm devices, and student patrols.

Bethel is a member of the NAIA. **Intercollegiate sports** (some offering scholarships) include baseball (m), basketball (m,w), football (m), soccer (m,w), tennis (m,w), track and field (m,w), volleyball (w).

International Students
For fall 1997, 30 international students applied, 25 were accepted, and 7 enrolled. Students can start in fall and spring. The **admissions test** required for entrance is TOEFL (minimum score: 540). Application deadline is 4/1. On-campus **housing** is guaranteed. Services include an international student adviser on campus.

Applying
Bethel requires SAT I or ACT, a high school transcript, and a minimum high school GPA of 2.5, and in some cases an essay and 2 recommendations. It recommends an interview, 4 years of high school English, 3 years of high school math and science, 2 years of high school foreign language, and 3 years of high school social studies. Application deadline: 8/15; 3/1 priority date for financial aid. Deferred entrance is possible. **Contact:** Mr. Michael Lamb, Director of Admissions, 300 East 27th Street, North Newton, KS 67117, 316-283-2500 ext. 230 or toll-free 800-522-1887; fax 316-284-5286; e-mail admissions@bethelks.edu.

GETTING IN LAST YEAR
350 applied
92% were accepted
39% enrolled (124)
18% from top tenth of their h.s. class
8% had SAT verbal scores over 600
16% had SAT math scores over 600
51% had ACT scores over 24
2 National Merit Scholars
7 valedictorians

THE STUDENT BODY
610 undergraduates

From 31 states and territories,
  22 other countries
68% from Kansas
57.2% women, 42.8% men
4.4% international students

COSTS AND FINANCIAL INFORMATION
1997–98 tuition and fees $10,330
1997–98 room and board $4200
Average percent of need met 83%

Average amount received per student $11,021

AFTER FRESHMAN YEAR
61% returned for sophomore year
40% got a degree in 4 years
11% got a degree in 5 years

AFTER GRADUATION
15% pursued further study (8% arts and
  sciences, 3% medicine, 1% business)
52 organizations recruited on campus

BETHEL COLLEGE
St. Paul, Minnesota

http://www.bethel.edu/

No matter what your area of study, you will find Bethel's integration of faith and learning inspiring. Professors examine the connections between the physical sciences, business, literature, and the arts and historical Christianity. You will emerge not only a master of your discipline prepared to enter the marketplace but also with a deeper understanding and appreciation of your faith. That's what a Bethel education is all about.

Academics

Bethel offers a Christian liberal arts curriculum and core academic program. It awards associate, bachelor's, and master's **degrees**. Challenging opportunities include advanced placement, student-designed majors, freshman honors college, an honors program, double majors, independent study, and a senior project. **Special programs** include internships, summer session for credit, off-campus study, study-abroad, and Army, Navy, and Air Force ROTC.

The most popular **majors** include education, business, and biological sciences. A complete listing of majors at Bethel appears in the Majors Index beginning on page 141.

The **faculty** at Bethel has 125 full-time undergraduate teachers, 65% with terminal degrees. The student-faculty ratio is 16:1, and the average **class size** in required courses is 23.

Campus Resources

Students are not required to have a computer. Purchase and/or lease options are available. Student rooms are linked to a campus network. 305 **computers** available in the computer center, computer labs, the learning resource center, the library, dormitories, and student rooms provide access to on-campus e-mail addresses, off-campus e-mail addresses, and the Internet. Staffed computer lab on campus provides training in the use of computers, software, and the Internet.

The **library** has 136,429 books and 742 subscriptions.

Career Services

The career planning and placement office has 3 full-time, 1 part-time staff members. Services include job fairs, resume preparation, interview workshops, resume referral, career/interest testing, career counseling, careers library, and job interviews.

Campus Life

Active organizations on campus include a drama/theater group and student-run newspaper and radio station. No national or local **fraternities** or **sororities**. Student **safety services** include late-night transport/escort service, 24-hour emergency telephone alarm devices, 24-hour patrols by trained security personnel, student patrols, and electronically operated dormitory entrances.

Bethel is a member of the NCAA (Division III). **Intercollegiate sports** include baseball (m), basketball (m,w), cross-country running (m,w), football (m), golf (m), ice hockey (m), soccer (m,w), softball (w), tennis (m,w), track and field (m,w), volleyball (w).

International Students

Students can start in fall, winter, and spring. The **admissions test** required for entrance is TOEFL (minimum score: 525); recommended is SAT I or ACT. Application deadline is 8/1. On-campus **housing** available during summer. Services include an international student adviser on campus.

Applying

Bethel requires an essay, SAT I or ACT, PSAT, a high school transcript, and 2 recommendations, and in some cases an interview. It recommends an interview, 4 years of high school English, 3 years of high school math and science, 2 years of high school foreign language, and 4 years of high school social studies. Application deadline: rolling admissions; 4/1 priority application deadline, 4/15 priority date for financial aid. Early and deferred entrance are possible. **Contact:** Mr. John C. Lassen, Director of Admissions, 3900 Bethel Drive, St. Paul, MN 55112-6999, 651-638-6436 or toll-free 800-255-8706; e-mail bcoll-admit@bethel.edu.

GETTING IN LAST YEAR
31% from top tenth of their h.s. class
41% had SAT verbal scores over 600
42% had SAT math scores over 600

THE STUDENT BODY
Total 2,612, of whom 2,391 are undergraduates

From 38 states and territories
62% from Minnesota
62.4% women, 37.6% men

COSTS AND FINANCIAL INFORMATION
1998–99 tuition and fees $14,720
1998–99 room and board $5180

Average percent of need met 83%
Average amount received per student $11,475

AFTER FRESHMAN YEAR
81% returned for sophomore year

BIOLA UNIVERSITY
La Mirada, California

http://www.biola.edu/

Biola University's international reputation as a distinctive Christian institution is prominent. Of the 92 members of the Coalition of Christian Colleges & Universities, which require faculty members to be Christian, only 12 of those require that their students be Christian: Biola is one of those 12. The University has also been granted *U.S. News & World Report*'s highest ranking, that of a National University, and has been an ongoing member of the John Templeton Foundation Honor Roll for Character Building Colleges. Requiring 30 units of Bible, Biola's hallmark is a solid biblical foundation to prepare students for all the challenges of life.

Academics

Biola offers a core academic program; more than half of graduate courses are open to undergraduates. It awards bachelor's, master's, and doctoral **degrees**. Challenging opportunities include advanced placement, accelerated degree programs, tutorials, freshman honors college, an honors program, double majors, and a senior project. **Special programs** include cooperative education, internships, summer session for credit, off-campus study, study-abroad, and Army and Air Force ROTC.

The most popular **majors** include business administration, communication, and psychology. A complete listing of majors at Biola appears in the Majors Index beginning on page 141.

The **faculty** at Biola has 143 full-time graduate and undergraduate teachers, 66% with terminal degrees. The student-faculty ratio is 17:1.

Campus Resources

Students are not required to have a computer. Purchase and/or lease options are available. Student rooms are linked to a campus network. 60 **computers** available in the computer center, computer labs, and the library provide access to on-campus e-mail addresses, off-campus e-mail addresses, and the Internet. Staffed computer lab on campus provides training in the use of computers, software, and the Internet.

The **library** has 251,000 books and 1,188 subscriptions.

Career Services

The career planning and placement office has 1 full-time, 2 part-time staff members. Services include job fairs, resume preparation, resume referral, career/interest testing, career counseling, careers library, job bank, and job interviews.

Campus Life

There are 31 active organizations on campus, including a drama/theater group and student-run newspaper and radio station. No national or local **fraternities** or **sororities**. Student **safety services** include access gates to roads through the middle of campus, late-night transport/escort service, 24-hour emergency telephone alarm devices, 24-hour patrols by trained security personnel, and electronically operated dormitory entrances.

Biola is a member of the NAIA. **Intercollegiate sports** (some offering scholarships) include baseball (m), basketball (m,w), cross-country running (m,w), soccer (m,w), swimming and diving (m,w), tennis (m,w), track and field (m,w), volleyball (w).

International Students

Students can start in fall, spring, and summer. The **admissions test** required for entrance is TOEFL (minimum score: 500). Application deadline is 4/1. On-campus **housing** is guaranteed, also available during summer. Services include an international student adviser on campus.

Applying

Biola requires an essay, SAT I or ACT, a high school transcript, an interview, 2 recommendations, 3 years of high school English, 2 years of high school math, 1 year of high school science, 2 years of high school foreign language, 2 years of high school history, and 6 years of high school academic electives. It recommends 3 years of high school math and science, 4 years of high school foreign language, and a minimum high school GPA of 2.8. Application deadline: 6/1; 2/1 priority date for financial aid. Early and deferred entrance are possible. **Contact:** Mr. Greg Vaughan, Director of Enrollment Management, 13800 Biola Avenue, La Mirada, CA 90639-0001, 562-903-4727 or toll-free 800-652-4652; fax 562-903-4709; e-mail admissions@biola.edu.

GETTING IN LAST YEAR
1,654 applied
88% were accepted
44% enrolled (634)
35% had SAT verbal scores over 600
32% had SAT math scores over 600

THE STUDENT BODY
Total 3,257, of whom 2,153
   are undergraduates

From 35 states and territories,
   30 other countries
75% from California
60.3% women, 39.7% men
4.2% international students

COSTS AND FINANCIAL INFORMATION
1997–98 tuition and fees $14,286
1997–98 room and board $4902
Average percent of need met 78%

Average amount received per student $14,218

AFTER FRESHMAN YEAR
78% returned for sophomore year

AFTER GRADUATION
60% pursued further study
50% had job offers within 6 months
75 organizations recruited on campus

BLUFFTON COLLEGE
Bluffton, Ohio

http://www.bluffton.edu/

Unique to Bluffton College is a seriously Mennonite peace church orientation with genuine openness to students of all racial, ethnic, and denominational backgrounds, including international and American minority students. Within this widely diverse and deeply caring Christian community, faculty and staff members and students seek to apply the insights of both the academic disciplines and the Christian faith to the problems of offender ministries, racial discrimination, oppression and poverty, and violence and war. Academic integrity, broad social concern, a caring community, spiritual nurturing, and a beautiful natural environment are all distinguishing characteristics of Bluffton.

Academics
Bluffton College offers an interdisciplinary curriculum and core academic program. It awards bachelor's and master's **degrees**. Challenging opportunities include advanced placement, accelerated degree programs, student-designed majors, tutorials, freshman honors college, an honors program, and a senior project. **Special programs** include internships, summer session for credit, off-campus study, and study-abroad.

The most popular **majors** include business administration, education, and social sciences. A complete listing of majors at Bluffton College appears in the Majors Index beginning on page 141.

The **faculty** at Bluffton College has 65 full-time undergraduate teachers, 78% with terminal degrees. The student-faculty ratio is 15:1.

Campus Resources
Students are not required to have a computer. Student rooms are linked to a campus network. 61 **computers** available in the computer center, computer labs, and departmental labs provide access to on-campus e-mail addresses, off-campus e-mail addresses, and the Internet. Staffed computer lab on campus provides training in the use of computers and software.

The **library** has 146,000 books and 1,000 subscriptions.

Career Services
The career planning and placement office has 1 full-time staff member. Services include job fairs, resume preparation, resume referral, career counseling, careers library, and job interviews.

Campus Life
There are 30 active organizations on campus, including a drama/theater group and student-run newspaper and radio station. No national or local **fraternities** or **sororities**. Student **safety services** include night security guards and late-night transport/escort service.

Bluffton College is a member of the NCAA (Division III). **Intercollegiate sports** include baseball (m), basketball (m,w), cross-country running (m,w), football (m), golf (m), soccer (m,w), softball (w), tennis (m,w), track and field (m,w), volleyball (w).

International Students
For fall 1997, 34 international students applied, 15 were accepted, and 9 enrolled. The **admissions tests** required for entrance are SAT I, TOEFL (minimum score: 500); recommended is ACT. Application deadline is 5/1. On-campus **housing** is guaranteed, also available during summer. Services include an international student adviser on campus.

Applying
Bluffton College requires SAT I or ACT, a high school transcript, 2 recommendations, and rank in upper 50% of high school class or 2.3 high school GPA, and in some cases an essay. It recommends an interview, 4 years of high school English, 3 years of high school math and science, 3 years of high school foreign language, and 3 years of high school social studies. Application deadline: 5/31; 5/1 priority date for financial aid. Early and deferred entrance are possible. **Contact:** Mr. Michael Hieronimus, Dean of Admissions, 280 West College Avenue, Bluffton, OH 45817-1196, 419-358-3254 or toll-free 800-488-3257; fax 419-358-3232; e-mail admissions@bluffton.edu.

GETTING IN LAST YEAR
705 applied
87% were accepted
41% enrolled (251)
19% from top tenth of their h.s. class
10% had SAT verbal scores over 600
24% had SAT math scores over 600
36% had ACT scores over 24

THE STUDENT BODY
Total 1,053, of whom 1,028
  are undergraduates

From 13 states and territories,
  13 other countries
92% from Ohio
54.8% women, 45.2% men
2.2% international students

COSTS AND FINANCIAL INFORMATION
1998–99 tuition and fees $12,375
1998–99 room and board $5121
Average percent of need met 100%
Average amount received per student $11,113

AFTER FRESHMAN YEAR
78% returned for sophomore year
45% got a degree in 4 years
10% got a degree in 5 years
1% got a degree in 6 years

AFTER GRADUATION
9% pursued further study (3% arts and
  sciences, 1% law, 1% medicine)
74% had job offers within 6 months
200 organizations recruited on campus

BRYAN COLLEGE
Dayton, Tennessee

http://www.bryan.edu/

Bryan's motto, "Christ Above All," clarifies its priorities as a Christian liberal arts college. This is a lofty goal, but one that challenges the Bryan community to be exceptional and dynamic in faith and practice. The liberal arts curriculum exposes students to a broad scope of knowledge as well as key skills of communication, interpersonal relations, and critical thinking skills. A major thrust of a Bryan education is biblical world view. Students investigate various world view philosophies, then scrutinize them under the lens of Scripture. The scenic 120-acre campus is located 40 miles north of Chattanooga.

Academics
Bryan offers a liberal arts curriculum and core academic program. It awards associate and bachelor's **degrees**. Challenging opportunities include advanced placement, tutorials, an honors program, and a senior project. **Special programs** include internships, summer session for credit, and study-abroad.

The most popular **majors** include education, business administration, and biology. A complete listing of majors at Bryan appears in the Majors Index beginning on page 141. The **faculty** at Bryan has 30 full-time teachers, 83% with terminal degrees. The student-faculty ratio is 13:1, and the average **class size** in required courses is 30.

Campus Resources
Students are not required to have a computer. Student rooms are linked to a campus network. 74 **computers** available in the computer center, the learning resource center, the library, and dormitories provide access to on-campus e-mail addresses, off-campus e-mail addresses, and the Internet. Staffed computer lab on campus provides training in the use of computers, software, and the Internet.

The **library** has 83,000 books and 700 subscriptions.

Career Services
The career planning and placement office has 1 full-time staff member. Services include job fairs, resume preparation, resume referral, career counseling, careers library, job bank, and job interviews.

Campus Life
There are 7 active organizations on campus, including a drama/theater group and student-run newspaper. 65% of students participate in student government elections. No national or local **fraternities** or **sororities**. Student **safety services** include police patrols, late-night transport/escort service, student patrols, and electronically operated dormitory entrances.

Bryan is a member of the NAIA and NCCAA. **Intercollegiate sports** (some offering scholarships) include basketball (m,w), soccer (m,w), tennis (m,w), volleyball (w).

International Students
For fall 1997, 8 international students applied, 5 were accepted, and 3 enrolled. Students can start in fall and spring. The **admissions test** required for entrance is TOEFL (minimum score: 500). Application deadline is 5/1. On-campus **housing** is guaranteed, also available during summer. Services include an international student adviser on campus.

Applying
Bryan requires an essay, ACT, SAT I or ACT, a high school transcript, 3 recommendations, and a minimum high school GPA of 2.0, and in some cases an interview. It recommends SAT I. Application deadline: rolling admissions; 5/1 priority date for financial aid. Early and deferred entrance are possible. **Contact:** Mr. Thomas A. Shaw, Dean of Enrollment Management, PO Box 7000, Dayton, TN 37321-7000, 423-775-2041 or toll-free 800-277-9522; fax 423-775-7330; e-mail admiss@bryan.edu.

GETTING IN LAST YEAR
381 applied
79% were accepted
46% enrolled (139)
33% from top tenth of their h.s. class
32% had SAT verbal scores over 600
29% had SAT math scores over 600
51% had ACT scores over 24
4 valedictorians

THE STUDENT BODY
500 undergraduates
From 33 states and territories,
  10 other countries
55.4% women, 44.6% men
4% international students

COSTS AND FINANCIAL INFORMATION
1998–99 tuition and fees $10,400
1998–99 room and board $3950
Average percent of need met 84%
Average amount received per student $3480

AFTER FRESHMAN YEAR
71% returned for sophomore year

CALIFORNIA BAPTIST UNIVERSITY

Riverside, California

http://www.calbaptist.edu/

California Baptist University is located in southern California's Inland Empire, which is one of the most rapidly growing areas in the nation. Cal Baptist emphasizes a life of assisting others, whether in service-oriented careers such as counseling and teaching or in business, which is based on biblical principles. The University is diverse in its ethnicity, denominational affiliation, and the ages of its students, providing students with a global outlook in all areas of campus life. Cal Baptist, with offerings of twenty undergraduate majors and master's degrees in marriage, family, and child counseling; education; and business administration, provides students with a diverse and challenging academic program and the opportunity for active participation in experiential learning and development. At California Baptist University, knowledge is enhanced through personal experience.

Academics

Cal Baptist offers an interdisciplinary curriculum and core academic program; a few graduate courses are open to undergraduates. It awards bachelor's and master's **degrees**. Challenging opportunities include advanced placement, accelerated degree programs, tutorials, an honors program, double majors, independent study, and a senior project. **Special programs** include cooperative education, internships, summer session for credit, off-campus study, study-abroad, and Army and Air Force ROTC.

The most popular **majors** include business administration, psychology, and education. A complete listing of majors at Cal Baptist appears in the Majors Index beginning on page 141.

The **faculty** at Cal Baptist has 86 full-time graduate and undergraduate teachers, 75% with terminal degrees. The student-faculty ratio is 18:1, and the average **class size** in required courses is 16.

Campus Resources

Students are not required to have a computer. Purchase and/or lease options are available. 225 **computers** available in the computer center, computer labs, business administration department, education technology/information systems and graphic arts lab, and the library provide access to the Internet. Staffed computer lab on campus provides training in the use of computers, software, and the Internet.

The **library** has 85,900 books and 825 subscriptions.

Career Services

The career planning and placement office has 1 full-time, 1 part-time staff members. Services include job fairs, resume preparation, interview workshops, resume referral, career/interest testing, career counseling, careers library, job bank, job interviews, and software programs.

Campus Life

There are 14 active organizations on campus, including a drama/theater group and student-run newspaper. 41% of students participate in student government elections. No national or local **fraternities** or **sororities**. Student **safety services** include late-night transport/escort service, 24-hour emergency telephone alarm devices, 24-hour patrols by trained security personnel, student patrols, and electronically operated dormitory entrances.

Cal Baptist is a member of the NAIA. **Intercollegiate sports** (some offering scholarships) include baseball (m), basketball (m,w), cross-country running (m,w), golf (m), soccer (m,w), softball (w), swimming (m,w), tennis (m,w), track and field (m,w), volleyball (m,w), water polo (m,w).

International Students

For fall 1998, 36 international students applied, 25 were accepted, and 18 enrolled. Students can start in fall and spring. The **admissions test** required for entrance is TOEFL (minimum score: 520). Application deadline is 7/15. On-campus **housing** is guaranteed, also available during summer. Services include an international student adviser on campus.

Applying

Cal Baptist requires an essay, SAT I or ACT, a high school transcript, 2 recommendations, 4 years of high school English, 3 years of high school math, 2 years of high school science, 2 years of high school social studies, 1 year of high school history, and a minimum high school GPA of 2.5. It recommends an interview, 3 years of high school science, and 2 years of high school foreign language. Application deadline: rolling admissions; 3/2 priority date for financial aid. Early and deferred entrance are possible. **Contact:** Ms. Keri Overstreet, Director of Recruitment, 8432 Magnolia Avenue, Riverside, CA 92504-3206, 909-343-4212 or toll-free 877-228-8866; fax 909-343-4525.

GETTING IN LAST YEAR
624 applied
70% were accepted
79% enrolled (348)
26% from top tenth of their h.s. class
13% had SAT verbal scores over 600
13% had SAT math scores over 600
11 class presidents
8 valedictorians

THE STUDENT BODY
Total 2,009, of whom 1,675
  are undergraduates
From 33 states and territories,
  16 other countries
91% from California
58.2% women, 41.8% men
2.1% international students

COSTS AND FINANCIAL INFORMATION
1998–99 tuition and fees $9200

1998–99 room and board $4594
Average percent of need met 75%
Average amount received per student $5700

AFTER FRESHMAN YEAR
71% returned for sophomore year

AFTER GRADUATION
12 organizations recruited on campus

CALVIN COLLEGE

Grand Rapids, Michigan   *http://www.calvin.edu/*

Calvin College is one of the largest, oldest, and most respected of the Coalition schools. Calvin's modern 400-acre campus provides the setting for 4,000 students and 270 faculty members to explore a broad range of majors and programs. While awarding over half of its degrees in accredited professional programs such as education, engineering, nursing, and business, Calvin remains committed to a liberal arts approach to learning. Eager to become a partner with students in their Christian maturation, the College encourages students to make faithful and responsible decisions about how they will use their time and talents—without imposing an excessive list of rules and regulations.

Academics

Calvin offers a Christ-centered liberal arts curriculum and core academic program; fewer than half of graduate courses are open to undergraduates. It awards bachelor's and master's **degrees**. Challenging opportunities include advanced placement, student-designed majors, tutorials, academically-based service learning, an honors program, and a senior project. **Special programs** include cooperative education, internships, summer session for credit, off-campus study, and study-abroad.

The most popular **majors** include education, business administration, and English. A complete listing of majors at Calvin appears in the Majors Index beginning on page 141.

The **faculty** at Calvin has 270 full-time graduate and undergraduate teachers, 81% with terminal degrees. The student-faculty ratio is 17:1.

Campus Resources

Students are not required to have a computer. Purchase and/or lease options are available. 710 **computers** available in the computer center, computer labs, the research center, classrooms, the library, the student center, and dormitories provide access to on-campus e-mail addresses, off-campus e-mail addresses, and the Internet. Staffed computer lab on campus (open 24 hours a day) provides training in the use of computers and software.

The **library** has 700,000 books and 2,700 subscriptions.

Career Services

The career planning and placement office has 6 full-time, 3 part-time staff members. Services include job fairs, resume preparation, resume referral, career counseling, careers library, job bank, and job interviews.

Campus Life

There are 32 active organizations on campus, including a drama/theater group and student-run newspaper and radio station. No national or local **fraternities** or **sororities**. Student **safety services** include crime prevention programs, crime alert bulletins, late-night transport/escort service, 24-hour patrols by trained security personnel, and student patrols.

Calvin is a member of the NCAA (Division III). **Intercollegiate sports** include baseball (m), basketball (m,w), cross-country running (m,w), golf (m,w), ice hockey (m), lacrosse (m), soccer (m,w), softball (w), swimming and diving (m,w), tennis (m,w), track and field (m,w), volleyball (m,w).

International Students

For fall 1997, 144 international students applied, 131 were accepted, and 67 enrolled. The **admissions tests** required for entrance are TOEFL (minimum score: 550) and SAT I or ACT. Application deadline is 8/1. On-campus **housing** is guaranteed, also available during summer. Services include an international student adviser on campus.

Applying

Calvin requires application essays, SAT I or ACT, a high school transcript, 1 recommendation, and a minimum high school GPA of 2.5. It recommends an interview, 3 years of high school math and science, and 2 years of high school foreign language. Application deadline: rolling admissions; 2/15 priority date for financial aid. Early and deferred entrance are possible. **Contact:** Mr. Dale D. Kuiper, Director of Admissions, 3201 Burton Street, SE, Grand Rapids, MI 49546-4388, 616-957-6106 or toll-free 800-668-0122; e-mail admissions@calvin.edu.

GETTING IN LAST YEAR
1,973 applied
98% were accepted
55% enrolled (1,061)
38% from top tenth of their h.s. class
55% had SAT verbal scores over 600
53% had SAT math scores over 600
70% had ACT scores over 24
38 National Merit Scholars
38 valedictorians

THE STUDENT BODY
Total 4,071, of whom 4,029
  are undergraduates

From 47 states and territories,
  26 other countries
52% from Michigan
56.6% women, 43.4% men
7.9% international students

COSTS AND FINANCIAL INFORMATION
1998–99 tuition and fees $12,915
1998–99 room and board $4500
Average percent of need met 84%
Average amount received per student $9680

AFTER FRESHMAN YEAR
86% returned for sophomore year

48% got a degree in 4 years
16% got a degree in 5 years
3% got a degree in 6 years

AFTER GRADUATION
22% pursued further study (13% arts and
  sciences, 2% education, 2% law)
68% had job offers within 6 months
120 organizations recruited on campus

CAMPBELLSVILLE UNIVERSITY

Campbellsville, Kentucky

http://www.campbellsvil.edu/

Campbellsville University is a private, comprehensive, graduate/undergraduate, (Level III) coeducational university undergirded by a strong liberal arts component. Affiliated with the Kentucky Baptist Convention, Campbellsville is open to students of all denominations. The 60-acre campus is situated precisely in the center of Kentucky and is 1« hours from Louisville and Lexington and just 2 hours from Nashville. Enrollment has soared more than 106% in just the last 8 years. Programs recently added include Social Work, Marketing Management, Physics, Semester in London program, Women's soccer, and much more. Summer international studies opportunities are also available.

Academics

Campbellsville University offers a core academic program. It awards associate, bachelor's, and master's **degrees**. Challenging opportunities include advanced placement, accelerated degree programs, and an honors program. **Special programs** include internships, summer session for credit, and study-abroad.

The most popular **majors** include elementary education, business administration, and social sciences. A complete listing of majors at Campbellsville University appears in the Majors Index beginning on page 141.

The **faculty** at Campbellsville University has 55 full-time graduate and undergraduate teachers, 72% with terminal degrees. The student-faculty ratio is 16:1.

Campus Resources

Students are not required to have a computer. 120 **computers** available in the computer center, computer labs, the learning resource center, classrooms, the library, and dormitories provide access to on-campus e-mail addresses, off-campus e-mail addresses, and the Internet. Staffed computer lab on campus provides training in the use of computers, software, and the Internet.

The **library** has 108,000 books and 500 subscriptions.

Career Services

The career planning and placement office has 1 full-time, 1 part-time staff members. Services include job fairs, resume preparation, resume referral, career counseling, careers library, job bank, and job interviews.

Campus Life

There are 40 active organizations on campus, including a drama/theater group and student-run newspaper and radio station. 80% of students participate in student government elections. No national or local **fraternities** or **sororities**. Student **safety services** include late-night transport/escort service, 24-hour emergency telephone alarm devices, 24-hour patrols by trained security personnel, and student patrols.

Campbellsville University is a member of the NAIA. **Intercollegiate sports** (some offering scholarships) include baseball (m), basketball (m,w), cross-country running (m,w), football (m), golf (m,w), soccer (m,w), softball (w), swimming and diving (m,w), tennis (m,w), volleyball (w).

International Students

For fall 1997, 60 international students applied, 45 were accepted, and 45 enrolled. Students can start in fall, spring, and summer. The **admissions tests** required for entrance are SAT I or ACT, TOEFL (minimum score: 500; minimum score for ESL admission: 420). Application deadline is 6/1. On-campus **housing** is guaranteed, also available during summer. Services include an international student adviser on campus.

Applying

Campbellsville University requires SAT I or ACT, a high school transcript, and a minimum high school GPA of 2.0. It recommends an essay, an interview, recommendations, 4 years of high school English, 3 years of high school math, 4 years of high school science, 1 year of high school foreign language, 2 years of high school social studies, 1 year of high school history, 6 years of high school academic electives, and a minimum high school GPA of 3.0. Application deadline: rolling admissions; 3/1 priority date for financial aid. Deferred entrance is possible. **Contact:** Mr. R. Trent Argo, Director of Admissions, 1 University Drive, Campbellsville, KY 42718-2799, 502-789-5220 or toll-free 800-264-6014; fax 502-789-5071; e-mail admissions@ campbellsvil.edu.

GETTING IN LAST YEAR
835 applied
82% were accepted
30% from top tenth of their h.s. class
1 National Merit Scholars
8 class presidents
22 valedictorians

THE STUDENT BODY
Total 1,521, of whom 1,465
   are undergraduates

From 29 states and territories,
   23 other countries
89% from Kentucky
55.4% women, 44.6% men
3.1% international students

COSTS AND FINANCIAL INFORMATION
1997–98 tuition and fees $7302
1997–98 room and board $3440
Average percent of need met 80%

Average amount received per student $7976

AFTER FRESHMAN YEAR
78% returned for sophomore year

AFTER GRADUATION
48% pursued further study
60 organizations recruited on campus

CAMPBELL UNIVERSITY

Buies Creek, North Carolina

 *http://www.campbell.edu/*

Campbell University is a private liberal arts institution in southeastern North Carolina, born of a vision over 100 years ago—a vision that lives on today. Campbell's curriculum meets individual needs and interests and offers the range of majors that today's students expect from a high-quality institution, including preprofessional and professional studies. A comprehensive financial aid program helps families meet educational costs. The University has adapted to changing times and needs without losing sight of its heritage and mission to provide educational opportunities in a Christian environment.

Academics

Campbell offers a core academic program; a few graduate courses are open to undergraduates. It awards associate, bachelor's, master's, doctoral, and first professional **degrees**. Challenging opportunities include advanced placement, accelerated degree programs, tutorials, an honors program, double majors, independent study, and a senior project. **Special programs** include cooperative education, internships, summer session for credit, study-abroad, and Army ROTC.

The most popular **majors** include business administration, (pre)pharmacy, and mass communications. A complete listing of majors at Campbell appears in the Majors Index beginning on page 141.

The **faculty** at Campbell has 175 full-time graduate and undergraduate teachers, 85% with terminal degrees. The student-faculty ratio is 18:1, and the average **class size** in required courses is 25.

Campus Resources

Students are not required to have a computer. 250 **computers** available in the computer center, computer labs, departmental labs, classrooms, and the library provide access to the Internet. Staffed computer lab on campus provides training in the use of computers, software, and the Internet.

The 3 **libraries** have 186,000 books and 995 subscriptions.

Career Services

The career planning and placement office has 2 full-time staff members. Services include job fairs, resume preparation, resume referral, career counseling, careers library, and job interviews.

Campus Life

There are 40 active organizations on campus, including a drama/theater group and student-run newspaper and radio station. 72% of students participate in student government elections. No national or local **fraternities** or **sororities**. Student **safety services** include late-night transport/escort service, 24-hour emergency telephone alarm devices, 24-hour patrols by trained security personnel, and electronically operated dormitory entrances.

Campbell is a member of the NCAA (Division I). **Intercollegiate sports** (some offering scholarships) include baseball (m), basketball (m,w), cross-country running (m,w), golf (m,w), soccer (m,w), softball (w), tennis (m,w), track and field (m,w), volleyball (w), wrestling (m).

International Students

For fall 1998, 147 international students applied, 100 were accepted, and 43 enrolled. Students can start in fall. The **admissions test** required for entrance is TOEFL (minimum score: 500). Application deadline is 8/1. On-campus **housing** is guaranteed, also available during summer. Services include an international student adviser on campus.

Applying

Campbell requires SAT I or ACT, a high school transcript, 4 years of high school English, 3 years of high school math and science, 2 years of high school social studies, and a minimum high school GPA of 2.0, and in some cases 3 recommendations. It recommends an interview and 2 years of high school foreign language. Application deadline: rolling admissions; 3/15 priority date for financial aid. Early and deferred entrance are possible. **Contact:** Mr. Herbert V. Kerner Jr., Dean of Admissions, Financial Aid, and Veterans Affairs, PO Box 546, Buies Creek, NC 27506, 910-893-1291 or toll-free 800-334-4111 (out-of-state); fax 910-893-1288; e-mail satterfiel@mailcenter.campbell.edu.

GETTING IN LAST YEAR
1,922 applied
60% were accepted
53% enrolled (620)
20% from top tenth of their h.s. class
19% had SAT verbal scores over 600
20% had SAT math scores over 600

THE STUDENT BODY
Total 3,359, of whom 2,231 are undergraduates

From 50 states and territories,
44 other countries
63% from North Carolina
55.4% women, 44.6% men
8% international students

COSTS AND FINANCIAL INFORMATION
1998–99 tuition and fees $10,215
1998–99 room and board $3740
Average percent of need met 100%

Average amount received per student $17,309

AFTER FRESHMAN YEAR
85% returned for sophomore year

AFTER GRADUATION
24% pursued further study (9% business, 6% arts and sciences, 4% law)
80% had job offers within 6 months
20 organizations recruited on campus

CEDARVILLE COLLEGE

Cedarville, Ohio

http://www.cedarville.edu/

Cedarville College's mission is "to offer an education consistent with biblical truth." Commitment and achievement characterize this education. All students and faculty members testify to personal faith in Christ. A Bible minor complements every major. Relevant daily chapels encourage spiritual growth. Over 150 local and worldwide ministries provide avenues for outreach. Cedarville teams consistently finish among top universities in national academic competitions. National, regional, and local employers and graduate schools recruit students who pursue any of 90 academic programs. Cedarville's campuswide computer network has been recognized as one of the nation's top 2. Reasonable costs and financial aid make Cedarville affordable.

Academics

Cedarville offers a biblically-integrated comprehensive liberal arts curriculum and core academic program. It awards associate and bachelor's **degrees**. Challenging opportunities include advanced placement, accelerated degree programs, an honors program, double majors, and a senior project. **Special programs** include internships, summer session for credit, study-abroad, and Army and Air Force ROTC.

The most popular **majors** include elementary education, nursing, and biology. A complete listing of majors at Cedarville appears in the Majors Index beginning on page 141.

The **faculty** at Cedarville has 133 full-time teachers, 70% with terminal degrees. The student-faculty ratio is 16:1.

Campus Resources

Students are not required to have a computer. Student rooms are linked to a campus network. 1,500 **computers** available in the computer center, computer labs, academic buildings, classrooms, the library, dormitories, and student rooms provide access to software packages, on-campus e-mail addresses, off-campus e-mail addresses, and the Internet. Staffed computer lab on campus provides training in the use of computers, software, and the Internet.

The **library** has 132,061 books and 2,268 subscriptions.

Career Services

The career planning and placement office has 3 full-time staff members. Services include job fairs, resume preparation, interview workshops, resume referral, career/interest testing, career counseling, careers library, job bank (available on line), and job interviews.

Campus Life

There are 50 active organizations on campus, including a drama/theater group and student-run newspaper and radio station. No national or local **fraternities** or **sororities**. Student **safety services** include late-night transport/escort service, 24-hour emergency telephone alarm devices, 24-hour patrols by trained security personnel, and student patrols.

Cedarville is a member of the NAIA and NCCAA. **Intercollegiate sports** (some offering scholarships) include baseball (m), basketball (m,w), cross-country running (m,w), golf (m), soccer (m,w), softball (w), tennis (m,w), track and field (m,w), volleyball (w).

International Students

For fall 1997, 19 international students applied, 10 were accepted, and 5 enrolled. Students can start in fall, winter, spring, and summer. The **admissions tests** required for entrance are SAT I or ACT, TOEFL (minimum score: 550). Application deadline is rolling. On-campus **housing** is guaranteed, also available during summer. Services include an international student adviser on campus.

Applying

Cedarville requires an essay, SAT I or ACT, a high school transcript, 2 recommendations, and a minimum high school GPA of 3.0, and in some cases an interview. It recommends 4 years of high school English, 3 years of high school math and science, 2 years of high school foreign language, and 3 years of high school social studies. Application deadline: rolling admissions; 3/1 priority date for financial aid. Early and deferred entrance are possible.
Contact: Mr. Roscoe Smith, Director of Admissions, PO Box 601, Cedarville, OH 45314-0601, 937-766-7700 or toll-free 800-CEDARVILLE; fax 937-766-7575; e-mail admiss@cedarville.edu.

GETTING IN LAST YEAR
1,609 applied
82% were accepted
45% enrolled (589)
33% from top tenth of their h.s. class
43% had SAT verbal scores over 600
39% had SAT math scores over 600
66% had ACT scores over 24
8 National Merit Scholars
70 valedictorians

THE STUDENT BODY
2,559 undergraduates
From 49 states and territories,
   12 other countries
54% women, 46% men
.9% international students

COSTS AND FINANCIAL INFORMATION
1998–99 tuition and fees $10,074
1998–99 room and board $4716

Average percent of need met 42%
Average amount received per student $8752

AFTER FRESHMAN YEAR
80% returned for sophomore year

AFTER GRADUATION
10% pursued further study (3% theology, 2% law, 1% business)
93% had job offers within 6 months
115 organizations recruited on campus

COLLEGE OF THE OZARKS

Point Lookout, Missouri   *http://www.cofo.edu/*

Called "Hard Work U" by *The Wall Street Journal*, all students at this unique Missouri institution work, rather than pay tuition, for their education. This self-help philosophy is a long-standing tradition and affirms a no-nonsense approach to academics and character education. Students major in a variety of fields, but all must meet a demanding liberal arts core taught by capable faculty. The combination of high academic standards, the work ethic, a pervasive sense of history and values, and a Christian environment creates an atmosphere of high expectations and provides many opportunities for students.

Academics

C of O offers an interdisciplinary liberal arts curriculum and core academic program. It awards bachelor's **degrees**. Challenging opportunities include advanced placement, accelerated degree programs, student-designed majors, tutorials, an honors program, and a senior project. **Special programs** include cooperative education, internships, summer session for credit, study-abroad, and Army ROTC.

The most popular **majors** include education, business administration, and psychology. A complete listing of majors at C of O appears in the Majors Index beginning on page 141.

The **faculty** at C of O has 83 full-time teachers, 52% with terminal degrees. The student-faculty ratio is 14:1, and the average **class size** in required courses is 35.

Campus Resources

Students are not required to have a computer. Purchase and/or lease options are available. Student rooms are linked to a campus network. 80 **computers** available in the computer center, computer labs, the research center, the learning resource center, Center for Writing and Thinking, classrooms, and the library provide access to on-campus e-mail addresses, off-campus e-mail addresses, and the Internet. Staffed computer lab on campus provides training in the use of computers and software.

The 2 **libraries** have 111,750 books and 736 subscriptions.

Career Services

The career planning and placement office has 1 full-time, 6 part-time staff members. Services include job fairs, resume preparation, resume referral, career counseling, careers library, job bank, and job interviews.

Campus Life

There are 49 active organizations on campus, including a drama/theater group and student-run newspaper and radio station. 67% of students participate in student government elections. No national or local **fraternities** or **sororities**. Student **safety services** include front gate closed 1 a.m.—6 a.m., gate security 5:30 p.m.—1 a.m, 24-hour emergency telephone alarm devices, 24-hour patrols by trained security personnel, and electronically operated dormitory entrances.

C of O is a member of the NAIA. **Intercollegiate sports** (some offering scholarships) include baseball (m), basketball (m,w), volleyball (w).

International Students

For fall 1997, 1,500 international students applied, 5 were accepted, and 5 enrolled. The **admissions test** required for entrance is TOEFL (minimum score: 560). Application deadline is The **admissions test** required for entrance is TOEFL (minimum score: 560).

Applying

C of O requires SAT I or ACT, a high school transcript, 2 recommendations, and medical history, financial statement, and in some cases an interview. It recommends an essay, an interview, 3 years of high school math and science, 2 years of high school foreign language, and a minimum high school GPA of 2.0. Application deadline: rolling admissions; 3/15 priority date for financial aid. Early entrance is possible. **Contact:** Mrs. Janet Miller, Admissions Secretary, Point Lookout, MO 65726, 417-334-6411 ext. 4217 or toll-free 800-222-0525; fax 417-335-2618; e-mail admiss4@cofo.edu.

GETTING IN LAST YEAR
2,823 applied
14% were accepted
77% enrolled (306)
15% from top tenth of their h.s. class
38% had ACT scores over 24

THE STUDENT BODY
1,563 undergraduates
From 39 states and territories,
    22 other countries

67% from Missouri
55% women, 45% men
2.2% international students

COSTS AND FINANCIAL INFORMATION
1997–98 tuition and fees $150
1997–98 room and board $2200
Average percent of need met 81%
Average amount received per student $9650

AFTER FRESHMAN YEAR
69% returned for sophomore year

AFTER GRADUATION
12% pursued further study (7% arts and
    sciences, 2% business, 2% education)
94% had job offers within 6 months
354 organizations recruited on campus

COLORADO CHRISTIAN UNIVERSITY

Lakewood, Colorado

http://www.ccu.edu/

Colorado Christian University is located in suburban Denver, one of the most attractive, recreation-centered, major metropolitan regions in the nation. At the foot of the Rockies, the picturesque campus offers students solid academic preparation for opportunities requiring the spiritual, social, and technical skills to compete successfully in today's marketplaces. CCU has established a strong regional reputation for academic quality. The university's graduate, technical, and professional programs are widely recognized in the region for the success of their graduates. Music and theater ensemble opportunities provide interested students with excellent opportunities for participation at a variety of levels. As an NCAA Division II school, CCU stresses achievement and excellence in its athletic programs. On-campus housing is apartment-style living.

Academics

CCU offers a core academic program; a few graduate courses are open to undergraduates. It awards associate, bachelor's, and master's **degrees**. Challenging opportunities include advanced placement, accelerated degree programs, student-designed majors, tutorials, an honors program, double majors, and a senior project. **Special programs** include cooperative education, internships, summer session for credit, off-campus study, study-abroad, and Army and Air Force ROTC.

The most popular **majors** include business administration, information sciences/systems, and elementary education. A complete listing of majors at CCU appears in the Majors Index beginning on page 141.

The **faculty** at CCU has 48 full-time graduate and undergraduate teachers, 37% with terminal degrees. The student-faculty ratio is 17:1, and the average **class size** in required courses is 25.

Campus Resources

Students are not required to have a computer. Student rooms are linked to a campus network. 92 **computers** available in the computer center, computer labs, classrooms, the library, and student rooms provide access to on-campus e-mail addresses,

off-campus e-mail addresses, and the Internet. Staffed computer lab on campus provides training in the use of computers, software, and the Internet.

The **library** has 55,000 books and 1,800 subscriptions.

Career Services

The career planning and placement office has 1 full-time staff member. Services include resume preparation, career counseling, careers library, and job bank.

Campus Life

There are 20 active organizations on campus, including a drama/theater group and student-run newspaper. No national or local **fraternities** or **sororities**. Student **safety services** include 24-hour emergency telephone alarm devices and 24-hour patrols by trained security personnel.

CCU is a member of the NCAA (Division II). **Intercollegiate sports** (some offering scholarships) include basketball (m,w), cross-country running (m,w), golf (m), soccer (m,w), tennis (m,w), volleyball (w).

International Students

For fall 1997, 34 international students applied, 18 were accepted, and 15 enrolled. Students can start in fall, spring, and summer. The **admissions test** required for entrance is Michigan Test of English Language Proficiency; recommended is TOEFL. Application deadline is rolling. On-campus **housing** available during summer. Services include an international student adviser on campus.

Applying

CCU requires an essay, SAT I or ACT, a high school transcript, 2 recommendations, and a minimum high school GPA of 2.0, and in some cases an interview and 3 recommendations. It recommends 3 years of high school math and science. Application deadline: 8/15; 3/1 priority date for financial aid. Deferred entrance is possible. **Contact:** Ms. Rebecca Leavenworth, Admissions Office Manager, 180 South Garrison Street, Lakewood, CO 80226-7499, 303-202-0100 ext. 165 or toll-free 800-44-FAITH; fax 303-238-2191; e-mail admissions@ccu.edu.

GETTING IN LAST YEAR
621 applied
80% were accepted
42% enrolled (211)
21% had SAT verbal scores over 600
12% had SAT math scores over 600
31% had ACT scores over 24

1 National Merit Scholars

THE STUDENT BODY
Total 1,910, of whom 1,726
  are undergraduates
From 39 states and territories,
  33 other countries

52.4% women, 47.6% men

COSTS AND FINANCIAL INFORMATION
1997–98 tuition and fees $10,010
1997–98 room and board $4560
Average percent of need met 62%
Average amount received per student $4607

CORNERSTONE COLLEGE

Grand Rapids, Michigan *http://www.cornerstone.edu/*

Cornerstone College, formerly Grand Rapids Baptist College, is unique for its internships. While most colleges have internship programs for some majors, Cornerstone College requires and arranges a practical internship for every student in all of its majors. The school's location in a large metropolitan area makes it possible for each student to have high-quality on-the-job experience before graduation. A major aim of the internship program is to allow students the opportunity to put their Christianity into practice in real-world circumstances. This unique feature provides the student with excellent preparation for life and for work after graduation.

Academics

Cornerstone College offers an interdisciplinary curriculum and core academic program. It awards associate and bachelor's **degrees**. Challenging opportunities include advanced placement and an honors program. **Special programs** include internships, summer session for credit, off-campus study, study-abroad, and Army ROTC.

The most popular **majors** include business administration, biblical studies, and psychology. A complete listing of majors at Cornerstone College appears in the Majors Index beginning on page 141.

The **faculty** at Cornerstone College has 55 full-time teachers, 60% with terminal degrees. The student-faculty ratio is 17:1.

Campus Resources

Students are not required to have a computer. 168 **computers** available in the computer center, computer labs, the learning resource center, the library, and dormitories provide access to on-campus e-mail addresses, off-campus e-mail addresses, and the Internet. Staffed computer lab on campus provides training in the use of computers and software.

The **library** has 113,678 books and 803 subscriptions.

Career Services

The career planning and placement office has 3 full-time staff members. Services include job fairs, resume preparation, resume referral, career counseling, careers library, job bank, and job interviews.

Campus Life

Active organizations on campus include a drama/theater group and student-run newspaper. 75% of students participate in student government elections. No national or local **fraternities** or **sororities**. Student **safety services** include late-night transport/escort service, 24-hour emergency telephone alarm devices, 24-hour patrols by trained security personnel, and student patrols.

Cornerstone College is a member of the NAIA. **Intercollegiate sports** (some offering scholarships) include basketball (m,w), cross-country running (m,w), golf (m), soccer (m,w), softball (w), tennis (m), volleyball (w).

International Students

For fall 1997, 14 international students applied, 6 were accepted, and 4 enrolled. Students can start in fall and spring. The **admissions tests** required for entrance are SAT I or ACT, TOEFL (minimum score: 500). Application deadline is 7/1. On-campus **housing** is guaranteed, also available during summer. Services include an international student adviser on campus.

Applying

Cornerstone College requires an essay, SAT I or ACT, a high school transcript, 1 recommendation, and a minimum high school GPA of 2.25. It recommends an interview, 4 years of high school English, 3 years of high school math, 2 years of high school science, 2 years of high school foreign language, 2 years of high school social studies, 2 years of high school history, and 4 years of high school academic electives. Application deadline: rolling admissions; 3/21 priority date for financial aid. Early and deferred entrance are possible. **Contact:** Mr. Brent Rudin, Director of Enrollment Management, 1001 East Beltline Avenue, NE, Grand Rapids, MI 49525-5597, 616-222-1426 or toll-free 800-968-4722; fax 616-949-0875; e-mail admissions@cornerstone.edu.

GETTING IN LAST YEAR
624 applied
87% were accepted
57% enrolled (312)
15% from top tenth of their h.s. class
35% had ACT scores over 24
7 valedictorians

THE STUDENT BODY
1,160 undergraduates

From 27 states and territories,
 4 other countries
.7% international students

COSTS AND FINANCIAL INFORMATION
1998–99 tuition and fees $10,026
1998–99 room and board $4392
Average percent of need met 72%

Average amount received per student $8900

AFTER FRESHMAN YEAR
67% returned for sophomore year

AFTER GRADUATION
14% pursued further study
95% had job offers within 6 months
35 organizations recruited on campus

COVENANT COLLEGE

Lookout Mountain, Georgia

http://www.covenant.edu/

Covenant's primary goal is to provide an environment of academic excellence that encourages students to develop a Christian world view. A Covenant education produces skills and values that equip students to serve effectively and live responsibly in a changing world. Covenant is more than a safe enclave for Christian students. It requires a distinctive experience that motivates and enables its young men and women to make an impact on the world for Christ. Covenant must not conform to the selfish dullness of the world, but must promote a rigorous discipline that, applied to academics, produces learning and, applied to spiritual life, produces wisdom.

Academics

Covenant offers a broad-based liberal arts curriculum and core academic program. It awards associate, bachelor's, and master's **degrees** (master's degree in education only). Challenging opportunities include advanced placement, accelerated degree programs, tutorials, an honors program, and a senior project. **Special programs** include cooperative education, internships, summer session for credit, and study-abroad.

The most popular **majors** include elementary education, business administration, and history. A complete listing of majors at Covenant appears in the Majors Index beginning on page 141.

The **faculty** at Covenant has 48 full-time graduate and undergraduate teachers, 79% with terminal degrees. The student-faculty ratio is 15:1, and the average **class size** in required courses is 25.

Campus Resources

Students are not required to have a computer. Purchase and/or lease options are available. 75 **computers** available in the computer center, academic building, the library, and dormitories provide access to on-campus e-mail addresses, off-campus e-mail addresses, and the Internet. Staffed computer lab on campus.

The **library** has 76,600 books and 422 subscriptions.

Career Services

The career planning and placement office has 2 full-time staff members. Services include job fairs, resume preparation, resume referral, and career counseling.

Campus Life

There are 45 active organizations on campus, including a drama/theater group and student-run newspaper. 80% of students participate in student government elections. No national or local **fraternities** or **sororities**. Student **safety services** include night security guards.

Covenant is a member of the NAIA. **Intercollegiate sports** (some offering scholarships) include basketball (m,w), cross-country running (m,w), soccer (m,w), volleyball (w).

International Students

For fall 1997, 39 international students applied, 19 were accepted, and 10 enrolled. Students can start in fall and spring. The **admissions test** required for entrance is SAT I, ACT, or TOEFL. Application deadline is 3/1. On-campus **housing** is guaranteed. Services include an international student adviser on campus.

Applying

Covenant requires an essay, SAT I or ACT, a high school transcript, an interview, 2 recommendations, and a minimum high school GPA of 2.5. It recommends 4 years of high school English, 3 years of high school math, 2 years of high school science, 2 years of high school foreign language, 2 years of high school social studies, and 3 years of high school academic electives. Application deadline: rolling admissions; 3/31 priority date for financial aid. Early and deferred entrance are possible. **Contact:** Mr. Joe Stephens, Director of Admissions, 14049 Scenic Highway, Lookout Mountain, GA 30750, 706-820-1560 ext. 1643 or toll-free 800-926-8362; e-mail admissions@covenant.edu.

GETTING IN LAST YEAR
498 applied
83% were accepted
47% enrolled (195)
19% from top tenth of their h.s. class
49% had SAT verbal scores over 600
40% had SAT math scores over 600
66% had ACT scores over 24

THE STUDENT BODY
Total 945, of whom 884
  are undergraduates

From 44 states and territories,
  13 other countries
17% from Georgia
52% women, 48% men
2.1% international students

COSTS AND FINANCIAL INFORMATION
1998–99 tuition and fees $13,750
1998–99 room and board $4250

AFTER FRESHMAN YEAR
82% returned for sophomore year
40% got a degree in 4 years
6% got a degree in 5 years
3% got a degree in 6 years

AFTER GRADUATION
17 organizations recruited on campus

DALLAS BAPTIST UNIVERSITY

Dallas, Texas

http://www.dbu.edu/

Servant-leadership is at the heart of the Dallas Baptist University educational experience. The academic commitment to the integration of faith and learning, coupled with an attitude of humility and service, provides the foundation for the development of Christian leadership that will extend into the 21st century. DBU's mission is to develop servant-leaders who will impact the world for Christ in their chosen profession. The University relies heavily on the *Intercessory Prayer Ministry* and the prayers of 1,200 senior adults who pray daily for the University to accomplish this mission.

Academics

DBU offers a comprehensive liberal arts curriculum and core academic program; fewer than half of graduate courses are open to undergraduates. It awards associate, bachelor's, and master's **degrees**. Challenging opportunities include advanced placement, double majors, independent study, and a senior project. **Special programs** include internships, summer session for credit, off-campus study, study-abroad, and Army and Air Force ROTC.

The most popular **majors** include business administration, education, and music. A complete listing of majors at DBU appears in the Majors Index beginning on page 141.

The **faculty** at DBU has 72 full-time graduate and undergraduate teachers, 68% with terminal degrees. The student-faculty ratio is 18:1.

Campus Resources

Students are not required to have a computer. Student rooms are linked to a campus network. 100 **computers** available in the computer center provide access to on-campus e-mail addresses, off-campus e-mail addresses, and the Internet. Staffed computer lab on campus provides training in the use of software and the Internet.

The **library** has 117,725 books and 656 subscriptions.

Career Services

The career planning and placement office has 1 full-time, 1 part-time staff members. Services include job fairs, interview workshops, resume referral, career/interest testing, career counseling, careers library, and job bank.

Campus Life

There are 32 active organizations on campus, including a drama/theater group. DBU has 1 local **fraternity** and 1 local **sorority**. Student **safety services** include 24-hour emergency telephone alarm devices, 24-hour patrols by trained security personnel, and electronically operated dormitory entrances.

DBU is a member of the NAIA. **Intercollegiate sports** (some offering scholarships) include baseball (m), cross-country running (m,w), soccer (m,w), tennis (m,w), volleyball (w).

International Students

For fall 1997, 152 international students applied, 103 were accepted, and 65 enrolled. Students can start in fall, winter, spring, and summer. The **admissions test** required for entrance is TOEFL (minimum score: 525). Application deadline is rolling. On-campus **housing** available during summer. Services include an international student adviser on campus.

Applying

DBU requires an essay, SAT I or ACT, a high school transcript, and rank in upper 50% of high school class or 3.0 high school GPA. It recommends an interview, recommendations, and 3 years of high school math and science. Application deadline: rolling admissions; 3/15 priority date for financial aid. Early and deferred entrance are possible. **Contact:** Mr. Jeremy Dutschke, Director of Admissions, 3000 Mountain Creek Parkway, Dallas, TX 75211-9299, 214-333-5360; fax 214-333-5447; e-mail admiss@dbu.edu.

GETTING IN LAST YEAR
15% from top tenth of their h.s. class
21% had SAT verbal scores over 600
20% had SAT math scores over 600
2 valedictorians

THE STUDENT BODY
Total 3,493, of whom 2,695
  are undergraduates

From 21 states and territories,
  30 other countries
59.5% women, 40.5% men

COSTS AND FINANCIAL INFORMATION
1998–99 tuition and fees $8250
1998–99 room and board $3554
Average percent of need met 94%

Average amount received per student $9650

AFTER GRADUATION
10 organizations recruited on campus

DORDT COLLEGE

Sioux Center, Iowa

http://www.dordt.edu/

Dordt College does not adhere to the traditional distinctions between liberal arts and professional training. The College instead focuses on transmitting "serviceable insight," a biblically based understanding of both the structure of creation and the nature and demands of a wide range of vocations and professions. This is why the College has majors such as agriculture, business, and computer science; why there are accredited programs in social work and engineering; why opportunities for internships and off-campus study abound; and why every course at Dordt will challenge students to think about the real-world applications of their learning.

Academics

Dordt offers a core academic program. It awards associate, bachelor's, and master's **degrees**. Challenging opportunities include advanced placement, student-designed majors, tutorials, double majors, independent study, and a senior project. **Special programs** include internships, off-campus study, and study-abroad.

The most popular **majors** include education, business administration, and engineering. A complete listing of majors at Dordt appears in the Majors Index beginning on page 141.

The **faculty** at Dordt has 75 full-time undergraduate teachers, 70% with terminal degrees. The student-faculty ratio is 15:1, and the average **class size** in required courses is 40.

Campus Resources

Students are not required to have a computer. Student rooms are linked to a campus network. 150 **computers** available in the computer center, computer labs, the learning resource center, classrooms, the library, the student center, and dormitories provide access to on-campus e-mail addresses, off-campus e-mail addresses, and the Internet. Staffed computer lab on campus provides training in the use of computers, software, and the Internet.

The 2 **libraries** have 181,788 books and 719 subscriptions.

Career Services

The career planning and placement office has 2 full-time staff members. Services include job fairs, resume preparation, resume referral, career counseling, careers library, job bank, and job interviews.

Campus Life

There are 40 active organizations on campus, including a drama/theater group and student-run newspaper and radio station. 75% of students participate in student government elections. No national or local **fraternities** or **sororities**. Student **safety services** include late-night transport/escort service, 24-hour emergency telephone alarm devices, student patrols, and electronically operated dormitory entrances.

Dordt is a member of the NAIA. **Intercollegiate sports** (some offering scholarships) include basketball (m,w), cross-country running (m,w), golf (m), ice hockey (m), soccer (m,w), softball (w), tennis (m,w), track and field (m,w), volleyball (w).

International Students

For fall 1997, 125 international students applied, 50 were accepted, and 50 enrolled. Students can start in fall and spring. The **admissions tests** required for entrance are TOEFL (minimum score: 500; minimum score for ESL admission: 500), ELS; recommended is SAT I or ACT. Application deadline is 6/1. On-campus **housing** is guaranteed, also available during summer. Services include an international student adviser on campus.

Applying

Dordt requires SAT I or ACT, a high school transcript, 3 years of high school English, 2 years of high school math and science, 2 years of high school foreign language, 2 years of high school history, 6 years of high school academic electives, and a minimum high school GPA of 2.25, and in some cases an interview. It recommends 1 year of high school social studies. Application deadline: 8/1; 4/1 priority date for financial aid. Early and deferred entrance are possible. **Contact:** Mr. Quentin Van Essen, Executive Director of Admissions, 498 4th Avenue, NE, Sioux Center, IA 51250-1697, 712-722-6080 or toll-free 800-343-6738; fax 712-722-1967; e-mail admissions@dordt.edu.

GETTING IN LAST YEAR
905 applied
90% were accepted
48% enrolled (391)
16% from top tenth of their h.s. class
39% had SAT verbal scores over 600
38% had SAT math scores over 600
58% had ACT scores over 24

THE STUDENT BODY
1,301 undergraduates

From 34 states and territories,
    13 other countries
36% from Iowa
49.9% women, 50.1% men
13.3% international students

COSTS AND FINANCIAL INFORMATION
1997–98 tuition and fees $11,450
1997–98 room and board $3030
Average percent of need met 90%

Average amount received per student $10,900

AFTER FRESHMAN YEAR
88% returned for sophomore year

AFTER GRADUATION
13% pursued further study (6% arts and
    sciences, 2% business, 2% engineering)
97% had job offers within 6 months
50 organizations recruited on campus

EASTERN COLLEGE
St. Davids, Pennsylvania
http://www.eastern.edu/

Eastern College is known for its innovative academic programs, caring Christian community, commitment to social action, and exceptionally beautiful campus. Class sizes are kept small, and professors are both role models to their students and highly accomplished experts in their fields. In addition to integrating faith and learning, Eastern's creative academic programs encourage students to learn from many disciplines. The campus community is highly diverse, with a multiethnic student body that includes representatives from over 30 countries. A strong campus ministries program and Eastern's proximity to the city of Philadelphia provide many opportunities for Christian service. The life of the Eastern College community is firmly centered in Jesus Christ.

Academics
Eastern offers an interdisciplinary curriculum and core academic program; fewer than half of graduate courses are open to undergraduates. It awards associate, bachelor's, and master's **degrees**. Challenging opportunities include advanced placement, accelerated degree programs, student-designed majors, tutorials, an honors program, independent study, and a senior project. **Special programs** include internships, summer session for credit, off-campus study, study-abroad, and Army and Air Force ROTC. A complete listing of majors at Eastern appears in the Majors Index beginning on page 141.

The **faculty** at Eastern has 230 graduate and undergraduate teachers, 68% with terminal degrees. The student-faculty ratio is 15:1.

Campus Resources
Students are not required to have a computer. Student rooms are linked to a campus network. 57 **computers** available in computer labs, the library, dormitories, and student rooms provide access to on-campus e-mail addresses, off-campus e-mail addresses, and the Internet. Staffed computer lab on campus provides training in the use of computers, software, and the Internet.

The 2 **libraries** have 209,361 books and 1,205 subscriptions.

Career Services
The career planning and placement office has 2 part-time staff members. Services include job fairs, resume preparation, interview workshops, resume referral, career counseling, careers library, and job bank.

Campus Life
There are 43 active organizations on campus, including a drama/theater group and student-run newspaper and radio station. 30% of students participate in student government elections. No national or local **fraternities** or **sororities**. Student **safety services** include closed circuit TV monitors, late-night transport/escort service, 24-hour emergency telephone alarm devices, 24-hour patrols by trained security personnel, and electronically operated dormitory entrances.

Eastern is a member of the NCAA (Division III). **Intercollegiate sports** include baseball (m), basketball (m,w), cross-country running (w), field hockey (w), golf (m,w), lacrosse (m,w), soccer (m,w), softball (w), tennis (m,w), volleyball (m,w).

International Students
For fall 1997, 48 international students applied and 8 enrolled. Students can start in fall, winter, spring, and summer. The **admissions tests** required for entrance are SAT I or ACT, TOEFL (minimum score: 500), ELS (minimum score 109). Application deadline is rolling. On-campus **housing** is guaranteed. Services include an international student adviser on campus.

Applying
Eastern requires an essay, SAT I or ACT, a high school transcript, 1 recommendation, and a minimum high school GPA of 2.0. It recommends an interview and a minimum high school GPA of 3.0. Application deadline: rolling admissions. Early and deferred entrance are possible. **Contact:** Mr. Mark Seymour, Executive Director for Enrollment Management, 1300 Eagle Road, St. Davids, PA 19087-3696, 610-341-5967 or toll-free 800-452-0996 (in-state); fax 610-341-1723; e-mail ugadm@eastern.edu.

GETTING IN LAST YEAR
809 applied
51% were accepted
75% enrolled (308)
20% from top tenth of their h.s. class
33% had SAT verbal scores over 600
26% had SAT math scores over 600
8% had ACT scores over 24
9 National Merit Scholars

THE STUDENT BODY
Total 2,496, of whom 1,744 are undergraduates

From 36 states and territories, 19 other countries
67% from Pennsylvania
65.4% women, 34.6% men
1.9% international students

COSTS AND FINANCIAL INFORMATION
1998–99 tuition and fees $13,200
1998–99 room and board $5654
Average percent of need met 90%

Average amount received per student $13,728

AFTER FRESHMAN YEAR
76% returned for sophomore year
41% got a degree in 4 years
10% got a degree in 5 years
1% got a degree in 6 years

AFTER GRADUATION
18% pursued further study
83% had job offers within 6 months

EASTERN MENNONITE UNIVERSITY

Harrisonburg, Virginia

http://www.emu.edu/

EASTERN
MENNONITE
UNIVERSITY
Harrisonburg
VA 22802-8462

Eastern Mennonite (EMU), a private Christian university, provides a high-quality liberal arts education that emphasizes spiritual growth and cross-cultural awareness. EMU's Global Village curriculum prepares students to make a difference in a multicultural world. All students spend time in another culture stateside or overseas. The nurturing environment of EMU's student-oriented campus not only prepares students for a wide variety of careers, but also challenges students to answer Christ's call to a life of nonviolence, witness, service, and peacebuilding. All of this happens on a friendly campus community in the heart of the scenic Shenandoah Valley of Virginia.

Academics

EMU offers a global village curriculum and core academic program; a few graduate courses are open to undergraduates. It awards associate, bachelor's, master's, and first professional **degrees**. Challenging opportunities include advanced placement, student-designed majors, an honors program, independent study, and a senior project. **Special programs** include internships, summer session for credit, off-campus study, and study-abroad.

The most popular **majors** include education, biology, and nursing. A complete listing of majors at EMU appears in the Majors Index beginning on page 141.

The **faculty** at EMU has 78 full-time graduate and undergraduate teachers, 71% with terminal degrees. The student-faculty ratio is 13:1, and the average **class size** in required courses is 38.

Campus Resources

Students are not required to have a computer. Student rooms are linked to a campus network. 85 **computers** available in computer labs, the learning resource center, science center, and the library provide access to on-campus e-mail addresses, off-campus e-mail addresses, and the Internet. Staffed computer lab on campus provides training in the use of computers and software.

The **library** has 144,546 books and 1,135 subscriptions.

Career Services

The career planning and placement office has 1 full-time staff member. Services include job fairs, resume preparation, interview workshops, resume referral, career/interest testing, career counseling, careers library, job bank, and job interviews.

Campus Life

There are 26 active organizations on campus, including a drama/theater group and student-run newspaper and radio station. 25% of students participate in student government elections. No national or local **fraternities** or **sororities**. Student **safety services** include night watchman.

EMU is a member of the NCAA (Division III). **Intercollegiate sports** include baseball (m), basketball (m,w), cross-country running (m,w), field hockey (w), soccer (m,w), softball (w), tennis (m,w), track and field (m,w), volleyball (m,w).

International Students

For fall 1997, 37 international students applied, 25 were accepted, and 16 enrolled. Students can start in fall and spring. The **admissions test** required for entrance is TOEFL (minimum score: 550; minimum score for ESL admission: 350). Application deadline is 4/1. On-campus **housing** is guaranteed. Services include an international student adviser on campus.

Applying

EMU requires SAT I or ACT, a high school transcript, 1 recommendation, statement of commitment, and a minimum high school GPA of 2.0. It recommends an interview, 4 years of high school English, 3 years of high school math and science, 2 years of high school foreign language, 3 years of high school social studies, 1 year of high school history, and 6 years of high school academic electives. Application deadline: 8/1; 3/15 priority date for financial aid. Early and deferred entrance are possible. **Contact:** Ms. Ellen B. Miller, Director of Admissions, 1200 Park Road, Harrisonburg, VA 22802-2462, 540-432-4118 or toll-free 800-368-2665 (out-of-state); fax 540-432-4444; e-mail admiss@emu. edu.

GETTING IN LAST YEAR
574 applied
91% were accepted
48% enrolled (249)
20% from top tenth of their h.s. class
32% had SAT verbal scores over 600
26% had SAT math scores over 600
48% had ACT scores over 24
3 National Merit Scholars
13 valedictorians

THE STUDENT BODY
Total 1,225, of whom 1,013
  are undergraduates

From 37 states and territories,
  22 other countries
39% from Virginia
60.7% women, 39.3% men
5% international students

COSTS AND FINANCIAL INFORMATION
1998–99 tuition and fees $12,600
1998–99 room and board $4700

Average percent of need met 81%
Average amount received per student $10,296

AFTER FRESHMAN YEAR
73% returned for sophomore year
48% got a degree in 4 years
12% got a degree in 5 years
4% got a degree in 6 years

AFTER GRADUATION
10% pursued further study
76% had job offers within 6 months
12 organizations recruited on campus

EASTERN NAZARENE COLLEGE

Quincy, Massachusetts

http://www.enc.edu/

Eastern Nazarene College seeks Christian scholars who wish to pursue rigorous academic studies in a small-school, Christian-oriented setting. Located just 6 miles south of Boston, our students are able to culturally, academically, and socially benefit from the city's libraries, universities, conservatories, museums, historic sights, and churches. Sponsored by the Church of the Nazarene, ENC has over 30 denominations represented on campus. ENC seeks to develop in each person a Christian world view and to encourage each person to become God's creative and redemptive agent in today's world.

Academics

ENC offers a core academic program; a few graduate courses are open to undergraduates. It awards associate, bachelor's, and master's **degrees**. Challenging opportunities include advanced placement, accelerated degree programs, tutorials, and a senior project. **Special programs** include internships, summer session for credit, off-campus study, and study-abroad.

The most popular **majors** include business administration, education, and psychology. A complete listing of majors at ENC appears in the Majors Index beginning on page 141.

The **faculty** at ENC has 52 full-time undergraduate teachers, 57% with terminal degrees. The student-faculty ratio is 12:1, and the average **class size** in required courses is 45.

Campus Resources

Students are not required to have a computer. Purchase and/or lease options are available. Student rooms are linked to a campus network. 70 **computers** available in the computer center, the learning resource center, the library, and dormitories provide access to on-campus e-mail addresses, off-campus e-mail addresses, and the Internet. Staffed computer lab on campus provides training in the use of computers and software.

The **library** has 126,000 books and 602 subscriptions.

Career Services

The career planning and placement office has 1 full-time, 1 part-time staff members. Services include resume preparation, career counseling, and careers library.

Campus Life

Active organizations on campus include a drama/theater group and student-run newspaper and radio station. No national or local **fraternities** or **sororities**. Student **safety services** include late-night transport/escort service, 24-hour emergency telephone alarm devices, 24-hour patrols by trained security personnel, and electronically operated dormitory entrances.

ENC is a member of the NCAA (Division III). **Intercollegiate sports** include baseball (m), basketball (m,w), cross-country running (m,w), lacrosse (m), soccer (m,w), softball (w), tennis (m,w), volleyball (m,w).

International Students

The **admissions test** required for entrance is TOEFL (minimum score: 500); recommended is SAT I or ACT. Application deadline is 6/1. On-campus **housing** is guaranteed. Services include an international student adviser on campus.

Applying

ENC requires SAT I or ACT, a high school transcript, and 3 recommendations. It recommends an essay, an interview, 3 years of high school math and science, and 2 years of high school foreign language. Application deadline: rolling admissions; 3/1 priority date for financial aid. Early and deferred entrance are possible. **Contact:** Mr. Keith Conant, Director of Admissions, 23 East Elm Avenue, Quincy, MA 02170-2999, 617-745-3868; fax 617-745-3490; e-mail admissions@enc.edu.

GETTING IN LAST YEAR
18% from top tenth of their h.s. class
25% had SAT verbal scores over 600
17% had SAT math scores over 600
8 valedictorians

THE STUDENT BODY
Total 1,508, of whom 1,363
  are undergraduates

From 27 states and territories,
  26 other countries
56.7% women, 43.3% men

COSTS AND FINANCIAL INFORMATION
1997–98 tuition and fees $11,440

1997–98 room and board $3975
Average percent of need met 80%

AFTER FRESHMAN YEAR
67% returned for sophomore year

EAST TEXAS BAPTIST UNIVERSITY

Marshall, Texas

http://www.etbu.edu/

East Texas Baptist University is a coeducational institution operated in association with the Baptist General Convention of Texas. The University is committed to fiscal soundness and Christian stewardship and to providing and maintaining an environment conducive to learning. East Texas Baptist University serves students of varied ages and with diverse social, geographic, economic, cultural, and religious backgrounds. We seek students who demonstrate a potential for success in our supportive and challenging environment, and we employ faculty members who are dedicated to teaching, scholarship, advising, and the principles of the Christian faith. Our purpose is the development of intellectual inquiry, social consciousness, wellness, and Christian character, for we believe that these endeavors prepare students to accept the obligations and opportunities of the age in which they live to serve humanity and the Kingdom of God. We affirm that the liberal arts form the surest foundation for education and that the Christian faith provides the surest foundation for life. Our primary focus is baccalaureate studies in the humanities, natural and social sciences, fine arts, and various professional areas; we also offer graduate study in selected disciplines. As a Christian University, we are committed to the integration of academic discipline and personal faith in the pursuit of truth.

Academics

ETBU offers no core academic program; a few graduate courses are open to undergraduates. It awards associate, bachelor's, and master's **degrees**. Challenging opportunities include advanced placement, accelerated degree programs, tutorials, an honors program, double majors, independent study, and a senior project. **Special programs** include internships, summer session for credit, off-campus study, study-abroad, and Army ROTC. A complete listing of majors at ETBU appears in the Majors Index beginning on page 141.

The **faculty** at ETBU has 62 full-time graduate and undergraduate teachers, 61% with terminal degrees. The student-faculty ratio is 16:1.

Campus Resources

Students are not required to have a computer. Purchase and/or lease options are available. Student rooms are linked to a campus network. 106 **computers** available in the computer center,

computer labs, the learning resource center, and the library provide access to on-campus e-mail addresses and the Internet. Staffed computer lab on campus provides training in the use of computers, software, and the Internet.

The **library** has 110,983 books and 615 subscriptions.

Career Services

The career planning and placement office has 1 full-time, 2 part-time staff members. Services include job fairs, resume preparation, career/interest testing, career counseling, careers library, and job bank.

Campus Life

Active organizations on campus include a drama/theater group and student-run newspaper. 30% of students participate in student government elections. 5% of eligible men and 2% of eligible women are members of 1 local **fraternity** and 1 local **sorority**. Student **safety services** include 24-hour emergency telephone alarm devices and electronically operated dormitory entrances.

ETBU is a member of the NAIA. **Intercollegiate sports** (some offering scholarships) include baseball (m), basketball (m,w), soccer (m,w), softball (w), tennis (w), volleyball (w).

International Students

For fall 1997, 25 international students applied, 25 were accepted, and 18 enrolled. Students can start in fall, winter, spring, and summer. The **admissions tests** required for entrance are ACT, TOEFL (minimum score: 500). Application deadline is rolling. On-campus **housing** is guaranteed, also available during summer. Services include an international student adviser on campus.

Applying

ETBU requires an essay, ACT, SAT I or ACT, a high school transcript, 4 years of high school English, 2 years of high school math and science, 2 years of high school social studies, 6 years of high school academic electives, and a minimum high school GPA of 2.0, and in some cases an interview. It recommends ACT, 4 years of high school math, 3 years of high school science, and 9 years of high school academic electives. Application deadline: rolling admissions; 6/1 priority date for financial aid. Early entrance is possible. **Contact:** Mr. David Howard, Director of Admissions, 1209 North Grove, Marshall, TX 75670-1498, 903-935-7963 ext. 225 or toll-free 800-804-3828; fax 903-938-1705; e-mail mbender@etbu.edu.

GETTING IN LAST YEAR
26% from top tenth of their h.s. class
38% had ACT scores over 24

THE STUDENT BODY
Total 1,292, of whom 1,269
  are undergraduates
From 22 states and territories,
  26 other countries

86% from Texas
58.8% women, 41.2% men
3.6% international students

COSTS AND FINANCIAL INFORMATION
1997–98 tuition and fees $6750
1997–98 room and board $3098
Average amount received per student $6000

AFTER FRESHMAN YEAR
61% returned for sophomore year
20% got a degree in 4 years
11% got a degree in 5 years
5% got a degree in 6 years

AFTER GRADUATION
117 organizations recruited on campus

ERSKINE COLLEGE
Due West, South Carolina

http://www.erskine.edu/

Why is the whole academic village that is Erkskine College called a neighborhood? A group of Erskine students, up late in their dorm studying together for an important chemistry exam the next day, were having trouble with one particular concept. After trying to work through the problem together, the group decided, after midnight, to call for help. Awakened by this request, a chemistry professor mat the students in the science hall, where he worked with them until they understood. For 160 years, Erskine College has been committed 24 hours a day to an atmosphere of leading-edge learning in a Christian environment. It is a traditional commitment to students in the Erskine "neighborhood" that extends beyond the classroom.

Academics
Erskine offers a liberal arts curriculum and core academic program. It awards bachelor's **degrees**. Challenging opportunities include advanced placement, accelerated degree programs, tutorials, and a senior project. **Special programs** include internships, summer session for credit, off-campus study, and study-abroad.

The most popular **majors** include biology, business administration, and chemistry. A complete listing of majors at Erskine appears in the Majors Index beginning on page 141.

The **faculty** at Erskine has 41 full-time teachers, 83% with terminal degrees. The student-faculty ratio is 12:1, and the average **class size** in required courses is 20.

Campus Resources
Students are not required to have a computer. Purchase and/or lease options are available. Student rooms are linked to a campus network. 96 **computers** available in the computer center, computer labs, classrooms, and the library provide access to on-campus e-mail addresses, off-campus e-mail addresses, and the Internet. Staffed computer lab on campus (open 24 hours a day) provides training in the use of computers and software.

The **library** has 198,767 books and 808 subscriptions.

Career Services
The career planning and placement office has 1 full-time, 1 part-time staff members. Services include job fairs, resume preparation, resume referral, career counseling, careers library, job bank, and job interviews.

Campus Life
There are 34 active organizations on campus, including a drama/theater group and student-run newspaper and radio station. 60% of students participate in student government elections. 30% of eligible men and 35% of eligible women are members of 3 local **fraternities**, 3 local **sororities**, and 2 Little Sisters. Student **safety services** include late-night transport/escort service, 24-hour patrols by trained security personnel, and electronically operated dormitory entrances.

Erskine is a member of the NCAA (Division II). **Intercollegiate sports** (some offering scholarships) include baseball (m), basketball (m,w), cross-country running (m,w), equestrian sports (m,w), soccer (m,w), softball (w), tennis (m,w).

International Students
For fall 1997, 3 international students applied, 3 were accepted, and 2 enrolled. Students can start in fall, winter, spring, and summer. The **admissions test** required for entrance is TOEFL (minimum score: 550); recommended is SAT I or ACT. Application deadline is 6/30. On-campus **housing** is guaranteed, also available during summer. Services include an international student adviser on campus.

Applying
Erskine requires SAT I or ACT, a high school transcript, 1 recommendation, 4 years of high school English, and 2 years of high school math, and in some cases an essay, SAT II Subject Tests, and an interview. It recommends an interview, 4 years of high school math and science, 2 years of high school foreign language, and 3 years of high school social studies. Application deadline: rolling admissions; 5/1 priority date for financial aid. Deferred entrance is possible. **Contact:** Mr. Jeff Craft, Director of Admissions, PO Box 176, Due West, SC 29639, 864-379-8830 or toll-free 800-241-8721; fax 864-379-8759; e-mail admissions@erskine.edu.

GETTING IN LAST YEAR
550 applied
88% were accepted
44% from top tenth of their h.s. class
34% had SAT verbal scores over 600
37% had SAT math scores over 600
1 National Merit Scholars
6 class presidents
8 valedictorians

THE STUDENT BODY
477 undergraduates

From 9 states and territories,
 5 other countries
77% from South Carolina
58.3% women, 41.7% men
1% international students

COSTS AND FINANCIAL INFORMATION
1997–98 tuition and fees $13,902
1997–98 room and board $4760
Average percent of need met 94%
Average amount received per student $13,154

AFTER FRESHMAN YEAR
82% returned for sophomore year
79% got a degree in 4 years
17% got a degree in 5 years
1% got a degree in 6 years

AFTER GRADUATION
24% pursued further study (18% arts and
 sciences, 2% law, 2% theology)
75.2% had job offers within 6 months
41 organizations recruited on campus

EVANGEL UNIVERSITY
Springfield, Missouri

http://www.evangel.edu/

Evangel University, the national Assemblies of God university of arts, sciences, and professions, offers more than 40 academic programs that are intended to prepare students for today's professional fields. The centerpiece of the campus is a new 72,000-square foot academic building, featuring state-of-the-art classrooms and computer labs plus an entire floor dedicated to science and technology. Evangel's theme, "Christ is Lord," touches every aspect of campus life— spiritual, intellectual, social, and physical. It is a residential college—75% of its students live on campus in modern residence halls—and draws from all 50 states and several foreign countries. Springfield, Missouri, is a medium-sized city with a low crime rate and ample employment opportunities. Located in the heart of the Ozark Mountains' recreational haven, Evangel is close to numerous lakes, parks, and the highly acclaimed Branson entertainment area.

Academics
Evangel University offers a core academic program. It awards associate, bachelor's, and master's **degrees**. Challenging opportunities include advanced placement and a senior project. **Special programs** include summer session for credit, study-abroad, and Army ROTC.

The most popular **majors** include business administration, education, and mass communications. A complete listing of majors at Evangel University appears in the Majors Index beginning on page 141.

The **faculty** at Evangel University has 90 full-time teachers, 50% with terminal degrees. The student-faculty ratio is 17:1.

Campus Resources
Students are not required to have a computer. 121 **computers** available in the computer center, computer labs, the learning resource center, the library, and dormitories. Staffed computer lab on campus provides training in the use of computers and software.

The **library** has 96,000 books and 750 subscriptions.

Career Services
The career planning and placement office has 2 full-time staff members. Services include resume preparation, interview workshops, resume referral, career/interest testing, career counseling, careers library, job bank, and job interviews.

Campus Life
Active organizations on campus include a drama/theater group and student-run newspaper and radio station. 67% of students participate in student government elections. No national or local **fraternities** or **sororities**. Student **safety services** include late-night transport/escort service, 24-hour emergency telephone alarm devices, 24-hour patrols by trained security personnel, student patrols, and electronically operated dormitory entrances.

Evangel College is a member of the NAIA. **Intercollegiate sports** (some offering scholarships) include baseball (m), basketball (m,w), cross-country running (m,w), football (m), golf (m,w), softball (w), track and field (m,w), volleyball (w).

International Students
For fall 1997, 14 international students applied, 12 were accepted, and 7 enrolled. Students can start in fall and spring. The **admissions tests** required for entrance are SAT I or ACT, TOEFL (minimum score: 490). Application deadline is 6/1. On-campus **housing** is guaranteed. Services include an international student adviser on campus.

Applying
Evangel University requires SAT I or ACT, a high school transcript, 3 years of high school English, 2 years of high school math, 3 years of high school science, and 2 years of high school social studies. It recommends 3 years of high school math and a minimum high school GPA of 2.0. Application deadline: 8/15; 4/1 priority date for financial aid. Deferred entrance is possible. **Contact:** Mr. David I. Schoolfield, Director of Enrollment Management, 1111 North Glenstone, Springfield, MO 65802-2191, 417-865-2811 ext. 7202 or toll-free 800-382-6435 (in-state); fax 417-865-9599; e-mail admissions@mail4.evangel.edu.

GETTING IN LAST YEAR
736 applied
88% were accepted
65% enrolled (422)
19% from top tenth of their h.s. class
38% had ACT scores over 24
12 valedictorians

THE STUDENT BODY
1,616 undergraduates
From 49 states and territories,
 17 other countries
40% from Missouri
56.4% women, 43.6% men
1.9% international students

COSTS AND FINANCIAL INFORMATION
1998–99 tuition and fees $8850
1998–99 room and board $3550

AFTER FRESHMAN YEAR
76% returned for sophomore year

FRESNO PACIFIC UNIVERSITY

Fresno, California   *http://www.fresno.edu/*

Fresno Pacific has been regularly ranked as one of the 10 best regional liberal arts colleges in the West by *U.S. News & World Report's* "America's Best Colleges." The tree-covered campus is located in the heart of the vast agricultural valley of central California, an hour's drive from the College's retreat center in the High Sierras and 2 hours from Pacific Ocean beaches. Pacific's academic program features a unique core sequence in Christian thinking as well as practical Christian service and professional internships. At Fresno Pacific, special emphasis is placed upon faculty-student mentoring, developing responsible personal freedom, and building strong Christian community. Prospective students should visit campus and meet faculty members and students. People make the difference at Fresno Pacific College.

Academics

Fresno Pacific offers a core academic program; fewer than half of graduate courses are open to undergraduates. It awards associate, bachelor's, and master's **degrees**. Challenging opportunities include advanced placement, student-designed majors, double majors, and a senior project. **Special programs** include internships, summer session for credit, off-campus study, and study-abroad.

The most popular **majors** include business administration, liberal arts and studies, and social sciences. A complete listing of majors at Fresno Pacific appears in the Majors Index beginning on page 141.

The **faculty** at Fresno Pacific has 169 graduate and undergraduate teachers, 46% with terminal degrees. The student-faculty ratio is 13:1.

Campus Resources

Students are not required to have a computer. Purchase and/or lease options are available. 68 **computers** available in computer labs and the library provide access to on-campus e-mail addresses, off-campus e-mail addresses, and the Internet.

The **library** has 145,000 books and 1,400 subscriptions.

Career Services

The career planning and placement office has 1 full-time staff member. Services include resume preparation, interview workshops, career/interest testing, career counseling, careers library, job bank, and job interviews.

Campus Life

There are 12 active organizations on campus, including a drama/theater group and student-run newspaper. No national or local **fraternities** or **sororities**. Student **safety services** include late-night transport/escort service, 24-hour emergency telephone alarm devices, 24-hour patrols by trained security personnel, and electronically operated dormitory entrances.

Fresno Pacific is a member of the NAIA. **Intercollegiate sports** (some offering scholarships) include basketball (m,w), cross-country running (m,w), soccer (m), track and field (m,w), volleyball (w).

International Students

For fall 1997, 60 international students applied, 30 were accepted, and 20 enrolled. Students can start in fall and spring. The **admissions test** required for entrance is TOEFL (minimum score: 500); recommended is SAT I or ACT. Application deadline is 7/31. Services include an international student adviser on campus.

Applying

Fresno Pacific requires an essay, SAT I or ACT, a high school transcript, 1 recommendation, 4 years of high school English, 3 years of high school math, 1 year of high school science, 2 years of high school foreign language, and 2 years of high school social studies, and in some cases an interview. Application deadline: rolling admissions; 3/2 priority date for financial aid. Early and deferred entrance are possible. **Contact:** Mr. Cary Templeton, Director of Admissions, 1717 South Chestnut Avenue, Fresno, CA 93702-4709, 209-453-2030 or toll-free 800-660-6089 (in-state); fax 209-453-2007; e-mail ugradmiss@fresno.edu.

GETTING IN LAST YEAR
343 applied
78% were accepted
50% from top tenth of their h.s. class

THE STUDENT BODY
Total 1,546, of whom 659
 are undergraduates

From 9 states and territories,
 9 other countries
63.7% women, 36.3% men
4.4% international students

COSTS AND FINANCIAL INFORMATION
1997–98 tuition and fees $11,936
1997–98 room and board $4100

Average percent of need met 82%
Average amount received per student $9583

AFTER FRESHMAN YEAR
79% returned for sophomore year

AFTER GRADUATION
30% had job offers within 6 months
7 organizations recruited on campus

GENEVA COLLEGE
Beaver Falls, Pennsylvania

http://www.geneva.edu/

Founded in 1848, Geneva College is one of the oldest evangelical Christian colleges in the nation, the second oldest in the Coalition of Christian Colleges & Universities. It offers an education that articulates the implications of Christ's sovereignty over all his creation. Geneva is one of 14 model sites chosen for the Coalition Racial and Ethnic Diversity Project. Students of color are encouraged to explore educational opportunities at Geneva. Majors include engineering, speech pathology, and cardiovascular technology. Through a cooperative program, students can combine degrees in aviation, air traffic control, or aerospace management with our business degree. All students complete a core program, which integrates courses in history, music, art, literature, and culture with biblical Christianity. Cocurricular activities include intercollegiate programs in all major sports, theater, choir, an FM radio station, and marching and concert bands. Although Geneva seeks students with a biblical world and life view, all students are welcome.

Academics
Geneva offers a Christian liberal arts and sciences curriculum and core academic program; a few graduate courses are open to undergraduates. It awards associate, bachelor's, and master's **degrees**. Challenging opportunities include advanced placement, accelerated degree programs, student-designed majors, tutorials, freshman honors college, an honors program, double majors, independent study, and a senior project. **Special programs** include cooperative education, internships, summer session for credit, off-campus study, and study-abroad.

The most popular **majors** include elementary education, business administration, and biology. A complete listing of majors at Geneva appears in the Majors Index beginning on page 141.

The **faculty** at Geneva has 60 full-time undergraduate teachers, 72% with terminal degrees. The student-faculty ratio is 18:1, and the average **class size** in required courses is 35.

Campus Resources
Students are not required to have a computer. 150 **computers** available in the computer center, computer labs, classrooms, the library, and the student center provide access to on-campus e-mail addresses, off-campus e-mail addresses, and the Internet. Staffed computer lab on campus provides training in the use of computers, software, and the Internet.

The 5 **libraries** have 158,045 books and 855 subscriptions.

Career Services
The career planning and placement office has 3 full-time staff members. Services include job fairs, resume preparation, interview workshops, resume referral, career/interest testing, career counseling, careers library, job bank (available on line), and job interviews.

Campus Life
There are 25 active organizations on campus, including a drama/theater group and student-run newspaper and radio station. 80% of students participate in student government elections. No national or local **fraternities** or **sororities**. Student **safety services** include late-night transport/escort service, 24-hour emergency telephone alarm devices, 24-hour patrols by trained security personnel, and electronically operated dormitory entrances.

Geneva is a member of the NAIA and NCCAA. **Intercollegiate sports** (some offering scholarships) include baseball (m), basketball (m,w), cross-country running (m,w), football (m), soccer (m,w), softball (w), tennis (m,w), track and field (m,w), volleyball (m,w).

International Students
For fall 1997, 63 international students applied, 32 were accepted, and 25 enrolled. Students can start in fall, spring, and summer. The **admissions test** required for entrance is TOEFL (minimum score: 550); recommended is SAT I or ACT. Application deadline is rolling. On-campus **housing** is guaranteed, also available during summer. Services include an international student adviser on campus.

Applying
Geneva requires an essay, SAT I or ACT, a high school transcript, recommendations, 4 years of high school English, 2 years of high school math, 1 year of high school science, 2 years of high school foreign language, 3 years of high school social studies, 4 years of high school academic electives, and a minimum high school GPA of 2.0, and in some cases an interview. It recommends a minimum high school GPA of 3.0. Application deadline: rolling admissions; 4/15 priority date for financial aid. Early and deferred entrance are possible. **Contact:** Mr. David Layton, Director of Admissions, 3200 College Avenue, Beaver Falls, PA 15010-3599, 724-847-6500 or toll-free 800-847-8255 (out-of-state); fax 724-847-6776; e-mail admissions@geneva.edu.

GETTING IN LAST YEAR
875 applied
54% were accepted
13% from top tenth of their h.s. class
21% had SAT verbal scores over 600
22% had SAT math scores over 600
65% had ACT scores over 24
1 National Merit Scholars
5 valedictorians

THE STUDENT BODY
Total 1,956, of whom 1,763
 are undergraduates

From 36 states and territories,
 15 other countries
80% from Pennsylvania
53.2% women, 46.9% men
2.3% international students

COSTS AND FINANCIAL INFORMATION
1997–98 tuition and fees $11,534
1997–98 room and board $4750

Average percent of need met 75%
Average amount received per student $9000

AFTER FRESHMAN YEAR
78% returned for sophomore year

AFTER GRADUATION
15% pursued further study (6% arts and
 sciences, 4% medicine, 3% education)
74% had job offers within 6 months
35 organizations recruited on campus

GEORGE FOX UNIVERSITY

Newberg, Oregon

http://www.georgefox.edu/

Freedom or faith. A college decision may seem like a choice between the two: sacrifice your faith or put your mind on the shelf. At George Fox University, academic freedom and Christian faith go hand in hand. Students find faculty members who encourage questions, who value their uniqueness, and who challenge them to explore truth from a foundation of faith. Students find a community of friends who accept them as they are, not as they are "supposed to be." Graduates of George Fox leave with more than a competitive degree from a well-respected school. They leave with the ability to think critically, to express themselves, and to take their faith into today's world. At George Fox University, students have the freedom to think and the freedom to believe.

Academics

George Fox offers a core academic program; a few graduate courses are open to undergraduates. It awards bachelor's, master's, and doctoral **degrees**. Challenging opportunities include advanced placement, accelerated degree programs, student-designed majors, tutorials, an honors program, double majors, independent study, and a senior project. **Special programs** include internships, off-campus study, study-abroad, and Air Force ROTC.

The most popular **majors** include education, business administration, and biology. A complete listing of majors at George Fox appears in the Majors Index beginning on page 141.

The **faculty** at George Fox has 117 full-time graduate and undergraduate teachers, 69% with terminal degrees. The student-faculty ratio is 16:1, and the average **class size** in required courses is 19.

Campus Resources

Students are required to have a computer. Purchase and/or lease options are available. Student rooms are linked to a campus network. 1,390 **computers** available in the computer center, computer labs, the learning resource center, classrooms, the library, and student rooms provide access to on-campus e-mail addresses, off-campus e-mail addresses, and the Internet. Staffed computer lab on campus provides training in the use of computers, software, and the Internet.

The 2 **libraries** have 176,236 books and 1,187 subscriptions.

Career Services

The career planning and placement office has 3 full-time staff members. Services include job fairs, resume preparation, interview workshops, career/interest testing, career counseling, careers library, job bank (available on line), job interviews, and career courses.

Campus Life

There are 18 active organizations on campus, including a drama/theater group and student-run newspaper and radio station. 40% of students participate in student government elections. No national or local **fraternities** or **sororities**. Student **safety services** include late-night transport/escort service, 24-hour emergency telephone alarm devices, 24-hour patrols by trained security personnel, student patrols, and electronically operated dormitory entrances.

George Fox is a member of the NCAA Division III. **Intercollegiate sports** include baseball (m), basketball (m,w), cross-country running (m,w), soccer (m,w), softball (w), tennis (m,w), track and field (m,w), volleyball (w).

International Students

For fall 1997, 47 international students applied, 38 were accepted, and 33 enrolled. Students can start in fall and spring. Application deadline is 3/1. On-campus **housing** is guaranteed. Services include an international student adviser on campus.

Applying

George Fox requires an essay, SAT I or ACT, a high school transcript, 2 recommendations, and 1 year of high school health/physical education, and in some cases an interview. It recommends 4 years of high school English, 2 years of high school math and science, 2 years of high school foreign language, 2 years of high school social studies, and 3 years of high school academic electives. Application deadline: 6/1; 3/1 priority date for financial aid. Early and deferred entrance are possible. **Contact:** Mr. Dale Seipp, Director of Undergraduate Admissions, 414 North Meridian, Newberg, OR 97132-2697, 503-538-8383 ext. 2240 or toll-free 800-765-4369; fax 503-538-7234; e-mail admissions@georgefox.edu.

GETTING IN LAST YEAR
939 applied
91% were accepted
40% enrolled (345)
28% from top tenth of their h.s. class
38% had SAT verbal scores over 600
29% had SAT math scores over 600
5 National Merit Scholars
31 class presidents
46 valedictorians

THE STUDENT BODY
Total 2,235, of whom 1,667
  are undergraduates

From 26 states and territories,
  10 other countries
62% from Oregon
59.8% women, 40.2% men
3.1% international students

COSTS AND FINANCIAL INFORMATION
1998–99 tuition and fees $15,950
1998–99 room and board $5120

Average percent of need met 59%
Average amount received per student $14,765

AFTER FRESHMAN YEAR
74% returned for sophomore year
36% got a degree in 4 years
9% got a degree in 5 years
2% got a degree in 6 years

AFTER GRADUATION
19% pursued further study
69% had job offers within 6 months
172 organizations recruited on campus

GORDON COLLEGE
Wenham, Massachusetts

http://www.gordon.edu/

Gordon College, on Boston's scenic North Shore, is New England's only nondenominational Christian college. It offers 33 majors, 17 national and international off-campus study options, and a Cooperative Education (Co-op) Program. Its 1,375 students, drawn from 39 states and 16 countries, are encouraged to participate in 22 ministry and service activities throughout the year. Gordon has won recognition for its high quality. Edward Fiske lists it in his *Selective Guide*. Both Fiske and Barron's rate it as a "Best Buy," and *U.S. News & World Report* ranks it among the top national liberal arts colleges.

Academics

Gordon offers a liberal arts curriculum and core academic program. It awards bachelor's and master's **degrees**. Challenging opportunities include advanced placement, student-designed majors, tutorials, an honors program, double majors, independent study, and a senior project. **Special programs** include cooperative education, internships, off-campus study, study-abroad, and Air Force ROTC.

The most popular **majors** include English, psychology, and biblical studies. A complete listing of majors at Gordon appears in the Majors Index beginning on page 141.

The **faculty** at Gordon has 83 full-time graduate and undergraduate teachers, 85% with terminal degrees. The student-faculty ratio is 14:1, and the average **class size** in required courses is 31.

Campus Resources

Students are not required to have a computer. Purchase and/or lease options are available. Student rooms are linked to a campus network. 123 **computers** available in the computer center, computer labs, the learning resource center, the library, and dormitories provide access to on-campus e-mail addresses, off-campus e-mail addresses, and the Internet. Staffed computer lab on campus provides training in the use of computers and software.

The **library** has 282,593 books and 1,571 subscriptions.

Career Services

The career planning and placement office has 3 full-time, 1 part-time staff members. Services include job fairs, resume preparation, interview workshops, resume referral, career/interest testing, career counseling, careers library, job bank, and job interviews.

Campus Life

There are 35 active organizations on campus, including a drama/theater group and student-run newspaper. No national or local **fraternities** or **sororities**. Student **safety services** include late-night transport/escort service, 24-hour emergency telephone alarm devices, and 24-hour patrols by trained security personnel.

Gordon is a member of the NCAA (Division III). **Intercollegiate sports** include baseball (m), basketball (m,w), cross-country running (m,w), field hockey (w), lacrosse (m,w), soccer (m,w), softball (w), swimming and diving (m,w), tennis (m,w).

International Students

For fall 1997, 45 international students applied, 22 were accepted, and 11 enrolled. Students can start in fall. The **admissions test** required for entrance is TOEFL (minimum score: 550); recommended is SAT I or ACT. Application deadline is 4/1. On-campus **housing** is guaranteed, also available during summer. Services include an international student adviser on campus.

Applying

Gordon requires an essay, SAT I or ACT, a high school transcript, an interview, 2 recommendations, pastoral recommendation and statement of Christian faith, 4 years of high school English, 2 years of high school math and science, 4 years of high school foreign language, 2 years of high school social studies, and 5 years of high school academic electives. It recommends SAT II Subject Tests, 3 years of high school math and science, 3 years of high school social studies, and a minimum high school GPA of 2.5. Application deadline: rolling admissions; 3/15 priority date for financial aid. Early and deferred entrance are possible.
Contact: Mr. Silvio Vazquez, Dean of Admissions, 255 Grapevine Road, Wenham, MA 01984-1899, 978-927-2300 ext. 4217 or toll-free 800-343-1379; fax 978-524-3704; e-mail admissions@gordon.edu.

GETTING IN LAST YEAR
1,073 applied
79% were accepted
47% enrolled (402)
24% from top tenth of their h.s. class
44% had SAT verbal scores over 600
36% had SAT math scores over 600
7 National Merit Scholars

THE STUDENT BODY
Total 1,375, of whom 1,348
 are undergraduates

From 42 states and territories,
 16 other countries
30% from Massachusetts
64.8% women, 35.2% men
1.8% international students

COSTS AND FINANCIAL INFORMATION
1998–99 tuition and fees $15,100
1998–99 room and board $4950
Average percent of need met 77%

Average amount received per student $12,080

AFTER FRESHMAN YEAR
85% returned for sophomore year
43% got a degree in 4 years
17% got a degree in 5 years
3% got a degree in 6 years

AFTER GRADUATION
15% pursued further study

GOSHEN COLLEGE

Goshen, Indiana   *http://www.goshen.edu/*

New to campus is the $6.3-million Gingerich Recreation-Fitness Center, home to a swimming pool, 200-meter track, racquetball courts, a large weight room, multi-court space with 3 basketball courts, and an exercise-science laboratory. Also new is the Schrock Science Annex, with new laboratories and classrooms for all of the sciences. It also houses the Turner Precision X-Ray Laboratory, the first of its kind in the nation. GC is one of 3 schools with fewer than 1,200 students that is included in the Pew Science Program in Undergraduate Education. More than 80% of GC students spend 13 weeks on Study-Service Term in a "significantly different" country, usually for the same cost as a term on campus.

Academics

Goshen offers a liberal arts curriculum with international emphasis and core academic program. It awards bachelor's **degrees**. Challenging opportunities include advanced placement, accelerated degree programs, student-designed majors, tutorials, freshman honors college, an honors program, double majors, independent study, and a senior project. **Special programs** include cooperative education, internships, summer session for credit, off-campus study, and study-abroad.

The most popular **majors** include business administration, nursing, and elementary education. A complete listing of majors at Goshen appears in the Majors Index beginning on page 141.

The **faculty** at Goshen has 71 full-time teachers, 65% with terminal degrees. The student-faculty ratio is 13:1, and the average **class size** in required courses is 31.

Campus Resources

Students are not required to have a computer. Student rooms are linked to a campus network. 80 **computers** available in the computer center, computer labs, the library, and dormitories provide access to on-campus e-mail addresses, off-campus e-mail addresses, and the Internet. Staffed computer lab on campus (open 24 hours a day) provides training in the use of computers, software, and the Internet.

The 3 **libraries** have 118,000 books and 750 subscriptions.

Career Services

The career planning and placement office has 1 full-time, 1 part-time staff members. Services include job fairs, resume preparation, resume referral, career/interest testing, career counseling, careers library, job bank (available on line), and job interviews.

Campus Life

There are 25 active organizations on campus, including a drama/theater group and student-run newspaper and radio station. 75% of students participate in student government elections. No national or local **fraternities** or **sororities**. Student **safety services** include night security, late-night transport/escort service, and 24-hour emergency telephone alarm devices.

Goshen is a member of the NAIA. **Intercollegiate sports** (some offering scholarships) include baseball (m), basketball (m,w), cross-country running (m,w), golf (m), soccer (m,w), softball (w), tennis (m,w), track and field (m,w), volleyball (w).

International Students

For fall 1997, 123 international students applied, 25 were accepted, and 18 enrolled. Students can start in fall, winter, spring, and summer. The **admissions tests** required for entrance are TOEFL (minimum score: 550; minimum score for ESL admission: 525), ELS (minimum score 109). Application deadline is rolling. On-campus **housing** is guaranteed. Services include an international student adviser on campus.

Applying

Goshen requires an essay, SAT I or ACT, a high school transcript, and 1 recommendation. It recommends an interview, 4 years of high school English, 3 years of high school math and science, 2 years of high school foreign language, 2 years of high school social studies, and 2 years of high school history. Application deadline: rolling admissions; 3/1 priority date for financial aid. Early and deferred entrance are possible. **Contact:** Ms. Martha Lehman, Director of Admissions, 1700 South Main Street, Goshen, IN 46526-4794, 219-535-7535 or toll-free 800-348-7422; fax 219-535-7609; e-mail admissions@goshen.edu.

GETTING IN LAST YEAR
573 applied
77% were accepted
61% enrolled (267)
25% from top tenth of their h.s. class
28% had SAT verbal scores over 600
23% had SAT math scores over 600
3 National Merit Scholars
51 class presidents
12 valedictorians

THE STUDENT BODY
1,016 undergraduates

From 31 states and territories,
  30 other countries
51% from Indiana
58.6% women, 41.4% men
6.1% international students

COSTS AND FINANCIAL INFORMATION
1997–98 tuition and fees $11,450
1997–98 room and board $4000
Average percent of need met 94%

Average amount received per student $13,070

AFTER FRESHMAN YEAR
74% returned for sophomore year
44% got a degree in 4 years
18% got a degree in 5 years
2% got a degree in 6 years

AFTER GRADUATION
40% pursued further study (15% arts and
  sciences, 11% medicine, 5% business)
40 organizations recruited on campus

GRACE COLLEGE
Winona Lake, Indiana

http://www.grace.edu/

The mission at Grace College is to impact students' lives by strengthening their character, sharpening their competence, and preparing them for service. Every year, hundreds of Grace students volunteer their time in the local community. There are over 20 ministry opportunities to choose from at Grace, including athletic outreach, inner-city missions, Halloween Funfest, and Youth for Christ. Grace students learn how they can have an effective ministry in any career, from youth pastor to business executive. Students who want to be a part of a community that makes ministry a priority should consider Grace.

Academics
Grace offers a traditional liberal arts curriculum and core academic program; a few graduate courses are open to undergraduates. It awards associate, bachelor's, and master's **degrees**. Challenging opportunities include advanced placement, double majors, independent study, and a senior project. **Special programs** include internships, summer session for credit, off-campus study, and study-abroad.

The most popular **majors** include elementary education, psychology, and business administration. A complete listing of majors at Grace appears in the Majors Index beginning on page 141.

The **faculty** at Grace has 44 full-time undergraduate teachers, 67% with terminal degrees. The average **class size** in required courses is 40.

Campus Resources
Students are not required to have a computer. 75+ **computers** available in computer labs, classrooms, and the library provide access to on-campus e-mail addresses, off-campus e-mail addresses, and the Internet. Staffed computer lab on campus provides training in the use of computers, software, and the Internet.

The **library** has 140,658 books and 350 subscriptions.

Career Services
The career planning and placement office has 1 full-time staff member. Services include job fairs, resume preparation, interview workshops, resume referral, career/interest testing, career counseling, careers library, job bank, and job interviews.

Campus Life
There are 30 active organizations on campus, including a drama/theater group and student-run newspaper. 62% of students participate in student government elections. No national or local **fraternities** or **sororities**. Student **safety services** include evening patrols by trained security personnel, late-night transport/escort service, student patrols, and electronically operated dormitory entrances.

Grace is a member of the NAIA. **Intercollegiate sports** (some offering scholarships) include baseball (m), basketball (m,w), cross-country running (m,w), golf (m), soccer (m,w), softball (w), tennis (m,w), track and field (m,w), volleyball (w).

International Students
For fall 1997, 7 international students applied, 4 were accepted, and 2 enrolled. Students can start in fall and spring. The **admissions test** required for entrance is TOEFL (minimum score: 500; minimum score for ESL admission: 500); recommended is either SAT I or ACT. Application deadline is 6/1. **Housing** is guaranteed. Services include an international student adviser on campus.

Applying
Grace requires SAT I or ACT, a high school transcript, 2 recommendations, and a minimum high school GPA of 2.0, and in some cases an interview. It recommends 4 years of high school English, 2 years of high school math and science, 2 years of high school foreign language, 2 years of high school social studies, 1 year of high school history, and 1 year of high school academic electives. Application deadline: 8/1; 4/1 priority date for financial aid. Early and deferred entrance are possible. **Contact:** Mr. Ron Henry, Dean of Enrollment, 200 Seminary Drive, Winona Lake, IN 46590-1294, 219-372-5131 or toll-free 800-54-GRACE; fax 219-372-5114; e-mail rhenry@grace.edu.

GETTING IN LAST YEAR
442 applied
88% were accepted
50% enrolled (195)
22% from top tenth of their h.s. class
25% had SAT verbal scores over 600
20% had SAT math scores over 600
50% had ACT scores over 24
8 class presidents
14 valedictorians

THE STUDENT BODY
Total 800, of whom 765
  are undergraduates

From 35 states and territories,
  7 other countries
60% from Indiana
53.1% women, 46.9% men
.9% international students

COSTS AND FINANCIAL INFORMATION
1998–99 tuition and fees $10,106
1998–99 room and board $4432

Average percent of need met 38%
Average amount received per student $8500

AFTER FRESHMAN YEAR
83.7% returned for sophomore year

AFTER GRADUATION
20% pursued further study (8% arts and
  sciences, 7% theology, 3% medicine)
70% had job offers within 6 months
30 organizations recruited on campus

GRAND CANYON UNIVERSITY

Phoenix, Arizona

http://www.grand-canyon.edu/

Grand Canyon University is an institution that seeks the cutting edge in educational opportunities for its students while cherishing the traditional values of a liberal arts community. The University has added the College of Science and Allied Health to equip its graduates with training in health care—the fastest growing field. Student internships abound in regional and nationally recognized companies, many leading directly to full-time employment upon graduation. Over 500 students and faculty and staff members participate in international exchange programs. Every innovative program is founded in a strong Christian heritage that allows each individual to find and utilize his or her God-given talents and abilities.

Academics

Grand Canyon University offers a core academic program; fewer than half of graduate courses are open to undergraduates. It awards bachelor's and master's **degrees**. Challenging opportunities include advanced placement, accelerated degree programs, tutorials, freshman honors college, an honors program, double majors, independent study, and a senior project. **Special programs** include internships, summer session for credit, off-campus study, study-abroad, and Army and Air Force ROTC.

The most popular **majors** include elementary education, nursing, and psychology. A complete listing of majors at Grand Canyon University appears in the Majors Index beginning on page 141.

The **faculty** at Grand Canyon University has 100 full-time graduate and undergraduate teachers, 80% with terminal degrees. The student-faculty ratio is 17:1, and the average **class size** in required courses is 24.

Campus Resources

Students are not required to have a computer. 119 **computers** available in the computer center, computer labs, the learning resource center, audiovisual lab, classrooms, and the library provide access to the Internet. Staffed computer lab on campus provides training in the use of computers and software.

The **library** has 76,011 books and 1,139 subscriptions.

Career Services

The career planning and placement office has 1 full-time, 1 part-time staff members. Services include resume referral and job interviews.

Campus Life

Active organizations on campus include a drama/theater group and student-run newspaper. No national or local **fraternities** or **sororities**. Student **safety services** include late-night transport/escort service, 24-hour emergency telephone alarm devices, 24-hour patrols by trained security personnel, student patrols, and electronically operated dormitory entrances.

Grand Canyon University is a member of the NCAA (Division II). **Intercollegiate sports** (some offering scholarships) include baseball (m), basketball (m,w), cross-country running (m,w), golf (m), soccer (m,w), tennis (w), volleyball (w).

International Students

Students can start in fall, spring, and summer. The **admissions test** required for entrance is TOEFL (minimum score: 550; minimum score for ESL admission: 500); recommended is SAT I or ACT. Application deadline is 7/15. On-campus **housing** is guaranteed, also available during summer. Services include an international student adviser on campus.

Applying

Grand Canyon University requires SAT I or ACT, a high school transcript, 4 years of high school English, 3 years of high school math, 2 years of high school science, 2 years of high school social studies, and a minimum high school GPA of 3.0, and in some cases an essay, an interview, and 3 recommendations. It recommends a minimum high school GPA of 3.0. Application deadline: 8/15. Early and deferred entrance are possible. **Contact:** Mr. Carl Tichenor, Director of Admissions, 3300 W Camelback Road, PO Box 11097, Phoenix, AZ 86017-3030, 602-589-2855; fax 602-589-2580; e-mail admiss@grand-canyon.edu.

GETTING IN LAST YEAR
604 applied
83% were accepted
39% enrolled (197)
37% from top tenth of their h.s. class
18% had SAT verbal scores over 600
22% had SAT math scores over 600
39% had ACT scores over 24
1 National Merit Scholars
12 valedictorians

THE STUDENT BODY
Total 2,245, of whom 1,789 are undergraduates

From 42 states and territories, 14 other countries
81% from Arizona
64.3% women, 35.7% men
3.6% international students

COSTS AND FINANCIAL INFORMATION
1998–99 tuition and fees $7526
1998–99 room and board $3740

Average percent of need met 77%
Average amount received per student $9297

AFTER FRESHMAN YEAR
72% returned for sophomore year
16% got a degree in 4 years
15% got a degree in 5 years
2% got a degree in 6 years

AFTER GRADUATION
67% had job offers within 6 months
50 organizations recruited on campus

GREENVILLE COLLEGE

Greenville, Illinois

http://www.greenville.edu/

Located in a quaint and friendly rural community, Greenville College offers a nurturing environment for academic, personal, social, and spiritual growth. This quiet setting, however, is just 45 minutes from downtown St. Louis, where students minister to inner-city kids, serve in internships for major corporations, and take advantage of the city's many rich cultural resources. Traditionally strong in the physical sciences, teacher education, music, and business, Greenville offers a wide range of majors. Its faculty are committed to academic excellence within the context of the mission of Greenville College: to equip students for lives of effective leadership and redemptive servanthood.

Academics

GC offers a liberal arts curriculum and core academic program. It awards bachelor's **degrees**. Challenging opportunities include advanced placement, accelerated degree programs, student-designed majors, tutorials, an honors program, and a senior project. **Special programs** include cooperative education, internships, summer session for credit, off-campus study, and study-abroad.

The most popular **majors** include education, business administration, and biology. A complete listing of majors at GC appears in the Majors Index beginning on page 141.

The **faculty** at GC has 57 full-time teachers, 54% with terminal degrees. The student-faculty ratio is 16:1, and the average **class size** in required courses is 40.

Campus Resources

Students are not required to have a computer. Purchase and/or lease options are available. 100 **computers** available in the computer center, computer labs, the research center, the learning resource center, faculty offices, the library, and dormitories provide access to on-campus e-mail addresses, off-campus e-mail addresses, and the Internet. Staffed computer lab on campus (open 24 hours a day) provides training in the use of computers and software.

The **library** has 124,576 books and 490 subscriptions.

Career Services

The career planning and placement office has 2 full-time staff members. Services include job fairs, resume preparation, career counseling, careers library, and job interviews.

Campus Life

There are 40 active organizations on campus, including a drama/theater group and student-run newspaper and radio station. 70% of students participate in student government elections. No national or local **fraternities** or **sororities**. Student **safety services** include 24-hour emergency telephone alarm devices and 24-hour patrols by trained security personnel.

GC is a member of the NAIA and NCCAA. **Intercollegiate sports** include basketball (m,w), cross-country running (m,w), football (m), golf (m), soccer (m,w), tennis (m,w), track and field (m,w), volleyball (w).

International Students

For fall 1997, 20 international students applied, 8 were accepted, and 5 enrolled. The **admissions test** required for entrance is TOEFL (minimum score: 500). Application deadline is 7/1. On-campus **housing** is guaranteed, also available during summer. Services include an international student adviser on campus.

Applying

GC requires an essay, SAT I or ACT, a high school transcript, 2 recommendations, agreement to code of conduct, and a minimum high school GPA of 2.0, and in some cases an interview. It recommends 4 years of high school English, 2 years of high school math and science, 2 years of high school foreign language, and 1 year of high school history. Application deadline: rolling admissions. Early and deferred entrance are possible. **Contact:** Mr. Randy Comfort, Dean of Admissions, 315 East College, PO Box 159, Greenville, IL 62246-0159, 618-664-2800 ext. 4401 or toll-free 800-248-2288 (in-state), 800-345-4440 (out-of-state); fax 618-664-9841; e-mail admissions@greenville.edu.

GETTING IN LAST YEAR
650 applied
74% were accepted
41% enrolled (196)
23% from top tenth of their h.s. class
28% had SAT verbal scores over 600
28% had SAT math scores over 600
47% had ACT scores over 24

THE STUDENT BODY
955 undergraduates

From 41 states and territories,
  9 other countries
68% from Illinois
56.3% women, 43.7% men
.9% international students

COSTS AND FINANCIAL INFORMATION
1997–98 tuition and fees $12,586
1997–98 room and board $4850
Average percent of need met 90%
Average amount received per student $13,219

AFTER FRESHMAN YEAR
69% returned for sophomore year
41% got a degree in 4 years
3% got a degree in 5 years

AFTER GRADUATION
17% pursued further study (4% arts and
  sciences, 3% business, 3% education)
80% had job offers within 6 months
22 organizations recruited on campus

HOPE INTERNATIONAL UNIVERSITY

Fullerton, California *http://www.hiu.edu/*

Hope International University exists to prepare students to be servant leaders in the church and in society. The southern California location makes possible cross-cultural experiences with persons from around the world while also offering a variety of internship and recreational opportunities for students. A formal relationship with Cal State University, which is adjacent to campus, allows students to study at both institutions. Students can be involved in service opportunities that include the local school system and missions projects in Mexico. At Hope International University, students prepare for life and career in a spiritual atmosphere with a caring faculty and staff.

Academics

Hope International University offers a writing-oriented curriculum and core academic program; a few graduate courses are open to undergraduates. It awards associate, bachelor's, and master's **degrees**. Challenging opportunities include advanced placement, accelerated degree programs, student-designed majors, an honors program, double majors, independent study, and a senior project. **Special programs** include internships, summer session for credit, off-campus study, and study-abroad.

The most popular **majors** include business administration and biblical studies. A complete listing of majors at Hope International University appears in the Majors Index beginning on page 141.

The **faculty** at Hope International University has 36 full-time graduate and undergraduate teachers, 60% with terminal degrees. The student-faculty ratio is 16:1.

Campus Resources

Students are not required to have a computer. 17 **computers** available in computer labs and the library provide access to on-campus e-mail addresses and off-campus e-mail addresses. Staffed computer lab on campus provides training in the use of computers and software.

The **library** has 72,000 books and 468 subscriptions.

Career Services

The career planning and placement office has 2 part-time staff members. Services include job fairs, resume preparation, and interview workshops.

Campus Life

Active organizations on campus include a drama/theater group and student-run newspaper. 50% of students participate in student government elections. No national or local **fraternities** or **sororities**. Student **safety services** include 24-hour emergency telephone alarm devices and student patrols.

Hope International University is a member of the NAIA. **Intercollegiate sports** (some offering scholarships) include basketball (m,w), soccer (m,w), softball (w), tennis (m,w), volleyball (m,w).

International Students

For fall 1997, 11 international students applied, 9 were accepted, and 4 enrolled. Students can start in fall, winter, spring, and summer. The **admissions test** required for entrance is TOEFL (minimum score: 500; minimum score for ESL admission: 450). Application deadline is 6/1. On-campus **housing** is guaranteed, also available during summer. Services include an international student adviser on campus.

Applying

Hope International University requires an essay, SAT I or ACT, a high school transcript, 2 recommendations, and a minimum high school GPA of 2.5, and in some cases an interview. It recommends 4 years of high school English, 2 years of high school math, 1 year of high school science, 1 year of high school foreign language, 1 year of high school social studies, .5 years of high school history, and 3 years of high school academic electives. Application deadline: 7/1. Early and deferred entrance are possible. **Contact:** Admissions Office, 2500 East Nutwood Avenue, Fullerton, CA 92831-3138, 714-879-3901 or toll-free 800-762-1294; fax 714-526-0231; e-mail twinston@hiu.edu.

GETTING IN LAST YEAR
21% had SAT verbal scores over 600
22% had SAT math scores over 600
56% had ACT scores over 24

THE STUDENT BODY
Total 1,022, of whom 847
   are undergraduates
From 24 states and territories,
   24 other countries

69% from California
52.1% women, 47.9% men
17.2% international students

COSTS AND FINANCIAL INFORMATION
1997–98 tuition and fees $9190
1997–98 room and board $3619
Average percent of need met 36%

Average amount received per student $7500

AFTER FRESHMAN YEAR
63% returned for sophomore year

AFTER GRADUATION
40% pursued further study (10% arts and
   sciences, 10% business, 10% education)
30% had job offers within 6 months

HOUGHTON COLLEGE

Houghton, New York   *http://www.houghton.edu/*

HOUGHTON
A Christian College of Liberal Arts and Sciences

Since 1883, Houghton College has provided an educational experience that integrates high academic quality with the Christian faith. Houghton is selective in admission, attracting a very capable student body from across the country and around the world. The College routinely receives widespread national recognition for the quality of its student profile, faculty, and facilities, as well as affordability. Enrolling 1,200 full-time students, Houghton is located on a scenic 1,300-sq.-mile campus in the beautiful countryside of western New York. The College's unique campus includes a 386 acre equestrian center and ski facilities. Houghton's traditional liberal arts curriculum offers 40 diverse majors and programs. Approximately 100 international students and missionary dependents attend Houghton. The First-Year Honors Program offers highly qualified students the opportunity to study in England during the second semester of their first year.

Academics

Houghton offers an interdisciplinary curriculum and core academic program. It awards associate and bachelor's **degrees**. Challenging opportunities include advanced placement, tutorials, an honors program, double majors, independent study, and a senior project. **Special programs** include internships, summer session for credit, off-campus study, study-abroad, Army ROTC, and equestrian program.

The most popular **majors** include elementary education, biology, and psychology. A complete listing of majors at Houghton appears in the Majors Index beginning on page 141.

The **faculty** at Houghton has 102 full-time teachers, 80% with terminal degrees. The student-faculty ratio is 15:1, and the average **class size** in required courses is 36.

Campus Resources

Students are required to have a computer. Purchase and/or lease options are available. Student rooms are linked to a campus network. 130 **computers** available in the computer center, computer labs, divisional offices, the library, the student center, and dormitories provide access to on-campus e-mail addresses, off-campus e-mail addresses, and the Internet. Computer lab on campus (open 24 hours a day) provides training in the use of computers and software.

The **library** has 222,000 books and 1,266 subscriptions.

Career Services

The career planning and placement office has 2 full-time staff members. Services include job fairs, resume preparation, interview workshops, resume referral, career/interest testing, career counseling, careers library, job bank (available on line), and job interviews.

Campus Life

There are 50 active organizations on campus, including a drama/theater group and student-run newspaper and radio station. 45% of students participate in student government elections. No national or local **fraternities** or **sororities**. Student **safety services** include phone connection to security patrols, late-night transport/escort service, 24-hour patrols by trained security personnel, and electronically operated dormitory entrances.

Houghton is a member of the NAIA. **Intercollegiate sports** (all offering scholarships) include basketball (m,w), cross-country running (m,w), field hockey (w), soccer (m,w), track and field (m,w), volleyball (w).

International Students

For fall 1997, 44 international students applied, 38 were accepted, and 23 enrolled. Students can start in fall and spring. The **admissions test** required for entrance is TOEFL (minimum score: 550). Application deadline is 3/1. On-campus **housing** is guaranteed, also available during summer. Services include an international student adviser on campus.

Applying

Houghton requires an essay, SAT I or ACT, a high school transcript, and pastoral recommendation. It recommends an interview, 4 years of high school English, 3 years of high school math, 2 years of high school science, 2 years of high school foreign language, 1 year of high school social studies, 2 years of high school history, and a minimum high school GPA of 3.0. Application deadline: 6/1; 3/1 priority date for financial aid. Early and deferred entrance are possible. **Contact:** Director of Admissions, PO Box 128, Houghton, NY 14744, 716-567-9353 or toll-free 800-777-2556; fax 716-567-9522; e-mail admission@houghton.edu.

GETTING IN LAST YEAR
997 applied
85% were accepted
36% enrolled (302)
40% from top tenth of their h.s. class
49% had SAT verbal scores over 600
44% had SAT math scores over 600
75% had ACT scores over 24
19 National Merit Scholars
19 valedictorians

THE STUDENT BODY
1,411 undergraduates
From 36 states and territories,
   25 other countries
62% from New York
62.3% women, 37.7% men
5.7% international students

COSTS AND FINANCIAL INFORMATION
1997–98 tuition and fees $12,765
1997–98 room and board $4238

Average percent of need met 92%
Average amount received per student $11,976

AFTER FRESHMAN YEAR
87.5% returned for sophomore year

AFTER GRADUATION
25% pursued further study (12% arts and
   sciences, 4% education, 4% theology)
80% had job offers within 6 months
34 organizations recruited on campus

HUNTINGTON COLLEGE

Huntington, Indiana

http://www.huntington.edu/

Huntington
College

Founded in 1897, Huntington College is dedicated to the principles of academic leadership and spiritual vitality. The Huntington Plan is a guaranteed tuition program in which students pay a one-time fee equal to 10% of the current year's tuition to lock in tuition at that rate through graduation. Huntington is home to the nationally recognized Link Institute for Faithful and Effective Youth Ministry and also features an outstanding theatre arts program. Huntington's campus facilities were described as being "among the finest among liberal arts colleges" by a North Central Association Accreditation Team. Call for a free copy of Huntington's new CD-ROM.

Academics

Huntington offers a core academic program; fewer than half of graduate courses are open to undergraduates. It awards bachelor's and master's **degrees**. Challenging opportunities include advanced placement, accelerated degree programs, student-designed majors, tutorials, and a senior project. **Special programs** include internships, summer session for credit, off-campus study, and study-abroad.

The most popular **majors** include elementary education, business administration, and youth ministries. A complete listing of majors at Huntington appears in the Majors Index beginning on page 141.

The **faculty** at Huntington has 48 full-time graduate and undergraduate teachers, 83% with terminal degrees. The student-faculty ratio is 15:1.

Campus Resources

Students are not required to have a computer. Purchase and/or lease options are available. Student rooms are linked to a campus network. 75 **computers** available in the computer center, computer labs, classrooms, the library, and dormitories provide access to the Internet. Staffed computer lab on campus provides training in the use of computers and software.

The **library** has 92,000 books and 553 subscriptions.

Career Services

The career planning and placement office has 1 full-time, 2 part-time staff members. Services include job fairs, resume preparation, resume referral, career counseling, careers library, job bank, and job interviews.

Campus Life

There are 35 active organizations on campus, including a drama/theater group and student-run newspaper and radio station. 80% of students participate in student government elections. Student **safety services** include night patrols by trained security personnel, late-night transport/escort service, and 24-hour emergency telephone alarm devices.

Huntington is a member of the NAIA. **Intercollegiate sports** (some offering scholarships) include baseball (m), basketball (m,w), cross-country running (m,w), golf (m,w), soccer (m,w), softball (w), tennis (m,w), track and field (m,w), volleyball (w).

International Students

For fall 1998, 13 international students applied, 8 were accepted, and 6 enrolled. The **admissions test** required for entrance is TOEFL (minimum score: 525; minimum score for ESL admission: 500); recommended is SAT I or ACT. Application deadline is 7/1. On-campus **housing** is guaranteed. Services include an international student adviser on campus.

Applying

Huntington requires an essay, SAT I or ACT, a high school transcript, and a minimum high school GPA of 2.3. It recommends an interview, 3 years of high school math and science, and 1 year of high school foreign language. Application deadline: 8/15; 3/1 priority date for financial aid. Early and deferred entrance are possible. **Contact:** Mr. Jeff Berggren, Dean of Enrollment, 2303 College Avenue, Huntington, IN 46750-1299, 219-359-4000 or toll-free 800-642-6493; fax 219-356-9448; e-mail admissions@huntington.edu.

GETTING IN LAST YEAR
565 applied
91% were accepted
44% enrolled (225)
30% from top tenth of their h.s. class
12% had SAT verbal scores over 600
21% had SAT math scores over 600

THE STUDENT BODY
Total 900, of whom 850
  are undergraduates

From 22 states and territories,
  12 other countries
57.5% women, 42.5% men

COSTS AND FINANCIAL INFORMATION
1998–99 tuition and fees $12,800
1998–99 room and board $4770

Average percent of need met 98%
Average amount received per student $10,490

AFTER FRESHMAN YEAR
82% returned for sophomore year

AFTER GRADUATION
15% pursued further study

INDIANA WESLEYAN UNIVERSITY
Marion, Indiana

Uniqueness, a distinctly Christian approach, and dynamic growth characterize Indiana Wesleyan University. IWU's uniqueness is demonstrated by its academic programs (over 60 majors), which include addictions counseling, athletic training, criminal justice, medical technology, nursing, sports management, and social work. Integration of biblical principles and faith in Christ occurs in the classrooms, athletics, and extracurricular activities. Bible classes and chapel, along with accountability, discipleship, and Bible study groups also enhance spiritual growth. New residence halls (all with air conditioning), town houses for upperclass students, a new art/communications classroom building, a new student center, a new performing arts center, new academic majors, a 65-acre "state-of-the-art" outdoor athletic complex, and construction of a Wellness/Recreation Center, featuring a competition-size pool, a running track, racquetball courts, a climbing wall, basketball courts, and a golf center, to be completed in fall 1999, have produced dynamic enrollment growth. Enrollment has increased from 1,085 students in 1988 to over 1,900 in 1998.

Academics
IWU offers a liberal arts curriculum and core academic program. It awards associate, bachelor's, and master's **degrees**. Challenging opportunities include advanced placement, accelerated degree programs, student-designed majors, an honors program, and a senior project. **Special programs** include internships, summer session for credit, off-campus study, and study-abroad.

The most popular **majors** include nursing, divinity/ministry, and elementary education. A complete listing of majors at IWU appears in the Majors Index beginning on page 141.

The **faculty** at IWU has 96 full-time graduate and undergraduate teachers, 53% with terminal degrees. The student-faculty ratio is 17:1.

Campus Resources
Students are not required to have a computer. Purchase and/or lease options are available. Student rooms are linked to a campus network. 70 **computers** available in the computer center, computer labs, the learning resource center, the library, the student center, and dormitories provide access to on-campus e-mail addresses, off-campus e-mail addresses, and the Internet. Staffed computer lab on campus provides training in the use of computers, software, and the Internet.

The **library** has 95,424 books.

Career Services
The career planning and placement office has 1 full-time, 1 part-time staff members. Services include job fairs, resume preparation, interview workshops, career/interest testing, career counseling, careers library, job bank (available on line), and job interviews.

Campus Life
There are 31 active organizations on campus, including a drama/theater group and student-run newspaper and radio station. 28% of students participate in student government elections. No national or local **fraternities** or **sororities**. Student **safety services** include 12-hour evening patrols by trained security personnel and late-night transport/escort service.

IWU is a member of the NAIA and NCCAA. **Intercollegiate sports** (some offering scholarships) include baseball (m), basketball (m,w), cross-country running (m,w), golf (m), soccer (m,w), softball (w), tennis (m,w), track and field (m,w), volleyball (w), cheer team (m,w).

International Students
Students can start in fall and spring. The **admissions tests** required for entrance are SAT I or ACT, TOEFL (minimum score: 550). Application deadline is 7/1. On-campus **housing** is guaranteed, also available during summer. Services include an international student adviser on campus.

Applying
IWU requires SAT I or ACT, a high school transcript, 1 recommendation, and a minimum high school GPA of 2.0, and in some cases an interview. It recommends an interview. Application deadline: rolling admissions. Early and deferred entrance are possible. **Contact:** Ms. Gaytha Holloway, Director of Admissions, 4201 South Washington Street, Marion, IN 46953-4974, 765-677-2138 or toll-free 800-332-6901; fax 765-677-2333; e-mail admissions@indwes.edu.

GETTING IN LAST YEAR
1,517 applied
71% were accepted

THE STUDENT BODY
Total 6,063, of whom 4,343
 are undergraduates
From 48 states and territories,
 10 other countries

55% from Indiana
65% women, 35% men
.5% international students

COSTS AND FINANCIAL INFORMATION
1998–99 tuition and fees (estimated) $11,204
1998–99 room and board (estimated) $4310

AFTER FRESHMAN YEAR
69% returned for sophomore year

AFTER GRADUATION
40 organizations recruited on campus

JOHN BROWN UNIVERSITY

Siloam Springs, Arkansas

http://www.jbu.edu/

There are two mottos which best describe the mission of John Brown University. The "Christ Over All" motto is demonstrated in our overall mission and purpose under submission to the Lordship of Jesus Christ. Our "Head, Heart, and Hand" motto describes our educational philosophy. We have a balanced approach to academic excellence (Head), spiritual development (Heart), and practical hands-on professional training (Hand). JBU is a diverse Christian community with students from 40 states and 30 countries. With approximately 100 missionary children from third world cultures, JBU offers a global approach to Christian higher education in the beauty of Northwest Arkansas.

Academics

JBU offers a values-oriented curriculum and core academic program. It awards associate, bachelor's, and master's **degrees**. Challenging opportunities include advanced placement, tutorials, freshman honors college, an honors program, double majors, independent study, and a senior project. **Special programs** include internships, study-abroad, and Army ROTC.

The most popular **majors** include business administration, elementary education, and engineering. A complete listing of majors at JBU appears in the Majors Index beginning on page 141.

The **faculty** at JBU has 71 full-time graduate and undergraduate teachers, 70% with terminal degrees. The student-faculty ratio is 16:1, and the average **class size** in required courses is 30.

Campus Resources

Students are not required to have a computer. 75 **computers** available in the computer center, computer labs, the learning resource center, classrooms, and the library provide access to on-campus e-mail addresses, off-campus e-mail addresses, and the Internet. Staffed computer lab on campus provides training in the use of computers, software, and the Internet.

The 4 **libraries** have 100,000 books and 850 subscriptions.

Career Services

The career planning and placement office has 1 full-time, 1 part-time staff members. Services include job fairs, resume preparation, career counseling, careers library, and job bank (available on line).

Campus Life

There are 20 active organizations on campus, including a drama/theater group and student-run newspaper and radio station. 50% of students participate in student government elections. No national or local **fraternities** or **sororities**. Student **safety services** include late-night transport/escort service, 24-hour emergency telephone alarm devices, and 24-hour patrols by trained security personnel.

JBU is a member of the NAIA. **Intercollegiate sports** (some offering scholarships) include basketball (m,w), soccer (m), swimming and diving (m,w), tennis (m,w), volleyball (w).

International Students

For fall 1997, 73 international students applied, 51 were accepted, and 28 enrolled. Students can start in fall and spring. The **admissions tests** required for entrance are SAT II, TOEFL (minimum score: 550), O levels, Caribbean Examination Counsel, SAT I, or ACT; recommended is ELS. Application deadline is 4/1. On-campus **housing** is guaranteed. Services include an international student adviser on campus.

Applying

JBU requires an essay, SAT I or ACT, a high school transcript, 2 recommendations, 4 years of high school English, 4 years of high school math, 3 years of high school science, 1 year of high school social studies, 1 year of high school history, and a minimum high school GPA of 2.5. It recommends an interview and 1 year of high school foreign language. Application deadline: 3/1; 3/1 priority date for financial aid. Early and deferred entrance are possible. **Contact:** Ms. Karyn Byrne, Application Coordinator, 2000 West University Street, Siloam Springs, AR 72761-2121, 501-524-7121 or toll-free 877-JBU-INFO; fax 501-524-4196; e-mail jbuinfo@acc.jbu.edu.

GETTING IN LAST YEAR
507 applied
71% were accepted
63% enrolled (226)
35% from top tenth of their h.s. class
33% had SAT verbal scores over 600
24% had SAT math scores over 600
49% had ACT scores over 24
1 National Merit Scholars
21 valedictorians

THE STUDENT BODY
Total 1,403, of whom 1,325
  are undergraduates

From 43 states and territories,
  27 other countries
42% from Arkansas
55.9% women, 44.1% men
8.1% international students

COSTS AND FINANCIAL INFORMATION
1998–99 tuition and fees $9802
1998–99 room and board $4478

Average percent of need met 55%
Average amount received per student $8030

AFTER FRESHMAN YEAR
79% returned for sophomore year

AFTER GRADUATION
25% pursued further study (8% business, 6% education, 3% theology)
84% had job offers within 6 months
50 organizations recruited on campus

JUDSON COLLEGE

Elgin, Illinois

http://www.judson-il.edu/

Judson offers students opportunities for practical experience in their fields to ensure they will be strong candidates for jobs or graduate school. Located 40 miles northwest of Chicago and just minutes from the region's Golden Corridor of corporate headquarters, numerous possibilities for internships in business, the visual arts, the sciences, and communications exist. Multiple school districts, social service agencies, and churches provide ample practica options in education, psychology, and ministry. In addition, Judson's faculty members, many of whom have decades of work experience in their fields, are committed to serving as professional and Christian mentors to their students.

Academics

Judson offers a liberal arts curriculum and core academic program. It awards bachelor's **degrees**. Challenging opportunities include advanced placement, accelerated degree programs, student-designed majors, tutorials, an honors program, double majors, independent study, and a senior project. **Special programs** include internships, summer session for credit, off-campus study, study-abroad, and Army ROTC.

The most popular **majors** include architecture, youth ministry/adolescent studies, graphic design, business administration, and education. A complete listing of majors at Judson appears in the Majors Index beginning on page 141. The **faculty** at Judson has 38 full-time teachers, 65% with terminal degrees. The student-faculty ratio is 15:1, and the average **class size** in required courses is 25.

Campus Resources

Students are not required to have a computer. 90 **computers** available in the computer center, computer labs, the learning resource center, and the library provide access to on- and off-campus e-mail addresses and the Internet. Staffed computer lab on campus provides training in the use of computers, software, and the Internet.

The **library** has 90,000 books and 430 subscriptions.

Career Services

The career planning and placement office has 1 full-time, 1 part-time staff members. Services include job fairs, resume preparation, career counseling, and careers library.

Campus Life

Active organizations on campus include a drama/theater group and student-run newspaper and radio station. No national or local **fraternities** or **sororities**. Student **safety services** include 24-hour emergency telephone alarm devices, 24-hour patrols by trained security personnel, and electronically operated dormitory entrances.

Judson is a member of the NAIA and NCCAA. **Intercollegiate sports** (some offering scholarships) include baseball (m), basketball (m,w), cross-country running (m,w), soccer (m,w), softball (w), tennis (m,w), volleyball (w).

International Students

Students can start in fall, spring, and summer (ESL only). The **admissions tests** required for entrance are TOEFL (minimum score: 550; minimum score for ESL admission: 450) or ELS (minimum score: 109). ESL courses are only offered in the summer and fall terms. Application deadline is one month prior to the beginning of the term. On-campus **housing** available during summer.

Applying

Judson requires an essay, SAT I or ACT, a high school transcript, and a minimum high school GPA of 2.0, and in some cases an interview and 1 recommendation. It recommends 4 years of high school English, 3 years of high school math and science, and 2 years of high school social studies. Application deadline: 8/15. Deferred entrance is possible. **Contact:** Mr. Brad Hughes, Director of Admissions, 1151 North State Street, Elgin, IL 60123-1498, 847-695-2500 ext. 2310 or toll-free 800-879-5376; fax 847-695-0216; e-mail admission@mail.judson-il.edu.

GETTING IN LAST YEAR
576 applied
90% were accepted
11% from top tenth of their h.s. class
2 valedictorians

THE STUDENT BODY
993 undergraduates

From 21 states and territories,
18 other countries
62.1% women, 37.9% men
3.5% international students

COSTS AND FINANCIAL INFORMATION
1998–99 tuition and fees $12,310
1998–99 room and board $4910

Average percent of need met 68%
Average amount received per student $15,655

AFTER FRESHMAN YEAR
83% returned for sophomore year

AFTER GRADUATION
79% had job offers within 6 months

KING COLLEGE

Bristol, Tennessee

http://www.king.edu

King College provides an atmosphere where real learning can take place. Rather than teaching you what to think, King's nationally recognized liberal arts education teaches you how to think. A challenging course of study prepares students to make a living in a fast-paced and ever-changing world. However, your academic experience is not separate from your spiritual formation. Ultimately, you will find your faith encouraged by King's commitment to the Truth. Through intellectual and spiritual growth among a community of Christian mentors, you will learn to connect what you believe with how you live your life.

Academics

King offers a classical and scientific curriculum and core academic program. It awards bachelor's **degrees**. Challenging opportunities include advanced placement, double majors, independent study, and a senior project. **Special programs** include internships, summer session for credit, off-campus study, study-abroad, and Army ROTC.

The most popular **majors** include behavioral sciences, economics, and psychology. A complete listing of majors at King appears in the Majors Index beginning on page 141.

The **faculty** at King has 32 full-time teachers, 88% with terminal degrees. The student-faculty ratio is 15:1, and the average **class size** in required courses is 25.

Campus Resources

Students are not required to have a computer, but campus network and Internet access is provided from virtually every room on campus. 50 **computers** available in the computer labs, academic buildings, the library, the student center, and residence halls provide access to e-mail and the Internet. Staffed computer lab on campus provides training in the use of computers, software, and the Internet.

The **library** has 97,500 books and 625 subscriptions.

Career Services

The career planning and placement office has 1 full-time, 1 part-time staff members. Services include job fairs, resume preparation, interview workshops, resume referral, career/interest testing, career counseling, internships, and job interviews.

Campus Life

There are 25 active organizations on campus, including a drama/theater group and student-run newspaper. 75% of students participate in student government elections. No national or local **fraternities** or **sororities**. Student **safety services** include late-night transport/escort service.

King is a member of the NAIA. **Intercollegiate sports** (some offering scholarships) include baseball (m), basketball (m,w), golf (m), soccer (m,w), tennis (m,w), volleyball (w).

International Students

For fall 1997, 42 international students applied, 24 were accepted, and 9 enrolled. Application deadline is rolling. On-campus **housing** is guaranteed. Services include an international student adviser on campus.

Applying

King requires an essay, SAT I or ACT, a high school transcript, 4 years of high school English, 3 years of high school math, 1 year of high school science, 2 years of high school foreign language, 2 years of high school social studies, 4 years of high school academic electives, and a minimum high school GPA of 2.4, and in some cases an interview and recommendations. It recommends an interview. Application deadline: rolling admissions; 3/1 priority date for financial aid. Early and deferred entrance are possible. **Contact:** Ms. Mindy Clark, Director of Admissions, 1350 King College Road, Bristol, TN 37620-2699, 423-652-4861 or toll-free 800-362-0014; fax 423-652-4727; e-mail admissions@king.edu.

GETTING IN LAST YEAR
563 applied
74% were accepted
31% enrolled (130)
37% from top tenth of their h.s. class
36% had SAT verbal scores over 600
24% had SAT math scores over 600
47% had ACT scores over 24
11 valedictorians

THE STUDENT BODY
516 undergraduates

From 28 states and territories,
   19 other countries
35% from Tennessee
56.4% women, 43.6% men
7.4% international students

COSTS AND FINANCIAL INFORMATION
1997–98 tuition and fees $10,550
1997–98 room and board $3444
Average percent of need met 80%
Average amount received per student $11,250

AFTER FRESHMAN YEAR
78% returned for sophomore year
44% got a degree in 4 years
5% got a degree in 5 years
1% got a degree in 6 years

AFTER GRADUATION
27% pursued further study (8% arts and
   sciences, 6% law, 5% education)
60% had job offers within 6 months
15 organizations recruited on campus

THE KING'S UNIVERSITY COLLEGE

Edmonton, Alberta, Canada

THE KING'S UNIVERSITY COLLEGE
Christian University Education

http://www.kingsu.ab.ca/

The King's University College is an independent, degree-granting institution, delivering Christian university education. King's students learn how to be "in the world, but not of the world" through an education that integrates the Christian faith with life and learning, with an emphasis on the unique task of the Christian in a secular society. As a full partner in the Alberta postsecondary system, King's students benefit from shared resources such as library borrowing privileges and full recognition of King's degrees and course work. King's small size and highly qualified faculty contribute to a caring and intellectually stimulating environment for learning and personal growth. New degree programs and an attractive new campus mean exciting years of growth for the College and its students.

Academics

King's offers a Christian university curriculum and core academic program. It awards bachelor's **degrees**. Challenging opportunities include double concentrations, independent study, and a senior project. **Special programs** include internships, off-campus study, and study-abroad.

The most popular **concentrations** include education, psychology, and social sciences. A complete listing of majors at King's appears in the Majors Index beginning on page 141.

The **faculty** at King's has 27 full-time teachers, 100% with terminal degrees. The student-faculty ratio is 7:1, and the average **class size** in required courses is 25.

Campus Resources

Students are not required to have a computer. Student rooms are linked to a campus network. 37 **computers** available in computer labs, the library, and dormitories provide access to on-campus e-mail addresses, off-campus e-mail addresses, and the Internet. Staffed computer lab on campus provides training in the use of computers, software, and the Internet.

The **library** has 62,000 books and 350 subscriptions.

Career Services

The career planning and placement office has 1 full-time staff member. Services include career counseling and careers library.

Campus Life

There are 15 active organizations on campus, including a drama/theater group and student-run newspaper. 35% of students participate in student government elections. No national or local **fraternities** or **sororities**. Student **safety services** include 24-hour emergency telephone alarm devices, student patrols, and electronically operated dormitory entrances.

Intercollegiate sports (some offering scholarships) include basketball (m,w), soccer (m,w), volleyball (m,w).

International Students

Students can start in fall and winter. The **admissions test** required for entrance is TOEFL (minimum score: 580). Application deadlines are 8/15 and 12/1. On-campus **housing** is available, also during summer.

Applying

King's requires a high school transcript, 1 recommendation, and 1 year of high school English, and in some cases an essay and an interview. It recommends SAT I and SAT II or ACT, 1 year of high school math and science, 1 year of high school foreign language, and 1 year of high school social studies. Application deadline: rolling admissions; 3/31 for financial aid. **Contact:** Mr. Glenn Keeler, Registrar/Director of Admissions, 9125-50 Street, Edmonton, AB T6B 2H3, Canada, 403-465-8330 or toll-free 800-661-8582 (in-state); fax 403-465-3534; e-mail registrar@kingsu.ab.ca.

GETTING IN LAST YEAR
384 applied
66% were accepted
90% enrolled (229)

THE STUDENT BODY
518 undergraduates

From 4 states and territories,
   7 other countries
98% from Alberta

COSTS AND FINANCIAL INFORMATION
1998–99 tuition and fees $5075
1998–99 room and board $4598

AFTER FRESHMAN YEAR
68% returned for sophomore year
20% got a degree in 4 years
2% got a degree in 5 years
1% got a degree in 6 years

LEE UNIVERSITY
Cleveland, Tennessee

http://www.leeuniversity.edu/

The dynamic growth of Lee University—to 2,870 students today from 960 just 12 years ago—marks it as an institution "on the move." Lee's beautiful campus in east Tennessee has doubled in size during that same period with the addition of a 500-seat theater/recital hall, a student recreation/fitness complex, 3 new dorms, and 2 classroom buildings. Lee offers its own study programs in England, Ukraine, China, and Germany. Lee is well known for the vitality of its student life. Over one third of its students play intramural sports, and 400 of them perform in traveling musical groups. It has ranked at the top of all Coalition colleges in tuition affordability for 4 straight years.

Academics

Lee offers a traditional liberal arts curriculum with Christian perspective and core academic program. It awards bachelor's and master's **degrees**. Challenging opportunities include advanced placement, an honors program, and a senior project. **Special programs** include cooperative education, internships, summer session for credit, off-campus study, and study-abroad.

The most popular **majors** include individual/family development, biology, and psychology. A complete listing of majors at Lee appears in the Majors Index beginning on page 141.

The **faculty** at Lee has 96 full-time graduate and undergraduate teachers, 54% with terminal degrees. The student-faculty ratio is 22:1.

Campus Resources

Students are not required to have a computer. Purchase and/or lease options are available. **Computers** available in the computer center, computer labs, the learning resource center, the library, and dormitories provide access to the Internet. Staffed computer lab on campus provides training in the use of computers, software, and the Internet.

The **library** has 142,525 books and 1,231 subscriptions.

Career Services

The career planning and placement office has 1 part-time staff member. Services include job fairs, career/interest testing, and job bank.

Campus Life

There are 48 active organizations on campus, including a drama/theater group and student-run newspaper. 80% of students participate in student government elections. 2% of eligible men and 2% of eligible women are members of 4 local **fraternities** and 4 local **sororities**. Student **safety services** include late-night transport/escort service, 24-hour emergency telephone alarm devices, and 24-hour patrols by trained security personnel.

Lee is a member of the NAIA and NCCAA. **Intercollegiate sports** (some offering scholarships) include basketball (m,w), cross-country running (m,w), golf (m), soccer (m,w), softball (w), tennis (m,w), volleyball (w).

International Students

Students can start in fall, winter, spring, and summer. The **admissions test** required for entrance is TOEFL (minimum score: 450). Application deadline is The **admissions test** required for entrance is TOEFL (minimum score: 450).

Applying

Lee requires SAT I or ACT, a high school transcript, MMR immunization record, and a minimum high school GPA of 2.0, and in some cases 1 recommendation. It recommends 3 recommendations, 4 years of high school English, 3 years of high school math and science, 2 years of high school foreign language, 2 years of high school social studies, and 2 years of high school history. Application deadline: rolling admissions; 4/15 priority date for financial aid. Early and deferred entrance are possible. **Contact:** Admissions Coordinator, PO Box 3450, Cleveland, TN 37320-3450, 423-614-8500 or toll-free 800-LEE-9930; fax 423-614-8533; e-mail admissions@leeuniversity.edu.

GETTING IN LAST YEAR
1,593 applied
63% were accepted
73% enrolled (728)
29% from top tenth of their h.s. class
19% had SAT verbal scores over 600
17% had SAT math scores over 600
37% had ACT scores over 24

THE STUDENT BODY
Total 2,870, of whom 2,827
 are undergraduates

From 46 states and territories,
 25 other countries
36% from Tennessee
55.8% women, 44.2% men
1% international students

COSTS AND FINANCIAL INFORMATION
1998–99 tuition and fees $5826
1998–99 room and board $3760

Average percent of need met 66%
Average amount received per student $6292

AFTER FRESHMAN YEAR
70% returned for sophomore year

AFTER GRADUATION
40 organizations recruited on campus

LeTourneau University

Longview, Texas

http://www.letu.edu/

Set apart by a special "spirit of ingenuity," LeTourneau University continues to build on the excellence and inventive zeal of its heritage. From nationally acclaimed academics in technological fields like engineering, aviation, and computer science to excellent programs in the liberal arts and sciences, the University emphasizes problem solving, applied knowledge and analytical thinking. Set in the beautiful pine woods and lakes of east Texas, the spacious contemporary campus is home to innovative students from 48 states and more than 20 nations. At LeTourneau, "Faith brings us together, ingenuity sets us apart."

Academics

LeTourneau offers a core academic program. It awards associate, bachelor's, and master's **degrees**. Challenging opportunities include advanced placement and a senior project. **Special programs** include cooperative education, internships, summer session for credit, off-campus study, and study-abroad.

The most popular **majors** include aeronautical science, mechanical engineering, and electrical/electronics engineering. A complete listing of majors at LeTourneau appears in the Majors Index beginning on page 141.

The **faculty** at LeTourneau has 52 full-time graduate and undergraduate teachers, 71% with terminal degrees. The student-faculty ratio is 20:1, and the average **class size** in required courses is 24.

Campus Resources

Students are not required to have a computer. Purchase and/or lease options are available. Student rooms are linked to a campus network. 120 **computers** available in the computer center, computer labs, and the library provide access to on-campus e-mail addresses, off-campus e-mail addresses, and the Internet. Staffed computer lab on campus.

The **library** has 250,025 books and 442 subscriptions.

Career Services

The career planning and placement office has 1 full-time, 1 part-time staff members. Services include job fairs, resume preparation, resume referral, career counseling, careers library, job bank, and job interviews.

Campus Life

There are 25 active organizations on campus, including a drama/theater group and student-run newspaper. 58% of students participate in student government elections. 8% of eligible men are members of 3 societies for men. Student **safety services** include late-night transport/escort service, 24-hour emergency telephone alarm devices, 24-hour patrols by trained security personnel, and electronically operated dormitory entrances.

LeTourneau is a member of the NCAA (Division III) and NCCAA. **Intercollegiate sports** include baseball (m), basketball (m,w), cross-country running (m,w), soccer (m,w), softball (w), tennis (m,w), volleyball (w).

International Students

For fall 1997, 10 enrolled. Students can start in fall, spring, and summer. The **admissions tests** required for entrance are SAT I, TOEFL (minimum score: 500). Application deadline is rolling. On-campus **housing** is guaranteed. Services include an international student adviser on campus.

Applying

LeTourneau requires an essay, SAT I or ACT, a high school transcript, 2 recommendations, 1 year of fine arts, 1 year of computer literacy, and a minimum high school GPA of 2.0, and in some cases an interview. It recommends 4 years of high school English, 3 years of high school math and science, 1 year of high school foreign language, 3 years of high school social studies, and 3 years of high school history. Application deadline: 8/1; 2/15 priority date for financial aid. Early and deferred entrance are possible. **Contact:** Ms. Linda Fitzhugh, Vice President for Enrollment Services, PO Box 7001, Longview, TX 75607-7001, 903-233-3472 or toll-free 800-759-8811; fax 903-233-3411; e-mail admissions@james.letu.edu.

GETTING IN LAST YEAR
564 applied
89% were accepted
42% enrolled (210)
43% had SAT verbal scores over 600
47% had SAT math scores over 600
57% had ACT scores over 24
3 National Merit Scholars

THE STUDENT BODY
Total 2,204, of whom 1,881
  are undergraduates

From 48 states and territories,
  25 other countries
41.5% women, 58.5% men
3.6% international students

COSTS AND FINANCIAL INFORMATION
1997–98 tuition and fees $10,744
1997–98 room and board $4770
Average percent of need met 83%
Average amount received per student $11,295

AFTER FRESHMAN YEAR
64% returned for sophomore year
32% got a degree in 4 years
12% got a degree in 5 years
2% got a degree in 6 years

AFTER GRADUATION
5% pursued further study (5% engineering, 1% business, 1% medicine)
88% had job offers within 6 months
31 organizations recruited on campus

MALONE COLLEGE

Canton, Ohio

http://www.malone.edu/

Malone College is a Christian College for the Arts, Sciences, and Professions. Affiliated with the Evangelical Friends church, Malone is committed to offering an education of the highest quality in an environment that encourages a steadfast devotion to God. Malone students are given the opportunity to develop academically, spiritually, and socially. Through their interaction with Christian faculty members, participation in varsity and intramural athletics, outreach music and drama groups, and mission trips, each student leaves Malone with more than just a diploma. The combination of strong academics, spiritual development, and a "city close, country quiet" campus makes Malone an attractive and challenging opportunity.

Academics

Malone offers an arts, sciences, professional curriculum and core academic program; fewer than half of graduate courses are open to undergraduates. It awards bachelor's and master's **degrees**. Challenging opportunities include advanced placement, accelerated degree programs, student-designed majors, tutorials, double majors, independent study, and a senior project. **Special programs** include cooperative education, internships, summer session for credit, off-campus study, and study-abroad.

The most popular **majors** include nursing, elementary education, communication, and business administration. A complete listing of majors at Malone appears in the Majors Index beginning on page 141.

The **faculty** at Malone has 89 full-time graduate and undergraduate teachers, 54% with terminal degrees. The student-faculty ratio is 15:1, and the average **class size** in required courses is 27.

Campus Resources

Students are not required to have a computer. 129 **computers** available in the computer center, computer labs, writing lab, the library, and dormitories provide access to on-campus e-mail addresses, off-campus e-mail addresses, and the Internet. Staffed computer lab on campus provides training in the use of computers, software, and the Internet.

The **library** has 140,000 books and 1,284 subscriptions.

Career Services

The career planning and placement office has 2 full-time, 1 part-time staff members. Services include job fairs, resume preparation, interview workshops, resume referral, career/interest testing, career counseling, careers library, job bank, and job interviews.

Campus Life

There are 45 active organizations on campus, including a drama/theater group, a student-run newspaper, and a radio station. 34% of students participate in student government elections. No national or local **fraternities** or **sororities**. Student **safety services** include late-night transport/escort service, 24-hour emergency telephone alarm devices, and 24-hour patrols by trained security personnel.

Malone is a member of the NAIA and NCCAA. **Intercollegiate sports** (some offering scholarships) include baseball (m), basketball (m,w), cross-country running (m,w), football (m), golf (m,w), soccer (m,w), softball (w), tennis (m,w), track and field (m,w), volleyball (w).

International Students

For fall 1998, 18 international students applied, 13 were accepted, and 12 enrolled. Students can start in fall and spring. The **admissions test** required for entrance is TOEFL (minimum score: 520). Application deadline is 7/1. On-campus **housing** available during summer. Services include an international student adviser on campus.

Applying

Malone requires an essay, SAT I or ACT, a high school transcript, and a minimum high school GPA of 2.5, and in some cases an interview. It recommends 4 years of high school English, 3 years of high school math and science, 2 years of high school foreign language, and 3 years of high school social studies. Application deadline: 7/1; 3/1 priority date for financial aid. Early and deferred entrance are possible. **Contact:** Mr. John Chopka, Dean of Admissions, 515 25th Street, NW, Canton, OH 44709-3897, 330-471-8145 or toll-free 800-521-1146; fax 330-471-8149; e-mail admissions@malone.edu.

GETTING IN LAST YEAR
950 applied
87% were accepted
56% enrolled (468)
26% from top tenth of their h.s. class
24% had SAT verbal scores over 600
20% had SAT math scores over 600
36% had ACT scores over 24
11 valedictorians

THE STUDENT BODY
Total 2,242, of whom 2,016
are undergraduates

From 20 states and territories,
10 other countries
93% from Ohio
62.1% women, 37.9% men
.7% international students

COSTS AND FINANCIAL INFORMATION
1998–99 tuition and fees $11,795
1998–99 room and board $4925
Average percent of need met 93%
Average amount received per student $9782

AFTER FRESHMAN YEAR
67% returned for sophomore year
29% got a degree in 4 years
12% got a degree in 5 years
3% got a degree in 6 years

AFTER GRADUATION
9% pursued further study (6% business, 2% arts
and sciences, 1% medicine)
68% had job offers within 6 months
23 organizations recruited on campus

THE MASTER'S COLLEGE AND SEMINARY

Santa Clarita, California

http://www.masters.edu/

THE MASTER'S COLLEGE
21726 Placerita Canyon Road
Santa Clarita, CA 91321

The Master's College exists to empower students for a life of enduring commitment to Christ, biblical fidelity, moral integrity, intellectual growth, and lasting contribution to the kingdom of God. A dynamic campus community, numerous ministry opportunities, and an outstanding, accessible faculty are key components of this mission. Located on a beautiful 103-acre campus in the Santa Clarita Valley, TMC offers a BA in 35 programs, a BS in 12 programs and an MA in biblical counseling. Also offered are a Professional Studies Program for working adults, a one-year diploma in Bible, and a unique one-semester field study program in Israel.

Academics
Master's offers a Bible-based curriculum and core academic program. It awards bachelor's and master's **degrees**. Challenging opportunities include advanced placement, accelerated degree programs, tutorials, double majors, independent study, and a senior project. **Special programs** include cooperative education, internships, summer session for credit, off-campus study, and study-abroad.

The most popular **majors** include biblical studies, education, and business administration. A complete listing of majors at Master's appears in the Majors Index beginning on page 141.

The **faculty** at Master's has 60 full-time graduate and undergraduate teachers, 76% with terminal degrees. The student-faculty ratio is 16:1.

Campus Resources
Students are not required to have a computer. 65 **computers** available in the computer center, computer labs, and the library provide access to on-campus e-mail addresses, off-campus e-mail addresses, and the Internet. Staffed computer lab on campus provides training in the use of computers, software, and the Internet.

The 2 **libraries** have 200,000 books and 900 subscriptions.

Career Services
The career planning and placement office has 2 full-time, 1 part-time staff members. Services include job fairs, resume preparation, resume referral, career counseling, careers library, and job bank.

Campus Life
Active organizations on campus include a drama/theater group and student-run radio station. 80% of students participate in student government elections. No national or local **fraternities** or **sororities**. Student **safety services** include 24-hour patrols by trained security personnel.

Master's is a member of the NAIA. **Intercollegiate sports** (all offering scholarships) include baseball (m), basketball (m,w), cross-country running (m,w), soccer (m,w), volleyball (w).

International Students
For fall 1997, 15 international students applied, 9 were accepted, and 7 enrolled. Students can start in fall and spring. The **admissions test** required for entrance is TOEFL (minimum score: 525). Application deadline is 5/31. On-campus **housing** is guaranteed, also available during summer. Services include an international student adviser on campus.

Applying
Master's requires an essay, SAT I or ACT, a high school transcript, an interview, 2 recommendations, 4 years of high school English, 3 years of high school math and science, 2 years of high school history, 5 years of high school academic electives, and a minimum high school GPA of 2.5. Application deadline: 3/6; 3/2 priority date for financial aid. Early and deferred entrance are possible. **Contact:** Mr. Yaphet Peterson, Director of Enrollment, 21726 Placerita Canyon Road, Santa Clarita, CA 91321-1200, 805-259-3540 ext. 368 or toll-free 800-568-6248; fax 805-254-1998; e-mail enrollment@masters.edu.

GETTING IN LAST YEAR
410 applied
82% were accepted
68% enrolled (229)
35% from top tenth of their h.s. class
26% had SAT verbal scores over 600
34% had SAT math scores over 600
44% had ACT scores over 24
3 National Merit Scholars
10 class presidents
15 valedictorians

THE STUDENT BODY
Total 1,198, of whom 917
    are undergraduates
From 40 states and territories,
    8 other countries
51.9% women, 48.1% men
1.2% international students

COSTS AND FINANCIAL INFORMATION
1997–98 tuition and fees $12,180
1997–98 room and board $4798

Average percent of need met 87%

AFTER FRESHMAN YEAR
78% returned for sophomore year

AFTER GRADUATION
35% pursued further study (25% theology, 4% arts and sciences, 2% business)
95% had job offers within 6 months
30 organizations recruited on campus

MESSIAH COLLEGE
Grantham, Pennsylvania

http://www.messiah.edu/

Messiah College is a Christian college of the liberal and applied arts and sciences. The College is committed to an embracing evangelical spirit rooted in the Anabaptist, Pietist, and Wesleyan traditions of the Christian Church. The College's mission is to educate men and women toward maturity of intellect, character, and Christian faith in preparation for lives of service, leadership, and reconciliation in church and society. The College's primary campus of 400 acres is located in south-central Pennsylvania, 10 miles south of Harrisburg. More than 55 academic programs are available. Since 1968, the College has supported a second campus in Philadelphia that is adjacent to and in alliance with Temple University.

Academics
Messiah College offers a liberal arts and sciences curriculum and core academic program. It awards bachelor's **degrees**. Challenging opportunities include advanced placement, accelerated degree programs, student-designed majors, tutorials, an honors program, double majors, independent study, and a senior project. **Special programs** include internships, summer session for credit, off-campus study, and study-abroad.

The most popular **majors** include elementary education, biology, and nursing. A complete listing of majors at Messiah College appears in the Majors Index beginning on page 141.

The **faculty** at Messiah College has 139 full-time teachers, 73% with terminal degrees. The student-faculty ratio is 15:1, and the average **class size** in required courses is 24.

Campus Resources
Students are not required to have a computer. Purchase and/or lease options are available. Student rooms are linked to a campus network. 272 **computers** available in the computer center, computer labs, the research center, the learning resource center, classrooms, the library, and dormitories provide access to on-campus e-mail addresses, off-campus e-mail addresses, and the Internet. Staffed computer lab on campus provides training in the use of computers and software.

The **library** has 224,694 books and 1,312 subscriptions.

Career Services
The career planning and placement office has 4 full-time, 1 part-time staff members. Services include job fairs, resume preparation, interview workshops, resume referral, career/interest testing, career counseling, careers library, job bank (available on line), and job interviews.

Campus Life
There are 76 active organizations on campus, including a drama/theater group and student-run newspaper and radio station. 35% of students participate in student government elections. No national or local **fraternities** or **sororities**. Student **safety services** include late-night transport/escort service, 24-hour emergency telephone alarm devices, 24-hour patrols by trained security personnel, student patrols, and electronically operated dormitory entrances.

Messiah College is a member of the NCAA (Division III). **Intercollegiate sports** include baseball (m), basketball (m,w), cross-country running (m,w), field hockey (w), golf (m), lacrosse (m,w), soccer (m,w), softball (w), tennis (m,w), track and field (m,w), volleyball (w), wrestling (m).

International Students
For fall 1997, 39 international students applied, 20 were accepted, and 11 enrolled. Students can start in fall and spring. The **admissions test** required for entrance is TOEFL (minimum score: 550; minimum score for ESL admission: 550); recommended is SAT I or ACT. Application deadline is rolling. On-campus **housing** is guaranteed, also available during summer. Services include an international student adviser on campus.

Applying
Messiah College requires an essay, SAT I or ACT, a high school transcript, 2 recommendations, 4 years of high school English, 2 years of high school math and science, 2 years of high school foreign language, 2 years of high school social studies, and 4 years of high school academic electives. It recommends an interview, 3 years of high school math and science, 3 years of high school foreign language, 2 years of high school history, and a minimum high school GPA of 3.0. Application deadline: rolling admissions; 4/1 for financial aid. Early and deferred entrance are possible. **Contact:** Mr. William G. Strausbaugh, Dean for Enrollment Management, 1 College Avenue, Grantham, PA 17027, 717-691-6000 or toll-free 800-382-1349 (in-state), 800-233-4220 (out-of-state); fax 717-796-5374; e-mail admiss@messiah.edu.

GETTING IN LAST YEAR
1,940 applied
87% were accepted
41% enrolled (690)
29% from top tenth of their h.s. class
40% had SAT verbal scores over 600
37% had SAT math scores over 600
63% had ACT scores over 24
8 National Merit Scholars
30 valedictorians

THE STUDENT BODY
2,616 undergraduates

From 40 states and territories,
14 other countries
52% from Pennsylvania
61.2% women, 38.8% men
1.5% international students

COSTS AND FINANCIAL INFORMATION
1997–98 tuition and fees $12,990
1997–98 room and board $5500
Average percent of need met 74%
Average amount received per student $10,104

AFTER FRESHMAN YEAR
84% returned for sophomore year
64% got a degree in 4 years
5% got a degree in 5 years
1% got a degree in 6 years

AFTER GRADUATION
9% pursued further study (7% arts and sciences, 1% business, 1% education)
95% had job offers within 6 months
385 organizations recruited on campus
1 Rhodes scholar

MidAmerica Nazarene University

Olathe, Kansas   *http://www.mnu.edu/*

MidAmerica Nazarene University is a private holiness university in the Wesleyan tradition. Sponsored by the Church of the Nazarene, it is a coeducational, career-oriented, liberal arts college offering 5 degree options: Associate of Arts, Bachelor of Arts, Bachelor of Science in Nursing, Master of Education, and Master of Business Administration. Among the most popular new programs is the management and human relations degree-completion program. The 105-acre campus is 19 miles southwest of Kansas City. The University has as its purpose the Christian education of individuals in a liberal arts context for personal development, service to God and humanity, and career preparation.

Academics
MNU offers an American heritage curriculum and core academic program. It awards associate, bachelor's, and master's **degrees** (master's degree in education and business administration). Challenging opportunities include advanced placement, accelerated degree programs, double majors, independent study, and a senior project. **Special programs** include internships, summer session for credit, off-campus study, study-abroad, and Army and Air Force ROTC.

The most popular **majors** include management and human relations, elementary education, business administration, and nursing. A complete listing of majors at MNU appears in the Majors Index beginning on page 141.

The **faculty** at MNU has 67 full-time graduate and undergraduate teachers, 42% with terminal degrees. The student-faculty ratio is 17:1.

Campus Resources
Students are not required to have a computer. Purchase and/or lease options are available. Student rooms are linked to a campus network. 40 **computers** available in the computer center, computer labs, and the library provide access to on-campus e-mail addresses, off-campus e-mail addresses, and the Internet. Staffed computer lab on campus provides training in the use of computers and software.

The **library** has 88,486 books and 225 subscriptions.

Career Services
The career planning and placement office has 2 full-time, 1 part-time staff members. Services include job fairs, resume preparation, interview workshops, career/interest testing, career counseling, careers library, job bank, and job interviews.

Campus Life
Active organizations on campus include a drama/theater group and student-run newspaper and radio station. 35% of students participate in student government elections. No national or local **fraternities** or **sororities**. Student **safety services** include late-night transport/escort service, 24-hour emergency telephone alarm devices, student patrols, and electronically operated dormitory entrances.

MNU is a member of the NAIA and NCCAA. **Intercollegiate sports** (some offering scholarships) include baseball (m), basketball (m,w), cross-country running (m,w), football (m), softball (w), track and field (m,w), volleyball (w).

International Students
For fall 1997, 60 international students applied, 12 were accepted, and 3 enrolled. Students can start in fall, spring, and summer. The **admissions test** required for entrance is TOEFL (minimum score: 500; minimum score for ESL admission: 500); recommended are SAT I or ACT. Application deadline is 5/15 for fall and 9/15 for spring. On-campus **housing** is guaranteed, also available during summer. Services include an international student adviser on campus.

Applying
MNU requires SAT I or ACT, a high school transcript, 2 recommendations, and a minimum high school GPA of 2.0. It recommends 4 years of high school English, 3 years of high school math and science, 1 year of high school foreign language, and 3 years of high school social studies. Application deadline: 8/1; 3/1 priority date for financial aid. Early and deferred entrance are possible. **Contact:** Mr. Dennis Troyer, Admissions Counselor, 2030 East College Way, Olathe, KS 66062-1899, 913-782-3750 ext. 481 or toll-free 800-800-8887; fax 913-791-3481; e-mail admissions@mnu.edu.

GETTING IN LAST YEAR
363 applied
90% were accepted
76% enrolled (249)
18% from top tenth of their h.s. class
20% had SAT verbal scores over 600
23% had SAT math scores over 600

THE STUDENT BODY
Total 1,400, of whom 1,229
  are undergraduates

From 33 states and territories,
  13 other countries
59% from Kansas
57.5% women, 42.6% men
1.2% international students

COSTS AND FINANCIAL INFORMATION
1998–99 tuition and fees $10,022
1998–99 room and board $4810
Average percent of need met 37%

Average amount received per student $4220

AFTER FRESHMAN YEAR
72% returned for sophomore year
26% got a degree in 4 years
14% got a degree in 5 years
5% got a degree in 6 years

AFTER GRADUATION
40 organizations recruited on campus

MILLIGAN COLLEGE

Milligan College, Tennessee

http://www.milligan.edu/

Milligan College combines the 3 areas of learning: God's world (taught through science), God's man (taught through the humanities), and God Himself (taught through revelation). Christ is central at Milligan College—both in its curriculum and in campus life. Milligan is a Christian liberal arts college dedicated to the integration of faith and learning in all facets of its college program. Milligan's mission is to prepare today's young people for a complicated world, and to do it in a Christian environment. Milligan's motto is "Christian education: the hope of the world!"

Academics

Milligan offers a Christian liberal arts curriculum and core academic program; fewer than half of graduate courses are open to undergraduates. It awards associate, bachelor's, and master's **degrees**. Challenging opportunities include advanced placement, accelerated degree programs, and tutorials. **Special programs** include cooperative education, internships, summer session for credit, off-campus study, study-abroad, and Army ROTC.

The most popular **majors** include mass communications and biblical studies. A complete listing of majors at Milligan appears in the Majors Index beginning on page 141.

The **faculty** at Milligan has 64 full-time graduate and undergraduate teachers, 59% with terminal degrees. The student-faculty ratio is 12:1.

Campus Resources

Students are not required to have a computer. Purchase and/or lease options are available. Student rooms are linked to a campus network. 80 **computers** available in the computer center, computer labs, the learning resource center, classrooms, and the library provide access to on-campus e-mail addresses, off-campus e-mail addresses, and the Internet. Staffed computer lab on campus provides training in the use of computers, software, and the Internet.

The **library** has 105,417 books and 598 subscriptions.

Career Services

The career planning and placement office has 1 part-time staff member. Services include job fairs, resume preparation, career counseling, careers library, and job interviews.

Campus Life

There are 27 active organizations on campus, including a drama/theater group and student-run newspaper and radio station. 80% of students participate in student government elections. No national or local **fraternities** or **sororities**. Student **safety services** include late-night transport/escort service and 24-hour patrols by trained security personnel.

Milligan is a member of the NAIA. **Intercollegiate sports** (some offering scholarships) include baseball (m), basketball (m,w), golf (m), soccer (m,w), softball (w), tennis (m,w), volleyball (w).

International Students

For fall 1997, 7 international students applied, 3 were accepted, and 2 enrolled. Students can start in fall, spring, and summer. The **admissions test** required for entrance is TOEFL (minimum score: 550); recommended is SAT I or ACT. Application deadline is rolling. On-campus **housing** is guaranteed, also available during summer.

Applying

Milligan requires an essay, SAT I or ACT, a high school transcript, 2 recommendations, and a minimum high school GPA of 2.0, and in some cases an interview. It recommends 3 years of high school math and science, 2 years of high school foreign language, and a minimum high school GPA of 3.0. Application deadline: rolling admissions; 3/1 priority date for financial aid. Early and deferred entrance are possible. **Contact:** Mr. Michael A. Johnson, Vice President for Enrollment Management, PO Box 210, Milligan College, TN 37682, 423-461-8730 or toll-free 800-262-8337 (in-state); fax 423-461-8960.

GETTING IN LAST YEAR
636 applied
81% were accepted
32% had SAT verbal scores over 600
23% had SAT math scores over 600
44% had ACT scores over 24

THE STUDENT BODY
Total 911, of whom 842
  are undergraduates

From 36 states and territories,
  9 other countries
40% from Tennessee
61.6% women, 38.4% men
1.5% international students

COSTS AND FINANCIAL INFORMATION
1998–99 tuition and fees $10,800
1998–99 room and board $3800

Average percent of need met 77%
Average amount received per student $10,868

AFTER FRESHMAN YEAR
74.2% returned for sophomore year
33% got a degree in 4 years
11% got a degree in 5 years
1% got a degree in 6 years

MONTREAT COLLEGE
Montreat, North Carolina

http://www.montreat.edu/

Montreat College's beautiful mountain campus is located 15 miles east of Asheville, NC, in the heart of one of America's most spectacularly scenic areas—the Blue Ridge Mountains. With challenging programs and a favorable student/faculty ratio of 12:1, Montreat College enrollment is rapidly growing. The student body typically represents 25 states and 10 foreign countries. Students on the Montreat campus (the traditional program) may choose from more than two dozen majors and minors. Montreat College's off-campus School of Professional and Adult Studies, which holds classes in Asheville, Charlotte, and various other NC locations, offers BBA and MBA degrees. Montreat College places great emphasis on the idea of servant leadership. Students are provided with numerous opportunities for practical leadership and service experience.

Academics
Montreat College offers a Christian liberal arts curriculum and core academic program. It awards associate, bachelor's, and master's **degrees**. Challenging opportunities include advanced placement, double majors, independent study, and a senior project. **Special programs** include cooperative education, internships, off-campus study, and study-abroad.

The most popular **majors** include business administration, environmental science, and religious studies. A complete listing of majors at Montreat College appears in the Majors Index beginning on page 141.

The **faculty** at Montreat College has 32 full-time graduate and undergraduate teachers, 67% with terminal degrees.

Campus Resources
Students are not required to have a computer. Purchase and/or lease options are available. Student rooms are linked to a campus network. 36 **computers** available in computer labs, gymnasium, classrooms, the library, and the student center provide access to on-campus e-mail addresses, off-campus e-mail addresses, and the Internet. Staffed computer lab on campus provides training in the use of computers and software.

The **library** has 67,378 books and 426 subscriptions.

Career Services
The career planning and placement office has 1 full-time staff member. Services include resume preparation, career counseling, and careers library.

Campus Life
There are 14 active organizations on campus, including a drama/theater group and student-run newspaper. 25% of students participate in student government elections. No national or local **fraternities** or **sororities**. Student **safety services** include 24-hour emergency telephone alarm devices, 24-hour patrols by trained security personnel, and electronically operated dormitory entrances.

Montreat College is a member of the NAIA. **Intercollegiate sports** (some offering scholarships) include baseball (m), basketball (m,w), cross-country running (m,w), golf (m), soccer (m,w), softball (w), tennis (m,w), volleyball (w).

International Students
For fall 1998, 37 international students applied, 10 were accepted, and 6 enrolled. Students can start in fall and spring. The **admissions test** required for entrance is TOEFL (minimum score: 500); recommended are SAT I or ACT, SAT II. Application deadline is 8/15. On-campus **housing** is guaranteed. Services include an international student adviser on campus.

Applying
Montreat College requires an essay, SAT I or ACT, a high school transcript, 1 recommendation, 3 years of high school math and science, and 1 year of high school foreign language, and in some cases an interview. Application deadline: 5/15 priority date for financial aid. Early and deferred entrance are possible. **Contact:** Ms. Anita Darby, Director of Admissions, PO Box 1267, Montreat, NC 28757-1267, 828-669-8012 ext. 3784 or toll-free 800-622-6968 (in-state); fax 828-669-0120; e-mail admissions@montreat.edu.

GETTING IN LAST YEAR
399 applied
72% were accepted
36% enrolled (143)
12% from top tenth of their h.s. class
16% had SAT verbal scores over 600
12% had SAT math scores over 600

THE STUDENT BODY
Total 1,021, of whom 970
    are undergraduates

From 30 states and territories,
    9 other countries
53.8% women, 46.2% men
.9% international students

COSTS AND FINANCIAL INFORMATION
1998–99 tuition and fees $10,444
1998–99 room and board $4098
Average percent of need met 80%

Average amount received per student $10,078

AFTER FRESHMAN YEAR
81% returned for sophomore year

AFTER GRADUATION
17% pursued further study
70% had job offers within 6 months
17 organizations recruited on campus

MOUNT VERNON NAZARENE COLLEGE

Mount Vernon, Ohio

http://www.mvnc.edu

At Mount Vernon Nazarene College, you'll encounter a high-quality higher education learning environment within a Christian worldview. Ours is a history of change and innovation; over the past three decades, we've become a leader in Christian higher education. Here you'll access more than 60 high-quality academic programs covering the full range of today's career fields, in-depth preprofessional preparation, and friends you will cherish the rest of your life—everything you need to build a successful future serving God and humanity in the 21st century!

Academics

MVNC offers a distribution curriculum and core academic program. It awards associate, bachelor's, and master's **degrees**. Challenging opportunities include advanced placement, tutorials, freshman honors college, an honors program, and a senior project. **Special programs** include internships, summer session for credit, off-campus study, and study-abroad.

The most popular **majors** include social sciences, business administration, and education. A complete listing of majors at MVNC appears in the Majors Index beginning on page 141.

The **faculty** at MVNC has 74 full-time graduate and undergraduate teachers, 60% with terminal degrees. The average **class size** in required courses is 22.

Campus Resources

Students are not required to have a computer. Student rooms are linked to a campus network. 162 **computers** available in the computer center, computer labs, the learning resource center, business, education labs, the library, and dormitories provide access to on-campus e-mail addresses, off-campus e-mail addresses, and the Internet. Staffed computer lab on campus provides training in the use of computers and software.

The **library** has 81,268 books and 575 subscriptions.

Career Services

The career planning and placement office has 1 full-time, 1 part-time staff members. Services include resume preparation, resume referral, career counseling, careers library, job bank, and job interviews.

Campus Life

There are 30 active organizations on campus, including a drama/theater group and student-run newspaper and radio station. No national or local **fraternities** or **sororities**. Student **safety services** include late-night transport/escort service, 24-hour emergency telephone alarm devices, and 24-hour patrols by trained security personnel.

MVNC is a member of the NAIA and NCCAA. **Intercollegiate sports** (some offering scholarships) include baseball (m), basketball (m,w), soccer (m,w), softball (w), volleyball (w).

International Students

The **admissions test** required for entrance is TOEFL (minimum score: 500). Application deadline is 5/15. On-campus **housing** is guaranteed, also available during summer. Services include a multicultural affairs office to assist with enrollment and retention.

Applying

MVNC requires an essay, ACT, a high school transcript, 2 recommendations, 3 years of high school English, 2 years of high school math, 1 year of high school science, 2 years of high school social studies, and a minimum high school GPA of 2.0. It recommends an interview, 4 years of high school English, 3 years of high school math, 2 years of high school science, and 2 years of high school foreign language. Application deadline: 5/15. Early and deferred entrance are possible. **Contact:** Ms. Doris Webb, Director of Admissions and Student Recruitment, 800 Martinsburg Road, Mount Vernon, OH 43050-9500, 740-397-9000 or toll-free 800-782-2435; e-mail admissions@mvnc.edu.

GETTING IN LAST YEAR
17% from top tenth of their h.s. class
3 National Merit Scholars
13 valedictorians

THE STUDENT BODY
Total 1,857, of whom 1,835
  are undergraduates

From 31 states and territories,
  6 other countries
.3% international students

COSTS AND FINANCIAL INFORMATION
1997–98 tuition and fees $9977
1997–98 room and board $3843
Average percent of need met 86%

Average amount received per student $10,943

AFTER FRESHMAN YEAR
67% returned for sophomore year

AFTER GRADUATION
16% pursued further study
73% had job offers within 6 months
40 organizations recruited on campus

NORTH PARK UNIVERSITY
Chicago, Illinois

http://www.northpark.edu/

Founded in 1891 by the Evangelical Covenant Church, North Park is Chicago's only Christian residential liberal arts university. Located in a park-like setting, North Park enrolls 1,350 undergraduate and 400 graduate students from across the country (36 states) and around the world (23 countries). North Park, well-known for its small classes and personal attention from faculty, has repeatedly been named one of "America's Best Colleges" by *U.S. News and World Report*. The College provides over 20 urban ministry programs, 300 internship opportunities, and on-campus African American, Korean, Latino, Middle Eastern, and Scandinavian cultural study centers.

Academics
North Park offers an interdisciplinary, thematic curriculum and core academic program. It awards bachelor's, master's, doctoral, and first professional **degrees**. Challenging opportunities include advanced placement, accelerated degree programs, student-designed majors, tutorials, freshman honors college, an honors program, and a senior project. **Special programs** include internships, summer session for credit, off-campus study, and study-abroad.

The most popular **majors** include business administration, nursing, and psychology. A complete listing of majors at North Park appears in the Majors Index beginning on page 141.

The **faculty** at North Park has 86 undergraduate teachers, 74% with terminal degrees. The student-faculty ratio is 16:1.

Campus Resources
Students are not required to have a computer. Purchase and/or lease options are available. Student rooms are linked to a campus network. 75 **computers** available in the computer center, computer labs, classrooms, the library, and dormitories provide access to on-campus e-mail addresses, off-campus e-mail addresses, and the Internet. Staffed computer lab on campus provides training in the use of computers and software.

The 5 **libraries** have 224,182 books and 1,131 subscriptions.

Career Services
The career planning and placement office has 1 full-time, 1 part-time staff members. Services include job fairs, resume preparation, resume referral, career counseling, careers library, job bank, and job interviews.

Campus Life
There are 10 active organizations on campus, including a drama/theater group and student-run newspaper. 50% of students participate in student government elections. No national or local **fraternities** or **sororities**. Student **safety services** include late-night transport/escort service, 24-hour emergency telephone alarm devices, and 24-hour patrols by trained security personnel.

North Park is a member of the NCAA (Division III). **Intercollegiate sports** include baseball (m), basketball (m,w), cross-country running (m,w), football (m), golf (m), soccer (m,w), softball (w), tennis (w), track and field (m,w), volleyball (m,w).

International Students
For fall 1997, 90 enrolled. The **admissions test** required for entrance is TOEFL (minimum score: 550). Application deadline is rolling. On-campus **housing** is guaranteed, also available during summer. Services include an international student adviser on campus.

Applying
North Park requires an essay, SAT I or ACT, a high school transcript, 1 recommendation, and a minimum high school GPA of 2.0, and in some cases an interview. It recommends 3 years of high school math and science and a minimum high school GPA of 3.0. Application deadline: rolling admissions; 5/1 priority date for financial aid. Early entrance is possible. **Contact:** Office of Admissions, 3225 West Foster Avenue, Chicago, IL 60625-4895, 773-244-5500 or toll-free 800-888-NPC8; fax 773-583-0858; e-mail afao@northpark.edu.

GETTING IN LAST YEAR
713 applied
85% were accepted
52% enrolled (316)
17% from top tenth of their h.s. class
39% had ACT scores over 24
5 National Merit Scholars

THE STUDENT BODY
Total 2,004, of whom 1,582
  are undergraduates

From 36 states and territories,
  23 other countries
61.6% women, 38.4% men
7.1% international students

COSTS AND FINANCIAL INFORMATION
1997–98 tuition and fees $14,690
1997–98 room and board $4820

AFTER FRESHMAN YEAR
67% returned for sophomore year

43% got a degree in 4 years
15% got a degree in 5 years
1% got a degree in 6 years

AFTER GRADUATION
20% pursued further study (10% arts and
  sciences, 4% theology, 3% medicine)
60% had job offers within 6 months
30 organizations recruited on campus

NORTHWEST CHRISTIAN COLLEGE

Eugene, Oregon   *http://www.nwcc.edu/*

For over 100 years, Northwest Christian College has provided a quality education in a vibrant and supportive academic community. Excellent programs of study linked to career preparation open doors in business, communications, counseling, ministry, and teaching. Because the College is deliberately small, students receive personal attention every step of the way. Superb professors take a personal interest, not just in the classroom, but in every day settings where informal learning takes place. Students can expect an educational experience that develops their strengths, deepens their faith, and builds their professional potential.

Academics
NCC offers a broad-based liberal arts curriculum and core academic program. It awards associate, bachelor's, and master's **degrees**. Challenging opportunities include advanced placement, accelerated degree programs, student-designed majors, tutorials, double majors, independent study, and a senior project. **Special programs** include cooperative education, internships, off-campus study, study-abroad, and Army ROTC.

The most popular **majors** include elementary education, business administration, and psychology. A complete listing of majors at NCC appears in the Majors Index beginning on page 141.

The **faculty** at NCC has 18 full-time graduate and undergraduate teachers, 67% with terminal degrees. The student-faculty ratio is 17:1, and the average **class size** in required courses is 25.

Campus Resources
Students are not required to have a computer. Purchase and/or lease options are available. 40 **computers** available in computer labs, classrooms, and the library provide access to on-campus e-mail addresses and the Internet. Staffed computer lab on campus provides training in the use of computers, software, and the Internet.

The **library** has 60,247 books and 261 subscriptions.

Career Services
The career planning and placement office has 1 full-time, 1 part-time staff members. Services include job fairs, resume preparation, career counseling, careers library, and job bank.

Campus Life
There are 8 active organizations on campus, including a drama/theater group, music ensembles, and a student-run newspaper. 30% of students participate in student government elections. No national or local **fraternities** or **sororities**. Student **safety services** include late-night transport/escort service, 24-hour emergency telephone alarm devices, student patrols, and electronically operated dormitory entrances.

NCC is a member of the NCCAA. **Intercollegiate sports** (some offering scholarships) include basketball (m), cross-country running (w), softball (w).

International Students
For fall 1997, 6 international students applied, 1 was accepted, and 1 enrolled. Students can start in fall, winter, and spring. The **admissions test** required for entrance is TOEFL (minimum score: 500). Application deadline is 6/1. On-campus **housing** is guaranteed, also available during summer. Services include an international student adviser on campus.

Applying
NCC requires an essay, SAT I or ACT, a high school transcript, 2 recommendations, and a minimum high school GPA of 2.5, and in some cases SAT II Subject Tests. It recommends an interview, 4 years of high school English, 2 years of high school math, 3 years of high school science, 2 years of high school foreign language, 2 years of high school social studies, and 1 year of high school history. Application deadline: rolling admissions; 3/1 priority date for financial aid. Deferred entrance is possible. **Contact:** Dr. Randy Jones, Vice President for Admissions, 828 East 11th Avenue, Eugene, OR 97401-3727, 541-684-7201; fax 541-684-7317.

GETTING IN LAST YEAR
215 applied
94% were accepted
24% from top tenth of their h.s. class
26% had SAT verbal scores over 600
12% had SAT math scores over 600
47% had ACT scores over 24
4 valedictorians

THE STUDENT BODY
Total 438, of whom 384 are undergraduates

From 6 states and territories, 2 other countries
82% from Oregon
65.6% women, 34.4% men
.5% international students

COSTS AND FINANCIAL INFORMATION
1998–99 tuition and fees $11,640
1998–99 room and board $4986

AFTER FRESHMAN YEAR
58% returned for sophomore year

23% got a degree in 4 years
13% got a degree in 5 years
3% got a degree in 6 years

AFTER GRADUATION
10% pursued further study
20 organizations recruited on campus

NORTHWEST COLLEGE

Kirkland, Washington

http://www.nwcollege.edu/

Since 1934, Northwest has successfully prepared students for service and leadership. Situated on 65 beautiful acres, the campus overlooks Lake Washington, just 10 miles east of Seattle. Over 850 students choose from nearly 50 academic programs, including teacher education, biblical literature, psychology, church ministries, business management and administration, religion and philosophy, music, and teaching English as a second language. Sports include basketball, volleyball, soccer, cross-country, and track and field. Student ministries provide a range of options in music and drama as well as opportunities to serve children, prisoners, and inner city populations. Northwest College—intensely academic, distinctly Christian.

Academics

Northwest College offers an interdisciplinary curriculum and core academic program. It awards associate and bachelor's **degrees**. Challenging opportunities include advanced placement, accelerated degree programs, student-designed majors, double majors, independent study, and a senior project. **Special programs** include internships, summer session for credit, and study-abroad.

The most popular **majors** include psychology, church ministries, and elementary education. A complete listing of majors at Northwest College appears in the Majors Index beginning on page 141.

The **faculty** at Northwest College has 44 full-time teachers, 43% with terminal degrees. The student-faculty ratio is 17:1, and the average **class size** in required courses is 23.

Campus Resources

Students are not required to have a computer. Student rooms are linked to a campus network. 40 **computers** available in the computer center, computer labs, the library, and dormitories provide access to on-campus e-mail addresses, off-campus e-mail addresses, and the Internet. Staffed computer lab on campus provides training in the use of computers, software, and the Internet.

The **library** has 70,947 books and 790 subscriptions.

Career Services

The career planning and placement office has 1 full-time staff member. Services include resume preparation, interview workshops, career/interest testing, career counseling, careers library, job bank, and job interviews.

Campus Life

There are 10 active organizations on campus, including a drama/theater group and student-run newspaper and radio station. 70% of students participate in student government elections. No national or local **fraternities** or **sororities**. Student **safety services** include late-night transport/escort service, 24-hour emergency telephone alarm devices, 24-hour patrols by trained security personnel, and electronically operated dormitory entrances.

Northwest College is a member of the NAIA and NCCAA. **Intercollegiate sports** (offering scholarships) include basketball (m,w), cross-country running (m,w), soccer (m), track and field (m,w), volleyball (w).

International Students

Students can start in fall, spring, and summer. The **admissions test** required for entrance is TOEFL (minimum score: 500). Application deadline is 8/1. On-campus **housing** is guaranteed, also available during summer.

Applying

Northwest College requires an essay, SAT I or ACT, a high school transcript, 2 recommendations, and a minimum high school GPA of 2.3, and in some cases an interview. It recommends 4 years of high school English, 3 years of high school math, 2 years of high school science, 2 years of high school foreign language, 2 years of high school social studies, and 3 years of high school academic electives. Application deadline: 8/1; 3/1 priority date for financial aid. Early and deferred entrance are possible. **Contact:** Dr. Calvin L. White, Director of Enrollment Services, PO Box 579, Kirkland, WA 98083-0579, 425-889-5231 or toll-free 800-669-3781; fax 425-425-0148; e-mail admissions@ncag.edu.

GETTING IN LAST YEAR
222 applied
98% were accepted
76% enrolled (165)
19% had SAT verbal scores over 600
4% had SAT math scores over 600
22% had ACT scores over 24

THE STUDENT BODY
860 undergraduates
From 22 states and territories,
  9 other countries
73% from Washington
57.8% women, 42.2% men
1.7% international students

COSTS AND FINANCIAL INFORMATION
1997–98 tuition and fees $8940
1997–98 room and board $4310
Average percent of need met 86%
Average amount received per student $7696

AFTER FRESHMAN YEAR
71% returned for sophomore year

NORTHWESTERN COLLEGE
Orange City, Iowa
http://www.nwciowa.edu/

Northwestern College offers students and faculty members an academic journey that reflects on what it means to be a reformed, evangelical Christian in today's society. The academic program nurtures the development of a biblical perspective. Student development programs provide opportunities for holistic growth and Christian service. Eighty percent of Northwestern's academic facilities have been built or renovated since 1986, along with an award-winning chapel, intercollegiate athletic center, and cafeteria. A fiber-optic computer network connects nearly every campus building, linking 180 workstations and allowing students to explore the resources of Ramaker Library without leaving their residence hall.

Academics
Northwestern offers a Western civilization and interdisciplinary curriculum and core academic program. It awards associate and bachelor's **degrees**. Challenging opportunities include advanced placement, accelerated degree programs, student-designed majors, tutorials, freshman honors college, an honors program, and a senior project. **Special programs** include cooperative education, internships, summer session for credit, off-campus study, and study-abroad.

The most popular **majors** include business administration, elementary education, and biology. A complete listing of majors at Northwestern appears in the Majors Index beginning on page 141.

The **faculty** at Northwestern has 64 full-time teachers, 82% with terminal degrees. The student-faculty ratio is 16:1, and the average **class size** in required courses is 40.

Campus Resources
Students are not required to have a computer. Student rooms are linked to a campus network. 225 **computers** available in the computer center, computer labs, the learning resource center, Demco Business Center, Kresge Education Center, classrooms, the library, and dormitories provide access to on-campus e-mail addresses, off-campus e-mail addresses, and the Internet. Staffed computer lab on campus provides training in the use of computers and software.

The 2 **libraries** have 102,947 books and 536 subscriptions.

Career Services
The career planning and placement office has 1 full-time, 1 part-time staff members. Services include job fairs, resume preparation, interview workshops, resume referral, career counseling, careers library, job bank, and job interviews.

Campus Life
There are 30 active organizations on campus, including a drama/theater group and student-run newspaper and radio station. 65% of students participate in student government elections. No national or local **fraternities** or **sororities**. Student **safety services** include 24-hour emergency telephone alarm devices and electronically operated dormitory entrances.

Northwestern is a member of the NAIA. **Intercollegiate sports** (some offering scholarships) include baseball (m), basketball (m,w), cross-country running (m,w), football (m), golf (m,w), soccer (m,w), softball (w), tennis (m,w), track and field (m,w), volleyball (w), wrestling (m).

International Students
For fall 1997, 34 international students applied, 24 were accepted, and 9 enrolled. Students can start in fall and spring. The **admissions test** required for entrance is TOEFL (minimum score: 550); recommended are SAT I or ACT, ELS. Application deadline is The **admissions test** required for entrance is TOEFL (minimum score: 550). On-campus **housing** is guaranteed. Services include an international student adviser on campus.

Applying
Northwestern requires an essay, SAT I or ACT, a high school transcript, 1 recommendation, and a minimum high school GPA of 2.0. It recommends an interview, 4 years of high school English, 3 years of high school math and science, 2 years of high school foreign language, and 3 years of high school social studies. Application deadline: rolling admissions; 4/1 priority date for financial aid. Deferred entrance is possible. **Contact:** Mr. Ronald K. DeJong, Director of Admissions, 101 College Lane, Orange City, IA 51041-1996, 712-737-7000 or toll-free 800-747-4757 (in-state); fax 712-737-7164; e-mail markb@nwciowa.edu.

GETTING IN LAST YEAR
895 applied
93% were accepted
39% enrolled (329)
27% from top tenth of their h.s. class
35% had SAT verbal scores over 600
23% had SAT math scores over 600
54% had ACT scores over 24
2 National Merit Scholars
23 valedictorians

THE STUDENT BODY
1,177 undergraduates

From 31 states and territories,
13 other countries
63% from Iowa
58.7% women, 41.3% men
2.2% international students

COSTS AND FINANCIAL INFORMATION
1997–98 tuition and fees $11,300
1997–98 room and board $3300
Average percent of need met 90%
Average amount received per student $9699

AFTER FRESHMAN YEAR
67% returned for sophomore year
45% got a degree in 4 years
9% got a degree in 5 years
2% got a degree in 6 years

AFTER GRADUATION
9% pursued further study (3% medicine, 2% law, 2% theology)
88% had job offers within 6 months
28 organizations recruited on campus

NORTHWESTERN COLLEGE

St. Paul, Minnesota

http://www.nwc.edu/

Northwestern is an accredited, nondenominational Christian college with a unique curriculum. A student's choice of 36 academic majors is complemented by a second major in Bible. This allows students to see the influence of spiritual truth as it relates to intellectual pursuit. The warm and friendly atmosphere, challenging academic programs, and superb facilities offer each student an excellent environment in which to develop academically, physically, and spiritually.

Academics

Northwestern offers a core academic program. It awards associate and bachelor's **degrees**. Challenging opportunities include advanced placement, double majors, independent study, and a senior project. **Special programs** include internships, summer session for credit, off-campus study, study-abroad, and Army and Air Force ROTC.

The most popular **majors** include business administration, psychology, and organizational behavior. A complete listing of majors at Northwestern appears in the Majors Index beginning on page 141.

The **faculty** at Northwestern has 75 full-time teachers, 59% with terminal degrees. The student-faculty ratio is 15:1.

Campus Resources

Students are not required to have a computer. 104 **computers** available in computer labs, the library, and the student center provide access to off-campus e-mail addresses and the Internet. Staffed computer lab on campus provides training in the use of computers, software, and the Internet.

The **library** has 74,857 books and 1,695 subscriptions.

Career Services

The career planning and placement office has 2 full-time staff members. Services include job fairs, resume preparation, interview workshops, resume referral, career/interest testing, career counseling, careers library, job bank (available on line), and job interviews.

Campus Life

There are 25 active organizations on campus, including a drama/theater group and student-run newspaper and radio station. 25% of students participate in student government elections. No national or local **fraternities** or **sororities**. Student **safety services** include late-night transport/escort service, 24-hour patrols by trained security personnel, and student patrols.

Northwestern is a member of the NAIA and NCCAA. **Intercollegiate sports** include baseball (m), basketball (m,w), cross-country running (m,w), football (m), golf (m), soccer (m,w), softball (w), tennis (m,w), track and field (m,w), volleyball (w).

International Students

For fall 1997, 19 were accepted and 5 enrolled. Students can start in fall. The **admissions test** required for entrance is TOEFL (minimum score: 530); recommended is SAT I or ACT. Application deadline is 6/1. On-campus **housing** is guaranteed. Services include an international student adviser on campus.

Applying

Northwestern requires an essay, SAT I or ACT, a high school transcript, 2 recommendations, lifestyle agreement, statement of Christian faith, and a minimum high school GPA of 2.0, and in some cases an interview. It recommends PSAT, an interview, 4 years of high school English, 3 years of high school math and science, 2 years of high school foreign language, 3 years of high school social studies, and a minimum high school GPA of 3.0. Application deadline: 8/15; 3/1 priority date for financial aid. Early and deferred entrance are possible. **Contact:** Mr. Kenneth K. Faffler, Director of Recruitment, 3003 Snelling Avenue North, St. Paul, MN 55113-1598, 612-631-5209 or toll-free 800-827-6827; fax 612-631-5680; e-mail admissions@nwc.edu.

GETTING IN LAST YEAR
1,110 applied
70% were accepted
49% enrolled (379)
22% from top tenth of their h.s. class
36% had SAT verbal scores over 600
47% had SAT math scores over 600
48% had ACT scores over 24
14 valedictorians

THE STUDENT BODY
1,664 undergraduates

From 42 states and territories,
16 other countries
61% from Minnesota
60.2% women, 39.8% men
1.2% international students

COSTS AND FINANCIAL INFORMATION
1998–99 tuition and fees $13,920
1998–99 room and board $4173
Average percent of need met 79%
Average amount received per student $11,340

AFTER FRESHMAN YEAR
75% returned for sophomore year
36% got a degree in 4 years
10% got a degree in 5 years
2% got a degree in 6 years

AFTER GRADUATION
5% pursued further study (2% theology, 1% arts and sciences, 1% education)
77% had job offers within 6 months
147 organizations recruited on campus

NORTHWEST NAZARENE COLLEGE

Nampa, Idaho

http://www.nnc.edu/

Northwest Nazarene College emphasizes development of the whole person. Spiritual, physical, intellectual, and emotional well-being are treated as important aspects of the educational process. The success of this integrative process is reflected by *U.S. News & World Report* consistently placing NNC among the top ten liberal arts colleges in the western United States. Numerous cocurricular programs involve students in community service as well as assistance programs in foreign countries. The college has an honors program, an outstanding undergraduate research program open to all departments, and internship programs in many departments. Also, NNC hosts the NAIA National Basketball Tournament from 1993 to 2001.

Academics

NNC offers a core academic program; fewer than half of graduate courses are open to undergraduates. It awards bachelor's and master's **degrees**. Challenging opportunities include advanced placement, accelerated degree programs, student-designed majors, tutorials, freshman honors college, an honors program, independent study, and a senior project. **Special programs** include cooperative education, internships, summer session for credit, off-campus study, study-abroad, and Army ROTC.

The most popular **majors** include elementary education, business administration, and social sciences. A complete listing of majors at NNC appears in the Majors Index beginning on page 141.

The **faculty** at NNC has 76 full-time graduate and undergraduate teachers, 67% with terminal degrees. The student-faculty ratio is 14:1, and the average **class size** in required courses is 21.

Campus Resources

Students are not required to have a computer. Purchase and/or lease options are available. Student rooms are linked to a campus network. 350 **computers** available in the computer center, computer labs, classrooms, and the library provide access to various software packages, on-campus e-mail addresses, off-campus e-mail addresses, and the Internet. Staffed computer lab on campus provides training in the use of computers and software.

The **library** has 100,966 books and 821 subscriptions.

Career Services

Services include resume preparation, resume referral, career counseling, careers library, job bank, and job interviews.

Campus Life

Active organizations on campus include a drama/theater group and student-run newspaper. 51% of students participate in student government elections. No national or local **fraternities** or **sororities**. Student **safety services** include residence hall check-in system, late-night transport/escort service, 24-hour patrols by trained security personnel, student patrols, and electronically operated dormitory entrances.

NNC is a member of the NAIA. **Intercollegiate sports** (some offering scholarships) include baseball (m), basketball (m,w), soccer (m,w), tennis (w), volleyball (w).

International Students

Students can start in fall, winter, spring, and summer. The **admissions test** required for entrance is TOEFL (minimum score: 500; minimum score for ESL admission: 500); recommended is ACT. Application deadline is rolling. On-campus **housing** is guaranteed, also available during summer. Services include an international student adviser on campus.

Applying

NNC requires a high school transcript, 2 recommendations, and a minimum high school GPA of 2.5, and in some cases ACT and an interview. It recommends ACT, SAT I or ACT, WPCT, 3 years of high school math and science, and 2 years of high school foreign language. Application deadline: 9/19; 3/1 priority date for financial aid. Early and deferred entrance are possible. **Contact:** Ms. Stacey Berggren, Director of Admissions, 623 Holly Street, Nampa, ID 83686-5897, 208-467-8950 or toll-free 800-NNC-4-YOU; fax 208-467-8645; e-mail bwswanson@exodus.nnc.edu.

GETTING IN LAST YEAR
880 applied
46% were accepted
68% enrolled (275)
18% from top tenth of their h.s. class
45% had ACT scores over 24
3 National Merit Scholars
16 valedictorians

THE STUDENT BODY
Total 1,774, of whom 1,116 are undergraduates

From 29 states and territories
31% from Idaho
56.5% women, 43.5% men
.3% international students

COSTS AND FINANCIAL INFORMATION
1998–99 tuition and fees $12,456
1998–99 room and board $3519
Average percent of need met 78%

Average amount received per student $11,336

AFTER FRESHMAN YEAR
85% returned for sophomore year
22% got a degree in 4 years
13% got a degree in 5 years
4% got a degree in 6 years

AFTER GRADUATION
22% pursued further study (6% medicine, 5% law, 3% business)

NYACK COLLEGE
Nyack, New York

http://www.nyackcollege.edu/

Beautifully situated in a suburban community on the Hudson River, Nyack College partakes of the rich cultural and ethnic diversity of suburban New York. Founded in 1882 for missionaries and ministers, Nyack has a long tradition of providing education that blends scholarship and service. Though today's curriculum is more diverse, ranging from business to missiology to communications, a sound education and a thorough grounding in the faith still characterize the Nyack graduate.

Academics
Nyack offers a Christian liberal arts curriculum and core academic program. It awards associate, bachelor's, and master's **degrees**. Challenging opportunities include advanced placement, double majors, and independent study. **Special programs** include internships, summer session for credit, off-campus study, and study-abroad.

The most popular **majors** include elementary education, psychology, and business administration. A complete listing of majors at Nyack appears in the Majors Index beginning on page 141.

The **faculty** at Nyack has 51 full-time graduate and undergraduate teachers, 59% with terminal degrees. The student-faculty ratio is 25:1, and the average **class size** in required courses is 45.

Campus Resources
Students are not required to have a computer. 100 **computers** available in the computer center, computer labs, the learning resource center, and the library provide access to on-campus e-mail addresses, off-campus e-mail addresses, and the Internet. Staffed computer lab on campus provides training in the use of computers, software, and the Internet.

The 2 **libraries** have 72,000 books and 510 subscriptions.

Career Services
Services include job fairs, resume preparation, career counseling, careers library, and job bank.

Campus Life
Active organizations on campus include a drama/theater group and student-run newspaper and radio station. 70% of students participate in student government elections. No national or local **fraternities** or **sororities**. Student **safety services** include late-night transport/escort service, 24-hour emergency telephone alarm devices, 24-hour patrols by trained security personnel, and student patrols.

Nyack is a member of the NAIA and NCCAA. **Intercollegiate sports** (some offering scholarships) include baseball (m), basketball (m,w), cross-country running (m,w), soccer (m,w), softball (w), volleyball (m,w).

International Students
For fall 1997, 35 international students applied, 23 were accepted, and 11 enrolled. Students can start in fall and spring. The **admissions test** required for entrance is TOEFL or CELT; recommended is SAT I or ACT. Application deadline is rolling. On-campus **housing** is guaranteed, also available during summer. Services include an international student adviser on campus.

Applying
Nyack requires an essay, SAT I or ACT, a high school transcript, 3 recommendations, 3 years of high school math/science, 3 years of high school social science, and a minimum high school GPA of 2.0, and in some cases an interview. It recommends 4 years of high school English, 2 years of high school foreign language, and 4 years of high school academic electives. Application deadline: 9/11; 3/15 priority date for financial aid. Early and deferred entrance are possible. **Contact:** Mr. Miguel A. Sanchez, Director of Admissions, One South Boulevard, Nyack, NY 10960-3698, 914-358-1710 ext. 350 or toll-free 800-33-NYACK; fax 914-358-3047; e-mail enroll@nyack.edu.

GETTING IN LAST YEAR
901 applied
70% were accepted
11% from top tenth of their h.s. class
21% had SAT verbal scores over 600
11% had SAT math scores over 600
17% had ACT scores over 24

THE STUDENT BODY
Total 1,433, of whom 1,121 are undergraduates

From 36 states and territories, 27 other countries
65% from New York
55.6% women, 44.4% men
5.4% international students

COSTS AND FINANCIAL INFORMATION
1998–99 tuition and fees $11,650
1998–99 room and board $5340
Average percent of need met 50%

Average amount received per student $8000

AFTER FRESHMAN YEAR
62% returned for sophomore year

AFTER GRADUATION
65% had job offers within 6 months
50 organizations recruited on campus

OKLAHOMA BAPTIST UNIVERSITY

Shawnee, Oklahoma

http://www.okbu.edu/

Unique academic programs and an emphasis on learning through doing are hallmarks of Oklahoma Baptist University. Growing from the vision of Baptists of the Oklahoma Territory, OBU is a leader in ministry training, business, teacher education, nursing, premedicine, music, and many other fields. OBU's innovative Unified Studies program provides a carefully constructed common core that integrates what students learn in various academic disciplines, providing a well-rounded liberal arts foundation for living in a rapidly changing world. Students excel in national exams and competitions and in their commitment to international service. OBU is a leader among Southern Baptist institutions in the number of mission volunteers. Nationally competitive in athletics, OBU has compiled 16 top-5 finishes in the 1990s.

Academics

OBU offers a liberal arts and sciences, Western Civilization curriculum and core academic program. It awards bachelor's and master's **degrees**. Challenging opportunities include advanced placement, student-designed majors, tutorials, freshman honors college, an honors program, double majors, independent study, and a senior project. **Special programs** include cooperative education, internships, summer session for credit, off-campus study, study-abroad, and Air Force ROTC.

The most popular **majors** include nursing, biblical studies, and psychology. A complete listing of majors at OBU appears in the Majors Index beginning on page 141.

The **faculty** at OBU has 114 full-time graduate and undergraduate teachers, 73% with terminal degrees. The student-faculty ratio is 14:1, and the average **class size** in required courses is 26.

Campus Resources

Students are not required to have a computer. 170 **computers** available in the computer center, computer labs, the learning resource center, classrooms, the library, and dormitories provide access to on-campus e-mail addresses, off-campus e-mail addresses, and the Internet. Staffed computer lab on campus provides training in the use of computers, software, and the Internet.

The **library** has 275,000 books and 600 subscriptions.

Career Services

The career planning and placement office has 2 full-time staff members. Services include job fairs, resume preparation, resume referral, career counseling, careers library, job bank, and job interviews.

Campus Life

There are 50 active organizations on campus, including a drama/theater group and student-run newspaper. 40% of students participate in student government elections. 18% of eligible men and 16% of eligible women are members of 5 local **fraternities** and 5 local **sororities**. Student **safety services** include late-night transport/escort service, 24-hour emergency telephone alarm devices, 24-hour patrols by trained security personnel, and electronically operated dormitory entrances.

OBU is a member of the NAIA. **Intercollegiate sports** (all offering scholarships) include baseball (m), basketball (m,w), cross-country running (m,w), golf (m,w), softball (w), tennis (m,w), track and field (m,w).

International Students

For fall 1997, 28 international students applied, 16 were accepted, and 6 enrolled. Students can start in fall, winter, spring, and summer. The **admissions test** required for entrance is TOEFL (minimum score: 500); recommended are SAT I or ACT, ELS. Application deadline is 3/1. On-campus **housing** is guaranteed, also available during summer. Services include an international student adviser on campus.

Applying

OBU requires SAT I or ACT, a high school transcript, and a minimum high school GPA of 2.5, and in some cases an essay, an interview, and recommendations. It recommends 4 years of high school English, 3 years of high school math and science, 2 years of high school foreign language, 1 year of high school social studies, 2 years of high school history, and 2 years of high school academic electives. Application deadline: 8/1; 3/1 priority date for financial aid. Deferred entrance is possible. **Contact:** Mr. Michael Cappo, Dean of Admissions, 500 West University, Shawnee, OK 74801-2558, 405-878-2033 or toll-free 800-654-3285; fax 405-878-2046; e-mail admissions@mail.okbu.edu.

GETTING IN LAST YEAR
917 applied
97% were accepted
53% enrolled (466)
39% from top tenth of their h.s. class
31% had SAT verbal scores over 600
31% had SAT math scores over 600
55% had ACT scores over 24
3 National Merit Scholars
43 valedictorians

THE STUDENT BODY
Total 2,211, of whom 2,181 are undergraduates

From 38 states and territories, 33 other countries
61% from Oklahoma
53.8% women, 46.2% men
2.4% international students

COSTS AND FINANCIAL INFORMATION
1998–99 tuition and fees $8336
1998–99 room and board $3250

Average percent of need met 70%
Average amount received per student $5922

AFTER FRESHMAN YEAR
79% returned for sophomore year

AFTER GRADUATION
35% pursued further study (15% theology, 10% arts and sciences, 5% business)
45 organizations recruited on campus

OKLAHOMA CHRISTIAN UNIVERSITY OF SCIENCE AND ARTS

Oklahoma City, Oklahoma

Oklahoma Christian (OC) is rated a Best Value in American Education by *U.S. News & World Report* and was commended for excellent faculty by the North Central Association of Colleges and Secondary Schools. OC is a four-year liberal arts University dedicated to providing an education that will prepare students for the spiritual and educational challenges of the 21st century. From ecology students that get their hands dirty to composition classes that are completely paperless to Computer Science students that work on projects for the university, Oklahoma Christian students learn by doing. In addition, Oklahoma Christian is second to none in international studies. With semester abroad programs in Latin America, Vienna, Austria, Japan, and Great Britain, OC offers you the world.

Academics

Oklahoma Christian offers a core academic program. It awards bachelor's and master's **degrees**. Challenging opportunities include advanced placement, accelerated degree programs, an honors program, and a senior project. **Special programs** include internships, summer session for credit, off-campus study, study-abroad, and Army and Air Force ROTC.

The most popular **majors** include business administration, elementary education, and biology. A complete listing of majors at Oklahoma Christian appears in the Majors Index beginning on page 141.

The **faculty** at Oklahoma Christian has 78 full-time graduate and undergraduate teachers, 67% with terminal degrees. The student-faculty ratio is 15:1, and the average **class size** in required courses is 25.

Campus Resources

Students are not required to have a computer. Purchase and/or lease options are available. Student rooms are linked to a campus network. 135 **computers** available in computer labs, business, science buildings, and the library provide access to on-campus e-mail addresses, off-campus e-mail addresses, and the Internet. Staffed computer lab on campus provides training in the use of computers and software.

The **library** has 95,789 books and 415 subscriptions.

Career Services

The career planning and placement office has 1 full-time, 2 part-time staff members. Services include job fairs, resume preparation, resume referral, career counseling, careers library, job bank, and job interviews.

Campus Life

Active organizations on campus include a drama/theater group and student-run newspaper and radio station. No national or local **fraternities** or **sororities**. Student **safety services** include late-night transport/escort service, 24-hour emergency telephone alarm devices, and 24-hour patrols by trained security personnel.

Oklahoma Christian is a member of the NAIA. **Intercollegiate sports** (some offering scholarships) include baseball (m), basketball (m,w), cross-country running (m,w), soccer (m,w), softball (w), tennis (m), track and field (m,w).

International Students

The **admissions test** required for entrance is TOEFL (minimum score: 500). Application deadline is 9/1. On-campus **housing** is guaranteed, also available during summer. Services include an international student adviser on campus.

Applying

Oklahoma Christian requires SAT I or ACT and a high school transcript. Application deadline: rolling admissions; 3/15 priority date for financial aid. Early and deferred entrance are possible. **Contact:** Mr. Kyle Ray, Director of Admissions, Box 11000, Oklahoma City, OK 73136-1100, 405-425-5050 or toll-free 800-877-5010 (in-state); fax 405-425-5208; e-mail info@oc.edu.

GETTING IN LAST YEAR
1,210 applied
100% were accepted
12% had SAT verbal scores over 600
26% had SAT math scores over 600

THE STUDENT BODY
Total 1,904, of whom 1,885
  are undergraduates

From 44 states and territories,
  28 other countries

COSTS AND FINANCIAL INFORMATION
1997–98 tuition and fees $8278
1997–98 room and board $3840
Average percent of need met 72%

Average amount received per student $7225

AFTER FRESHMAN YEAR
67% returned for sophomore year

AFTER GRADUATION
82% had job offers within 6 months
75 organizations recruited on campus

Olivet Nazarene University

Bourbonnais, Illinois
http://www.olivet.edu/

Olivet Nazarene University exists to provide Education with a Christian Purpose. The academic depth and practical opportunities in a broad range of disciplines result in 85% of alumni reporting employment in a field related to their major. Located 1 hour south of downtown Chicago, the 168-acre campus supplies a small-town atmosphere and access to a world-class city. The 29 major buildings include a 3,000-seat athletic center, 35,000-watt WONU-FM radio (live on the Internet), and a planetarium. Some 400 students participate in music (choirs, band, orchestra, ensembles) and more than 500 in intramural sports. The campus is fully networked, including two Internet connection ports in each dorm room.

Academics
Olivet offers a core academic program; a few graduate courses are open to undergraduates. It awards bachelor's and master's **degrees**. Challenging opportunities include advanced placement, accelerated degree programs, student-designed majors, double majors, independent study, and a senior project. **Special programs** include cooperative education, internships, summer session for credit, study-abroad, and Army ROTC.

The most popular **majors** include elementary education, nursing, and psychology. A complete listing of majors at Olivet appears in the Majors Index beginning on page 141.

The **faculty** at Olivet has 100 full-time undergraduate teachers, 65% with terminal degrees. The student-faculty ratio is 17:1.

Campus Resources
Students are not required to have a computer. Purchase and/or lease options are available. 149 **computers** available in the computer center, computer labs, the learning resource center, departmental labs, classrooms, and the library provide access to on-campus e-mail addresses and the Internet. Staffed computer lab on campus provides training in the use of computers and software.

The **library** has 144,513 books and 998 subscriptions.

Career Services
The career planning and placement office has 2 full-time, 1 part-time staff members. Services include job fairs, resume preparation, interview workshops, resume referral, career/interest testing, career counseling, careers library, job bank, and job interviews.

Campus Life
There are 30 active organizations on campus, including a drama/theater group and student-run newspaper and radio station. 50% of students participate in student government elections. No national or local **fraternities** or **sororities**. Student **safety services** include late-night transport/escort service and 24-hour patrols by trained security personnel.

Olivet is a member of the NAIA. **Intercollegiate sports** (some offering scholarships) include baseball (m), basketball (m,w), cross-country running (m,w), football (m), golf (m), soccer (m,w), softball (w), tennis (m,w), track and field (m,w), volleyball (w).

International Students
For fall 1997, 18 international students applied, 4 were accepted, and 1 enrolled. The **admissions test** required for entrance is TOEFL (minimum score: 500). Application deadline is 6/1. On-campus **housing** is guaranteed, also available during summer. Services include an international student adviser on campus.

Applying
Olivet requires ACT, a high school transcript, 2 recommendations, 3 years of high school English, 5 years of high school academic electives, and a minimum high school GPA of 2.0. It recommends an interview and 3 years of high school science. Application deadline: 8/1; 3/1 priority date for financial aid. Early and deferred entrance are possible. **Contact:** John Mongerson, Director of Admissions, PO Box 592, Kankakee, IL 60901, 815-939-5203 or toll-free 800-648-1463; e-mail admissions@olivet.edu.

GETTING IN LAST YEAR
944 applied
92% were accepted
23% from top tenth of their h.s. class
41% had ACT scores over 24

THE STUDENT BODY
Total 2,285, of whom 1,874
  are undergraduates
From 40 states and territories,
  19 other countries

40% from Illinois
57.6% women, 42.4% men

COSTS AND FINANCIAL INFORMATION
1997–98 tuition and fees $10,838
1997–98 room and board $4560
Average percent of need met 76%
Average amount received per student $10,458

AFTER FRESHMAN YEAR
71% returned for sophomore year

37% got a degree in 4 years
10% got a degree in 5 years
2% got a degree in 6 years

AFTER GRADUATION
10% pursued further study
15 organizations recruited on campus

Peterson's Christian Colleges & Universities

ORAL ROBERTS UNIVERSITY

Tulsa, Oklahoma　　　　　*http://www.oru.edu/*

Because of a unique approach to education, ORU graduates are prepared to excel in today's workforce. At ORU, students do more than just earn a degree. They learn that a formal college education is just the beginning of a lifelong education. In addition to learning the specifics of your chosen field, you will learn the importance of character and ethics, as well as integrity, in your relationships with others. ORU provides an environment of excellence and a culture of commitment. Excellence is the hallmark of ORU's progressive and innovative academic programs. Offering more than 70 undergraduate majors, as well as preprofessional and graduate programs, ORU integrates exceptional learning opportunities with true Christian principles. At the same time, commitment to Jesus Christ is at the center of everything at ORU.

Academics
ORU offers a core academic program. It awards bachelor's, master's, and doctoral **degrees**. Challenging opportunities include advanced placement, accelerated degree programs, student-designed majors, freshman honors college, and an honors program. **Special programs** include internships, summer session for credit, and study-abroad.

The most popular **majors** include business administration, telecommunications, and elementary education. A complete listing of majors at ORU appears in the Majors Index beginning on page 141.

The **faculty** at ORU has 187 full-time graduate and undergraduate teachers, 52% with terminal degrees. The student-faculty ratio is 16:1.

Campus Resources
Students are not required to have a computer. Student rooms are linked to a campus network. 250 **computers** available in the computer center, computer labs, the learning resource center, classrooms, the library, and dormitories provide access to on-campus e-mail addresses, off-campus e-mail addresses, and the Internet. Staffed computer lab on campus provides training in the use of computers and software.

The 3 **libraries** have 306,005 books and 1,500 subscriptions.

Career Services
The career planning and placement office has 2 full-time, 4 part-time staff members. Services include job fairs, resume preparation, resume referral, career counseling, careers library, job bank, and job interviews.

Campus Life
Active organizations on campus include a drama/theater group and student-run newspaper and radio station. 70% of students participate in student government elections. No national or local **fraternities** or **sororities**. Student **safety services** include late-night transport/escort service, 24-hour emergency telephone alarm devices, and 24-hour patrols by trained security personnel.

ORU is a member of the NCAA (Division I). **Intercollegiate sports** (some offering scholarships) include baseball (m,w), basketball (m,w), cross-country running (m,w), golf (m,w), soccer (m,w), tennis (m,w), track and field (m,w), volleyball (w).

International Students
For fall 1997, 200 international students applied, 90 were accepted, and 85 enrolled. Students can start in fall and spring. The **admissions test** required for entrance is TOEFL (minimum score: 500); recommended are SAT I or ACT, ELS. Application deadline is rolling. On-campus **housing** is guaranteed, also available during summer. Services include an international student adviser on campus.

Applying
ORU requires an essay, SAT I or ACT, a high school transcript, 1 recommendation, 4 years of high school English, 2 years of high school math and science, 2 years of high school foreign language, 2 years of high school social studies, 2 years of high school history, 4 years of high school academic electives, and a minimum high school GPA of 2.6, and in some cases an interview. It recommends 3 years of high school math and 3 years of high school foreign language. Application deadline: rolling admissions; 4/15 priority date for financial aid. Early and deferred entrance are possible. **Contact:** Mrs. LeAnne Langley, Director of Undergraduate Admissions, 7777 South Lewis Avenue, Tulsa, OK 74171-0001, 918-495-6518 or toll-free 800-678-8876 (out-of-state); fax 918-495-6222; e-mail admissions@oru.edu.

GETTING IN LAST YEAR
2,262 applied
60% were accepted
21% from top tenth of their h.s. class
18% had SAT verbal scores over 600
23% had SAT math scores over 600
7 National Merit Scholars
15 valedictorians

THE STUDENT BODY
Total 3,966, of whom 3,229
　　are undergraduates
From 52 states and territories,
　　43 other countries
38% from Oklahoma

COSTS AND FINANCIAL INFORMATION
1998–99 tuition and fees $10,460

1998–99 room and board $4728
Average percent of need met 80%
Average amount received per student $12,636

AFTER FRESHMAN YEAR
74% returned for sophomore year

PALM BEACH ATLANTIC COLLEGE

West Palm Beach, Florida   *http://www.pbac.edu/*

Palm Beach Atlantic College combines the Christian tradition of service with twenty-first century technology. PBA was among the first colleges, more than 25 years ago, to ask students to put their Christian beliefs into action with a program requiring them to contribute at least 45 hours of community service annually to nonprofit agencies, churches, and schools. PBA is also on the information highway. Every residence hall bedroom is equipped with a computer connected to PalmNET, a campus-wide fiber optic network that gives students access to e-mail, the Internet, World Wide Web, and numerous electronic databases. Academic and extracurricular opportunities range from internships and real-world projects at area businesses to mission efforts around the world to a variety of on- and off-campus ministry opportunities.

Academics

PBA offers a core academic program. It awards bachelor's and master's **degrees**. Challenging opportunities include advanced placement, tutorials, freshman honors college, an honors program, and a senior project. **Special programs** include internships, summer session for credit, and study-abroad.

The most popular **majors** include business administration, education, and psychology. A complete listing of majors at PBA appears in the Majors Index beginning on page 141.

The **faculty** at PBA has 80 full-time graduate and undergraduate teachers, 68% with terminal degrees. The student-faculty ratio is 16:1.

Campus Resources

Students are not required to have a computer. Student rooms are linked to a campus network. 550 **computers** available in the computer center, computer labs, the library, dormitories, and student rooms provide access to on-campus e-mail addresses, off-campus e-mail addresses, and the Internet. Staffed computer lab on campus provides training in the use of computers and software.

The **library** has 117,795 books and 1,457 subscriptions.

Career Services

The career planning and placement office has 1 full-time staff member. Services include job fairs, resume preparation, resume referral, career counseling, careers library, job bank, job interviews, and internship referrals.

Campus Life

Active organizations on campus include a drama/theater group and student-run newspaper. 31% of students participate in student government elections. No national or local **fraternities** or **sororities**. Student **safety services** include late-night transport/escort service, 24-hour emergency telephone alarm devices, 24-hour patrols by trained security personnel, and electronically operated dormitory entrances.

PBA is a member of the NAIA. **Intercollegiate sports** (some offering scholarships) include baseball (m), basketball (m), cross-country running (m,w), golf (m,w), soccer (m,w), softball (w), tennis (m,w), volleyball (w).

International Students

The **admissions test** required for entrance is TOEFL (minimum score: 550). Application deadline is August 1. The **admissions test** required for entrance is TOEFL (minimum score: 550). On-campus **housing** is guaranteed. Services include an international student adviser on campus.

Applying

PBA requires an essay, SAT I or ACT, a high school transcript, 2 recommendations, and a minimum high school GPA of 2.0. It recommends an interview, 3 years of high school math and science, and a minimum high school GPA of 3.0. Application deadline: 8/1; 5/1 priority date for financial aid. Early and deferred entrance are possible. **Contact:** Mr. Buck James, Dean of Enrollment Services, 901 South Flagler Dr, PO Box 24708, West Palm Beach, FL 33416-4708, 561-803-2100 or toll-free 800-238-3998; e-mail admit@pbac.edu.

GETTING IN LAST YEAR
20% from top tenth of their h.s. class
19% had SAT verbal scores over 600
17% had SAT math scores over 600
1 valedictorians

THE STUDENT BODY
Total 2,071, of whom 1,773
 are undergraduates

From 39 states and territories,
 50 other countries

COSTS AND FINANCIAL INFORMATION
1998–99 tuition and fees $10,580
1998–99 room and board $4638
Average percent of need met 85%

Average amount received per student $11,150

AFTER FRESHMAN YEAR
55% returned for sophomore year

AFTER GRADUATION
75 organizations recruited on campus

POINT LOMA NAZARENE UNIVERSITY

San Diego, California

http://www.ptloma.edu/

PLNC is a distinctly Christian college that has provided a high-quality education for almost 100 years. Located on the crest of historic Point Loma, collegians enjoy a clear view westward overlooking the Pacific Ocean and eastward across downtown San Diego, where many cultural and employment opportunities are available. President Jim Bond states "the primary goal of Point Loma Nazarene College is to provide a broad-based experience in the liberal arts, within an environment of vital Christianity, designed to equip men and women with the skills to cope effectively in a complex and constantly changing world."

Academics

PLNU offers a Christian liberal arts curriculum and core academic program; fewer than half of graduate courses are open to undergraduates. It awards bachelor's and master's **degrees**. Challenging opportunities include advanced placement, accelerated degree programs, tutorials, an honors program, independent study, and a senior project. **Special programs** include internships, summer session for credit, off-campus study, study-abroad, and Army, Navy, and Air Force ROTC.

The most popular **majors** include liberal arts and studies, business administration, and nursing. A complete listing of majors at PLNU appears in the Majors Index beginning on page 141.

The **faculty** at PLNU has 133 full-time graduate and undergraduate teachers, 80% with terminal degrees. The student-faculty ratio is 15:1, and the average **class size** in required courses is 25.

Campus Resources

Students are not required to have a computer. Purchase and/or lease options are available. Student rooms are linked to a campus network. 125 **computers** available in the computer center, computer labs, the learning resource center, and dormitories provide access to on-campus e-mail addresses, off-campus e-mail addresses, and the Internet. Staffed computer lab on campus provides training in the use of computers, software, and the Internet.

The **library** has 151,263 books and 8,396 subscriptions.

Career Services

The career planning and placement office has 1 full-time staff member. Services include job fairs, resume preparation, interview workshops, resume referral, career/interest testing, career counseling, careers library, job bank (available on line), and job interviews.

Campus Life

There are 50 active organizations on campus, including a drama/theater group and student-run newspaper and radio station. 25% of students participate in student government elections. 8% of eligible men and 5% of eligible women are members of 1 national **sorority**, 3 local **fraternities**, and 2 local sororities. Student **safety services** include late-night transport/escort service, 24-hour patrols by trained security personnel, and student patrols.

PLNU is a member of the NAIA. **Intercollegiate sports** (some offering scholarships) include baseball (m), basketball (m,w), cross-country running (m,w), golf (m), soccer (m,w), softball (w), tennis (m,w), track and field (m,w), volleyball (w).

International Students

For fall 1997, 55 enrolled. Students can start in fall, spring, and summer. The **admissions tests** required for entrance are SAT I, ACT, TOEFL (minimum score: 550). Application deadline is 3/1. On-campus **housing** is guaranteed, also available during summer. Services include an international student adviser on campus.

Applying

PLNU requires an essay, SAT I or ACT, a high school transcript, 2 recommendations, and a minimum high school GPA of 2.8, and in some cases an interview. It recommends SAT I, 4 years of high school English, 2 years of high school math, 2 years of high school foreign language, and 1 year of high school history. Application deadline: 3/1; 3/15 priority date for financial aid. Deferred entrance is possible. **Contact:** Executive Director for Enrollment Services, 3900 Lomaland Drive, San Diego, CA 92106-2899, 619-849-2225; fax 619-849-2579; e-mail cnlsr3ad@ptloma.edu.

GETTING IN LAST YEAR
1,251 applied
88% were accepted
45% enrolled (495)
30% from top tenth of their h.s. class
20% had SAT verbal scores over 600
22% had SAT math scores over 600
36% had ACT scores over 24
19 valedictorians

THE STUDENT BODY
Total 2,358, of whom 2,027
  are undergraduates

From 34 states and territories,
  21 other countries
83% from California
61% women, 39% men

COSTS AND FINANCIAL INFORMATION
1998–99 tuition and fees $12,650
1998–99 room and board $5220

Average percent of need met 80%
Average amount received per student $12,612

AFTER FRESHMAN YEAR
69% returned for sophomore year
31% got a degree in 4 years
14% got a degree in 5 years
2% got a degree in 6 years

AFTER GRADUATION
100 organizations recruited on campus

REDEEMER COLLEGE

Ancaster, Ontario, Canada   *http://www.redeemer.on.ca/*

Just an hour's drive from Buffalo and Toronto, Redeemer College offers an undergraduate liberal arts and science university education that explores the relationship of faith to learning and serving. A unique housing arrangement that features fully furnished town-house residences, a wide range of extracurricular and service opportunities, and the opportunity to work alongside skilled and committed faculty means that Redeemer students are part of a dynamic, Christian academic community. Work-study grants, scholarship programs based on community service as well as academic ability, and innovative financial aid programs make tuition surprisingly affordable, and the current exchange rate for the Canadian dollar can provide American applicants with savings of approximately 50 percent.

Academics

Redeemer offers a liberal arts curriculum and core academic program. It awards bachelor's **degrees**. Challenging opportunities include an honors program, double majors, independent study, and a senior project. **Special programs** include cooperative education, internships, summer session for credit, off-campus study, and study-abroad.

The most popular **majors** include education, health/physical education, and English. A complete listing of majors at Redeemer appears in the Majors Index beginning on page 141.

The **faculty** at Redeemer has 31 full-time teachers, 93% with terminal degrees. The student-faculty ratio is 14:1.

Campus Resources

Students are not required to have a computer. 35 **computers** available in the computer center, student lounge, the library, and dormitories provide access to on-campus e-mail addresses, off-campus e-mail addresses, and the Internet. Staffed computer lab on campus provides training in the use of computers, software, and the Internet.

The **library** has 93,500 books and 419 subscriptions.

Career Services

The career planning and placement office has 1 full-time staff member. Services include resume preparation, interview workshops, career/interest testing, career counseling, careers library, and job bank.

Campus Life

There are 25 active organizations on campus, including a drama/theater group and student-run newspaper. 63% of students participate in student government elections. No national or local **fraternities** or **sororities**. Student **safety services** include late-night transport/escort service, 24-hour emergency telephone service, and student patrols.

Intercollegiate sports include basketball (m,w), golf (m), hockey (m), indoor soccer (m,w), soccer (m,w), volleyball (m,w).

International Students

Students can start in fall and winter. The **admissions test** required for entrance is TOEFL (minimum score: 550; minimum score for ESL admission: 450); recommended is SAT I or ACT. Application deadline is The **admissions test** required for entrance is TOEFL (minimum score: 550; minimum score for ESL admission: 450). Services include an international student adviser on campus.

Applying

Redeemer requires a high school transcript, 2 recommendations, and pastoral reference, and in some cases an essay, SAT I or ACT, and an interview. It recommends 4 years of high school math and science, 4 years of high school foreign language, and 1 year of high school history. Application deadline: rolling admissions. Deferred entrance is possible. **Contact:** Ms. Marian Ryks-Szelekovszky, Registrar and Admissions Director, 777 Garner Road East, Ancaster, ON L9K 1J4, Canada, 905-648-2131 ext. 224 or toll-free 800-263-6467 (North America); fax 905-648-2134; e-mail adm@redeemer.on.ca.

GETTING IN LAST YEAR
269 applied
84% were accepted

THE STUDENT BODY
464 undergraduates
From 8 states and territories,
  12 other countries
59.3% women, 40.7% men

3.7% international students

COSTS AND FINANCIAL INFORMATION
1998–99 tuition and fees $8313
1998–99 room and board $4180

AFTER FRESHMAN YEAR
79% returned for sophomore year
28% got a degree in 4 years

22% got a degree in 5 years
6% got a degree in 6 years

AFTER GRADUATION
29% pursued further study (12% arts and
  sciences, 9% education, 8% theology)
70% had job offers within 6 months
25 organizations recruited on campus

ROBERTS WESLEYAN COLLEGE

Rochester, New York

http://www.rwc.edu/

Roberts Wesleyan College, a Christian liberal arts college, is located just 10 miles from the center of Rochester, New York. The College's broadly based curriculum of 40 majors and preprofessional programs includes 4 with national professional accreditation: art, music, nursing, and social work. Roberts is proud to be the only Christian college offering a Master of Social Work degree. In the fall of 1996, the doors to the new Cultural Life Center, a fine arts facility with state of the art acoustics, along with two new town house complexes, will open.

Academics

Roberts Wesleyan offers a Christian liberal arts curriculum and core academic program; a few graduate courses are open to undergraduates. It awards associate, bachelor's, and master's **degrees**. Challenging opportunities include advanced placement, tutorials, freshman honors college, an honors program, double majors, independent study, and a senior project. **Special programs** include cooperative education, internships, summer session for credit, off-campus study, study-abroad, and Army and Air Force ROTC.

The most popular **majors** include education, nursing, and business administration. A complete listing of majors at Roberts Wesleyan appears in the Majors Index beginning on page 141.

The **faculty** at Roberts Wesleyan has 66 full-time graduate and undergraduate teachers, 46% with terminal degrees. The student-faculty ratio is 14:1, and the average **class size** in required courses is 45.

Campus Resources

Students are not required to have a computer. Student rooms are linked to a campus network. 160 **computers** available in the computer center, computer labs, the learning resource center, the library, and dormitories provide access to on-campus e-mail addresses, off-campus e-mail addresses, and the Internet. Staffed computer lab on campus provides training in the use of computers, software, and the Internet.

The **library** has 103,376 books and 797 subscriptions.

Career Services

The career planning and placement office has 1 full-time staff member. Services include job fairs, resume preparation, interview workshops, career/interest testing, career counseling, careers library, job bank, and job interviews.

Campus Life

There are 25 active organizations on campus, including a drama/theater group and student-run newspaper. 30% of students participate in student government elections. No national or local **fraternities** or **sororities**. Student **safety services** include 24-hour Resident Life staff on-call, late-night transport/escort service, 24-hour emergency telephone alarm devices, 24-hour patrols by trained security personnel, and electronically operated dormitory entrances.

Roberts Wesleyan is a member of the NAIA and NCCAA. **Intercollegiate sports** (some offering scholarships) include basketball (m,w), cross-country running (m,w), soccer (m,w), track and field (m,w), volleyball (w).

International Students

For fall 1997, 13 enrolled. Students can start in fall. The **admissions test** required for entrance is TOEFL (minimum score: 550). Application deadline is 2/1. On-campus **housing** is guaranteed, also available during summer. Services include an international student adviser on campus.

Applying

Roberts Wesleyan requires an essay, SAT I or ACT, a high school transcript, and 2 recommendations. It recommends an interview, 3 years of high school math and science, 3 years of high school foreign language, and a minimum high school GPA of 2.5. Application deadline: 2/1; 3/15 priority date for financial aid. Early and deferred entrance are possible. **Contact:** Ms. Linda Kurtz, Director of Admissions, 2301 Westside Drive, Rochester, NY 14624-1997, 716-594-6400 or toll-free 800-777-4RWC; fax 716-594-6371.

GETTING IN LAST YEAR
653 applied
91% were accepted
53% enrolled (313)
16% from top tenth of their h.s. class
23% had SAT verbal scores over 600
18% had SAT math scores over 600
39% had ACT scores over 24
4 valedictorians

THE STUDENT BODY
Total 1,414, of whom 1,136
  are undergraduates
From 25 states and territories,
  16 other countries
85% from New York
62.9% women, 37.1% men
9.1% international students

COSTS AND FINANCIAL INFORMATION
1997–98 tuition and fees $12,400
1997–98 room and board $4260

AFTER FRESHMAN YEAR
78% returned for sophomore year

AFTER GRADUATION
82% had job offers within 6 months
96 organizations recruited on campus

SEATTLE PACIFIC UNIVERSITY

Seattle, Washington

http://www.spu.edu/

Seattle Pacific University

Seattle Pacific University is rated by *U.S. News & World Report* as one of America's best universities in terms of academic programs and value. Located in the beautiful Pacific Northwest, SPU is a fully accredited, distinctly Christian university of arts, sciences, and professional studies. The University enjoys national accreditation in electrical engineering, music, nursing, and teacher education. SPU faculty members are respected scholars whose primary commitments are teaching and nurturing students. Just minutes from downtown Seattle, SPU is ideally located for internship, service-learning, and ministry opportunities. Overall, SPU students are educated, supported, and encouraged to pursue roles of Christian leadership and service in society.

Academics

SPU offers a Christian foundations and general education curriculum and core academic program; a few graduate courses are open to undergraduates. It awards bachelor's, master's, and doctoral **degrees**. Challenging opportunities include advanced placement, student-designed majors, tutorials, an honors program, double majors, independent study, and a senior project. **Special programs** include cooperative education, internships, summer session for credit, off-campus study, study-abroad, and Army, Navy, and Air Force ROTC.

The most popular **majors** include nursing, business administration, and psychology. A complete listing of majors at SPU appears in the Majors Index beginning on page 141.

The **faculty** at SPU has 159 full-time graduate and undergraduate teachers, 85% with terminal degrees. The student-faculty ratio is 15:1, and the average **class size** in required courses is 21.

Campus Resources

Students are not required to have a computer. Purchase and/or lease options are available. Student rooms are linked to a campus network. 150 **computers** available in computer labs, the learning resource center, media center, and the library provide access to on-campus e-mail addresses, off-campus e-mail addresses, and the Internet. Staffed computer lab on campus provides training in the use of computers, software, and the Internet.

The **library** has 200,000 books and 1,400 subscriptions.

Career Services

The career planning and placement office has 4 full-time, 4 part-time staff members. Services include job fairs, resume preparation, interview workshops, career/interest testing, career counseling, careers library, job bank, and job interviews.

Campus Life

There are 50 active organizations on campus, including a drama/theater group and student-run newspaper. No national or local **fraternities** or **sororities**. Student **safety services** include closed circuit TV monitors, late-night transport/escort service, 24-hour emergency telephone alarm devices, 24-hour patrols by trained security personnel, and student patrols.

SPU is a member of the NCAA (Division II). **Intercollegiate sports** (some offering scholarships) include basketball (m,w), crew (m,w), cross-country running (m,w), gymnastics (w), soccer (m,w), track and field (m,w), volleyball (w).

International Students

For fall 1997, 98 international students applied, 28 were accepted, and 25 enrolled. Students can start in fall, winter, spring, and summer. The **admissions test** required for entrance is TOEFL (minimum score: 550; minimum score for ESL admission: 500); recommended is SAT I or ACT. Application deadline is 8/1. On-campus **housing** is guaranteed, also available during summer. Services include an international student adviser on campus.

Applying

SPU requires an essay, SAT I or ACT, a high school transcript, 2 recommendations, and a minimum high school GPA of 2.5. It recommends 3 years of high school math and science and 3 years of high school foreign language. Application deadline: 9/1; 1/31 priority date for financial aid. Early entrance is possible. **Contact:** Mr. Ken Cornell, Director of Admissions, 3307 Third Avenue West, Seattle, WA 98119-1997, 206-281-2021 or toll-free 800-366-3344; e-mail admissions@spu.edu.

GETTING IN LAST YEAR
1,516 applied
92% were accepted
42% enrolled (585)
36% had SAT verbal scores over 600
34% had SAT math scores over 600
53% had ACT scores over 24
11 National Merit Scholars
35 valedictorians

THE STUDENT BODY
Total 3,321, of whom 2,610
   are undergraduates

From 45 states and territories,
   31 other countries
61% from Washington
65% women, 35% men
4.3% international students

COSTS AND FINANCIAL INFORMATION
1998–99 tuition and fees $14,541
1998–99 room and board $5574

Average percent of need met 89%
Average amount received per student $13,446

AFTER FRESHMAN YEAR
78% returned for sophomore year
29% got a degree in 4 years
19% got a degree in 5 years
3% got a degree in 6 years

AFTER GRADUATION
87 organizations recruited on campus

Simpson College and Graduate School

Redding, California

http://www.simpsonca.edu/

Newly relocated in the Shasta recreation area of Northern California, Simpson College blends more than 75 years of solid tradition with innovative thought. A Christian college of liberal arts and professional studies, Simpson takes seriously its mission to educate Christian students for service in a global context. Growing numbers of students come to the College's new campus to benefit from its vigorous educational programs and vibrant spiritual life.

Academics

Simpson offers a Christian liberal arts/professional studies curriculum and core academic program; fewer than half of graduate courses are open to undergraduates. It awards associate, bachelor's, and master's **degrees**. Challenging opportunities include advanced placement, accelerated degree programs, student-designed majors, tutorials, double majors, independent study, and a senior project. **Special programs** include internships, summer session for credit, off-campus study, and study-abroad.

The most popular **majors** include elementary education, business administration, and psychology. A complete listing of majors at Simpson appears in the Majors Index beginning on page 141.

The **faculty** at Simpson has 43 full-time graduate and undergraduate teachers, 50% with terminal degrees. The student-faculty ratio is 14:1, and the average **class size** in required courses is 26.

Campus Resources

Students are not required to have a computer. Purchase and/or lease options are available. 21 **computers** available in computer labs and the library provide access to on-campus e-mail addresses, off-campus e-mail addresses, and the Internet. Staffed computer lab on campus provides training in the use of computers, software, and the Internet.

The **library** has 63,163 books and 301 subscriptions.

Career Services

The career planning and placement office has 1 part-time staff member. Services include career counseling.

International Students

For fall 1997, 32 international students applied, 21 were accepted, and 15 enrolled. Students can start in fall, spring, and summer. The **admissions test** required for entrance is TOEFL (minimum score: 500). Application deadline is 6/1. On-campus **housing** available during summer. Services include an international student adviser on campus.

Applying

Simpson requires an essay, SAT I or ACT, a high school transcript, 2 recommendations, Christian commitment, and a minimum high school GPA of 2, and in some cases an interview. It recommends 4 years of high school English, 3 years of high school math, 2 years of high school science, 2 years of high school foreign language, and 3 years of high school social studies. Application deadline: rolling admissions; 3/2 priority date for financial aid. Deferred entrance is possible. **Contact:** Mrs. Beth Spencer, Administrative Assistant to Vice President for Enrollment, 2211 College View Drive, Redding, CA 96003-8606, 530-224-5606 ext. 2602 or toll-free 800-598-2493; fax 530-224-5627; e-mail admissions@simpsonca.edu.

GETTING IN LAST YEAR	THE STUDENT BODY	COSTS AND FINANCIAL INFORMATION
1,178 applied	Total 1,248, of whom 955	1998–99 tuition and fees $10,050
72% were accepted	are undergraduates	1998–99 room and board $4400
25% enrolled (211)	From 29 states and territories,	Average percent of need met 91%
29% from top tenth of their h.s. class	8 other countries	Average amount received per student $10,600
25% had SAT verbal scores over 600	72% from California	
21% had SAT math scores over 600	64.7% women, 35.3% men	**AFTER FRESHMAN YEAR**
21% had ACT scores over 24		66% returned for sophomore year

SOUTHERN CALIFORNIA COLLEGE

(Vanguard University of Southern California beginning in fall 1999)

Costa Mesa, California   *http://www.sccu.edu/*

Southern California College is located 5 miles from the Pacific Ocean in Costa Mesa, California. Founded in 1920 and affiliated with the Assemblies of God, SCC is the largest Christian college in the charismatic tradition west of the Rocky Mountains. SCC offers 29 academic majors and several opportunities for off-campus study, including the American Studies Program in Washington, DC, LA film studies, archaelogy trips to Israel, and language/missions study in San José, Costa Rica. The campus is ideally located in Orange County, where business and recreational activities provide students with countless jobs, internships, and leisure opportunities.

Academics

SCC offers a general education curriculum and core academic program; fewer than half of graduate courses are open to undergraduates. It awards bachelor's and master's **degrees**. Challenging opportunities include advanced placement, accelerated degree programs, and a senior project. **Special programs** include internships, summer session for credit, off-campus study, and study-abroad.

The most popular **majors** include business administration, interdisciplinary studies, and religious studies. A complete listing of majors at SCC appears in the Majors Index beginning on page 141.

The **faculty** at SCC has 52 full-time graduate and undergraduate teachers, 79% with terminal degrees. The student-faculty ratio is 16:1, and the average **class size** in required courses is 25.

Campus Resources

Students are not required to have a computer. Purchase and/or lease options are available. Student rooms are linked to a campus network. 60 **computers** available in the computer center, computer labs, the research center, the learning resource center, the library, and dormitories provide access to on-campus e-mail addresses, off-campus e-mail addresses, and the Internet. Staffed computer lab on campus provides training in the use of computers and software.

The **library** has 121,000 books and 825 subscriptions.

Career Services

Services include career counseling.

Campus Life

There are 55 active organizations on campus, including a drama/theater group and student-run newspaper. 35% of students participate in student government elections. No national or local **fraternities** or **sororities**. Student **safety services** include late-night transport/escort service, 24-hour emergency telephone alarm devices, and 24-hour patrols by trained security personnel.

SCC is a member of the NAIA. **Intercollegiate sports** (all offering scholarships) include baseball (m), basketball (m,w), cross-country running (m,w), soccer (m,w), softball (w), tennis (m,w), track and field (m,w), volleyball (w).

International Students

For fall 1997, 11 international students applied, 8 were accepted, and 7 enrolled. Students can start in fall and spring. The **admissions test** required for entrance is TOEFL (minimum score: 550); recommended is SAT I or ACT. Application deadline is rolling. On-campus **housing** is guaranteed, also available during summer. Services include an international student adviser on campus.

Applying

SCC requires an essay, SAT I or ACT, a high school transcript, 1 recommendation, and a minimum high school GPA of 2.5, and in some cases an interview. It recommends 4 years of high school English, 2 years of high school math and science, and 3 years of high school social studies. Application deadline: rolling admissions; 3/2 priority date for financial aid. Deferred entrance is possible. **Contact:** Ms. Jessica Mireles, Associate Director of Admissions, 55 Fair Drive, Costa Mesa, CA 92626-6597, 714-556-3610 ext. 327 or toll-free 800-722-6279; fax 714-668-6194; e-mail admissions@sccu.edu.

GETTING IN LAST YEAR
25% from top tenth of their h.s. class
22% had SAT verbal scores over 600
12% had SAT math scores over 600
2 National Merit Scholars
5 valedictorians

THE STUDENT BODY
Total 1,312, of whom 1,190
  are undergraduates

From 36 states and territories,
  14 other countries
75% from California
58.3% women, 41.7% men
1.6% international students

COSTS AND FINANCIAL INFORMATION
1997–98 tuition and fees $11,848
1997–98 room and board $4860

Average percent of need met 70%
Average amount received per student $9800

AFTER FRESHMAN YEAR
71% returned for sophomore year

SOUTHERN NAZARENE UNIVERSITY

Bethany, Oklahoma

http://www.snu.edu/

Southern Nazarene University, founded in 1899, is dedicated to building responsible Christian persons. Students from 38 states and 24 countries come to SNU to receive excellent professional and academic preparation in the context of a warm, Christian community. SNU offers fully accredited programs in more than 60 major fields of study, with a national reputation for its programs in the sciences, pre-medicine, physics, fine arts, education, and business. The School of Business has won international business competitions in 5 of the past 7 years. Additional academic offerings include programs in Washington, DC; Cairo, Egypt; Los Angeles, California; San José, Costa Rica; Moscow, Russia; and Oxford, England. Southern Nazarene University helps students prepare for their future and a life of service.

Academics
SNU offers a core academic program. It awards associate, bachelor's, and master's **degrees**. Challenging opportunities include advanced placement, accelerated degree programs, student-designed majors, and a senior project. **Special programs** include internships, summer session for credit, off-campus study, study-abroad, and Army ROTC.

The most popular **majors** include education, (pre)medicine, and business administration. A complete listing of majors at SNU appears in the Majors Index beginning on page 141.

The **faculty** at SNU has 64 full-time graduate and undergraduate teachers. The student-faculty ratio is 17:1.

Campus Resources
Students are not required to have a computer. Student rooms are linked to a campus network. 55 **computers** available in the computer center, classrooms, and the library provide access to the Internet. Staffed computer lab on campus provides training in the use of computers and software.

The **library** has 108,200 books and 610 subscriptions.

Career Services
The career planning and placement office has 1 full-time, 2 part-time staff members. Services include job fairs, resume preparation, resume referral, career counseling, careers library, job bank, and job interviews.

Campus Life
Active organizations on campus include a drama/theater group and student-run newspaper. No national or local **fraternities** or **sororities**. Student **safety services** include 24-hour emergency telephone alarm devices and electronically operated dormitory entrances.

SNU is a member of the NAIA. **Intercollegiate sports** (some offering scholarships) include baseball (m), basketball (m,w), cross-country running (m,w), golf (m,w), soccer (m,w), softball (w), tennis (m,w), track and field (m,w), volleyball (w).

International Students
For fall 1997, 25 international students applied, 3 were accepted, and 3 enrolled. The **admissions tests** required for entrance are TOEFL (minimum score: 500), ELS (minimum score 109); recommended is SAT I. Application deadline is 6/1. On-campus **housing** available during summer.

Applying
SNU requires SAT I or ACT and a high school transcript. It recommends an interview, 3 years of high school math and science, and 2 years of high school foreign language. Application deadline: 8/15; 3/1 priority date for financial aid. Deferred entrance is possible. **Contact:** Mr. Brad Townley, Director of Admissions, 6729 Northwest 39th Expressway, Bethany, OK 73008-2694, 405-491-6324 or toll-free 800-648-9899; fax 405-491-6381; e-mail admiss@snu.edu.

GETTING IN LAST YEAR
26% from top tenth of their h.s. class

THE STUDENT BODY
Total 1,799, of whom 1,524 are undergraduates

From 38 states and territories, 31 other countries

COSTS AND FINANCIAL INFORMATION
1998–99 tuition and fees $8832
1998–99 room and board $4176

AFTER FRESHMAN YEAR
70% returned for sophomore year

AFTER GRADUATION
22% pursued further study (10% theology, 8% business, 2% medicine)

SOUTHERN WESLEYAN UNIVERSITY

Central, South Carolina

http://www.swu.edu/

Southern Wesleyan University is committed to providing a high-quality education from a Christian perspective. The issues of faith are explored in each course of study and practiced in daily life. The faculty's personal dedication and skills enable it to serve students from a wide variety of backgrounds—ranging from those who might be underprepared to National Merit Finalists—by providing the right amount of support and the right amount of challenge. A cooperative program with nearby Clemson University allows Southern Wesleyan's students to experience the atmosphere and fellowship of a Christian campus and the academic diversity of a large university. Graduates have distinguished themselves in their careers while maintaining active involvement in service to their communities and churches. An education at Southern Wesleyan provides what's needed for a career and for a satisfying and balanced life.

Academics

SWU offers an interdisciplinary curriculum and core academic program. It awards associate, bachelor's, and master's **degrees**. Challenging opportunities include advanced placement, accelerated degree programs, tutorials, an honors program, double majors, independent study, and a senior project. **Special programs** include internships, summer session for credit, off-campus study, study-abroad, and Army and Air Force ROTC.

The most popular **majors** include business administration, education, and psychology. A complete listing of majors at SWU appears in the Majors Index beginning on page 141.

The **faculty** at SWU has 46 graduate and undergraduate teachers, 73% with terminal degrees. The student-faculty ratio is 14:1.

Campus Resources

Students are not required to have a computer. 64 **computers** available in the computer center, science, writing labs, and the library provide access to on-campus e-mail addresses, off-campus e-mail addresses, and the Internet. Staffed computer lab on campus provides training in the use of computers and software. The **library** has 67,823 books and 440 subscriptions.

Career Services

The career planning and placement office has 1 full-time, 1 part-time staff members. Services include job fairs, resume preparation, resume referral, career counseling, careers library, and job bank.

Campus Life

There are 10 active organizations on campus, including a drama/theater group. No national or local **fraternities** or **sororities**. Student **safety services** include late-night security patrols and 24-hour emergency telephone alarm devices.

SWU is a member of the NAIA and NCCAA. **Intercollegiate sports** (some offering scholarships) include baseball (m), basketball (m,w), cross-country running (m,w), golf (m), soccer (m,w), softball (w), volleyball (w).

International Students

For fall 1997, 10 international students applied, 6 were accepted, and 5 enrolled. Students can start in fall and spring. The **admissions tests** required for entrance are SAT I or ACT, TOEFL (minimum score: 550). Application deadline is 8/1. On-campus **housing** is guaranteed, also available during summer. Services include an international student adviser on campus.

Applying

SWU requires SAT I or ACT, a high school transcript, 2 recommendations, 4 years of high school English, 2 years of high school math and science, 2 years of high school social studies, and a minimum high school GPA of 2.0, and in some cases an interview. Application deadline: 8/10; 6/30 priority date for financial aid. Early and deferred entrance are possible. **Contact:** Mr. Mike Ennis, Director of Admissions, 907 Wesleyan Drive, PO Box 1020, Central, SC 29630-1020, 864-639-2453 ext. 327 or toll-free 800-CUATSWU; fax 864-639-0826 ext. 327; e-mail admissions@swu.edu.

GETTING IN LAST YEAR
11% from top tenth of their h.s. class
9% had SAT verbal scores over 600
15% had SAT math scores over 600

THE STUDENT BODY
Total 1,337, of whom 1,265
  are undergraduates

From 20 states and territories,
  4 other countries
58.3% women, 41.7% men

COSTS AND FINANCIAL INFORMATION
1997–98 tuition and fees $10,180
1997–98 room and board $3540
Average percent of need met 74%

Average amount received per student $8700

AFTER FRESHMAN YEAR
59% returned for sophomore year

AFTER GRADUATION
11 organizations recruited on campus

SOUTHWEST BAPTIST UNIVERSITY

Bolivar, Missouri

http://www.sbuniv.edu/

Southwest Baptist University is a community working together for academic excellence with values added. With a strong emphasis on integrating faith and values with a quality liberal arts academic preparation, SBU is a Christian university, not simply a university for Christians. SBU is committed to preparing the best leaders for today and tomorrow, and SBU graduates are recognized leaders serving in a variety of ministries and professions around the world. SBU has been named to the *Student's Guide to America's* 100 Best College Buys for 1996–97.

Academics

SBU offers a liberal arts curriculum and core academic program; a few graduate courses are open to undergraduates. It awards associate, bachelor's, and master's **degrees**. Challenging opportunities include advanced placement, accelerated degree programs, an honors program, double majors, independent study, and a senior project. **Special programs** include cooperative education, internships, summer session for credit, study-abroad, and Army ROTC.

The most popular **majors** include nursing, elementary education, and business administration. A complete listing of majors at SBU appears in the Majors Index beginning on page 141.

The **faculty** at SBU has 103 full-time undergraduate teachers, 59% with terminal degrees. The student-faculty ratio is 22:1.

Campus Resources

Students are not required to have a computer. Purchase and/or lease options are available. 130 **computers** available in the computer center, classrooms, and the library provide access to on-campus e-mail addresses, off-campus e-mail addresses, and the Internet. Staffed computer lab on campus provides training in the use of computers, software, and the Internet.

The **library** has 132,050 books and 1,649 subscriptions.

Career Services

The career planning and placement office has 2 full-time staff members. Services include job fairs, resume preparation, resume referral, career counseling, careers library, job bank, and job interviews.

Campus Life

There are 25 active organizations on campus, including a drama/theater group and student-run newspaper. 25% of students participate in student government elections. No national or local **fraternities** or **sororities**. Student **safety services** include 24-hour emergency telephone alarm devices and 24-hour patrols by trained security personnel.

SBU is a member of the NCAA (Division II). **Intercollegiate sports** (some offering scholarships) include baseball (m), basketball (m,w), cross-country running (m,w), football (m), golf (m), soccer (m,w), softball (w), tennis (m,w), track and field (m,w), volleyball (w).

International Students

For fall 1997, 4 international students applied, 4 were accepted, and 4 enrolled. Students can start in fall, winter, spring, and summer. The **admissions test** required for entrance is TOEFL (minimum score: 525). Application deadline is 8/21. On-campus **housing** is guaranteed, also available during summer.

Applying

SBU requires SAT I or ACT and a high school transcript. It recommends an interview and 3 years of high school math and science. Application deadline: 9/7; 3/1 priority date for financial aid. Early and deferred entrance are possible. **Contact:** Mr. Rob Harris, Director of Admissions, 1600 University Avenue, Bolivar, MO 65613-2597, 417-326-1814 or toll-free 800-526-5859; fax 417-326-1514; e-mail admitme@shuniv.edu.

GETTING IN LAST YEAR
18% from top tenth of their h.s. class
21% had SAT verbal scores over 600
23% had SAT math scores over 600
31% had ACT scores over 24

THE STUDENT BODY
Total 3,593, of whom 2,815 are undergraduates

From 38 states and territories
84% from Missouri
65.9% women, 34.1% men
.1% international students

COSTS AND FINANCIAL INFORMATION
1997–98 tuition and fees $8347
1997–98 room and board $2580

Average percent of need met 60%
Average amount received per student $7654

AFTER FRESHMAN YEAR
69% returned for sophomore year

AFTER GRADUATION
615 organizations recruited on campus

SPRING ARBOR COLLEGE
Spring Arbor, Michigan

At Spring Arbor College there is a community of learners with 3 essential commitments: the serious study of the liberal arts, Jesus Christ as the community's perspective for learning, and critical participation in the affairs of the contemporary world. Everything that is done at Spring Arbor is based on these ideas, from an interest in fostering lifelong learning and developing thinking skills with many different applications to chapel programming, ministry opportunities, and the recognition of the lordship of Christ over the environment and all of life to the College's cross-cultural study requirement and belief that students need to be informed world citizens with a global perspective.

Academics
Spring Arbor offers a Christian liberal arts/education curriculum and core academic program; a few graduate courses are open to undergraduates. It awards associate, bachelor's, and master's **degrees**. Challenging opportunities include advanced placement, student-designed majors, an honors program, and a senior project. **Special programs** include internships, off-campus study, and study-abroad.

The most popular **majors** include teacher education, psychology, and communications. A complete listing of majors at Spring Arbor appears in the Majors Index beginning on page 141.

The **faculty** at Spring Arbor has 70 full-time undergraduate teachers, 47% with terminal degrees. The student-faculty ratio is 15:1.

Campus Resources
Students are not required to have a computer. 100 **computers** available in the computer center, computer labs, the learning resource center, classrooms, the library, the student center, and dormitories provide access to on-campus e-mail addresses, off-campus e-mail addresses, and the Internet. Staffed computer labs on campus.

The **library** has 88,354 books and 1,413 subscriptions.

Career Services
The career planning and placement office has 2 full-time, 4 part-time staff members. Services include job fairs, resume preparation, career counseling, careers library, job bank, and job interviews.

Campus Life
Active organizations on campus include a drama/theater group and student-run newspaper and radio station. No national or local **fraternities** or **sororities**. Student **safety services** include late-night transport/escort service.

Spring Arbor is a member of the NAIA. **Intercollegiate sports** (some offering scholarships) include baseball (m), basketball (m,w), cross-country running (m,w), golf (m), soccer (m,w), softball (w), tennis (m,w), track and field (m,w), volleyball (w).

International Students
For fall 1998, 13 international students applied, 11 were accepted, and 6 enrolled. The **admissions test** required for entrance is TOEFL (minimum score: 525). Application deadline is 5/1. On-campus **housing** is guaranteed, also available during summer. Services include an international student adviser on campus.

Applying
Spring Arbor requires SAT I or ACT and a high school transcript, and in some cases recommendations. It recommends an essay, an interview, guidance counselor's evaluation form, and 2 years of high school foreign language. Application deadline: rolling admissions; 2/15 priority date for financial aid. Early and deferred entrance are possible. **Contact:** Mr. Jim Weidman, Director of Admissions, 106 Main Street, Spring Arbor, MI 49283-9799, 517-750-1200 ext. 1470 or toll-free 800-968-0011; fax 517-750-6620; e-mail jimw@admin.arbor.edu.

GETTING IN LAST YEAR
476 applied
89% were accepted
18% from top tenth of their h.s. class
1 National Merit Scholar
8 valedictorians

THE STUDENT BODY
Total 2,242, of whom 2,226 are undergraduates

From 26 states and territories, 8 other countries

COSTS AND FINANCIAL INFORMATION
1998–99 tuition and fees $11,106
1998–99 room and board $4310

Average amount received per student $6562

AFTER FRESHMAN YEAR
80% returned for sophomore year

AFTER GRADUATION
9% pursued further study

STERLING COLLEGE

Sterling, Kansas

http://www.stercolks.edu/

Sterling College is nationally recognized for developing creative and thoughtful leaders who understand a maturing Christian faith. The reason for this reputation is simple—Sterling cares about people. Sterling cares how its students are developing academically, socially, physically, and spiritually. Top-quality faculty members teach students how to think, not what to think. Strong theater, music, and art programs stretch students artistically and creatively. Dedicated staff members provide active and enthusiastic student-life activities. Concerned coaches help students maintain a proper balance between athletics and academics. All this individual attention is directed toward one aim—helping each student to learn, to grow, and to excel.

Academics

Sterling College offers a Christian liberal arts curriculum and core academic program. It awards bachelor's **degrees**. Challenging opportunities include advanced placement, student-designed majors, an honors program, double majors, independent study, and a senior project. **Special programs** include internships, summer session for credit, off-campus study, and study-abroad.

The most popular **majors** include education, business administration, and behavioral sciences. A complete listing of majors at Sterling College appears in the Majors Index beginning on page 141.

The **faculty** at Sterling College has 30 full-time teachers, 52% with terminal degrees. The student-faculty ratio is 15:1.

Campus Resources

Students are not required to have a computer. 56 **computers** available in the computer center, computer labs, classrooms, the library, the student center, and dormitories provide access to on-campus e-mail addresses, off-campus e-mail addresses, and the Internet. Staffed computer lab on campus provides training in the use of computers, software, and the Internet.

The **library** has 84,000 books and 450 subscriptions.

Career Services

The career planning and placement office has 1 full-time staff member. Services include job fairs, resume preparation, interview workshops, resume referral, career/interest testing, career counseling, careers library, job bank, and job interviews.

Campus Life

Active organizations on campus include a drama/theater group and student-run newspaper. No national or local **fraternities** or **sororities**.

Sterling College is a member of the NAIA. **Intercollegiate sports** (some offering scholarships) include baseball (m), basketball (m,w), cross-country running (m,w), football (m), soccer (m,w), softball (w), tennis (m,w), track and field (m,w), volleyball (w).

International Students

For fall 1997, 4 international students applied, 1 were accepted, and 1 enrolled. The **admissions test** required for entrance is TOEFL (minimum score: 520); recommended is SAT I or ACT. Application deadline is rolling. On-campus **housing** is guaranteed. Services include an international student adviser on campus.

Applying

Sterling College requires SAT I or ACT and a high school transcript. It recommends 3 years of high school math and science and 1 year of high school foreign language. Application deadline: rolling admissions; 3/15 priority date for financial aid. Early and deferred entrance are possible. **Contact:** Mr. Dennis W. Dutton, Director of Admissions, PO Box 98, Sterling, KS 67579-0098, 316-278-4364 or toll-free 800-346-1017; fax 316-278-3690; e-mail admissions@acc.stercolks.edu.

GETTING IN LAST YEAR
723 applied
70% were accepted
29% enrolled (147)
9% from top tenth of their h.s. class
3% had SAT verbal scores over 600
6% had SAT math scores over 600
31% had ACT scores over 24
1 National Merit Scholars
5 valedictorians

THE STUDENT BODY
457 undergraduates
From 24 states and territories,
  1 other country
62% from Kansas
47.5% women, 52.5% men
.4% international students

COSTS AND FINANCIAL INFORMATION
1997–98 tuition and fees $10,076

1997–98 room and board $4104
Average percent of need met 85%
Average amount received per student $10,310

AFTER FRESHMAN YEAR
63% returned for sophomore year
31% got a degree in 4 years
6% got a degree in 5 years
1% got a degree in 6 years

TABOR COLLEGE
Hillsboro, Kansas

http://www.tabor.edu/

Tabor's religious heritage places utmost importance on a voluntary, adult commitment to follow Christ. This includes a life of personal devotion and outer witness, serious corporate biblical study, and service to others, which is the foundation of Tabor's mission statement. The academic program, therefore, is designed to develop servants of Christ for all walks of life. This occurs in a Christian learning community, which emphasizes fellowship and mutual accountability. Themes of stewardship and service infuse the College's majors. The student development program stresses personal growth, self-discipline, acceptance of responsibility, and the development of decision-making skills. Tabor provides global travel/service experiences each Interterm and structured opportunities to serve others for Christ through a variety of local ministries.

Academics

Tabor offers an evangelical liberal arts curriculum and core academic program. It awards associate and bachelor's **degrees**. Challenging opportunities include advanced placement, student-designed majors, tutorials, an honors program, and a senior project. **Special programs** include internships, summer session for credit, off-campus study, and study-abroad.

The most popular **majors** include business administration, social sciences, and elementary education. A complete listing of majors at Tabor appears in the Majors Index beginning on page 141.

The **faculty** at Tabor has 33 full-time teachers, 59% with terminal degrees. The average **class size** in required courses is 27.

Campus Resources

Students are not required to have a computer. Student rooms are linked to a campus network. 57 **computers** available in the computer center, computer labs, administration and academic buildings, classrooms, and the library provide access to on-campus e-mail addresses, off-campus e-mail addresses, and the Internet. Staffed computer lab on campus provides training in the use of computers and software.

The 3 **libraries** have 76,730 books and 298 subscriptions.

Career Services

The career planning and placement office has 1 full-time, 1 part-time staff members. Services include job fairs, resume preparation, resume referral, career counseling, careers library, job bank, and job interviews.

Campus Life

There are 24 active organizations on campus, including a drama/theater group and student-run newspaper. 60% of students participate in student government elections. No national or local **fraternities** or **sororities**. Student **safety services** include student patrols and electronically operated dormitory entrances.

Tabor is a member of the NAIA. **Intercollegiate sports** (some offering scholarships) include baseball (m), basketball (m,w), cross-country running (m,w), football (m), golf (m,w), soccer (m,w), softball (w), tennis (m,w), track and field (m,w), volleyball (w).

International Students

For fall 1997, 11 international students applied, 9 were accepted, and 7 enrolled. The **admissions test** required for entrance is TOEFL (minimum score: 525); recommended is ACT. Application deadline is 8/1. On-campus **housing** is guaranteed. Services include an international student adviser on campus.

Applying

Tabor requires an essay, SAT I or ACT, a high school transcript, 2 recommendations, and a minimum high school GPA of 2.0. It recommends SAT II Subject Tests, SAT II: Writing Test, an interview, 4 years of high school English, 3 years of high school math and science, 1 year of high school foreign language, 3 years of high school social studies, and a minimum high school GPA of 3.0. Application deadline: rolling admissions; 3/1 priority date for financial aid. Deferred entrance is possible. **Contact:** Mr. Glenn Lygrisse, Vice President for Enrollment Management, 400 South Jefferson, Hillsboro, KS 67063, 316-947-3121 ext. 1723 or toll-free 800-822-6799; fax 316-947-2607; e-mail admissions@tcnet.tabor.edu.

GETTING IN LAST YEAR
333 applied
67% were accepted
58% enrolled (129)
16% from top tenth of their h.s. class
9% had SAT math scores over 600
42% had ACT scores over 24
3 National Merit Scholars

THE STUDENT BODY
516 undergraduates

From 19 states and territories,
  5 other countries
62% from Kansas
48.6% women, 51.4% men

COSTS AND FINANCIAL INFORMATION
1997–98 tuition and fees $10,560
1997–98 room and board $4000
Average percent of need met 87%
Average amount received per student $10,779

AFTER FRESHMAN YEAR
76% returned for sophomore year
31% got a degree in 4 years
10% got a degree in 5 years
1% got a degree in 6 years

AFTER GRADUATION
20% pursued further study
40 organizations recruited on campus

Peterson's Christian Colleges & Universities

TAYLOR UNIVERSITY

Upland, Indiana

http://www.tayloru.edu/

Taylor University seeks Christian scholars who wish to experience thoughtful and rigorous academic studies thoroughly integrated with biblical Christianity. It seeks students who will respond to a supportive campus community that expects responsible decision making in the context of Christian freedom. It seeks students who will endeavor to translate their 4-year experience into lifelong learning and ministering the redemptive love of Jesus Christ to a world in need. Taylor's President, Dr. Jay Kesler, and outstanding Christian faculty invite students to consider the call to become a part of Taylor's exceptional student body and begin their own Taylor Tradition.

Academics

Taylor offers a Christian liberal arts curriculum and core academic program. It awards associate and bachelor's **degrees**. Challenging opportunities include advanced placement, accelerated degree programs, student-designed majors, tutorials, an honors program, double majors, independent study, and a senior project. **Special programs** include internships, summer session for credit, off-campus study, and study-abroad.

The most popular **majors** include business administration, elementary education, and psychology. A complete listing of majors at Taylor appears in the Majors Index beginning on page 141.

The **faculty** at Taylor has 105 full-time teachers, 69% with terminal degrees. The student-faculty ratio is 18:1, and the average **class size** in required courses is 25.

Campus Resources

Students are not required to have a computer. Purchase and/or lease options are available. Student rooms are linked to a campus network. 234 **computers** available in computer labs, the learning resource center, the library, and dormitories provide access to on-campus e-mail addresses, off-campus e-mail addresses, and the Internet. Staffed computer lab on campus provides training in the use of computers, software, and the Internet.

The **library** has 184,000 books and 717 subscriptions.

Career Services

The career planning and placement office has 1 full-time, 1 part-time staff members. Services include job fairs, resume preparation, resume referral, career/interest testing, career counseling, careers library, job bank (available on line), and job interviews.

Campus Life

There are 30 active organizations on campus, including a drama/theater group and student-run newspaper and radio station. No national or local **fraternities** or **sororities**. Student **safety services** include late-night transport/escort service, 24-hour patrols by trained security personnel, and student patrols.

Taylor is a member of the NAIA and NCCAA. **Intercollegiate sports** (some offering scholarships) include baseball (m), basketball (m,w), cross-country running (m,w), equestrian sports (m,w), football (m), golf (m), soccer (m,w), softball (w), tennis (m,w), track and field (m,w), volleyball (w).

International Students

For fall 1997, 53 international students applied, 22 were accepted, and 15 enrolled. Students can start in fall and spring. The **admissions test** required for entrance is TOEFL (minimum score: 550); recommended is SAT I or ACT. Application deadline is rolling. On-campus **housing** is guaranteed, also available during summer. Services include an international student adviser on campus.

Applying

Taylor requires an essay, SAT I or ACT, a high school transcript, 2 recommendations, 4 years of high school English, 3 years of high school math and science, and 2 years of high school social studies. It recommends an interview, 2 years of high school foreign language, and a minimum high school GPA of 3.0. Application deadline: rolling admissions; 3/1 for financial aid. Deferred entrance is possible. **Contact:** Mr. Stephen R. Mortland, Director of Admissions, 500 West Reade Avenue, Upland, IN 46989-1001, 765-998-5134 or toll-free 800-882-3456; fax 765-998-4925; e-mail admissions_u@tayloru.edu.

GETTING IN LAST YEAR
1,693 applied
69% were accepted
42% enrolled (487)
43% from top tenth of their h.s. class
49% had SAT verbal scores over 600
49% had SAT math scores over 600
70% had ACT scores over 24
12 National Merit Scholars
40 valedictorians

THE STUDENT BODY
1,884 undergraduates

From 48 states and territories,
19 other countries
30% from Indiana
53.5% women, 46.6% men
2.4% international students

COSTS AND FINANCIAL INFORMATION
1998–99 tuition and fees $14,456
1998–99 room and board $4544
Average percent of need met 87%
Average amount received per student $11,136

AFTER FRESHMAN YEAR
89% returned for sophomore year
48% got a degree in 4 years
18% got a degree in 5 years
3% got a degree in 6 years

AFTER GRADUATION
13% pursued further study (6% arts and sciences, 3% theology, 2% medicine)
78% had job offers within 6 months
120 organizations recruited on campus

TREVECCA NAZARENE UNIVERSITY

Nashville, Tennessee   *http://www.trevecca.edu/*

Trevecca Nazarene's goal is to prepare students for Christian service in all areas of life by providing an education that integrates faith and learning. The College seeks to combine the best in liberal arts as "preparation for life" and the best in career education as "preparation to earn a living." It also provides many opportunities for spiritual growth through chapel services, student organizations, convocations and revivals, and visiting lecturers. In addition, students are actively involved with the Nashville community through local churches and service clubs, which reflects Trevecca's service-oriented philosophy.

Academics
Trevecca offers a core academic program. It awards associate, bachelor's, and master's **degrees**. Challenging opportunities include advanced placement, accelerated degree programs, and a senior project. **Special programs** include cooperative education, internships, summer session for credit, off-campus study, study-abroad, and Army ROTC.

The most popular **majors** include business administration, early childhood education, and religious studies. A complete listing of majors at Trevecca appears in the Majors Index beginning on page 141.

The **faculty** at Trevecca has 65 full-time graduate and undergraduate teachers, 57% with terminal degrees. The student-faculty ratio is 13:1.

Campus Resources
Students are not required to have a computer. Purchase and/or lease options are available. Student rooms are linked to a campus network. 150 **computers** available in the computer center, computer labs, the library, and dormitories provide access to on-campus e-mail addresses and the Internet. Staffed computer lab on campus provides training in the use of computers and software.

The **library** has 99,976 books and 1,200 subscriptions.

Career Services
The career planning and placement office has 2 full-time, 3 part-time staff members. Services include job fairs, resume preparation, interview workshops, career counseling, and job bank (available on line).

Campus Life
Active organizations on campus include a drama/theater group and student-run newspaper. No national or local **fraternities** or **sororities**. Student **safety services** include 24-hour patrols by trained security personnel and student patrols.

Trevecca is a member of the NAIA. **Intercollegiate sports** (some offering scholarships) include baseball (m), basketball (m,w), softball (w), volleyball (w).

International Students
For fall 1997, 10 enrolled. Students can start in fall, spring, and summer. The **admissions test** required for entrance is TOEFL (minimum score: 500). Application deadline is 7/1. On-campus **housing** is guaranteed.

Applying
Trevecca requires ACT, a high school transcript, and medical history and immunization records. It recommends recommendations, 3 years of high school math and science, and 2 years of high school foreign language. Application deadline: rolling admissions; 3/1 priority date for financial aid. Early and deferred entrance are possible. **Contact:** Ms. Patricia D. Cook, Director of Admissions, 333 Murfreesboro Road, Nashville, TN 37210-2834, 615-248-1320 or toll-free 888-210-4862; fax 615-248-7728; e-mail admissions_und@trevecca.edu.

GETTING IN LAST YEAR
781 applied
100% were accepted
24% enrolled (187)
11% from top tenth of their h.s. class
1 National Merit Scholars
2 valedictorians

THE STUDENT BODY
Total 1,516, of whom 1,049
   are undergraduates

From 37 states and territories,
   8 other countries
61% from Tennessee
55.7% women, 44.3% men
1% international students

COSTS AND FINANCIAL INFORMATION
1997–98 tuition and fees $9090
1997–98 room and board $4038
Average percent of need met 61%

Average amount received per student $12,200

AFTER FRESHMAN YEAR
58% returned for sophomore year
24% got a degree in 4 years
5% got a degree in 5 years
3% got a degree in 6 years

AFTER GRADUATION
31 organizations recruited on campus

TRINITY CHRISTIAN COLLEGE
Palos Heights, Illinois

http://www.trnty.edu/

Trinity Christian College is located in Palos Heights, a suburb southwest of Chicago. Its proximity to the city offers students access to cultural, educational, and employment opportunities through the College-wide internship program and the Chicago Metropolitan Studies Program. Trinity offers majors in 21 areas of study; in addition, there are 25 minor programs available. The nursing program is fully accredited by the National League for Nursing. Trinity graduates enjoy the benefits of a solid, Christian, liberal arts education. They have an excellent acceptance rate into graduate programs in business, education, science, and medicine as well as great success in career placement.

Academics
Trinity Christian College offers a global perspective curriculum and core academic program. It awards bachelor's **degrees**. Challenging opportunities include advanced placement, tutorials, an honors program, double majors, independent study, and a senior project. **Special programs** include internships, off-campus study, and study-abroad.

The most popular **majors** include nursing, elementary education, and business administration. A complete listing of majors at Trinity Christian College appears in the Majors Index beginning on page 141.

The **faculty** at Trinity Christian College has 40 full-time teachers, 75% with terminal degrees. The student-faculty ratio is 12:1, and the average **class size** in required courses is 26.

Campus Resources
Students are not required to have a computer. Student rooms are linked to a campus network. 65 **computers** available in the computer center, the library, and dormitories provide access to on-campus e-mail addresses, off-campus e-mail addresses, and the Internet. Staffed computer lab on campus provides training in the use of computers, software, and the Internet.

The **library** has 67,000 books and 400 subscriptions.

Career Services
The career planning and placement office has 2 full-time staff members. Services include job fairs, resume preparation, interview workshops, career/interest testing, career counseling, careers library, and job bank.

Campus Life
There are 15 active organizations on campus, including a drama/theater group and student-run newspaper. 77% of students participate in student government elections. No national or local **fraternities** or **sororities**. Student **safety services** include late-night transport/escort service and student patrols.

Trinity Christian College is a member of the NAIA and NCCAA. **Intercollegiate sports** (some offering scholarships) include baseball (m), basketball (m,w), soccer (m,w), softball (w), track and field (m,w), volleyball (m,w).

International Students
For fall 1997, 7 international students applied, 3 were accepted, and 3 enrolled. Students can start in fall and spring. The **admissions test** required for entrance is TOEFL (minimum score: 500); recommended is SAT I or ACT. Application deadline is rolling. On-campus **housing** is guaranteed, also available during summer. Services include an international student adviser on campus.

Applying
Trinity Christian College requires an essay, ACT, a high school transcript, an interview, and a minimum high school GPA of 2.0, and in some cases 1 recommendation. It recommends ACT, 3 years of high school English, 3 years of high school math, 2 years of high school science, 2 years of high school foreign language, and 2 years of high school social studies. Application deadline: 8/15; 2/15 priority date for financial aid. Early and deferred entrance are possible. **Contact:** Mr. Peter Hamstra, Dean of Admissions, 6601 West College Drive, Palos Heights, IL 60463-0929, 708-239-4709 or toll-free 800-748-0085; fax 708-239-3995; e-mail admissions@trnty.edu.

GETTING IN LAST YEAR
432 applied
89% were accepted
42% enrolled (162)
14% from top tenth of their h.s. class
37% had ACT scores over 24

THE STUDENT BODY
618 undergraduates
From 22 states and territories,
8 other countries

50% from Illinois
65.4% women, 34.6% men
2.8% international students

COSTS AND FINANCIAL INFORMATION
1998–99 tuition and fees $12,290
1998–99 room and board $4870

AFTER FRESHMAN YEAR
73% returned for sophomore year

46% got a degree in 4 years
50% got a degree in 5 years
52% got a degree in 6 years

AFTER GRADUATION
10% pursued further study (6% arts and sciences, 1% dentistry, 1% law)
89% had job offers within 6 months

TRINITY INTERNATIONAL UNIVERSITY

Deerfield, Illinois   *http://www.tiu.edu/*

Trinity will expand your intellect, challenge your faith, and prepare you for life. With 29 majors, Trinity provides many options for motivated students to integrate Christianity with academics. While excellence within the classroom is crucial, Trinity also expands your education beyond four walls. You have opportunities to test your knowledge and gain practical experience through internships and ministry opportunities. Music groups, athletics, and numerous other activities help you develop leadership and communications skills essential for the workplace. Upon graduation, you are ready for the work force, graduate school, and to impact your world for Christ.

Academics

Trinity offers a core academic program; some graduate courses are open to undergraduates. It awards bachelor's, master's, doctoral, and first professional **degrees**. Challenging opportunities include advanced placement, an honors program, double majors, independent study, and a senior project. **Special programs** include cooperative education, internships, summer session for credit, off-campus study, and study-abroad.

The most popular **majors** include education, psychology, Christian ministries, and business administration. A complete listing of majors at Trinity appears in the Majors Index beginning on page 141.

The **faculty** at Trinity has 79 full-time graduate and undergraduate teachers, 86% with terminal degrees. The student-faculty ratio is 17:1, and the average **class size** in required courses is 30.

Campus Resources

Students are not required to have a computer. 60 **computers** available in computer labs and the library provide access to on-campus e-mail addresses, off-campus e-mail addresses, and the Internet. Staffed computer labs on campus provide training in the use of computers and software.

The **library** has 233,000 books and 2,000 subscriptions.

Career Services

The career planning and placement office has 1 full-time staff member. Services include job fairs, resume preparation, interview workshops, resume referral, career/interest testing, career counseling, careers library, and job interviews.

Campus Life

There are 15 active organizations on campus, including a drama/theater group and student-run newspaper. No national or local **fraternities** or **sororities**. Student **safety services** include 24-hour patrols by trained security personnel.

Trinity is a member of the NAIA. **Intercollegiate sports** (some offering scholarships) include baseball (m), basketball (m,w), football (m), soccer (m,w), softball (w), tennis (m,w), track and field (m,w), volleyball (m,w).

International Students

For fall 1997, 16 international students applied, 11 were accepted, and 5 enrolled. The **admissions test** required for entrance is TOEFL (minimum score: 500); recommended is SAT I or ACT. On-campus **housing** is guaranteed. Services include an international student adviser on campus.

Applying

Trinity requires an essay, SAT I or ACT, a high school transcript, 1 recommendation, and a minimum high school GPA of 2.5, and in some cases an interview. It recommends 3 years of high school English, 2 years of high school math and science, 2 years of high school foreign language, 2 years of high school social studies, and a minimum high school GPA of 3.0. Application deadline: rolling admissions; 4/15 priority date for financial aid. **Contact:** Mr. Brian Pomeroy, Director of Undergraduate Admissions, 2065 Half Day Road, Deerfield, IL 60015-1284, 847-317-7000 or toll-free 800-822-3225 (out-of-state); fax 847-317-7081; e-mail tcdadm@tiu.edu.

GETTING IN LAST YEAR
9% from top tenth of their h.s. class
26% had SAT verbal scores over 600
20% had SAT math scores over 600
36% had ACT scores over 24
2 valedictorians

THE STUDENT BODY
Total 2,571, of whom 844 are undergraduates

From 33 states and territories, 6 other countries
53.2% women, 46.8% men

COSTS AND FINANCIAL INFORMATION
1998–99 tuition and fees $13,080
1998–99 room and board $4800
Average percent of need met 97%
Average amount received per student $12,960

AFTER FRESHMAN YEAR
70.4% returned for sophomore year

AFTER GRADUATION
17% pursued further study (12% arts and sciences, 2% medicine, 2% theology)
86% had job offers within 6 months
69 organizations recruited on campus

TRINITY WESTERN UNIVERSITY
Langley, British Columbia, Canada *http://www.twu.ca/*

Located in British Columbia's beautiful Fraser Valley, only 40 minutes from downtown Vancouver and 2½ hours from Seattle, Trinity Western University is one of Canada's most respected Christian liberal arts institutions. A commitment to developing the whole student—academically, socially, physically, and spiritually—distinguishes Trinity Western as a premier institute for leadership development. Taught by some of North America's finest scholars who have thoroughly integrated their studies with their faith, Trinity Western students acquire the thinking skills, expertise, professional abilities, and character qualities essential for today's world marketplace.

Academics
TWU offers a Christian worldview curriculum and core academic program. It awards bachelor's and master's **degrees**. Challenging opportunities include advanced placement, tutorials, an honors program, double majors, and a senior project. **Special programs** include cooperative education, internships, summer session for credit, off-campus study, and study-abroad.

The most popular **majors** include business administration, psychology, and education. A complete listing of majors at TWU appears in the Majors Index beginning on page 141.

The **faculty** at TWU has 71 full-time graduate and undergraduate teachers, 85% with terminal degrees. The student-faculty ratio is 18:1, and the average **class size** in required courses is 22.

Campus Resources
Students are not required to have a computer. Purchase and/or lease options are available. Student rooms are linked to a campus network. 50 **computers** available in the computer center, student lounges, and the library provide access to on-campus e-mail addresses, off-campus e-mail addresses, and the Internet. Staffed computer lab on campus provides training in the use of computers and software.

The **library** has 108,722 books and 634 subscriptions.

Career Services
The career planning and placement office has 4 full-time, 1 part-time staff members. Services include job fairs, resume preparation, resume referral, career counseling, careers library, job bank (available on line), and job interviews.

Campus Life
There are 33 active organizations on campus, including a drama/theater group and student-run newspaper. 30% of students participate in student government elections. No national or local **fraternities** or **sororities**. Student **safety services** include late-night transport/escort service, 24-hour emergency telephone alarm devices, and 24-hour patrols by trained security personnel.

Intercollegiate sports include basketball (m,w), rugby (m,w), soccer (m,w), volleyball (m,w).

International Students
For fall 1997, 67 international students applied and 46 were accepted. Students can start in fall and spring. The **admissions test** required for entrance is TOEFL (minimum score: 570). Application deadline is The **admissions test** required for entrance is TOEFL (minimum score: 570). Services include an international student adviser on campus.

Applying
TWU requires an essay, a high school transcript, 2 recommendations, community standards document, 4 years of high school English, 3 years of high school math, 2 years of high school science, 2 years of high school social studies, 2 years of high school academic electives, a minimum high school GPA of 2.5, and the SAT I or ACT. Application deadline: 6/15. Early and deferred entrance are possible. **Contact:** Mr. Cam Lee, Director of Admissions, 7600 Glover Road, Langley, BC V2Y 1Y1, Canada, 604-513-2019 ext. 3015 or toll-free 888-468-6898; fax 604-513-2064; e-mail admissions@twu.ca.

GETTING IN LAST YEAR
1,078 applied
67% were accepted

THE STUDENT BODY
Total 2,725, of whom 2,003
  are undergraduates

From 25 states and territories,
  20 other countries

COSTS AND FINANCIAL INFORMATION
1998–99 tuition and fees $5300 (US)
1998–99 room and board $3354 (US)

AFTER FRESHMAN YEAR
60% returned for sophomore year

AFTER GRADUATION
15% pursued further study

UNION UNIVERSITY

Jackson, Tennessee

http://www.uu.edu/

Equipping graduates for the challenges and changes of a new century is the heart of Union University's mission. In addition to superior liberal arts training, Union offers top professional programs in fields such as nursing, business administration, and education. Union's team of leading scholars provides a Christian world view that pervades the classroom as well as the chapel. In every discipline, Union's goal is to prepare Christian men and women to assume key leadership roles in their professions, communities, and churches, transforming their world in Christ's name.

Academics
Union offers a liberal arts curriculum and core academic program; a few graduate courses are open to undergraduates. It awards bachelor's and master's **degrees**. Challenging opportunities include advanced placement, accelerated degree programs, tutorials, an honors program, double majors, independent study, and a senior project. **Special programs** include internships, summer session for credit, off-campus study, and study-abroad.

The most popular **majors** include nursing, education, and business administration. A complete listing of majors at Union appears in the Majors Index beginning on page 141.

The **faculty** at Union has 123 full-time graduate and undergraduate teachers, 60% with terminal degrees. The student-faculty ratio is 12:1, and the average **class size** in required courses is 23.

Campus Resources
Students are not required to have a computer. Purchase and/or lease options are available. 175 **computers** available in the computer center, computer labs, classrooms, the library, and dormitories provide access to on-campus e-mail addresses, off-campus e-mail addresses, and the Internet. Staffed computer lab on campus provides training in the use of computers, software, and the Internet.

The **library** has 196,294 books and 1,311 subscriptions.

Career Services
The career planning and placement office has 2 full-time staff members. Services include job fairs, resume preparation, interview workshops, resume referral, career/interest testing, career counseling, careers library, job bank, and job interviews.

Campus Life
There are 73 active organizations on campus, including a drama/theater group and student-run newspaper. 45% of students participate in student government elections. 26% of eligible men and 23% of eligible women are members of 3 national **fraternities** and 3 national **sororities**. Student **safety services** include 24-hour patrols by trained security personnel and student patrols.

Union is a member of the NAIA. **Intercollegiate sports** (some offering scholarships) include baseball (m), basketball (m,w), golf (m), soccer (m), softball (w), tennis (m,w), volleyball (w).

International Students
For fall 1997, 37 international students applied, 6 were accepted, and 5 enrolled. Students can start in fall and spring. The **admissions test** required for entrance is TOEFL (minimum score: 500); recommended are SAT I or ACT, ELS. Application deadline is 8/1. On-campus **housing** is guaranteed, also available during summer. Services include an international student adviser on campus.

Applying
Union requires SAT I or ACT, a high school transcript, 3 years of high school English, 3 years of high school math and science, 3 years of high school social studies, and a minimum high school GPA of 2.5, and in some cases an essay, an interview, and recommendations. It recommends 4 years of high school English, 4 years of high school math and science, and 2 years of high school foreign language. Application deadline: 2/1; 2/1 priority date for financial aid. Early entrance is possible. **Contact:** Mr. Robert Graves, Director of Enrollment Services, 1050 Union University Drive, Jackson, TN 38305-3697, 901-661-5000 or toll-free 800-33-UNION; fax 901-661-5187; e-mail info@buster.uu.edu.

GETTING IN LAST YEAR
821 applied
85% were accepted
52% had ACT scores over 24
31 valedictorians

THE STUDENT BODY
Total 1,953, of whom 1,779
  are undergraduates
From 31 states and territories,
  10 other countries

76% from Tennessee
64.6% women, 35.4% men
1.2% international students

COSTS AND FINANCIAL INFORMATION
1997–98 tuition and fees $8180
1997–98 room and board $3005
Average percent of need met 80%
Average amount received per student $4900

AFTER FRESHMAN YEAR
93% returned for sophomore year
34% got a degree in 4 years
10% got a degree in 5 years
1% got a degree in 6 years

AFTER GRADUATION
40% pursued further study
87% had job offers within 6 months
65 organizations recruited on campus

UNIVERSITY OF SIOUX FALLS

Sioux Falls, South Dakota

http://www.thecoo.edu/

Sioux Falls College is a 4-year Christian liberal arts college affiliated with the American Baptist Churches. In an environment that both challenges and supports, students are encouraged to develop knowledge and wisdom for discerning truth and meeting human needs, to build a value system in keeping with Christ's teachings, to achieve emotional maturity, to pursue physical fitness, and to gain interpersonal skills. Students develop close, caring relationships with professors in and out of the classroom. Beyond the classroom, there are numerous cocurricular activities important to a college education. Sioux Falls is large enough to provide many opportunities for involvement and small enough to encourage participation.

Academics

USF offers a core academic program; all graduate courses are open to undergraduates. It awards associate, bachelor's, and master's **degrees**. Challenging opportunities include advanced placement, accelerated degree programs, student-designed majors, an honors program, and a senior project. **Special programs** include cooperative education, internships, summer session for credit, off-campus study, and study-abroad.

The most popular **majors** include business administration, education, and behavioral sciences. A complete listing of majors at USF appears in the Majors Index beginning on page 141.

The **faculty** at USF has 39 full-time graduate and undergraduate teachers, 72% with terminal degrees. The student-faculty ratio is 14:1.

Campus Resources

Students are not required to have a computer. 44 **computers** available in the computer center, computer labs, and the library provide access to on-campus e-mail addresses and the Internet. Staffed computer lab on campus provides training in the use of computers and software.

The **library** has 78,000 books and 336 subscriptions.

Career Services

The career planning and placement office has 2 full-time, 1 part-time staff members. Services include job fairs, resume preparation, resume referral, career counseling, careers library, job bank, and job interviews.

Campus Life

There are 12 active organizations on campus, including a drama/theater group and student-run newspaper and radio station. No national or local **fraternities** or **sororities**. Student **safety services** include late-night transport/escort service and electronically operated dormitory entrances.

USF is a member of the NAIA. **Intercollegiate sports** (some offering scholarships) include baseball (m), basketball (m,w), cross-country running (m,w), football (m), golf (m,w), soccer (m,w), softball (w), tennis (m,w), track and field (m,w), volleyball (w).

International Students

For fall 1997, 14 international students applied, 8 were accepted, and 3 enrolled. Students can start in fall and spring. The **admissions test** required for entrance is TOEFL (minimum score: 500); recommended is SAT I or ACT. Application deadline is 3/31. On-campus **housing** is guaranteed, also available during summer. Services include an international student adviser on campus.

Applying

USF requires ACT and a high school transcript, and in some cases an interview and 2 recommendations. It recommends an essay, SAT I, 3 years of high school math and science, and 1 year of high school foreign language. Application deadline: rolling admissions. Early and deferred entrance are possible. **Contact:** Mr. Terry Okken, Director of Admissions, 1101 West 22nd Street, Sioux Falls, SD 57105-1699, 605-331-6600 or toll-free 800-888-1047 (out-of-state); fax 605-331-6615; e-mail terry.okken@thecoo.edu.

GETTING IN LAST YEAR 398 applied 96% were accepted 13% from top tenth of their h.s. class	From 19 states and territories, 6 other countries 58.1% women, 41.9% men 2.2% international students	**AFTER FRESHMAN YEAR** 65% returned for sophomore year **AFTER GRADUATION** 14% pursued further study 94% had job offers within 6 months 188 organizations recruited on campus
THE STUDENT BODY Total 979, of whom 845 are undergraduates	**COSTS AND FINANCIAL INFORMATION** 1997–98 tuition and fees $10,750 1997–98 room and board $3450	

WARNER PACIFIC COLLEGE

Portland, Oregon

http://www.warnerpacific.edu/

Warner Pacific College is shaped by an assumption that there must be a strong and reinforcing relationship among faith, learning, and life. Faculty members are selected for their ability to teach; for evidence of thoughtful personal, spiritual, and professional growth; and for being experts in their subject areas. There is a conviction that students are expected to develop servant leadership and a global perspective through community and/or ministry-related outreach activities and optional international experiences such as the mission service program in Mexico. Well-trained residence and counseling staffs help students resolve normal difficulties. All students benefit from the Academic Support Center. Warner Pacific is located 15 minutes from downtown Portland, Oregon, and is less than 2 hours by car from Mt. Hood ski slopes and Pacific Ocean beaches.

Academics

Warner Pacific offers a Christian liberal arts curriculum and core academic program; fewer than half of graduate courses are open to undergraduates. It awards associate, bachelor's, and master's **degrees**. Challenging opportunities include advanced placement, student-designed majors, tutorials, an honors program, double majors, independent study, and a senior project. **Special programs** include cooperative education, internships, summer session for credit, off-campus study, study-abroad, and Army and Air Force ROTC.

The most popular **majors** include education, business administration, and human development. A complete listing of majors at Warner Pacific appears in the Majors Index beginning on page 141.

The **faculty** at Warner Pacific has 40 full-time graduate and undergraduate teachers, 50% with terminal degrees. The student-faculty ratio is 16:1, and the average **class size** in required courses is 25.

Campus Resources

Students are not required to have a computer. 9 **computers** available in the library provide access to off-campus e-mail addresses and the Internet. Staffed computer lab on campus provides training in the use of computers, software, and the Internet.

The 2 **libraries** have 54,000 books and 400 subscriptions.

Career Services

The career planning and placement office has 1 full-time, 2 part-time staff members. Services include job fairs, resume preparation, resume referral, career counseling, careers library, job bank, and job interviews.

Campus Life

Active organizations on campus include a student-run newspaper. 12% of students participate in student government elections. No national or local **fraternities** or **sororities**. Student **safety services** include 14-hour patrols by trained security personnel, late-night transport/escort service, and 24-hour emergency telephone alarm devices.

Intercollegiate sports include basketball (m), soccer (m), volleyball (w).

International Students

For fall 1997, 22 international students applied, 13 were accepted, and 11 enrolled. Students can start in fall, spring, and summer. The **admissions test** required for entrance is TOEFL (minimum score: 525); recommended is SAT I or ACT. Application deadline is rolling. On-campus **housing** is guaranteed, also available during summer. Services include an international student adviser on campus.

Applying

Warner Pacific requires an essay, SAT I or ACT, a high school transcript, 2 recommendations, and a minimum high school GPA of 2.0, and in some cases an interview. It recommends SAT II Subject Tests, SAT II: Writing Test, an interview, 4 years of high school English, 2 years of high school math and science, 3 years of high school social studies, and a minimum high school GPA of 3.0. Application deadline: rolling admissions; 5/1 priority date for financial aid. **Contact:** Mr. Guy R. Adams, Interim Director of Admissions, 2219 Southeast 68th Avenue, Portland, OR 97215-4099, 503-788-7495 or toll-free 800-582-7885; fax 503-788-7425; e-mail admiss@warnerpacific.edu.

GETTING IN LAST YEAR
330 applied
58% were accepted
86% enrolled (67)

THE STUDENT BODY
Total 639, of whom 630
  are undergraduates

From 17 states and territories,
  7 other countries
66% from Oregon
68% women, 32% men
3.8% international students

COSTS AND FINANCIAL INFORMATION
1998–99 tuition and fees $11,482

1998–99 room and board $4100
Average percent of need met 90%
Average amount received per student $10,020

WARNER SOUTHERN COLLEGE

Lake Wales, Florida

http://www.warner.edu/

Warner Southern College's 380-acre campus is located in central Florida. This four-year college fosters an environment that allows students to search for truth in the context of Christian faith and academic excellence. Students are a top priority. Administration, faculty, and staff members are all committed to helping students develop, excel, and become contributors to the betterment of their community. Students develop a close bond with their professors because of the low student-teacher ratio and with fellow students because of the friendly atmosphere. Students often remark that they enjoy the size of classes and the spiritual atmosphere on campus.

Academics

Warner Southern offers a traditional liberal arts curriculum and core academic program. It awards associate and bachelor's **degrees**. Challenging opportunities include advanced placement, accelerated degree programs, tutorials, double majors, independent study, and a senior project. **Special programs** include internships and summer session for credit.

The most popular **majors** include business administration, elementary education, and (pre)theology. A complete listing of majors at Warner Southern appears in the Majors Index beginning on page 141.

The **faculty** at Warner Southern has 23 full-time teachers, 39% with terminal degrees. The student-faculty ratio is 14:1.

Campus Resources

Students are not required to have a computer. **45 computers** available in computer labs, academic skills center, and the library. Staffed computer lab on campus.

The 2 **libraries** have 65,000 books and 301 subscriptions.

Career Services

The career planning and placement office has 1 part-time staff member. Services include resume preparation, career counseling, and careers library.

Campus Life

There are 4 active organizations on campus, including a student-run newspaper and radio station. 40% of students participate in student government elections. No national or local **fraternities** or **sororities**. Student **safety services** include late-night transport/escort service, 24-hour emergency telephone alarm devices, 24-hour patrols by trained security personnel, and electronically operated dormitory entrances.

Warner Southern is a member of the NAIA. **Intercollegiate sports** (some offering scholarships) include baseball (m), basketball (m,w), cross-country running (m,w), volleyball (w).

International Students

Students can start in fall and spring. The **admissions test** required for entrance is TOEFL (minimum score: 450). Application deadline is The **admissions test** required for entrance is TOEFL (minimum score: 450). On-campus **housing** is available.

Applying

Warner Southern requires SAT I or ACT, a high school transcript, 1 recommendation, and a minimum high school GPA of 2.25, and in some cases an interview. It recommends an essay, 4 years of high school English, 4 years of high school math and science, 2 years of high school foreign language, and 4 years of high school social studies. Application deadline: rolling admissions. Early and deferred entrance are possible. **Contact:** Ms. Karen Steverson, Director of Admissions, 5301 US Highway 27 South, Lake Wales, FL 33853-8725, 800-949-7248 ext. 7208.

GETTING IN LAST YEAR
270 applied
53% were accepted
42% enrolled (60)
12% from top tenth of their h.s. class

THE STUDENT BODY
646 undergraduates
From 26 states and territories,
  4 other countries

90% from Florida
57.3% women, 42.7% men
1.1% international students

COSTS AND FINANCIAL INFORMATION
1997–98 tuition and fees $8220
1997–98 room and board $3969
Average percent of need met 85%

Average amount received per student $8452

AFTER FRESHMAN YEAR
65% returned for sophomore year
11% got a degree in 4 years
7% got a degree in 5 years
2% got a degree in 6 years

WESTERN BAPTIST COLLEGE

Salem, Oregon

http://www.wbc.edu/

As soon as students step onto the beautiful 100 acre campus in Salem, Oregon, they discover the family atmosphere and caring community of professing Christians. Western provides a strong academic program in the liberal arts and professional studies that is Bible centered. The college's vision for all students is that they have a burning desire to make a difference in the world for Jesus Christ. Academic advisors meet with freshmen—usually in their homes before they ever enroll—to schedule classes and talk about the transition to college life. The goal is to see all students thrive at Western.

Academics

Western offers an interdisciplinary curriculum and core academic program. It awards associate and bachelor's **degrees**. Challenging opportunities include advanced placement, freshman honors college, an honors program, and a senior project. **Special programs** include internships, summer session for credit, off-campus study, study-abroad, and Army and Air Force ROTC.

The most popular **majors** include business administration, education, and psychology. A complete listing of majors at Western appears in the Majors Index beginning on page 141.

The **faculty** at Western has 24 full-time teachers, 25% with terminal degrees. The student-faculty ratio is 18:1.

Campus Resources

Students are not required to have a computer. Student rooms are linked to a campus network. 34 **computers** available in computer labs and dormitories provide access to on-campus e-mail addresses, off-campus e-mail addresses, and the Internet. Staffed computer lab on campus provides training in the use of computers and software.

The **library** has 70,638 books and 490 subscriptions.

Career Services

The career planning and placement office has 1 full-time, 1 part-time staff members. Services include job fairs, resume preparation, career counseling, careers library, job bank (available on line), and job interviews.

Campus Life

Active organizations on campus include a drama/theater group. No national or local **fraternities** or **sororities**. Student **safety services** include late-night transport/escort service, 24-hour emergency telephone alarm devices, and student patrols.

Western is a member of the NCCAA. **Intercollegiate sports** (some offering scholarships) include basketball (m,w), soccer (m,w), volleyball (w).

International Students

For fall 1997, 2 international students applied, 2 were accepted, and 1 enrolled. The **admissions test** required for entrance is TOEFL (minimum score: 552); recommended is SAT I or ACT. Application deadline is 6/1. On-campus **housing** is guaranteed, also available during summer. Services include an international student adviser on campus.

Applying

Western requires an essay, SAT I or ACT, a high school transcript, 3 recommendations, and a minimum high school GPA of 2.5. It recommends 4 years of high school English, 3 years of high school math, 2 years of high school science, 1 year of high school foreign language, and 3 years of high school social studies. Application deadline: rolling admissions; 3/1 for financial aid, with a 2/15 priority date. **Contact:** Mr. Daren Milionis, Director of Admissions, 5000 Deer Park Drive, SE, Salem, OR 97301-9392, 503-375-7005; fax 503-585-4316; e-mail dmilionis@wbc.edu.

GETTING IN LAST YEAR	THE STUDENT BODY	COSTS AND FINANCIAL INFORMATION
327 applied	701 undergraduates	1997–98 tuition and fees $12,350
91% were accepted	From 11 states and territories,	1997–98 room and board $4820
41% enrolled (123)	1 other country	Average percent of need met 25%
25% from top tenth of their h.s. class	73% from Oregon	Average amount received per student $10,772
18% had SAT verbal scores over 600	61.2% women, 38.8% men	
14% had SAT math scores over 600	.1% international students	**AFTER FRESHMAN YEAR**
20% had ACT scores over 24		65% returned for sophomore year

WESTMONT COLLEGE
Santa Barbara, California

http://www.westmont.edu/

Known nationally for unusually strong academics, Westmont blends a rigorous liberal arts curriculum with enthusiastic, evangelical Christian faith and community. Highly qualified faculty members with degrees from prestigious universities give priority to teaching and working closely with undergraduates while conducting significant scholarly research. Innovative, semester-long study programs at home and abroad offer a global perspective and cross-cultural experiences. On campus, students participate in leadership studies, creative and performing arts, student-led outreach programs in the local community and beyond, internships, and practica, and intercollegiate and intramural sports. The College encourages students to make responsible personal choices and provides great leadership and support in this area.

Academics
Westmont offers a humanities and sciences curriculum and core academic program. It awards bachelor's **degrees**. Challenging opportunities include advanced placement, accelerated degree programs, student-designed majors, tutorials, an honors program, double majors, independent study, and a senior project. **Special programs** include internships, summer session for credit, off-campus study, study-abroad, and Army and Air Force ROTC.

The most popular **majors** include business economics, English, and biology. A complete listing of majors at Westmont appears in the Majors Index beginning on page 141.

The **faculty** at Westmont has 78 full-time teachers, 86% with terminal degrees. The student-faculty ratio is 14:1, and the average **class size** in required courses is 25.

Campus Resources
Students are not required to have a computer. Purchase and/or lease options are available. Student rooms are linked to a campus network. 40 **computers** available in computer labs, academic buildings, the library, dormitories, and student rooms provide access to on-campus e-mail addresses, off-campus e-mail addresses, and the Internet. Staffed computer lab on campus provides training in the use of computers, software, and the Internet.

The **library** has 150,000 books and 700 subscriptions.

Career Services
The career planning and placement office has 5 full-time, 1 part-time staff members. Services include job fairs, resume preparation, resume referral, career counseling, careers library, job bank, and job interviews.

Campus Life
There are 50 active organizations on campus, including a drama/theater group and student-run newspaper and radio station. 80% of students participate in student government elections. No national or local **fraternities** or **sororities**. Student **safety services** include late-night transport/escort service, 24-hour emergency telephone alarm devices, 24-hour patrols by trained security personnel, and electronically operated dormitory entrances.

Westmont is a member of the NAIA. **Intercollegiate sports** (some offering scholarships) include baseball (m), basketball (m,w), cross-country running (m,w), soccer (m,w), tennis (m,w), track and field (m,w), volleyball (w).

International Students
For fall 1997, 10 international students applied, 5 were accepted, and 2 enrolled. Students can start in fall and spring. The **admissions tests** required for entrance are SAT I, TOEFL (minimum score: 560). Application deadline is 4/15. On-campus **housing** is guaranteed. Services include an international student adviser on campus.

Applying
Westmont requires an essay, SAT I or ACT, a high school transcript, and a minimum high school GPA of 2.0. It recommends an interview, recommendations, 4 years of high school English, 3 years of high school math and science, 2 years of high school foreign language, 1 year of high school social studies, 1 year of high school history, 4 years of high school academic electives, and a minimum high school GPA of 3.0. Application deadline: 3/1; 3/1 priority date for financial aid. Deferred entrance is possible. **Contact:** Mr. David Morley, Dean of Admissions, 955 La Paz Road, Santa Barbara, CA 93108-1099, 805-565-6200 ext. 6003 or toll-free 800-777-9011 (out-of-state); fax 805-565-6234; e-mail admissions@westmont.edu.

GETTING IN LAST YEAR
1,180 applied
77% were accepted
36% enrolled (331)
44% from top tenth of their h.s. class
42% had SAT verbal scores over 600
43% had SAT math scores over 600
63% had ACT scores over 24
2 National Merit Scholars

THE STUDENT BODY
1,263 undergraduates

From 30 states and territories,
    14 other countries
61.1% women, 38.9% men

COSTS AND FINANCIAL INFORMATION
1997–98 tuition and fees $17,998
1997–98 room and board $6048
Average percent of need met 84%
Average amount received per student $12,500

AFTER FRESHMAN YEAR
80.4% returned for sophomore year
61% got a degree in 4 years
4% got a degree in 5 years
1% got a degree in 6 years

AFTER GRADUATION
85% had job offers within 6 months
58 organizations recruited on campus

WHEATON COLLEGE
Wheaton, Illinois
http://www.wheaton.edu/

Convinced that "all truth is God's truth," Wheaton College actively pursues the integration of biblical Christianity with rigorous academic study in the liberal arts, with the goal of serving Christ in this world. Wheaton has a national reputation built upon a distinguished and dedicated faculty known for its outstanding teaching and scholarship and a student body committed to academic achievement, leadership, and Christian service. It offers students a wide range of overseas study programs and opportunities to engage in collaborative research. Outstanding athletic programs and a full calendar of student activities add to the friendly and supportive campus community.

Academics
Wheaton offers a liberal arts curriculum and core academic program; more than half of graduate courses are open to undergraduates. It awards bachelor's, master's, and doctoral **degrees**. Challenging opportunities include advanced placement, student-designed majors, double majors, independent study, and a senior project. **Special programs** include internships, summer session for credit, off-campus study, study-abroad, and Army ROTC.

The most popular **majors** include literature, biblical studies, and music. A complete listing of majors at Wheaton appears in the Majors Index beginning on page 141.

The **faculty** at Wheaton has 174 full-time graduate and undergraduate teachers, 89% with terminal degrees. The student-faculty ratio is 15:1, and the average **class size** in required courses is 28.

Campus Resources
Students are not required to have a computer. 126 **computers** available in computer labs and dormitories provide access to on-campus e-mail addresses, off-campus e-mail addresses, and the Internet. Staffed computer lab on campus provides training in the use of computers, software, and the Internet.

The 2 **libraries** have 199,115 books and 2,578 subscriptions.

Career Services
The career planning and placement office has 3 full-time, 2 part-time staff members. Services include job fairs, resume preparation, resume referral, career counseling, careers library, job bank, and job interviews.

Campus Life
There are 57 active organizations on campus, including a drama/theater group and student-run newspaper and radio station. 50% of students participate in student government elections. No national or local **fraternities** or **sororities**. Student **safety services** include late-night transport/escort service and 24-hour patrols by trained security personnel.

Wheaton is a member of the NCAA (Division III). **Intercollegiate sports** include baseball (m), basketball (m,w), cross-country running (m,w), football (m), golf (m), soccer (m,w), softball (w), swimming (m,w), tennis (m,w), track and field (m,w), volleyball (w), wrestling (m).

International Students
The **admissions test** required for entrance is TOEFL (minimum score: 550; minimum score for ESL admission: 550). Application deadline is 2/1. On-campus **housing** is guaranteed, also available during summer. Services include an international student adviser on campus.

Applying
Wheaton requires an essay, SAT I or ACT, a high school transcript, an interview, and 2 recommendations. It recommends SAT II Subject Tests, 4 years of high school English, 4 years of high school math and science, 3 years of high school foreign language, and 4 years of high school social studies. Application deadline: 1/15; 2/15 priority date for financial aid. Deferred entrance is possible. **Contact:** Mr. Dan Crabtree, Director of Admissions, 501 East College Avenue, Wheaton, IL 60187-5593, 630-752-5011 or toll-free 800-222-2419 (out-of-state); fax 630-752-5285; e-mail admissions@wheaton.edu.

GETTING IN LAST YEAR
1,927 applied
55% were accepted
52% enrolled (547)
58% from top tenth of their h.s. class
88% had SAT verbal scores over 600
74% had SAT math scores over 600
88% had ACT scores over 24
34 National Merit Scholars
48 valedictorians

THE STUDENT BODY
Total 2,725, of whom 2,321
  are undergraduates
From 50 states and territories,
  9 other countries
28% from Illinois
51.4% women, 48.6% men
.8% international students

COSTS AND FINANCIAL INFORMATION
1997–98 tuition and fees $13,780

1997–98 room and board $4740
Average percent of need met 85%
Average amount received per student $10,935

AFTER FRESHMAN YEAR
93% returned for sophomore year

AFTER GRADUATION
135 organizations recruited on campus

WHITWORTH COLLEGE

Spokane, Washington

http://www.whitworth.edu/

For over a century, Whitworth has dedicated itself to a blend of educational components: an integration of faith and learning in the classroom featuring rigorous academics taught by Christian scholars, active residential life, and a commitment to fostering an understanding of other cultures within the nation and the world. Study tours and exchanges provide opportunities for students to experience countries throughout Europe, Asia, and Central America. Cooperative education experiences and internships, which allow students to gain experience and build contacts in the professional community, are encouraged. Whitworth's stated mission is to equip its graduates to honor God, follow Christ, and serve humanity.

Academics

Whitworth offers a Western civilization curriculum and core academic program. It awards bachelor's and master's **degrees**. Challenging opportunities include advanced placement, student-designed majors, and tutorials. **Special programs** include cooperative education, internships, summer session for credit, off-campus study, study-abroad, and Army ROTC.

The most popular **majors** include elementary education, business administration, and history. A complete listing of majors at Whitworth appears in the Majors Index beginning on page 141.

The **faculty** at Whitworth has 84 full-time undergraduate teachers, 78% with terminal degrees. The student-faculty ratio is 16:1, and the average **class size** in required courses is 27.

Campus Resources

Students are not required to have a computer. Purchase and/or lease options are available. Student rooms are linked to a campus network. 150 **computers** available in the computer center and the library provide access to the Internet. Staffed computer lab on campus provides training in the use of computers and software.

The **library** has 135,373 books and 725 subscriptions.

Career Services

The career planning and placement office has 3 full-time, 4 part-time staff members. Services include job fairs, resume preparation, resume referral, career counseling, careers library, job bank, and job interviews.

Campus Life

Active organizations on campus include a drama/theater group and student-run newspaper and radio station. No national or local **fraternities** or **sororities**. Student **safety services** include late-night transport/escort service, 24-hour emergency telephone alarm devices, and 24-hour patrols by trained security personnel.

Whitworth is a member of the NAIA. **Intercollegiate sports** include baseball (m), basketball (m,w), cross-country running (m,w), football (m), golf (m), soccer (m,w), swimming and diving (m,w), tennis (m,w), track and field (m,w), volleyball (w).

Applying

Whitworth requires an essay, SAT I or ACT, a high school transcript, and recommendations, and in some cases an interview. It recommends 3 years of high school math and science. Application deadline: 3/1; 3/1 priority date for financial aid. Early and deferred entrance are possible. **Contact:** Mr. Fred Pfursich, Dean of Enrollment Services, 300 West Hawthorne Road, Spokane, WA 99251-0001, 509-466-3212 or toll-free 800-533-4668 (out-of-state); fax 509-466-3773; e-mail admissions@ whiteworth.edu.

GETTING IN LAST YEAR
1,446 applied
87% were accepted
44% from top tenth of their h.s. class
15% had SAT verbal scores over 600
30% had SAT math scores over 600
30 valedictorians

THE STUDENT BODY
Total 2,043, of whom 1,798
 are undergraduates

From 27 states and territories,
 26 other countries

COSTS AND FINANCIAL INFORMATION
1998–99 tuition and fees $15,593
1998–99 room and board $5300

Average amount received per student $14,190

AFTER FRESHMAN YEAR
82% returned for sophomore year

AFTER GRADUATION
125 organizations recruited on campus

WILLIAMS BAPTIST COLLEGE

Walnut Ridge, Arkansas

http://www.wbcoll.edu/

Williams vision is to be an exemplary Christian college with an integrated curriculum of liberal arts and professional studies shaped by a caring people committed to biblical precepts and the highest educational standards.

Academics

Williams offers a liberal arts curriculum and core academic program. It awards associate and bachelor's **degrees**. Challenging opportunities include advanced placement, student-designed majors, tutorials, an honors program, and a senior project. **Special programs** include internships, summer session for credit, off-campus study, study-abroad, and Army ROTC.

The most popular **majors** include elementary education, business administration, and psychology. A complete listing of majors at Williams appears in the Majors Index beginning on page 141.

The **faculty** at Williams has 27 full-time teachers, 50% with terminal degrees. The student-faculty ratio is 10:1, and the average **class size** in required courses is 22.

Campus Resources

Students are not required to have a computer. 40 **computers** available in the computer center, computer labs, and the library provide access to on-campus e-mail addresses, off-campus e-mail addresses, and the Internet. Staffed computer lab on campus provides training in the use of computers and software.

The **library** has 57,321 books and 284 subscriptions.

Career Services

The career planning and placement office has 2 part-time staff members. Services include job fairs, resume preparation, career counseling, and job bank.

Campus Life

There are 26 active organizations on campus, including a drama/theater group. 10% of eligible men and 10% of eligible women are members of 2 local **fraternities** and 2 local **sororities**. Student **safety services** include 24-hour emergency telephone alarm devices and student patrols.

Williams is a member of the NAIA and NCCAA. **Intercollegiate sports** (some offering scholarships) include baseball (m), basketball (m,w), cross-country running (m,w), golf (m), soccer (m), softball (w), volleyball (w).

International Students

For fall 1997, 19 international students applied, 16 were accepted, and 8 enrolled. The **admissions test** required for entrance is TOEFL (minimum score: 500). Application deadline is rolling. On-campus **housing** is guaranteed, also available during summer.

Applying

Williams requires SAT I or ACT, a high school transcript, and a minimum high school GPA of 2.25. It recommends an essay, an interview, and 3 years of high school math and science. Application deadline: rolling admissions; 4/15 priority date for financial aid. Early and deferred entrance are possible. **Contact:** Ms. Angela Flippo, Director of Admissions, 60 West Fulbright Avenue, Walnut Ridge, AR 72476, 870-886-6741 ext. 127; e-mail admissions@wbcoll.edu.

GETTING IN LAST YEAR
326 applied
79% were accepted
56% enrolled (143)
13% from top tenth of their h.s. class
27% had ACT scores over 24

THE STUDENT BODY
708 undergraduates

From 14 states and territories,
7 other countries
73% from Arkansas
52.5% women, 47.5% men
3.4% international students

COSTS AND FINANCIAL INFORMATION
1998–99 tuition and fees $5660
1998–99 room and board $3000

Average percent of need met 75%
Average amount received per student $3116

AFTER FRESHMAN YEAR
64% returned for sophomore year
6% got a degree in 4 years
27% got a degree in 5 years
4% got a degree in 6 years

WILLIAM TYNDALE COLLEGE

Farmington Hills, Michigan

http://www.tyndalecollege.edu/

Since its beginning in 1945, the mission of William Tyndale College has been to provide a Christ-centered education designed to produce effective Christian living and service. Tyndale provides an accredited, quality education in Christian studies, arts and sciences, and professional studies through small classes taught by highly qualified and caring faculty. The college strives to integrate all academic subjects and cocurricular experiences within a Christian world view so that graduates are prepared for Christian living and service in a variety of vocations and life-callings.

Academics

Tyndale offers a Christ-centered liberal arts curriculum and core academic program. It awards associate and bachelor's **degrees**. Challenging opportunities include advanced placement, accelerated degree programs, tutorials, double majors, independent study, and a senior project. **Special programs** include internships, summer session for credit, and study-abroad.

The most popular **majors** include business administration, biblical studies, and psychology. A complete listing of majors at Tyndale appears in the Majors Index beginning on page 141.

The **faculty** at Tyndale has 15 full-time teachers, 87% with terminal degrees. The student-faculty ratio is 7:1, and the average **class size** in required courses is 20.

Campus Resources

Students are not required to have a computer. 10 **computers** available in computer labs.

The **library** has 63,500 books and 230 subscriptions.

Career Services

Services include career counseling.

Campus Life

Active organizations on campus include a drama/theater group. 35% of students participate in student government elections. No national or local **fraternities** or **sororities**.

Intercollegiate sports include soccer (m).

International Students

For fall 1997, 4 international students applied, 3 were accepted, and 2 enrolled. Students can start in fall, winter, spring, and summer. The **admissions test** required for entrance is TOEFL (minimum score: 500). Application deadline is rolling.

Applying

Tyndale requires ACT, SAT I or ACT, a high school transcript, and a minimum high school GPA of 2.25, and in some cases an essay, an interview, and recommendations. It recommends 4 years of high school English, 3 years of high school math and science, 2 years of high school foreign language, 2 years of high school social studies, 2 years of high school history, 1 year of high school academic electives, and a minimum high school GPA of 3.0. Application deadline: rolling admissions; 5/1 for financial aid, with a 2/15 priority date. Early and deferred entrance are possible. **Contact:** Mrs. Elmarie Odendaal, Counselor, 37500 West Twelve Mile Road, Farmington Hills, MI 48331, 248-553-7200 or toll-free 800-483-0707; fax 248-553-5963.

GETTING IN LAST YEAR
4% from top tenth of their h.s. class
29% had ACT scores over 24

THE STUDENT BODY
615 undergraduates
From 5 states and territories,
  4 other countries

52.9% women, 47.2% men
1.5% international students

COSTS AND FINANCIAL INFORMATION
1998–99 tuition and fees (estimated) $6300
1998–99 room only (estimated) $1800
Average percent of need met 95%

Average amount received per student $5350

AFTER FRESHMAN YEAR
92% returned for sophomore year
8% got a degree in 4 years

Affiliates

■　Affiliates may include institutions which do not fully meet the criteria for Coalition membership, are not primarily four-year undergraduate colleges or are located outside of North America. These institutions may include graduate schools, two-year colleges and seminaries.

Non-Member Affiliates

Atlantic Baptist University
333 Gorge Road
Moncton, New Brunswick
CANADA E1C 8K2
Web site: http://www.abu.nb.ca
Admission contact
Ms. Shawna Peverill, Admissions Officer
506-858-8970
Atlantic Baptist University, begun as a Bible School over 40 years ago, is a Christ-centered university committed to providing a high quality educational experience grounded in the preeminence of Jesus Christ. The university provides liberal arts education leading to undergraduate degrees, diplomas and certifications in a broad range of academic subjects. Although owned and operated by the United Baptist Convention of the Atlantic Provinces, a variety of evangelical denominations are represented in their student body.

Bethune-Cookman College
640 Dr. Mary McLeod Bethune Blvd.
Daytona Beach, FL 32114-3099
Web site: http://bethune.cookman.edu
Admission contact
Mr. William Byrd, Assistant VP, Enrollment Management
904-255-1401 Ext. 358/378
Founded by Dr. Mary McLeod Bethune in 1904, Bethune-Cookman College is a historically black, United Methodist Church-related college offering baccalaureate degrees. The mission is to serve in the Christian tradition the educational, social and cultural needs of its students—traditional and nontraditional—and to develop in them the desire and capacity for continuous intellectual and professional growth, leadership, and service to others. The College has deep roots in the social history of America and continues to provide services to the broader community through its on- and off-campus outreach programs.

Central Baptist College
1501 College Avenue
Conway, AR 72032-6470
Admission contact
Mr. Dustin Lemke, Associate Director of Admissions
501-329-6872 Ext. 156
Mr. Eric Etchison, Associate Director of Admissions
501-329-6872 Ext. 153

Founded as a junior college in 1952, Central Baptist now offers a four-year program leading to a bachelor of arts degree in numerous vocational ministries, as well as associate degrees in such fields as music, business, mathematics and science. Its motto—A College with Christian Ideals—embodies the educational philosophy of the college and expresses the point of reference from which the college seeks to educate the whole person.

Chongshin University & Theological Seminary
31-3, Sadang-Dong
Dongjak-Ku
Seoul 156-763 KOREA
Web site: http://www.congshin.ac.kr
Admission contact
Mr. Tae-je Moon, Director of Admissions (University)
(011-82) 2-3479-0253
Chongshin University & Theological Seminary is an institution of Christian higher education built upon the foundation of reformed theology. The seminary has 2,500 students in an M.Div. equivalent program which trains pastoral candidates to work for approximately 5,600 churches under the supervision of the General Assembly of the Presbyterian Church in Korea.

Crichton College
6655 Winchester Road
Memphis, TN 38115
Admission contact
Mr. Charles Tillman, VP for Enrollment Management & Community Relations
901-366-2651
The mission of Crichton College is to provide a biblically oriented education emphasizing the liberal arts and career preparation. All elements of the curriculum are integrated to impart to students a Christian worldview and to focus on occupational preparedness, a broad understanding of the arts and sciences, and a personal evangelical faith. The biblical basis of all programs is a distinctive part of the Crichton curriculum.

The Criswell College
4010 Gaston Avenue
Dallas, TX 75246
Website: http://www.criswell.edu

Admission contact
Mr. Joel Wilson, VP for Enrollment & Student Services
214-818-1302

The Criswell College exists to provide biblical, theological and professional education on both the undergraduate and graduate levels, preparing men and women to serve in Christian ministry. The inerrant Word of God remains central to every facet of the program.

Crown College
6425 County Road 30
St. Bonifacius, MN 55375-9001
Web site: http://www.crown.edu
Admission contact
Mrs. Janelle Wood, Director of Admissions
612-446-4144

Crown College, situated on a 193-acre campus west of Minneapolis, is the Midwestern regional college of the C&MA. Crown's mission is to provide a biblically-based education for Christian leadership in the C&MA, the church-at-large, and the world. To accomplish this mission, Crown endeavors to prepare men and women for ministry, develop students as earnest Christians, facilitate students' intellectual, emotional, physical and social development, encourage the understanding and appreciation of cultural and ethnic diversity, and offer an education integrated with biblical studies.

Denver Seminary
3401 S. University Blvd.
Englewood, CO 80110
Web site: http://www.gospelcom.net/densem/
Admission contact
Dr. Gary Huckabay, Director of Admissions
303-761-2482 Ext. 234

Denver Seminary was founded in 1950 with an emphasis on a vibrant evangelicalism—commitment with freedom to think within the limits laid down in Scripture. Under President Clyde B. McDowell, the seminary has entered a major re-engineering process for equipping leaders, embodied by its new vision—to glorify God in partnership with his church by equipping leaders to know the truth, practice godliness and mobilize ministry. This new paradigm emphasizes high standards for academic content but also requires the development of godly character and Spirit-led competency through intensive mentoring by local churches and ministries.

Franciscan University of Steubenville
1235 University Blvd.
Steubenville, OH 43952-1763
Web site: http://www.franuniv.edu

Admission contact
Mrs. Margaret Weber, Director of Admissions
740-283-6226

Founded in 1946 by Franciscan Friars of the Third Order Regular, Franciscan University of Steubenville integrates strong academic programs with a lively faith environment. This attractive combination—termed "dynamic orthodoxy" by Boston's Cardinal Bernard Law—draws over 1,900 students from all 50 states and over 40 foreign countries. In addition to over 30 undergraduate and six graduate degree programs, Franciscan University offers the country's only Human Life Studies minor, which prepares students to think, speak and act intelligently in the defense of life in contemporary culture. Our theology major program attracts more undergrads than any other Catholic university in the United States.

Fuller Theological Seminary
135 North Oakland Avenue
Pasadena, CA 91182
Web site: http://www.fuller.edu
Admission contact
Mr. Howard G. Wilson, Director of Admissions
626-584-5434

Fuller Theological Seminary is an evangelical, multidenominational, international and multi-ethnic community dedicated to the preparation of men and women for the manifold ministries of Christ and his Church. As an educational arm of the church, Fuller's three graduate schools—Theology, Psychology, and World Mission—seek to serve the body of Christ in worldwide ministry, offering varied academic programs in Christian leadership.

I.C.A.S. Mare Nostrum University
PO Box 45
Ingeniero Muñoz
03590 Altea,
Alicante SPAIN
(011-34) 96-584-3400

The International Center for Advanced Studies (ICAS) Mare Nostrum is an international, privately-owned university committed to the highest standards of education from both continents, America and Europe. The university offers four-year degree courses as well as one two-year Associate of Liberal Arts degree which, linked with sister universities in the U.S.A. and U.K., enables students to continue their studies leading to a BA, BS, BSE, BME and BFA, among others, at these associated universities.

Institute For Christian Studies
229 College Street
Toronto, Ontario
CANADA M5T 1R4
Web site: http://www.icscanada.edu

Admission contact
Mrs. Wanda Coffey-Bailey, Director of Student Services
416-979-2331 Ext. 239

The Institute for Christian Studies seeks to honour and proclaim Jesus Christ as the Redeemer of life and the Renewer of thought and learning. To carry out this mission, ICS engages in scholarship that reveals the religious roots of all learning and contributes to a scripturally-directed understanding of our world, and equips men and women for scholarly and other vocations through unique programs of graduate level education.

The International University
Rennweg 1
A-1030 Vienna
AUSTRIA

Admission contact
Mrs. Ana Benassi, Admissions Officer
(011-43) 1-718-50-6813

To prepare students from around the world to serve in the world—that is the mission of The International University. Based in Vienna, IU offers its international students a globalized liberal arts curriculum, featuring international business, computer information systems, and international studies. IU has an extension in Kiev, in conjunction with the Kiev State Economic University, as well as Agreements of Cooperation offering student exchange in Amman, Bratislava, Osaka and Prague. IU-Kiev is the first non-Soviet university to receive full recognition from the Ministry of Education and contributes significantly to the re-development of Ukraine, both spiritually and economically.

Jerusalem University College
Mount Zion, PO Box 1276
3 Aravnah Ha Yevusi
91012 Jerusalem
ISRAEL
Web site: http://www.juc.edu

Admission contact
Mrs. Janet DeWaal, Director of Student Services
(011-972) 2-671-8628

Jerusalem University College is an independent, degree-granting Christian institution of higher education located in Jerusalem, Israel, which seeks to enhance its students' understanding of the Bible and the cultures of the Middle East. JUC offers graduate and undergraduate programs of study in Biblical history, geography, archaeology, and languages, in related literature, and in various cultural, philosophical and religious expressions of peoples of the modern Middle East. The school emphasizes a maximal use of, and personal interaction with, the unique academic and cultural resources available both in the classroom and field work in Israel and other Middle Eastern and eastern Mediterranean regions. By formally cooperating with over 100 colleges, universities and seminaries, JUC is able to bring its strengths to students throughout the world.

Lithuania Christian Fund College
Malunininku 4
5813 Klaipeda
LITHUANIA
Web site: http://www.lccbc.org

Admission contact
Ms. Alma Jankauskaite, Director of Admissions
(011-370) 6-310745

Lithuania Christian Fund College exists to provide recognized university education that integrates academic excellence with Christian character, world view, and service. LCFC offers a one-year English Language Institute and four-year programs of study in Bible and Religion, Business Administration, and English.

North Central University
901 Elliot Avenue South
Minneapolis, MN 55404
Web site: http://www.ncbc.edu

Admission contact
Mr. James Hubert, Director of Admissions
612-343-4483

North Central University is a four-year residential college located in downtown Minneapolis, whose purpose is to build Pentecostal leaders to serve God in the Church and in the world. Founded in 1930, NCU maintains an urban and international focus in its curriculum and cocurricular activities. Students choose from more than 20 academic majors ranging from pastoral studies and youth and children's ministries to communications and broadcasting to elementary education. Through teaching and scholarship, the faculty demonstrate a tradition of academic excellence combined with a strong commitment to develop spiritually mature alumni who understand and experience the challenge of God's inerrant Word.

Norwegian Teacher Academy
Post Box 74
Amalie Skrams vei 3
5035 Bergen-Sandviken
NORWAY
Web site: http://www.nla.no/

Admission contact
Mr. Arnfinn Norheim, Chief Enrollment Officer
(011-47) 55 54 07 52

Norsk Lærerakademi (The Norwegian Teacher Academy) is a private University College jointly run by seven Christian organizations within the (Lutheran) Church of Norway. Established in 1966, the Academy aims at equipping high school teachers, Christian youth workers and others with a deeper understanding of educational science in general and Christian Education in particular. In 1996 a College of Teacher Education for elementary school teachers was added. The Academy has Departments of Education and Religion offering both basic and intermediate (undergraduate) and graduate courses.

Philadelphia College of Bible
200 Manor Avenue
Langhorne, PA 19047-2990
Web site: http://www.pcb.edu

Admission contact
Mrs. Fran Emmons, VP of Admission Services
215-702-4239

Since 1913, Philadelphia College of Bible has been committed to teaching God's Word and preparing men and women for Christian ministry. In the process, PCB has distinguished itself as the nation's most accredited Bible college. At PCB every student majors in Bible, with some pursuing a second degree simultaneously in music, social work, education or business. All students choose from one of 42 programs designed to provide specific professional skills needed in ministry today. PCB continues to develop for the Christian church and its related ministries qualified leaders who possess a foundational knowledge of the Scriptures and a biblical world and life view.

Providence College & Seminary
Otterburne, Manitoba
CANADA R0A 1G0
Web site: http://www.providence.mb.ca

Admission contact
Mr. Mark Little, Chief Enrollment Officer
204-433-7488

The mission of Providence College is to educate students at a university level to think, live, and serve effectively as Christians in the church and society. Providence College differs from many Christian colleges in its commitment to conduct all of its education at the academic level of accredited university studies. A large and growing number of Canadian and international universities are recognizing this dimension of the Providence College educational program by granting a growing amount of transfer credit to alumni.

Regent University
1000 Regent University Drive
Virginia Beach, VA 23464-9800
Web site: http://www.regent.edu

Admission contact
Central Admissions Office
800-373-5504

Founded in 1977 as CBN University, Regent is a graduate institution preparing Christian leaders for the challenge of representing Christ in their professions. Through its offering of graduate degrees in business, communication, counseling, education, law, government, divinity, and organizational leadership. Regent seeks to send Christians into all professional spheres and to be a leading center of Christian thought and action.

Russian-American Christian University
kvartal 29/30, korpus 5
Noviye Cheryomushky
117420 Moscow
RUSSIA
Web site: http://www.racu.com

Admission contact
Ms. Darya K. Checareva, Admissions Director
(011-7) 095-719-7818

The Russian-American Christian University, established in the Russian Republic, is a comprehensive liberal arts university grounded in historic Biblical Christianity. Through the combined efforts of Russian and American educators, RACU offers to Russian students an educational program which trains them to be agents of renewal and reconciliation in the university, church, society and the world of business.

Southwestern Baptist Theological Seminary
P.O. Box 22000
Fort Worth, TX 76122-0150
Web site: http://www.swbts.edu

Admission contact
Ms. Judy Morris, Director of Admissions
817-923-1921 Ext. 2777

Southwestern Baptist Theological Seminary's balance of sound scholarship, spiritual vitality and practical ministry and its historic commitment to missions and evangelism have been evidenced in the lives and work of men and women around the world for most of this century. SWBTS is committed both to a renewed emphasis on the historic traditions of Southwestern and to bring a part of the fresh and exciting winds in theological education that God seems to be sending across our world today. Southern Baptists and students from 39 other denominations have come to study in the Schools of Theology, Educational Ministries, and Church Music. SWBTS is today the world's largest school for graduate theological training. Since 1908, over 60,000 SWBTS students have gone out to contribute immeasurably to the life and work of Christian organizations around the world.

Taylor University Fort Wayne

1025 West Rudisill Blvd.
Fort Wayne, IN 46807
Web site: http://www.tayloru.edu/fw

Admission contact
Mr. Leo G. Gonot, Director of Admission
219-456-2111 Ext. 32347

In 1992, Taylor University established a second campus in Fort Wayne as the result of a merger with Summit Christian College, previously known as Fort Wayne Bible College. The Fort Wayne campus is unique in that it implements the Taylor tradition of scholarship, leadership and Christian commitment within an urban environment. Taylor University is currently celebrating its 151st year of providing quality Christian higher education.

Tokyo Christian University

3-301-5-1 Uchino
Inzai City
Chiba 270-13 JAPAN
Web site: http://www.tci.ac.jp/english/tcu.htm

Admission contact
Dr. Akio Ito, Director of Admissions
(011-81) 476-46-1131 Ext. 62/169

Tokyo Christian University is a four-year theological university rooted in the liberal arts. Its Division of Theological Studies educates future pastors, missionaries and other church leaders to be "messengers of God" for the 21st century; the Division of International Christian Studies prepares students to be ministers of reconciliation to the world by emphasizing a Christian response to global human concerns. With the slogan "From Chiba to the World!" TCU is full of enthusiasm for global missions.

Tyndale College & Seminary

25 Ballyconnor Court
North York, Ontario
CANADA M2M 4B3
Web site: http://www.tyndale-canada.edu

Admission contact
Mr. Don Russell, Director of Admissions
416-226-6380 Ext. 2190

Tyndale College & Seminary, formerly Ontario Bible College and Ontario Theological Seminary, seeks to educate and equip Christians to serve the world with passion for Jesus Christ. Student bodies and faculties reflect the broad spectrum of evangelical denominations and the multicultural nature of Toronto. Degree programs are offered in a wide variety of formats so as to make Christian education available to both traditional and non-traditional students of every age and vocational group.

Universidad Evangélica Boliviana

Casilla 4027
Barrio Cruz del Sur
Santa Cruz BOLIVIA

Admission contact
Lic. Miriam Guzmán de Molina, Chief Enrollment Officer
(011-591) 3-560991

The Universidad Evangélica Boliviana is a ministry of the World Gospel Mission, Marion, Indiana, in conjunction with three other U.S.-based missions and eight Bolivian evangelical institutions. It is the only American-sponsored university recognized by the Bolivian government and the first evangelical university in Spanish-speaking South America.

Waynesburg College

51 West College Street
Waynesburg, PA 15370
Web site: http://www.waynesburg.edu

Admission contact
Mrs. Robin Moore, Director of Admissions
724-852-3333

Recognized for its institutional commitment to service-learning for all enrolled students, Waynesburg College provides educational opportunities for students through both traditional and professional programs based upon a liberal arts foundation. Students are challenged to pursue scholarship, leadership and service based upon Christian values. The College has established active partnerships with other international educational institutions, and emphasis on the educational uses of technology has placed the institution on the "cutting edge" of innovative educational ventures. Waynesburg pledges to provide the means and inspiration by which its students may pursue lives of purpose.

Special Programs

■   If reviewing a script for a movie director in Hollywood, studying environmental problems in the rain forests of Costa Rica, or working with lobbyists on Capitol Hill sounds like an appealing way to get your college degree, an off-campus study program may be right for you. In the United States and abroad, hundreds of students each year from Christian colleges and universities decide to make the world their classroom and spend a semester away from their home campus. This section contains descriptions of special off-campus study programs available to students at member schools of the Coalition for Christian Colleges & Universities. The Coalition sponsors seven programs: the American Studies Program, the China Studies Program, the Latin American Studies Program, the Los Angeles Film Studies Center, the Middle East Studies Program, the Oxford Honors Program, and the Russian Studies Program. It also coordinates the Oxford Summer School Program and the Summer Institute of Journalism in Washington, D.C. In addition, the Coalition endorses a number of programs. While these nine programs are not directly sponsored by the Coalition, oversight for each is guided by at least ten participating colleges within the Coalition membership.

American Studies Program

Students in today's complex, competitive world face many challenges: to expand their world, to gain the education and experience they need, to get perspective, and to put their beliefs into practice.

For over two decades, the Coalition's American Studies Program (ASP) has challenged students to integrate their faith with the realities of the marketplace and public life through a semester of experiential learning in Washington, D.C. In the ASP, students can gain the experience they need to live and work in a biblically faithful way in society and in their chosen field.

Students enrolled at any of the colleges listed in this guide are invited to participate in this unique work-study program. ASP students earn academic credit by working about 20 to 25 hours a week as an unpaid intern in their intended vocational field and by participating in inter-disciplinary, issue-oriented seminar classes.

Washington, D.C., is a stimulating educational laboratory that offers on-the-job training to help ASP students build a solid foundation for their future. ASP students live and study in the Coalition's Dellenback Center on Capitol Hill, which includes student apartments, a library, dining facilities, and a classroom.

Designed for juniors and seniors with a wide range of academic majors and career interests, the ASP provides many types of internships, including those in executive and congressional offices; business and trade associations; the law and social services; radio, TV, and print media; and think tanks, cultural institutions, and inner-city ministries. The American Studies Program works with students to tailor internships to fit their unique talents and aspirations.

While participating in the contemporary, issue-oriented seminar program, students and faculty members analyze current topics in domestic and international policy through two public policy units. In addition, each term begins and ends with a two-week unit on the foundation of Christian public involvement.

Over the years, the ASP has provided almost 1,700 college students with real-world experiences that have helped them gain the critical knowledge and preparation they need to begin understanding their life's vocation.

Because of its unique location in Washington, D.C., the program has a special way of challenging students to consider the meaning of the lordship of Christ in all areas of life, including career choices, public policy issues, and personal relationships.

ASP has had life-changing impact on its participants. As one alumnus says:

I loved the program because it challenged me to look deeper into beliefs I already had and to explore beliefs I'd never considered, substantiating them through Scripture and faith. The responsibilities expected of me, combined with the job skills I learned in the internship, provided a smoother transition from college to the workplace.

Additional information on the American Studies Program is available from the academic dean's office at any of the colleges listed in this guide or by contacting:

American Studies Program
Coalition for Christian Colleges & Universities

combined with the job skills I learned in the internship, provided a smoother transition from college to the workplace.

Additional information on the American Studies Program is available from the academic dean's office at any of the colleges listed in this guide or by contacting:

American Studies Program
Coalition for Christian Colleges & Universities
327 Eighth Street, NE
Washington, D.C. 20002
Telephone: 202-546-3086
E-mail: asp@cccu.org
World Wide Web: www.cccu.org/students/

China Studies Program

China is going through monumental changes that encompass all aspects of life: economic, social, religious, and political. Students from Coalition member institutions now have the unprecedented opportunity to gain knowledge and understanding of China's people, culture, and language firsthand through the Coalition's China Studies Program (CSP).

The CSP, an interdisciplinary semester program available to upperclass students, takes advantage of formal classes, travel, meeting and interacting with Chinese people from various backgrounds. Under the leadership of CSP's North American director, the program takes advantage of a number of strategic settings. Home base is a leading university in Shanghai, where students live for approximately nine weeks. During each

semester, CSP participants also spend significant time in Xi'an, Beijing, and Hong Kong, and visit other areas of this vast country as well.

The curriculum for the CSP is designed to maximize the educational and experiential dimensions of a cross-cultural program. Studies in the standard Chinese language run throughout the time in Shanghai. The course is designed to help students gain an appreciation and beginning usage of spoken Mandarin. Language acquisition also occurs as it is practiced during the semester with Chinese students, faculty members, and others whom participants meet during their time in China.

In addition to the 3-credit **Basic Conversational Chinese,** studies also include the following seminar courses, each worth 3 semester credits:

- **Geography and History,** an introductory overview that includes archaeological findings from the Stone and Bronze Age, study of the ancient dynasties, slavery and feudalism, the Opium War, and China in revolution (1919–1949).

- **Society and Culture** builds on the first seminar, with overviews of China's diverse ethnic groups, population, and China's population policy; the various religions found throughout China's history; and its education, literature, music and art.

- **Relations with the World** begins with China's relationship at home—mainland China, Taiwan, and Hong Kong. The study broadens to include its relations with the rest of Asia and the West Pacific, the U.S., and the Western World, especially focusing on the Chinese dispersion, international relations, and foreign investments in China.

- **China's Modern Development.** Shanghai is the setting for the study of China's modern development, including it's financial situation, economic reform, telecommunication, transportation, and modern industrial development. Students address questions related to China's future—with its own people and the world around it.

China Studies Program

The curriculum also includes a 1-credit special seminar on local folk art and customs in Shanghai.

Further information on the China Studies Program is available from the academic dean's office at any of the colleges listed in this guide or by contacting:

China Studies Program
Coalition for Christian Colleges & Universities
329 Eighth Street, NE
Washington, DC 20002
Telephone: 202-546-8713
E-mail: student-programs@cccu.org
World Wide Web: www.cccu.org/students/

Latin American Studies Program

An opportunity to live and learn in Latin America is available to students from Coalition member colleges in their junior or senior year through the Latin American Studies Program (LASP). Since 1986, the LASP, headquartered in San José, Costa Rica, has been committed to helping students examine and live out the lordship of Jesus Christ in an international context.

Each semester, a group of 36 to 40 students is selected to participate in this seminar/service travel experience in Latin America. The academic program, for which credit is awarded by the student's home institution, involves a combination of learning, serving, and observing.

In addition to the regular LASP experience, several tracks are available for students with specific major fields of study: the Advanced Language & Literature track (offered both fall and spring semesters), the International Business and Marketing track (offered each fall semester), and the Tropical Science track (offered each spring semester). Students participating in a track rather than the regular program take five weeks of the semester to focus on courses and experiential learning unique to their field.

All participants are involved in three full weeks of intensive language study at the beginning of each semester, in which class assignment is based on language proficiency. Students practice their language skills with local Costa Ricans, including the host families who provide a home away from home for each LASP student. These families are chosen for their Christian commitment and their willingness to share their culture and their friendship. At the same time, students take part in seminars coordinated by the LASP staff that deal with such issues as Third World development, Latin American history and culture, and the role of the church. Conducted in English and in Spanish, these seminar sessions enable students to interact with outside speakers, who bring a rich variety of perspectives to current issues.

The serving component involves hands-on experience working in a "servant role" in the Third World through participation in a service "opportunity." In order to get a better understanding of the complexities of Latin society, students are placed in a variety of service activities. The service opportunities may involve working in an orphanage or in an agency with abused children. The activities may also involve the fields of agriculture, economic development, education, environmental stewardship, and health. Track participants use this time to do hands-on activities in their field throughout the region.

In addition to living with Costa Rican families, students also have the opportunity to observe by traveling to at least two other Central American countries. By visiting Latin American countries outside Costa Rica, including Guatemala, Honduras, and Nicaragua, students enjoy a rich diversity of cultures in the cities, villages, and countryside of those areas. After participating in the Coalition's Latin American Studies Program, one student had this to say of his experience:

I feel this semester has been one of the hardest, most fun, most worthwhile experiences of my whole life, and I know that what I have learned will affect me always.

Applicants are required to have a minimum 2.75 GPA and the equivalent of 1 year of college-level Spanish. Additional information on the Latin American Studies Program is available from the academic dean's office at any of the colleges listed in this guide or by contacting:

Latin American Studies Program
Coalition for Christian Colleges & Universities
329 Eighth Street, NE
Washington, D.C. 20002
Telephone: 202-546-8713
E-mail: student-programs@cccu.org
World Wide Web: http://www.gospelcom.net/cccu/students/5prog.html

Los Angeles Film Studies Center

In January 1991, the Coalition for Christian Colleges & Universities inaugurated the Los Angeles Film Studies Center (LAFSC). This unique program serves as an introduction to the work and workings of the mainstream Hollywood film industry.

The LAFSC is conveniently located in Los Angeles near several of the major film and television studios. Accommodations are provided nearby in a corporate apartment complex featuring exceptional recreational facilities and comfortably furnished units.

The program is designed to allow students exposure to the industry, to the many academic disciplines that might be appropriate to it, and to critical thinking and reflection on what it means to be a Christian in the film world. As such, the curriculum is balanced between courses of a theoretical nature and courses that offer students an applied introduction to the world of film. LAFSC students participate in two required seminar courses, two of three elective options, and an internship in the film or television industry, as described below:

• **Inside Hollywood** (1 semester credit): This seminar examines the creative and operational aspects of the Hollywood film business, including the Christian's role in working within the entertainment business.

• **Faith, Film and Culture** (3 semester credits): This course studies the relationship between film and popular culture, with emphasis on Christianity's role in these arenas. The course examines how faith, film, and culture mutually influence one another. It includes an overview of the historical relationship between the church and the movies, an understanding of a theology of the arts, a cultural studies approach to the nature of the arts in popular culture, and the Christian's role in identifying, discerning, and ultimately influencing movie content.

• **Introduction to Filmmaking** (3-semester-credit elective): Students receive an introduction to the theory and practice of motion picture filmmaking. Topics include familiarity with filmmaking equipment, converting idea to image, the use of lighting, editing, and sound in film; and the role of acting, directing and good storytelling in the filmmaking process. Students make several short Super 8 mm films that manifest their faith in content and practice.

• **Screenwriting** (3-semester-credit elective): This course serves as an introduction to contemporary screenwriting, including an understanding of dramatic structure, character and dialogue development, and the writing process. Students complete a full-length screenplay for a feature film or "movie-of-the-week." Emphasis is given to the role of Christian faith and values as they relate to script content.

• **Seminar in Producing the Independent Film** (3-semester-credit elective): This is an introduction to the process of producing an independent feature film. Topics include legal structures, business plans, preproduction activities such as scheduling and budgeting, and an overview of the producer's role in production, postproduction, and distribution.

- **Internships:** All LAFSC students are assigned a nonpaid internship in some aspect of the Hollywood film or television industry as arranged by the LAFSC staff. These internships are primarily in an office setting such as development companies, agencies, personal management companies, production offices, etc. Students are expected to work 20–24 hours a week throughout the entire semester. The internship serves as a laboratory to provide students with real-life exposure to the industry and as a basis for discussion and reflection in the courses.

Here is how one student viewed her semester:

The LAFSC is a great opportunity to get a broad overview of the film industry. The best part was actually being involved in the industry through my internship. I learned more through 'hands on' experience at a production company than I would have in any classroom setting.

Students interested in the Los Angeles Film Studies Center are invited to request additional information from the academic dean's office at any of the colleges listed in this guide or to contact the LAFSC directly:

Los Angeles Film Studies Center
3800 Barham Boulevard, Suite 202
Los Angeles, CA 90068
Telephone 213-882-6224
E-mail: LAFSC@aol.com
World Wide Web: www.cccu.org/students/

Middle East Studies Program

The Middle East, often called "the cradle of civilization," has always been a fascinating and complex region. The Coalition for Christian Colleges & Universities' Middle East Studies Program (MESP), based in Cairo, Egypt, exists to help college students understand the history, peoples, and cultures of the Middle East. Upperclass students enrolled at any of the colleges listed in this guide are eligible to apply for this unique learning experience. There is no language prerequisite.

While living in Cairo, students study spoken Arabic and participate in three interdisciplinary seminar courses designed to provide insights into the historical, religious, political, and economic dimensions of life in the Middle East. Academic credit for participation in the Middle East Studies Program is awarded by the student's home institution.

- **Peoples and Cultures of the Middle East** introduces students to the many different societies and ways of life in the region.

- **Islam in the Modern World** explains the basic tenets of the Islamic faith and seeks to give students an understanding of how Christians relate to Muslim countries and individuals.

- **Conflict and Change in the Middle East Today** addresses the ongoing quest for peace in this region, identifying the obstacles and the triumphs.

In all three seminar classes, personal interaction with resident scholars, local business people, religious leaders, and government officials enhances the education experience and provides perspectives no textbook can equal.

MESP students also study Arabic language, focusing on spoken Arabic and on Arabic literature throughout the semester. This course is taught by native speakers of Arabic trained at the American University in Cairo, the program director, and guest lecturers. Ample opportunities exist to practice conversational skills with Egyptian students, other teachers, business people, and friends of the MESP.

Each week, students participate in a service opportunity in cooperation with one of the many organizations in Cairo, gaining valuable hands-on work experience and interaction with local Egyptians.

Safe and comfortable housing is provided in the international dormitory of the American University in Cairo and in nearby furnished apartments. All students live close to the MESP Center located on Zamalek, a large island in Cairo just minutes from the downtown area. Students have access to American University's library and computer facilities. During the semester, participants travel by bus to Israel/Palestine to see the historic land of the Bible and to explore the many dimensions of the ongoing efforts for peace between Arabs and Israelis. On free weekends, students are able to travel within Egypt to Sinai, Alexandria, and Giza as well as to other locations. Much of the seminar "Peoples and Cultures" is taught "on site" while traveling through the Sinai, Jordan, Syria, and Turkey.

Participants in the Middle East Studies Program have the opportunity to gather a wide array of experiences. Says one student:

The MESP has, above all else, exposed me to a culture whose basis is not in Christianity. I now have a good Muslim friend whose faith is as strong as mine. It's an interesting situation for me to be in, because whenever I've been with people of deep faith before, they've been Christian.

Additional information about the Middle East Studies Program is available from the academic dean's office at any of the colleges listed in this guide or by contacting:

Middle East Studies Program
Coalition for Christian Colleges & Universities
329 Eighth Street, NE
Washington, D.C. 20002
Telephone: 202-546-8713
E-mail: mesp@intouch.com or student-programs@cccu.
   org
World Wide Web: www.cccu.org/students/

Oxford Honors Program

■ The Oxford Honors Program (OHP) is a partnership program between the Coalition for Christian Colleges & Universities and the Centre for Medieval and Renaissance Studies, affiliated with Keble College of the University of Oxford.

Juniors and seniors at member institutions of the Coalition having a GPA of 3.5 or better have the opportunity to join 25 other students in the exploration of what it means to study "Oxford style." Under the guidance of the Coalition-appointed program director, participants take part in the following 4-credit study components:

• Two tutorials, each worth 4 credits, in areas of study individually chosen. Course options include architecture, art, art history, European history, Greek, Latin, European languages, literature, drama, classics, writing, law, philosophy, political science, and Biblical and religious studies. These British tutorials provide the opportunity to study one-on-one under Oxford dons (professors), who guide their students through research and wrestling with the issues involved, taking full advantage of this individual attention and supervision.

• An interactive seminar exploring the great questions of life during the Medieval, Reformation, and Counter-Reformation periods and other subject areas. In these small classes (made up of approximately 5 students), participants are challenged by different world views presented by Oxford dons, tutors and other students, while having the opportunity to share their own Christian perspectives.

• A semester-long integrative course designed specifically to engage the interconnections of faith, living, and learning under the leadership of the OHP director. This course covers such topics as the Renaissance and humanism, conflict between Church and State, and society in transformation. As part of the course, students create and present a major scholarly project/paper at a final symposium.

In addition to study at Oxford, students also travel to significant historic and cultural sites in England on four study tours included in the program. These include visits to Bath, Glastonbury Abbey/Wells Cathedral, The Cotswolds, Stratford-upon-Avon, and St. Augustine's Abbey and Canterbury.

The OHP serves as the "Oxford campus" of participants' home institutions. They receive credit from their sending campus for participation in the program.

Additional information about the Oxford Honors Program is available from the academic dean's office at any of the colleges listed in this guide or by contacting:

Oxford Honors Program
Coalition for Christian Colleges & Universities
329 Eighth Street, NE
Washington, DC 20002
Telephone: 202-546-8713
E-mail: student-programs@cccu.org
World Wide Web: www.cccu.org/students/

Russian Studies Program

Upperclass students enrolled at one of the colleges listed in this guide have the opportunity to discover firsthand the richness of the Russian language, culture, and history through the Russian Studies Program (RSP).

The RSP is unique in that it makes use of the excellent resources found in three distinct locations: Moscow, Nizhni Novgorod, and St. Petersburg. The first ten days of the semester are spent in Moscow, where students receive an orientation to life in Russia and take in the city's extraordinary museums, galleries, landmarks, and historical resources.

Students then travel to Nizhni Novgorod, formerly Gorky, which becomes home for the next twelve weeks. As the "test site" for many economic reforms, the city is an ideal learning environment. While there, they take part in both language classes and seminars that explore the country's history, cultural and religious life, and literature, as well as challenges facing Russians today.

- **History and Sociology of Religion in Russia** (3 credits) delves into the history of religion in Russia from the beginnings of Christianity in the tenth century to the present day. The course also looks at the current government regulations from various points of view. Included are visits to churches and cathedrals in Moscow, St. Petersburg and Nizhni Novgorod and guest lectures by representatives of Russian Orthodox, Protestant and other religious perspectives.

- **Russian Peoples, Culture and Literature** (4 credits) covers Russian history and culture using the rich resources of the three RSP sites, studying Russian people and culture throughout history using well-known works of Russian literature such as Tolstoy and Dostoyevsky.

- **Russia in Transition** (3 credits) focuses on contemporary Russia and her struggle to rebuild society following the collapse of Communism. Students are introduced to the complexities of economic transition from a centrally planned to a free-market economy and study efforts to build democratic institutions in Russia. This seminar includes service projects in selected educational institutions, orphanages, businesses, and other organizations in the Nizhni region, as well as travel throughout western Russia.

- **Russian Language** In addition to seminar classes, RSP students receive Russian language instruction by qualified native Russian language teachers, choosing either a 4-credit (80 hours in-class instruction) or 6-credit (120 hours) option. Prior knowledge of the Russian language is not required and students are placed in courses that correspond to their level of proficiency, from beginning to advanced. Students choosing the 4-credit option also take a 2-credit seminar on **Russian Business and International Relations.** Contacts with Russian students, particularly in Nizhni Novgorod, and the opportunity to live with Russian families for six weeks facilitate language acquisition.

After twelve weeks in Nizhni Novgorod, the RSP moves to St. Petersburg, Russian's former capital and its most westernized city. The richness of the historical and cultural resources of this beautiful city provide a venue for additional study of Russian/Soviet society and a fitting conclusion for the program.

One RSP student observed:

The thing that surprised me most about Russian culture is the existence of religious history. I had thought of Russia as an antireligious country, but not even seventy years of communism could break the power of their religious past.

Said another student:

What really amazed me was the genuine sense of caring radiating from the Russians.... It felt like home there.

Additional information about the Russian Studies Program is available from the academic dean's office at any of the colleges listed in this guide or by contacting:

Russian Studies Program
Coalition for Christian Colleges & Universities
329 Eighth Street, NE
Washington, D.C. 20002
Telephone: 202-546-8713
E-mail: wagler@wagler.kis.nnov.su or student-programs@cccu.org
World Wide Web: www.cccu.org/students/

Summer Programs

The Summer Institute of Journalism

Students at the colleges and universities listed in this guide are eligible to apply for participation in the Summer Institute of Journalism, a summer program managed by the Coalition for Christian Colleges & Universities.

Held for the first time in 1995, each summer 15 journalism students travel to Washington, D.C. for a monthlong program designed to support the journalism education offered at Christian colleges and help equip journalism students for future work in the profession. The program, sometimes referred to as "Capstone in the Capital," enables participating students to interact with professional journalists in Washington, D.C., through seminars with the media personnel and hands-on projects. Over 20 journalists representing the national media, including ABC News, the *Washington Post*, the Associated Press and *U.S. News & World Report*, typically participate in the program.

"This program is all about helping Christians develop the skills to be valid journalists," says Terry Mattingly, a journalism professor at Milligan College in Tennessee, who codirects the institute. "It is not about Christian journalism. It's about Christians being in journalism."

In addition to interacting with leading journalists, students have the opportunity to experience Washington, D.C., by visiting museums, monuments and art galleries. Students are housed at The Dellenback Center, located just blocks from Capitol Hill.

The program has positively influenced the students who have participated in it. Comments one participant:

My experience here (The Summer Institute of Journalism) has motivated me to pursue all kinds of things in journalism, like small-town reporting, magazine reporting, and newspaper design. I know now that *whatever I am doing, I am called by God to be there. This workshop has been confirmation of that.*

Further information is available from the academic dean's office at any of the colleges listed in this guide or by contacting:

The Summer Institute of Journalism
Coalition for Christian Colleges & Universities
329 Eighth St., NE
Washington, DC 20002
Telephone: 202-546-8713
E-mail: student-programs@cccu.org
World Wide Web: www.cccu.org/students/

Oxford Summer School Program

Students at the colleges and universities listed in this guide are eligible to apply for admission to the Oxford Summer School Program, a multidisciplinary program of study of the events of the Renaissance and Reformation. Located in Oxford, England, the program is cosponsored by the Coalition for Christian Colleges & Universities and the Centre for Medieval and Renaissance Studies, which is affiliated with Oxford's Keble College.

Inaugurated in 1975, the six-week program explores the Renaissance and Reformation through the study of the philosophy, art, literature, science, music, politics, and religion of this era. Many classes are conducted by Oxford dons, who also meet with students in seminars and in one-on-one tutorials that are typical of the Oxford method of education.

Lectures, classes, meals, and social activities are held in St. Michael's Hall, which also houses faculty offices and the Centre's library. Students take residence at St. Michael's or at Wycliffe Hall, located next to the University's beautiful park.

Weekly field trips to places of importance outside Oxford introduce students to great cathedrals, castles, and historic towns nearby. Special activities

Keble College, the annual Carl F. H. Henry Lecture, a weekly colloquium on faith and learning, and an evening at Shakespeare's Stratford-upon-Avon. The resources of Oxford, such as the world-famous Bodleian Library, are also available to students.

Participants in the OSS have commented on the excellent experience that they have had:

I would definitely suggest this program for all students, regardless of one's major. The Oxford summer program is an excellent opportunity for students to grow intellectually, but more importantly, to grow in their personal faith.

Further information is available from the academic dean's office at any of the colleges listed in this guide or by contacting:

Oxford Summer School Program
Coalition for Christian Colleges & Universities
329 Eighth Street, NE
Washington, D.C. 20002
Telephone: 202-546-8713
E-mail: student-programs@cccu.org

Endorsed Programs

The Coalition endorses the following educational programs. While not directly sponsored by the Coalition, oversight for each is guided by at least ten "participating colleges" within the Coalition membership.

The **AuSable Institute of Environmental Studies,** located in Michigan's lower peninsula, is an environmental stewardship program whose mission is to bring healing and wholeness to the biosphere and the whole of Creation. Students participate for college credit during January terms, May terms and summer schools. For more information:

AuSable Institute of Environmental Studies
7526 Sunset Trail, NE
Mancelona, MI 49659
Telephone: 616-587-8686
E-mail: MJAuSable@aol.com
Director: Dr. Cal DeWitt
Associate Director: Dr. David Mahan (contact person)

The **Christian Center for Urban Studies** (formerly the Wesleyan Urban Coalition) in Chicago, Illinois offers weekend, three-week and semester programs. Classes are offered in urban anthropology, culture, leadership, art, mission and service. For more information:

Christian Center for Urban Studies
Olive Branch Mission
6310 S. Claremont
Chicago, IL 60636-2427
Telephone: 773-476-6200, Ext. 39; 800-986-5483
Director: Rev. Oreon K. Trickey

The **Focus on the Family Institute** in Colorado Springs, Colorado offers a semester-long program of on-site instruction and field experiences aimed at addressing the causes and cures for fractured families, and helping students become equipped to reverse societal trends that cause harm to traditional family structures and beliefs.

Focus on the Family Institute
Focus on the Family
8606 Explorer Drive
Colorado Springs, CO 80920
Telephone: 719-548-4560
Director: Dr. Michael Rosebush

The **Global Stewardship Study Program** is based at an environmental center in the jungle of Belize, Central America. Students take four courses: Global Stewardship, Sustainable Development in Third World Communities, Tropical Ecology and Biblical Stewardship. Additional electives and practicums are available, as well as a summer school option.

Global Stewardship Study Program
Christian Environmental Association
3015-P Hopyard Road
Pleasanton, CA 94588
Telephone: 925-462-2439
E-mail: gssp@targetearth.org
Director: Dr. Christopher Elisara

The **International Business Institute** is designed to give students in economics, business and related areas a distinctive opportunity for study that incorporates the international dimension in these fields. This summer program is ten weeks in length and includes periods of residence in key locations as well as coordinated visits and presentations in the major political and economic centers of Western and Eastern Europe, Scandinavia, Finland and Russia.

International Business Institute
King College
1350 King College Road
Bristol, TN 37620
Telephone: 423-652-4817
E-mail: robertjbartel@king.edu
Director: Dr. Robert J. Bartel

The **Jerusalem University College** in Jerusalem, Israel, (formerly the Institute for Holy Land Studies) offers credit for semester and yearlong programs of study. Students study the history, language, culture, archaeology, geography, and literature of the region, with a focus on enhancing their understanding of the Scriptures.

Institute of Holy Land Studies
42498 East State Street, Suite 203
Rockford, IL 61108
Telephone: 800-891-9408
E-mail: 75454.1770@compuserve.com
President: Dr. Sidney DeWaal
VP for North America: Dr. Michael McDonald (contact)

The **Netherlandic Student Program in Contemporary Europe** provides the opportunity to live in Amsterdam, one of the centers of the Western European Community. Participants receive 16 semester credits from courses in language, literature, the arts, history and politics. Options also exist for individualized study in other disciplines.

Netherlandic-SPICE Program
Dordt College
498 4th Avenue, NE
Sioux Center, IA 51250-1697
Telephone: 712-722-6263
E-mail: kboot@dordt.edu
Director: Dr. K. J. Boot

The **San Francisco Urban Program** of Westmont College provides an opportunity for a semester of Christ-centered study in the unique context of this great city. Students study urbanization, working in a practicum related to their interests, and have opportunities for independent study.

San Francisco Urban Program
3016 Jackson Street
San Francisco, CA 94115-1021
Telephone: 800-61-URBAN
E-mail: urban@westmont.edu
Director: Steve Schultz

The Coalition for Christian Colleges & Universities assumes no responsibility for the ownership and management of these programs.

Majors Index by School

ABILENE CHRISTIAN UNIVERSITY
Accounting, advertising, agribusiness, American studies, animal sciences, art, art education, biblical studies, biochemistry, biology, biology education, broadcast journalism, business administration, business education, business marketing and marketing management, chemistry, chemistry education, child care/development, computer education, computer/information sciences, computer science, counseling psychology, criminal justice/law enforcement administration, (pre)dentistry, divinity/ministry, drafting, drama and dance education, electrical/electronics engineering, elementary education, engineering physics, engineering science, English, English education, environmental science, exercise sciences, family/consumer studies, fashion merchandising, finance, fine/studio arts, French, French language education, geology, German, German language education, graphic design/commercial art/illustration, Greek (Modern), health education, health/physical education, history, history education, home economics, home economics education, human resources management, individual/family development, industrial arts education, industrial technology, interdisciplinary studies, interior design, international relations, journalism, (pre)law, liberal arts and studies, mass communications, mathematics, mathematics education, (pre)medicine, missionary studies, music, music education, music (piano and organ performance), music (voice and choral/opera performance), nursing, nutrition science, organizational psychology, (pre)pharmacy studies, physical education, physics, physics education, political science, psychology, public administration, public relations, radio/television broadcasting, range management, reading education, religious studies, science education, secondary education, social science education, social studies education, social work, sociology, Spanish, Spanish language education, special education, speech education, speech-language pathology/audiology, speech/rhetorical studies, theater arts/drama, (pre)veterinary studies.

ANDERSON UNIVERSITY
Accounting, art education, athletic training/sports medicine, biblical studies, biology, business, business administration, business economics, business marketing and marketing management, chemistry, computer science, criminal justice/law enforcement administration, (pre)dentistry, education, elementary education, (pre)engineering, English, English education, family studies, finance, fine/studio arts, French, French language education, general studies, German, German language education, graphic design/commercial art/illustration, health education, health/physical education, history, (pre)law, management information systems/business data processing, mass communications, mathematics, mathematics/computer science, mathematics education, medical technology, (pre)medicine, music business management and merchandising, music education, music (general performance), nursing, philosophy, physical education, physics, political science, psychology, religious studies, sacred music, science education, social studies education, social work, sociology, Spanish, Spanish language education, speech education, theater arts/drama, theology, (pre)veterinary studies.

ASBURY COLLEGE
Accounting, applied mathematics, art education, biblical studies, biology, business, chemistry, classics, elementary education, engineering, English, fine/studio arts, French, Greek (Ancient and Medieval), history, journalism, Latin (Ancient and Medieval), mathematics, medical technology, middle school education, missionary studies, music, music education, nursing, philosophy, physical education, physical sciences, psychology, radio/television broadcasting technology, recreation/leisure facilities management, religious education, social sciences, social work, sociology, Spanish, speech/rhetorical studies.

AZUSA PACIFIC UNIVERSITY
Accounting, applied art, art, athletic training/sports medicine, biblical studies, biochemistry, biology, business administration, business marketing and marketing management, chemistry, computer science, divinity/ministry, English, environmental science, history, international relations, (pre)law, liberal arts and studies, management information systems/business data processing, mass communications, mathematics, music, nursing, philosophy, physical education, physics, political science, psychology, religious studies, social sciences, social work, sociology, Spanish, theology.

BARTLESVILLE WESLEYAN COLLEGE
Accounting, athletic training/sports medicine, behavioral sciences, biological and physical sciences, biology, business administration, business education, chemistry, (pre)dentistry, divinity/ministry, education, elementary education, English, exercise sciences, history, information sciences/systems, (pre)law, liberal arts and studies, linguistics, mass communications, mathematics, (pre)medicine, music, music (general performance), natural sciences, nursing, physical education, physical therapy, political science, religious studies, science education, secondary education, secretarial science, social sciences, teaching English as a second language, theology, (pre)veterinary studies.

BELHAVEN COLLEGE
Accounting, art, athletic training/sports medicine, biblical studies, biology, business administration, chemistry, communications, computer science, dance, (pre)dentistry, elementary education, engineering science, English, history, humanities, (pre)law, mathematics, (pre)medicine, music, philosophy, psychology, sport/fitness administration, theater arts/drama.

BETHEL COLLEGE (IN)
Accounting, aerospace engineering, art, biblical languages/literatures, biblical studies, biological and physical sciences, biology, business administration, business education, chemical engineering, chemistry, civil engineering, computer science, (pre)dentistry, divinity/ministry, early childhood education, economics, education, electrical/electronics engineering, elementary education, engineering science, English, French, gerontology, graphic design/commercial art/illustration, health education, history, human resources management, information sciences/systems, interior design, journalism, (pre)law, liberal arts and studies, mass communications, mathematics, mathematics education, mechanical engineering, (pre)medicine, metallurgical engineering, music, music education, music (piano and organ performance), music (voice and choral/opera performance), nursing, pastoral counseling, philosophy, physical education, physics education, psychology, recreation and leisure studies, religious studies, sacred music, science education, secondary education, secretarial science, sign language interpretation, social sciences, sociology, Spanish, theater arts/drama.

BETHEL COLLEGE (KS)
Accounting, art, art education, biblical studies, biological and physical sciences, biology, business administration, business education, chemistry, communications, computer science, (pre)dentistry, early childhood education, economics, education, elementary education, English, environmental science, German, health education, history, human ecology, interdisciplinary studies, international relations, (pre)law, mass communications, mathematics, (pre)medicine, music, music education, natural sciences, nursing, peace and conflict studies, physical education, physics, psychology, religious stud-

Bethel College (KS) (continued)

ies, science education, secondary education, social sciences, social work, sociology, Spanish, special education, speech/rhetorical studies, theater arts/drama, theology.

BETHEL COLLEGE (MN)

Accounting, adult/continuing education, art, art education, art history, athletic training/sports medicine, biblical studies, biochemistry, biology, business administration, chemistry, child care/development, computer science, creative writing, cultural studies, (pre)dentistry, divinity/ministry, early childhood education, economics, education, elementary education, (pre)engineering, English, environmental science, finance, fine/studio arts, health education, history, international relations, (pre)law, liberal arts and studies, literature, management information systems/business data processing, mass communications, mathematics, (pre)medicine, molecular biology, music, music education, nursing, philosophy, physical education, physics, political science, psychology, sacred music, science education, secondary education, social work, Spanish, speech/rhetorical studies, theater arts/drama, theology, (pre)veterinary studies.

BIOLA UNIVERSITY

Accounting, adult/continuing education, anthropology, applied art, applied mathematics, art, art education, art therapy, biblical studies, bilingual/bicultural education, biochemistry, biology, broadcast journalism, business administration, business economics, business education, business machine repair, business marketing and marketing management, chemistry, computer/information sciences, computer programming, computer science, divinity/ministry, drawing, economics, education, elementary education, English, European studies, film studies, finance, fine/studio arts, graphic design/commercial art/illustration, history, humanities, information sciences/systems, international relations, journalism, (pre)law, liberal arts and studies, literature, management information systems/business data processing, mass communications, mathematics, (pre)medicine, middle school education, modern languages, music, music education, music (piano and organ performance), music (voice and choral/opera performance), nursing, pastoral counseling, philosophy, physical education, physical sciences, physics, psychology, public relations, radio/television broadcasting, religious education, religious studies, science education, secondary education, social sciences, sociology, speech-language pathology/audiology, speech therapy, teaching English as a second language, theater arts/drama, theology.

BLUFFTON COLLEGE

Accounting, art, art education, biology, business administration, business economics, business education, chemistry, child care/development, clothing and textiles, computer science, criminal justice/law enforcement administration, developmental/child psychology, dietetics, divinity/ministry, early childhood education, economics, education, elementary education, English, exercise sciences, fashion design/illustration, fashion merchandising, graphic design/commercial art/illustration, health education, history, home economics, home economics education, humanities, (pre)law, liberal arts and studies, mass communications, mathematics, medical technology, (pre)medicine, music, music education, nutrition science, peace and conflict studies, philosophy, physical education, physics, political science, psychology, recreation and leisure studies, religious studies, retail management, secondary education, social sciences, social work, sociology, Spanish, special education, speech/rhetorical studies, sport/fitness administration.

BRYAN COLLEGE

Biblical studies, biology, business administration, computer science, early childhood education, education, elementary education, English, history, liberal arts and studies, literature, mass communications, mathematics, (pre)medicine, middle school education, music, music business management and merchandising, music education, music (piano and organ performance), music (voice and choral/opera performance), physical education, psychology, religious education, sacred music, science education, secondary education, wind and percussion instruments.

CALIFORNIA BAPTIST UNIVERSITY

Applied mathematics, art, athletic training/sports medicine, behavioral sciences, biblical studies, biology, business administration, chemistry, classics, (pre)dentistry, education, elementary education, English, history, information sciences/systems, journalism, liberal arts and studies, mathematics, music, philosophy, physical education, physical sciences, physics, political science, psychology, secondary education, social sciences, sociology, Spanish, theater arts/drama.

CALVIN COLLEGE

Accounting, art, art education, art history, athletic training/sports medicine, biblical studies, bilingual/bicultural education, biochemistry, biological and physical sciences, biology, business administration, business economics, chemistry, civil engineering, classics, computer science, criminal justice/law enforcement administration, (pre)dentistry, economics, education, electrical/electronics engineering, elementary education, engineering, English, environmental science, European studies, exercise sciences, film studies, fine/studio arts, French, geography, geology, German, Greek (Modern), history, humanities, interdisciplinary studies, Japanese, journalism, Latin (Ancient and Medieval), (pre)law, liberal arts and studies, linguistics, literature, mass communications, mathematics, mechanical engineering, medical technology, (pre)medicine, music, music education, music history, music (voice and choral/opera performance), natural sciences, occupational therapy, philosophy, physical education, physical sciences, physics, political science, psychology, recreation and leisure studies, religious education, religious studies, sacred music, science education, secondary education, social sciences, social work, sociology, Spanish, special education, speech-language pathology/audiology, speech/rhetorical studies, telecommunications, theater arts/drama, theology, (pre)veterinary studies.

CAMPBELLSVILLE UNIVERSITY

Accounting, art, art education, athletic training/sports medicine, biblical studies, biology, business administration, business economics, business education, business marketing and marketing management, chemistry, criminal justice/law enforcement administration, data processing technology, (pre)dentistry, divinity/ministry, economics, elementary education, English, health education, history, information sciences/systems, journalism, (pre)law, mass communications, mathematics, medical technology, (pre)medicine, music, music education, music (piano and organ performance), music (voice and choral/opera performance), pastoral counseling, physical education, physics, political science, psychology, recreation and leisure studies, religious education, religious studies, sacred music, science education, secondary education, secretarial science, social sciences, social work, sociology, (pre)veterinary studies.

CAMPBELL UNIVERSITY

Accounting, advertising, applied mathematics, art, athletic training/sports medicine, biblical studies, biochemistry, biology, biomedical technology, broadcast journalism, business administration, business economics, chemistry, child care/development, clothing and textiles, computer science, criminal justice/law enforcement administration, data processing technology, (pre)dentistry, divinity/ministry, economics, education, education administration, elementary education, (pre)engineering, English, exercise sciences, finance, fine/studio arts, food products retailing, French, graphic design/commercial art/illustration, health education, health science, history, home economics, home economics education, information sciences/systems, international business, international relations, journalism, (pre)law, liberal arts and studies, mass communications, mathematics, medical technology, (pre)medicine, middle school education, music, music education, music (piano and organ performance), music (voice and choral/opera performance), natural sciences, pastoral counseling, pharmacy, philosophy, physical education, physical therapy, physician assistant, political science, psychology, public administration, public relations, radio/television broadcasting, religious education, science education, secondary education, social sciences, social work, Spanish, sport/fitness administration, theater arts/drama, theology, (pre)veterinary studies.

CEDARVILLE COLLEGE

Accounting, American studies, athletic training/sports medicine, behavioral sciences, biblical studies, biological and physical sciences, biology, broadcast journalism, business administration, business economics, business marketing and marketing management, chemistry, criminal justice/law enforcement administration, (pre)dentistry, early childhood education, economics, education, electrical/electronics engineering, elementary education, English, environmental biology, finance, health education, history, information sciences/systems, international business, international economics, international relations, (pre)law, mass communications, mathematics, mechanical engineering, medical technology, (pre)medicine, music, music education, music (piano and organ performance), music (voice and choral/opera performance), nursing, pastoral counseling, philosophy, physical education, political science, psychology, public administration, radio/television broadcasting, sacred music, science education, secondary education, secretarial science, social sciences, social work, sociology, Spanish, special education, speech/rhetorical studies, technical writing, theater arts/drama, theology, (pre)veterinary studies.

COLLEGE OF THE OZARKS

Accounting, agricultural business, agricultural mechanization, agronomy/crop science, aircraft mechanic/airframe, aircraft pilot (professional), animal sciences, art, art education, aviation technology, biology, business administration, business education, business marketing and marketing management, chemistry, child care/development, computer science, consumer services, corrections, criminal justice/law enforcement administration, criminology, dietetics, education, elementary education, English, family/consumer studies, fine/studio arts, food sciences, forensic technology, French, German, gerontology, graphic design/commercial art/illustration, health science, history, home economics, home economics education, horticulture science, hotel and restaurant management, industrial arts, information sciences/systems, interdisciplinary studies, journalism, (pre)law, law enforcement/police science, mass communications, mathematics, medical technology, (pre)medicine, middle school education, music, music education, nursing, nutrition science, pharmacy, philosophy, physical education, political science, poultry science, psychology, public relations, recreation/leisure facilities management, religious studies, science education, secondary education, social work, sociology, Spanish, theater arts/drama, trade and industrial education, (pre)veterinary studies.

COLORADO CHRISTIAN UNIVERSITY

Accounting, adult/continuing education, art, biblical studies, biology, broadcast journalism, business, business administration, communications, computer/information sciences, divinity/ministry, elementary education, English, English education, history, humanities, human resources management, information sciences/systems, liberal arts and studies, management information systems/business data processing, mass communications, mathematics, mathematics education, music, music education, music (general performance), music (voice and choral/opera performance), pastoral counseling, political science, psychology, sacred music, science education, secondary education, social studies education, theater arts/drama, theology.

CORNERSTONE COLLEGE

Accounting, adult/continuing education, aircraft pilot (professional), biblical languages/literatures, biblical studies, biology, broadcast journalism, business administration, business education, business marketing and marketing management, (pre)dentistry, divinity/ministry, early childhood education, education, elementary education, English, history, information sciences/systems, interdisciplinary studies, (pre)law, mass communications, mathematics, (pre)medicine, music, music education, pastoral counseling, physical education, psychology, religious education, religious studies, science education, secondary education, social work, sociology, Spanish, speech/rhetorical studies, sport/fitness administration, (pre)veterinary studies.

COVENANT COLLEGE

Biblical studies, biology, business administration, chemistry, computer science, economics, elementary education, (pre)engineering, English, health science, history, interdisciplinary studies, (pre)law, (pre)medicine, music, natural sciences, nursing, philosophy, psychology, sociology.

DALLAS BAPTIST UNIVERSITY

Accounting, art, biblical studies, biology, business administration, business economics, business marketing and marketing management, computer/information sciences, computer science, criminal justice/law enforcement administration, early childhood education, education, elementary education, English, finance, health services administration, history, interdisciplinary studies, liberal arts and studies, management information systems/business data processing, mass communications, mathematics, music, music education, music (piano and organ performance), music (voice and choral/opera performance), pastoral counseling, philosophy, physical education, political science, psychology, religious education, sacred music, science education, secondary education, sociology.

DORDT COLLEGE

Accounting, agricultural business, agricultural sciences, animal sciences, art, biology, business administration, business education, chemistry, computer science, criminal justice/law enforcement administration, data processing technology, (pre)dentistry, education, electrical/electronics engineering, elementary education, engineering, engineering mechanics, English, environmental science, exercise sciences, German, graphic design/commercial art/illustration, history, journalism, management information systems/business data processing, mass communications, mathematics, medical technology, (pre)medicine, music, music education, natural sciences, philosophy, physical education, physics, political science, psychology, recreation and leisure studies, religious studies, secondary education, secretarial science, social sciences, social work, sociology, Spanish, teacher assistant/aide, theater arts/drama, theology, (pre)veterinary studies.

EASTERN COLLEGE

Accounting, art history, astronomy, biblical studies, biochemistry, biology, business administration, cardiovascular technology, chemistry, communications, creative writing, economics, elementary education, English, English education, environmental science, French, health/physical education, health services administration, history, intermedia, liberal arts and studies, mathematics, music, nursing, philosophy, political science, psychology, secondary education, social work, sociology, Spanish, theology, urban studies.

EASTERN MENNONITE UNIVERSITY

Accounting, agricultural sciences, art, biblical studies, biochemistry, biology, business administration, chemistry, community services, computer programming, computer science, data processing technology, (pre)dentistry, development economics, divinity/ministry, early childhood education, economics, education, elementary education, (pre)engineering, English, environmental science, French, German, health education, history, information sciences/systems, international business, liberal arts and studies, mathematics, medical technology, (pre)medicine, middle school education, music, music education, nursing, pastoral counseling, physical education, psychology, recreation and leisure studies, religious studies, science education, secondary education, social work, sociology, Spanish, special education, teacher assistant/aide, theology, (pre)veterinary studies.

EASTERN NAZARENE COLLEGE

Accounting, advertising, aerospace engineering, athletic training/sports medicine, bioengineering, biological and physical sciences, biology, business administration, chemistry, clinical psychology, computer engineering, computer science, (pre)dentistry, developmental/child psychology, divinity/ministry, early childhood education, education, electrical/electronics engineering, elementary education, engineering physics, English, environmental science, French, history, industrial engineering, journalism, (pre)law, liberal arts and studies, literature, mass communications, mathematics, mechanical engineering, (pre)medicine, middle school education, music, music education, pastoral counseling, pharmacy, physical education, physical therapy, physics, psychology, radio/television broadcasting, religious studies, sacred music, secondary education, social sciences, social work, sociology, Spanish, special education, systems engineering, theater arts/drama, (pre)veterinary studies.

EAST TEXAS BAPTIST UNIVERSITY

Accounting, behavioral sciences, biology, biology education, business administration, business education, chemistry, chemistry education, computer education, computer/information sciences, (pre)dentistry, drama and dance education, early childhood education, education (multiple levels), elementary education, English, English education, history, history education, liberal arts and studies, mathematics, mathematics education, medical technology, (pre)medicine, music, music education, music (voice and choral/opera performance), nursing, paralegal/legal assistant, pastoral counseling, physical education, psychology, religious education, religious studies, sacred music, science education, secondary education, social studies education, sociology, Spanish, Spanish language education, speech education, speech/rhetorical studies, theater arts/drama.

ERSKINE COLLEGE

Accounting, American studies, art history, arts management, athletic training/sports medicine, behavioral sciences, biblical studies, biological and physical sciences, biology, business administration, chemistry, early childhood education, elementary education, English, French, history, mathematics, medical technology, music, music business management and merchandising, music education, music (piano and organ performance), music (voice and choral/opera performance), natural sciences, physical education, physics, psychology, religious education, religious studies, sacred music, social studies education, Spanish, special education, sport/fitness administration.

EVANGEL UNIVERSITY

Accounting, art, art education, behavioral sciences, biblical studies, biology, broadcast journalism, business administration, business education, business marketing and marketing management, chemistry, child care/development, computer science, criminal justice/law enforcement administration, (pre)dentistry, early childhood education, education, elementary education, English, history, journalism, (pre)law, mass communications, mathematics, medical laboratory technologies, medical technology, (pre)medicine, mental health/rehabilitation, music, music education, physical education, political science, psychology, public administration, radio/television broadcasting, recreation and leisure studies, sacred music, science education, secondary education, secretarial science, social sciences, social work, sociology, Spanish, special education, speech/rhetorical studies, (pre)veterinary studies.

FRESNO PACIFIC UNIVERSITY

Accounting, applied mathematics, athletic training/sports medicine, biblical studies, bilingual/bicultural education, biology, business administration, business education, chemistry, developmental/child psychology, divinity/ministry, education, elementary education, English, history, humanities, human resources management, (pre)law, liberal arts and studies, literature, mass communications, mathematics, (pre)medicine, music, music education, natural sciences, pastoral counseling, physical education, political science, psychology, religious studies, sacred music, science education, secondary education, social sciences, social work, sociology, Spanish, sport/fitness administration.

GENEVA COLLEGE

Accounting, applied mathematics, aviation management, biblical studies, biology, broadcast journalism, business administration, chemical engineering, chemistry, computer science, counseling psychology, elementary education, engineering, English, history, human resources management, mathematics education, music, music business management and merchandising, music education, music (general performance), philosophy, physics, political science, psychology, radio/television broadcasting, secondary education, sociology, Spanish, speech-language pathology/audiology, speech/rhetorical studies, (pre)theology.

GEORGE FOX UNIVERSITY

Accounting, art, athletic training/sports medicine, biblical studies, biological and physical sciences, biology, business, business administration, business marketing and marketing management, chemistry, civil engineering, cognitive psychology and psycholinguistics, computer engineering, computer science, (pre)dentistry, divinity/ministry, economics, education, electrical/electronics engineering, elementary education, engineering, engineering science, English, fashion merchandising, food sciences,

history, home economics, home economics education, information sciences/systems, interdisciplinary studies, interior design, international business, international relations, (pre)law, liberal arts and studies, literature, management information systems/business data processing, mass communications, mathematics, (pre)medicine, music, music education, physical education, psychology, religious studies, science education, secondary education, social work, sociology, Spanish, telecommunications, (pre)theology, (pre)veterinary studies.

GORDON COLLEGE (MA)

Accounting, art, biblical studies, biology, business administration, chemistry, communications, computer science, divinity/ministry, early childhood education, economics, education, elementary education, English, exercise sciences, foreign languages/literatures, French, history, international relations, mass communications, mathematics, middle school education, modern languages, music, music education, music (general performance), philosophy, physics, political science, psychology, recreation and leisure studies, religious education, social work, sociology, Spanish, special education.

GOSHEN COLLEGE

Accounting, art, art education, art therapy, biblical studies, bilingual/bicultural education, biology, broadcast journalism, business administration, business education, chemistry, child care/development, computer science, (pre)dentistry, early childhood education, economics, education, elementary education, English, family/community studies, German, Hispanic-American studies, history, information sciences/systems, journalism, (pre)law, liberal arts and studies, mass communications, mathematics, (pre)medicine, music, music education, natural sciences, nursing, physical education, physical sciences, physics, political science, psychology, religious studies, science education, secondary education, social work, sociology, Spanish, teaching English as a second language, theater arts/drama, (pre)veterinary studies.

GRACE COLLEGE

Accounting, art, art education, behavioral sciences, biblical languages/literatures, biblical studies, biology, business administration, criminal justice/law enforcement administration, divinity/ministry, elementary education, English, French, German, graphic design/commercial art/illustration, Greek (Ancient and Medieval), (pre)law, management information systems/business data processing, mass communications, mathematics, (pre)medicine, music, music education, music (piano and organ performance), physical education, psychology, science education, secretarial science, sociology, Spanish, (pre)veterinary studies.

GRAND CANYON UNIVERSITY

Accounting, art, art education, athletic training/sports medicine, biblical studies, biology, business administration, business economics, business education, business marketing and marketing management, chemistry, criminal justice/law enforcement administration, (pre)dentistry, divinity/ministry, economics, elementary education, English, environmental biology, exercise sciences, finance, fine/studio arts, graphic design/commercial art/illustration, history, human resources management, international business, international relations, (pre)law, liberal arts and studies, literature, mass communications, mathematics, (pre)medicine, music, music business management and merchandising, music education, music (piano and organ performance), music (voice and choral/opera performance), nursing, physical education, physical sciences, political science, psychology, religious studies, sacred music, science education, secondary education, social sciences, sociology, special education, speech/rhetorical studies, theater arts/drama, theology, (pre)veterinary studies, wildlife biology, wind and percussion instruments.

GREENVILLE COLLEGE

Accounting, art, art education, biology, biology education, business administration, business marketing and marketing management, chemistry, chemistry education, computer science, (pre)dentistry, divinity/ministry, drama and dance education, early childhood education, education, elementary education, English, English education, environmental biology, foreign languages education, French, history, (pre)law, liberal arts and studies, management information systems/business data processing, mass communications, mathematics, mathematics education, (pre)medicine, modern languages, music, music education, pastoral counseling, philosophy, physical education, physics, physics education, political science, psychology, public relations, recreation and leisure studies, religious studies, sacred music, science education, secondary education, social studies education, social work, sociology, Spanish, Spanish language education, special education, speech education, speech/rhetorical studies, theater arts/drama, theology, (pre)veterinary studies.

HOPE INTERNATIONAL UNIVERSITY
Athletic training/sports medicine, biblical studies, business administration, child care/development, early childhood education, elementary education, English education, general studies, individual/family development, interdisciplinary studies, missionary studies, music education, physical therapy, physiological psychology/psychobiology, psychology, sacred music, social science education, social sciences, social work.

HOUGHTON COLLEGE
Accounting, art, art education, biblical studies, biological and physical sciences, biology, business administration, chemistry, computer science, creative writing, (pre)dentistry, divinity/ministry, education, elementary education, English, French, history, humanities, international relations, (pre)law, literature, mass communications, mathematics, medical technology, (pre)medicine, music, music education, music (piano and organ performance), music (voice and choral/opera performance), natural sciences, pastoral counseling, philosophy, physical education, physical sciences, physics, political science, psychology, recreation and leisure studies, religious education, religious studies, sacred music, science education, secondary education, social sciences, sociology, Spanish, stringed instruments, (pre)veterinary studies, wind and percussion instruments.

HUNTINGTON COLLEGE
Accounting, art, art education, biblical studies, biological and physical sciences, biology, broadcast journalism, business administration, business economics, business education, chemistry, computer science, (pre)dentistry, divinity/ministry, economics, education, elementary education, English, exercise sciences, graphic design/commercial art/illustration, history, (pre)law, mass communications, mathematics, (pre)medicine, music, music education, music (piano and organ performance), music (voice and choral/opera performance), natural resources management, philosophy, physical education, psychology, recreation and leisure studies, religious studies, science education, secondary education, sociology, special education, theater arts/drama, theology, (pre)veterinary studies.

INDIANA WESLEYAN UNIVERSITY
Accounting, alcohol/drug abuse counseling, art, art education, athletic training/sports medicine, biblical languages/literatures, biblical studies, biological and physical sciences, biology, business administration, business marketing and marketing management, chemistry, communications, creative writing, criminal justice studies, curriculum and instruction, (pre)dentistry, divinity/ministry, economics, education, elementary education, English, exercise sciences, finance, fine/studio arts, general studies, history, (pre)law, mass communications, mathematics, medical technology, (pre)medicine, middle school education, music, music education, nursing, pastoral counseling, philosophy, physical education, political science, psychology, recreation/leisure facilities management, religious education, sacred music, science education, secondary education, social sciences, social work, sociology, Spanish, special education, sport/fitness administration, theology, (pre)veterinary studies.

JOHN BROWN UNIVERSITY
Accounting, art, athletic training/sports medicine, biblical studies, biochemistry, biology, broadcast journalism, business administration, business education, chemistry, computer graphics, construction engineering, construction management, divinity/ministry, early childhood education, education, electrical/electronics engineering, elementary education, engineering, engineering/industrial management, engineering technology, English, environmental science, exercise sciences, graphic design/commercial art/illustration, health education, health services administration, history, interdisciplinary studies, international business, international relations, journalism, (pre)law, liberal

arts and studies, mass communications, mathematics, mechanical engineering, medical technology, (pre)medicine, middle school education, music, music education, music (piano and organ performance), music (voice and choral/opera performance), pastoral counseling, physical education, psychology, public relations, radio/television broadcasting, recreation/leisure facilities management, religious education, religious studies, secondary education, social sciences, special education, teaching English as a second language, theology, (pre)veterinary studies.

JUDSON COLLEGE (IL)
Accounting, anthropology, architecture, art, biblical studies, biological and physical sciences, biology, business administration, chemistry, computer graphics, computer science, criminal justice studies, drawing, early childhood education, education, elementary education, English, fine/studio arts, graphic design/commercial art/illustration, history, human resources management, human services, information sciences/systems, international business, journalism, (pre)law, linguistics, literature, management information systems/business data processing, mass communications, mathematics, (pre)medicine, music, music education, music (voice and choral/opera performance), nursing, philosophy, physical education, physical sciences, psychology, religious studies, science education, secondary education, social sciences, sociology, speech/rhetorical studies, sport/fitness administration, theater arts/drama.

KING COLLEGE
Accounting, American studies, behavioral sciences, biblical studies, biological and physical sciences, biology, biology education, business, business administration, business economics, chemistry, chemistry education, (pre)dentistry, early childhood education, economics, education, elementary education, English, English education, fine/studio arts, French, French language education, history, history education, international business, (pre)law, mathematics, mathematics/computer science, mathematics education, medical technology, (pre)medicine, middle school education, modern languages, music, (pre)pharmacy studies, physics, physics education, political science, psychology, religious studies, secondary education, Spanish, Spanish language education, theater arts/drama, (pre)veterinary studies.

THE KING'S UNIVERSITY COLLEGE
Biology, business administration, chemistry, education, English, environmental science, history, music, philosophy, psychology, social sciences, sociology.

LEE UNIVERSITY
Accounting, biblical studies, biological and physical sciences, biology, business administration, business education, chemistry, education, elementary education, English, health education, history, individual/family development, information sciences/systems, international relations, mass communications, mathematics, medical technology, modern languages, music, music education, music (piano and organ performance), music (voice and choral/opera performance), natural sciences, pastoral counseling, physical education, psychology, religious education, respiratory therapy, secondary education, secretarial science, social sciences, sociology, special education, theology.

LETOURNEAU UNIVERSITY
Accounting, aircraft mechanic/airframe, aircraft pilot (professional), aviation technology, biblical studies, biology, business administration, business marketing and marketing management, chemistry, computer engineering, computer engineering technology, computer science, (pre)dentistry, divinity/ministry, drafting, electrical/electronic engineering technology, electrical/electronics engineering, elementary education, engineering, engineering design, engineering technology, English, history, interdisciplinary studies, (pre)law, mathematics, mechanical design technology, mechanical engineering, mechanical engineering technology, (pre)medicine, natural sciences, physical education, physics, psychology, public administration, religious studies, secondary education, sport/fitness administration, (pre)veterinary studies, welding technology.

MALONE COLLEGE
Accounting, art, art education, biblical studies, biology, broadcast journalism, business administration, chemistry, communications, computer science,

Malone College (continued)

early childhood education, education of the specific learning disabled, elementary education, English, exercise sciences, health/physical education, history, international relations, journalism, (pre)law, liberal arts and studies, mathematics, medical technology, music, musical instrument technology, music education, pastoral counseling, physical education, psychology, sacred music, science education, social sciences, social studies education, social work, Spanish, speech education, theater arts/drama, urban studies.

THE MASTER'S COLLEGE AND SEMINARY
Accounting, actuarial science, American government, applied mathematics, biblical languages/literatures, biblical studies, biological and physical sciences, biology, broadcast journalism, business administration, divinity/ministry, education, elementary education, English, environmental biology, finance, history, home economics, liberal arts and studies, management information systems/business data processing, mass communications, mathematics, (pre)medicine, middle school education, music, music business management and merchandising, music education, music (piano and organ performance), music (voice and choral/opera performance), natural sciences, nutrition science, pastoral counseling, physical education, physical sciences, political science, public relations, radio/television broadcasting, religious education, religious studies, sacred music, science education, secondary education, special education, speech/rhetorical studies, theology.

MESSIAH COLLEGE
Accounting, adapted physical education, art education, art history, athletic training/sports medicine, biblical studies, biochemistry, biology, biology education, business administration, business economics, business marketing and marketing management, chemistry, chemistry education, civil engineering, computer/information sciences, (pre)dentistry, dietetics, early childhood education, economics, elementary education, engineering, English, English education, environmental education, exercise sciences, family/community studies, French, French language education, German, history, humanities, human resources management, information sciences/systems, international business, journalism, (pre)law, mathematics, mathematics education, medical technology, (pre)medicine, music, music education, nursing, philosophy, physical education, physics, political science, psychology, radio/television broadcasting, recreation and leisure studies, religious education, religious studies, social studies education, social work, sociology, Spanish, Spanish language education, theater arts/drama, (pre)theology, (pre)veterinary studies.

MIDAMERICA NAZARENE UNIVERSITY
Accounting, agricultural business, athletic training/sports medicine, biology, business administration, business education, chemistry, computer science, criminal justice/law enforcement administration, divinity/ministry, early childhood education, elementary education, English, exercise sciences, health education, history, human resources management, international business, liberal arts and studies, mass communications, mathematics, middle school education, modern languages, music, music education, music (voice and choral/opera performance), nursing, physical education, physics, psychology, public relations, religious education, religious studies, sacred music, science education, secondary education, sociology, Spanish.

MILLIGAN COLLEGE
Accounting, adult/continuing education, advertising, art, biblical studies, biological and physical sciences, biology, broadcast journalism, business administration, business economics, chemistry, computer science, (pre)dentistry, divinity/ministry, early childhood education, education, elementary education, engineering, English, exercise sciences, health education, health science, health services administration, history, humanities, human services, journalism, law and legal studies, liberal arts and studies, mass communications, mathematics, medical laboratory technician, (pre)medicine, mortuary science, music, music education, music (piano and organ performance), music (voice and choral/opera performance), nursing, paralegal/legal assistant, pastoral counseling, physical education, psychology, public relations, radio/television broadcasting, religious education, religious studies,

sacred music, science education, secondary education, social work, sociology, special education, theater arts/drama, theology, (pre)veterinary studies.

MONTREAT COLLEGE
Accounting, American studies, art, biblical studies, business administration, business economics, business marketing and marketing management, child care/development, (pre)dentistry, ecology, economics, education, (pre)engineering, English, environmental science, history, human services, (pre)law, liberal arts and studies, literature, management information systems/business data processing, mass communications, mathematics, (pre)medicine, music, music business management and merchandising, music education, music (piano and organ performance), music (voice and choral/opera performance), physical education, religious studies, secondary education, social sciences, Spanish, sport/fitness administration.

MOUNT VERNON NAZARENE COLLEGE
Accounting, applied art, art, art education, athletic training/sports medicine, biblical studies, biochemistry, biological and physical sciences, biology, broadcast journalism, business administration, business education, business marketing and marketing management, chemistry, computer engineering technology, computer science, criminal justice/law enforcement administration, data processing technology, (pre)dentistry, early childhood education, education, elementary education, (pre)engineering, English, health science, history, home economics, home economics education, human services, (pre)law, liberal arts and studies, literature, mass communications, mathematics, medical technology, (pre)medicine, modern languages, music, music education, music (piano and organ performance), music (voice and choral/opera performance), natural resources management, nursing, philosophy, physical education, psychology, religious education, religious studies, sacred music, science education, secondary education, secretarial science, social sciences, social work, sociology, Spanish, special education, sport/fitness administration, theater arts/drama, theology, (pre)veterinary studies, wind and percussion instruments.

NORTH PARK UNIVERSITY
Accounting, anthropology, art, art education, athletic training/sports medicine, biblical studies, biological and physical sciences, biology, business administration, business marketing and marketing management, chemistry, community services, (pre)dentistry, divinity/ministry, early childhood education, economics, education, elementary education, English, exercise sciences, finance, fine/studio arts, French, history, international business, international relations, (pre)law, literature, mass communications, mathematics, medical technology, (pre)medicine, modern languages, music, music business management and merchandising, music education, music (voice and choral/opera performance), natural sciences, nursing, philosophy, physical education, physics, political science, psychology, religious studies, sacred music, Scandinavian languages, secondary education, social sciences, sociology, Spanish, speech/rhetorical studies, theater arts/drama, theology, urban studies, (pre)veterinary studies.

NORTHWEST CHRISTIAN COLLEGE
Area studies, biblical studies, business administration, business communications, business marketing and marketing management, communication disorders, elementary education, general studies, history, humanities, interdisciplinary studies, mass communications, (pre)medicine, missionary studies, modern languages, music, pastoral counseling, psychology, social sciences, speech/rhetorical studies, (pre)theology.

NORTHWEST COLLEGE
Behavioral sciences, biblical studies, business administration, divinity/ministry, education, elementary education, English, environmental biology, health science, history, interdisciplinary studies, liberal arts and studies, middle school education, music, music education, music (piano and organ performance), music (voice and choral/opera performance), pastoral counseling, philosophy, psychology, religious education, religious studies, sacred music, secondary education, social sciences, teaching English as a second language, theology.

NORTHWESTERN COLLEGE (IA)

Accounting, art, art education, biology, business administration, business education, chemistry, computer science, economics, education, elementary education, English, environmental science, exercise sciences, French, history, humanities, mass communications, mathematics, medical technology, music, music education, philosophy, physical education, political science, psychology, religious education, religious studies, secondary education, secretarial science, social work, sociology, Spanish, theater arts/drama, theology.

NORTHWESTERN COLLEGE (MN)

Accounting, art education, athletic training/sports medicine, biblical studies, biology, business administration, business marketing and marketing management, child care/development, communications, computer/information sciences, criminal justice studies, elementary education, English, English education, finance, fine/studio arts, graphic design/commercial art/illustration, history, human resources management, international business, journalism, liberal arts and studies, management information systems/business data processing, mathematics, mathematics education, missionary studies, music education, music (general performance), office management, organizational behavior, pastoral counseling, physical education, psychology, radio/television broadcasting, religious education, secretarial science, social sciences, social studies education, Spanish, sport/fitness administration, teaching English as a second language, theater arts/drama, theology, (pre)theology.

NORTHWEST NAZARENE COLLEGE

Accounting, art, art education, athletic training/sports medicine, biblical languages/literatures, biological and physical sciences, biology, biology education, business administration, business marketing and marketing management, chemistry, chemistry education, computer science, (pre)dentistry, divinity/ministry, drawing, elementary education, engineering physics, English, English education, finance, graphic design/commercial art/illustration, health/physical education, history, history education, international business, international relations, (pre)law, liberal arts and studies, mathematics, mathematics education, (pre)medicine, missionary studies, music, music education, music (general performance), music theory and composition, pastoral counseling, philosophy, physical education, physical therapy, physics, political science, psychology, recreation and leisure studies, religious education, religious studies, sacred music, secondary education, social science education, social sciences, social work, special education, speech education, speech-language pathology/audiology, speech/rhetorical studies, theology, (pre)veterinary studies.

NYACK COLLEGE

Accounting, biblical studies, business administration, communications, elementary education, English, general studies, history, interdisciplinary studies, liberal arts and studies, missionary studies, music, music education, music (piano and organ performance), music theory and composition, music (voice and choral/opera performance), nonprofit/public management, pastoral counseling, philosophy, psychology, religious education, religious studies, sacred music, secondary education, social sciences, teaching English as a second language, theology.

OKLAHOMA BAPTIST UNIVERSITY

Accounting, advertising, applied art, art, art education, athletic training/sports medicine, biblical languages/literatures, biblical studies, biological and physical sciences, biology, biology education, broadcast journalism, business administration, business communications, business computer programming, business education, business marketing and marketing management, chemistry, chemistry education, child care/development, child guidance, computer/information sciences, computer management, computer science, computer systems analysis, (pre)dentistry, developmental/child psychology, divinity/ministry, drama and dance education, early childhood education, education, education of the emotionally handicapped, education of the mentally handicapped, education of the specific learning disabled, elementary education, English, English composition, English education, exercise sciences, finance, fine/studio arts, French, French language educa-

tion, German, German language education, health/physical education, health services administration, history, history education, humanities, human resources management, information sciences/systems, interdisciplinary studies, international business, international business marketing, journalism, (pre)law, management information systems/business data processing, marriage and family counseling, mass communications, mathematics, mathematics education, (pre)medicine, missionary studies, music, music education, music (piano and organ performance), music theory and composition, music (voice and choral/opera performance), natural sciences, nursing, pastoral counseling, (pre)pharmacy studies, philosophy, physical education, physical sciences, physics, political science, psychology, public relations, radio/television broadcasting, recreation and leisure studies, religious education, religious studies, sacred music, science education, secondary education, social science education, social sciences, social studies education, social work, sociology, Spanish, Spanish language education, special education, speech education, speech/rhetorical studies, stringed instruments, telecommunications, theater arts/drama, theology, (pre)veterinary studies, wind and percussion instruments.

OKLAHOMA CHRISTIAN UNIVERSITY OF SCIENCE AND ARTS

Accounting, advertising, art, art education, biblical studies, biochemistry, biological and physical sciences, biology, broadcast journalism, business administration, business education, business marketing and marketing management, chemistry, child care/development, community services, computer engineering, computer science, (pre)dentistry, developmental/child psychology, divinity/ministry, early childhood education, electrical/electronics engineering, elementary education, emergency medical technology, engineering, engineering physics, English, family/community studies, graphic design/commercial art/illustration, history, information sciences/systems, interior design, journalism, (pre)law, liberal arts and studies, mass communications, mathematics, mechanical engineering, medical technology, (pre)medicine, middle school education, music, music education, music (voice and choral/opera performance), pastoral counseling, physical education, psychology, public relations, radio/television broadcasting, religious education, religious studies, science education, secondary education, Spanish, special education, speech/rhetorical studies, teaching English as a second language, theater arts/drama, (pre)veterinary studies, wind and percussion instruments.

OLIVET NAZARENE UNIVERSITY

Accounting, art, art education, athletic training/sports medicine, biblical studies, biochemistry, biological and physical sciences, biology, broadcast journalism, business administration, business economics, business marketing and marketing management, chemistry, child care/development, clothing and textiles, computer science, criminal justice/law enforcement administration, (pre)dentistry, developmental/child psychology, dietetics, early childhood education, earth sciences, economics, education, elementary education, English, environmental science, family/community studies, fashion merchandising, film studies, finance, food sciences, French, geology, graphic design/commercial art/illustration, history, home economics, home economics education, human resources management, information sciences/systems, interdisciplinary studies, journalism, (pre)law, liberal arts and studies, literature, mass communications, mathematics, medical technology, (pre)medicine, modern languages, music, music education, music (piano and organ performance), music (voice and choral/opera performance), natural sciences, nursing, philosophy, physical education, physical sciences, psychology, radio/television broadcasting, religious education, religious studies, Romance languages, sacred music, science education, secondary education, social sciences, Spanish, speech/rhetorical studies, stringed instruments, theology, (pre)veterinary studies, wind and percussion instruments, zoology.

ORAL ROBERTS UNIVERSITY

Accounting, art, art education, behavioral sciences, biblical studies, biochemistry, bioengineering, biology, biomedical science, broadcast journalism, business administration, business education, business marketing and marketing management, chemical engineering, chemistry, computer science, dental hygiene, (pre)dentistry, divinity/ministry, drama therapy, early

Oral Roberts University (continued)

childhood education, education, electrical/electronics engineering, elementary education, engineering, engineering/industrial management, engineering science, English, exercise sciences, finance, fine/studio arts, French, German, graphic design/commercial art/illustration, health education, history, humanities, international business, journalism, (pre)law, liberal arts and studies, literature, management information systems/business data processing, marine biology, mass communications, mathematics, mechanical engineering, medical technology, (pre)medicine, modern languages, music, music education, music (piano and organ performance), music (voice and choral/opera performance), natural sciences, nursing, ophthalmic/optometric services, pastoral counseling, physical education, physical therapy, physics, political science, psychology, radio/television broadcasting, recreation and leisure studies, religious education, sacred music, science education, secondary education, social sciences, social work, sociology, Spanish, teaching English as a second language, telecommunications, theater arts/drama, theology, (pre)veterinary studies.

PALM BEACH ATLANTIC COLLEGE
Art, art education, biology, business administration, business marketing and marketing management, early childhood education, education, elementary education, English, finance, history, human resources management, information sciences/systems, international business, (pre)law, mathematics, (pre)medicine, music, music education, music (voice and choral/opera performance), philosophy, physical education, political science, psychology, religious studies, sacred music, secondary education, stringed instruments, theater arts/drama, wind and percussion instruments.

POINT LOMA NAZARENE UNIVERSITY
Accounting, art, biblical studies, biochemistry, biology, British literature, business administration, business communications, business home economics, chemistry, child care/development, communications, computer science, dietetics, economics, engineering physics, family studies, graphic design/commercial art/illustration, health/physical education, history, home economics, journalism, liberal arts and studies, management information systems/business data processing, mass communications, mathematics, music, music business management and merchandising, nursing, organizational psychology, philosophy, physics, political science, psychology, Romance languages, sacred music, social sciences, social work, sociology, Spanish, speech/rhetorical studies, theater arts/drama, theology.

REDEEMER COLLEGE
Accounting, art, behavioral sciences, biblical studies, biological and physical sciences, biology, business administration, clinical psychology, (pre)dentistry, education, elementary education, English, exercise sciences, experimental psychology, French, health/physical education, history, humanities, (pre)law, liberal arts and studies, mathematics, (pre)medicine, modern languages, music, natural sciences, pastoral counseling, philosophy, political science, psychology, recreation and leisure studies, religious studies, Romance languages, secondary education, sociology, theater arts/drama, theology, (pre)theology, (pre)veterinary studies.

ROBERTS WESLEYAN COLLEGE
Accounting, art, art education, biochemistry, biological and physical sciences, biology, business administration, chemistry, computer science, criminal justice/law enforcement administration, (pre)dentistry, divinity/ministry, education, elementary education, English, fine/studio arts, graphic design/commercial art/illustration, history, humanities, human resources management, mass communications, mathematics, medical technology, music, music education, music (piano and organ performance), music (voice and choral/opera performance), natural sciences, nursing, physical sciences, physics, psychology, religious studies, secondary education, social sciences, social work, sociology.

SEATTLE PACIFIC UNIVERSITY
Accounting, art education, biology, business administration, business economics, chemistry, clothing/apparel/textile studies, communications, computer/information sciences, electrical/electronics engineering, engineering, English,

English education, European studies, exercise sciences, general studies, history, home economics, mathematics, mathematics education, music, music education, nursing, nutrition studies, philosophy, physical education, physics, political science, psychology, religious education, religious studies, science education, social science education, sociology, special education, theater arts/drama, visual/performing arts.

SIMPSON COLLEGE AND GRADUATE SCHOOL
Accounting, biblical studies, business administration, communications, divinity/ministry, education, elementary education, English, English education, general studies, history, human resources management, liberal arts and studies, mathematics, missionary studies, music, music education, pastoral counseling, psychology, religious education, sacred music, secondary education, social science education, social sciences.

SOUTHERN CALIFORNIA COLLEGE
Accounting, anthropology, biblical studies, biological and physical sciences, biology, business administration, business marketing and marketing management, chemistry, education, English, film/video production, finance, history, interdisciplinary studies, international business, mass communications, mathematics, music, pastoral counseling, physical education, physical therapy, political science, psychology, radio/television broadcasting, religious education, religious studies, secondary education, social sciences, Spanish, speech/rhetorical studies, theater arts/drama.

SOUTHERN NAZARENE UNIVERSITY
Accounting, adult/continuing education, applied mathematics, art, art education, athletic training/sports medicine, aviation management, behavioral sciences, biblical languages/literatures, biblical studies, biological and physical sciences, biology, business administration, business education, business marketing and marketing management, chemistry, computer programming, computer science, criminal justice/law enforcement administration, (pre)dentistry, divinity/ministry, early childhood education, economics, education, elementary education, engineering, English, health education, health science, history, information sciences/systems, international relations, journalism, (pre)law, liberal arts and studies, literature, management information systems/business data processing, mass communications, mathematics, (pre)medicine, modern languages, music, music business management and merchandising, music education, music (piano and organ performance), music (voice and choral/opera performance), natural sciences, nursing, pastoral counseling, philosophy, physical education, physics, political science, psychology, reading education, religious education, religious studies, sacred music, science education, secondary education, social sciences, sociology, Spanish, speech/rhetorical studies, sport/fitness administration, theology, (pre)veterinary studies.

SOUTHERN WESLEYAN UNIVERSITY
Accounting, biology, business administration, chemistry, criminal justice/law enforcement administration, divinity/ministry, early childhood education, education, elementary education, English, Greek (Modern), history, mathematics, medical technology, music, music education, nursing, physical education, psychology, recreation and leisure studies, religious studies, social sciences, special education.

SOUTHWEST BAPTIST UNIVERSITY
Accounting, art, art education, biology, business administration, business education, chemistry, child care/development, computer science, early childhood education, elementary education, emergency medical technology, English, graphic design/commercial art/illustration, history, human services, information sciences/systems, interdisciplinary studies, mass communications, mathematics, medical technology, middle school education, music, music education, nursing, physical education, political science, psychology, recreation and leisure studies, religious education, religious studies, secondary education, secretarial science, social sciences, sociology, Spanish, sport/fitness administration, theater arts/drama, theology.

SPRING ARBOR COLLEGE
Accounting, art, biochemistry, biology, business administration, business economics, chemistry, computer science, divinity/ministry, early childhood

education, elementary education, English, French, history, liberal arts and studies, mass communications, mathematics, music, philosophy, physical education, physics, psychology, religious studies, secondary education, social sciences, social work, sociology, Spanish, speech/rhetorical studies.

STERLING COLLEGE (KS)

Accounting, art, behavioral sciences, biology, business administration, computer science, education, elementary education, English, history, liberal arts and studies, mathematics, music, music education, natural sciences, philosophy, physical education, political science, religious studies, religious studies, speech/rhetorical studies, theater arts/drama.

TABOR COLLEGE

Accounting, actuarial science, adult/continuing education, agricultural business, applied mathematics, art education, athletic training/sports medicine, biblical studies, biological and physical sciences, biology, business administration, business education, business marketing and marketing management, chemistry, communications, computer science, (pre)dentistry, divinity/ministry, early childhood education, education, elementary education, (pre)engineering, English, environmental biology, health education, history, humanities, interdisciplinary studies, international relations, (pre)law, legal administrative assistant, mass communications, mathematics, medical administrative assistant, medical technology, (pre)medicine, music, music business management and merchandising, music education, music (piano and organ performance), music (voice and choral/opera performance), natural sciences, pastoral counseling, philosophy, physical education, psychology, religious studies, science education, secondary education, secretarial science, social sciences, sociology, special education, theater design, (pre)veterinary studies, zoology.

TAYLOR UNIVERSITY

Accounting, art, art education, athletic training/sports medicine, biblical languages/literatures, biblical studies, biology, business administration, chemistry, computer programming, computer science, creative writing, (pre)dentistry, early childhood education, economics, education, elementary education, engineering physics, English, environmental biology, environmental science, French, graphic design/commercial art/illustration, history, information sciences/systems, international business, international economics, international relations, (pre)law, literature, management information systems/business data processing, mass communications, mathematics, medical technology, (pre)medicine, middle school education, music, music business management and merchandising, music education, music (piano and organ performance), music (voice and choral/opera performance), natural sciences, philosophy, physical education, physics, political science, psychology, recreation and leisure studies, religious education, religious studies, sacred music, science education, secondary education, social sciences, social work, sociology, Spanish, sport/fitness administration, theater arts/drama, theology, (pre)veterinary studies.

TREVECCA NAZARENE UNIVERSITY

Accounting, behavioral sciences, biological and physical sciences, biology, biology education, broadcast journalism, business administration, business marketing and marketing management, chemistry, chemistry education, child care/development, communications, early childhood education, economics, elementary education, English, English education, exercise sciences, history, history education, information sciences/systems, liberal arts and studies, mass communications, mathematics, mathematics education, medical technology, music, music business management and merchandising, music education, physical education, physician assistant, physics, psychology, religious studies, sacred music, sales operations, secondary education, social sciences, social work, speech/rhetorical studies, theater arts/drama.

TRINITY CHRISTIAN COLLEGE

Accounting, art, art education, biology, biology education, business, business administration, business education, business marketing and marketing management, ceramic arts, chemistry, chemistry education, communications, computer science, (pre)dentistry, drawing, education, education of the emotionally handicapped, education of the mentally handicapped, education of the specific learning disabled, elementary education, English, English

education, entrepreneurship, financial planning, graphic design/commercial art/illustration, history, history education, human resources management, information sciences/systems, management information systems/business data processing, mathematics, mathematics education, (pre)medicine, middle school education, music, music education, music (general performance), music (piano and organ performance), music (voice and choral/opera performance), nursing, painting, philosophy, photography, physical education, printmaking, psychology, religious education, religious studies, science education, sculpture, secondary education, sociology, special education, theology, (pre)theology, (pre)veterinary studies.

TRINITY INTERNATIONAL UNIVERSITY

Accounting, athletic training/sports medicine, biblical studies, biology, business administration, business marketing and marketing management, chemistry, computer science, divinity/ministry, economics, education, elementary education, English, history, humanities, human resources management, information sciences/systems, liberal arts and studies, mass communications, mathematics, (pre)medicine, music, music education, philosophy, physical education, psychology, sacred music, secondary education, social sciences, sociology.

TRINITY WESTERN UNIVERSITY

Applied mathematics, biblical studies, biological and physical sciences, biology, business administration, chemistry, computer science, (pre)dentistry, education, elementary education, English, environmental biology, geography, history, humanities, human services, international relations, (pre)law, liberal arts and studies, linguistics, mass communications, mathematics, (pre)medicine, music, natural sciences, nursing, philosophy, physical education, political science, psychology, recreation and leisure studies, religious studies, secondary education, social sciences, theater arts/drama, (pre)veterinary studies.

UNION UNIVERSITY

Accounting, art, art education, biological and physical sciences, biology, business administration, business economics, business education, business marketing and marketing management, chemistry, computer science, (pre)dentistry, early childhood education, economics, education, elementary education, English, finance, French, Greek (Modern), history, information sciences/systems, interdisciplinary studies, journalism, (pre)law, marine biology, mass communications, mathematics, medical technology, (pre)medicine, music, music education, music (piano and organ performance), music (voice and choral/opera performance), nursing, philosophy, physical education, psychology, radio/television broadcasting, religious studies, sacred music, science education, secondary education, social work, sociology, Spanish, special education, telecommunications, theater arts/drama, theology, (pre)veterinary studies.

UNIVERSITY OF SIOUX FALLS

Accounting, applied art, applied mathematics, art education, behavioral sciences, biology, business administration, business marketing and marketing management, chemistry, computer science, (pre)dentistry, developmental/child psychology, early childhood education, economics, education, elementary education, (pre)engineering, English, exercise sciences, graphic design/commercial art/illustration, health education, history, humanities, industrial radiologic technology, information sciences/systems, interdisciplinary studies, (pre)law, liberal arts and studies, management information systems/business data processing, mass communications, mathematics, medical technology, (pre)medicine, middle school education, music, music business management and merchandising, music (piano and organ performance), music (voice and choral/opera performance), pastoral counseling, philosophy, physical education, political science, psychology, public relations, radio/television broadcasting, religious studies, science education, secondary education, secretarial science, social sciences, social work, sociology, speech/rhetorical studies, theater arts/drama, (pre)veterinary studies, wind and percussion instruments.

WARNER PACIFIC COLLEGE

American studies, biblical studies, biological and physical sciences, biology, business administration, divinity/ministry, early childhood education, educa-

Warner Pacific College (continued)

tion, elementary education, English, exercise sciences, health science, history, individual/family development, (pre)law, liberal arts and studies, mathematics, (pre)medicine, middle school education, music, music business management and merchandising, music education, nursing, pastoral counseling, physical education, physical sciences, psychology, religious education, religious studies, science education, secondary education, social sciences, social work, theology, (pre)veterinary studies.

WARNER SOUTHERN COLLEGE
Accounting, biblical studies, biology, business administration, communications, elementary education, English, exercise sciences, general studies, history, music education, physical education, psychology, recreation and leisure studies, sacred music, science education, social science education, social sciences, social work, special education, sport/fitness administration, (pre)theology.

WESTERN BAPTIST COLLEGE
Accounting, biblical studies, business administration, community services, computer science, divinity/ministry, education, elementary education, English, finance, health science, humanities, interdisciplinary studies, (pre)law, liberal arts and studies, mathematics, music, music education, pastoral counseling, psychology, religious education, religious studies, secondary education, social sciences, sport/fitness administration, theology.

WESTMONT COLLEGE
Art, art education, biology, business economics, chemistry, communications, computer science, (pre)dentistry, elementary education, engineering physics, English, English education, exercise sciences, French, history, (pre)law, liberal arts and studies, mathematics, mathematics education, (pre)medicine, modern languages, music, music education, natural sciences, philosophy, physical education, physics, political science, psychology, religious studies, secondary education, social science education, social sciences, sociology, Spanish, theater arts/drama, (pre)veterinary studies.

WHEATON COLLEGE (IL)
Anthropology, archaeology, art, art education, art history, biblical languages/literatures, biblical studies, biology, business economics, chemistry, computer science, economics, elementary education, environmental science, fine/studio arts, French, geology, German, history, interdisciplinary studies, literature, mass communications, mathematics, music, music business management and merchandising, music education, music history, music (piano and organ performance), music (voice and choral/opera performance), philosophy, physical education, physics, political science, psychology, religious education, religious studies, sociology, Spanish, speech/rhetorical studies, stringed instruments, theater arts/drama, wind and percussion instruments.

WHITWORTH COLLEGE
Accounting, American studies, art, art education, art history, arts management, athletic training/sports medicine, biology, business administration, chemistry, computer science, (pre)dentistry, economics, elementary education, English, fine/studio arts, French, history, international business, international relations, journalism, (pre)law, mass communications, mathematics, (pre)medicine, music, music education, music (piano and organ performance), music (voice and choral/opera performance), nursing, peace and conflict studies, philosophy, physical education, physics, political science, psychology, religious studies, secondary education, sociology, Spanish, special education, speech/rhetorical studies, theater arts/drama, (pre)veterinary studies.

WILLIAMS BAPTIST COLLEGE
Art, art education, biology, business administration, (pre)dentistry, divinity/ministry, early childhood education, education, elementary education, English, fine/studio arts, history, (pre)law, liberal arts and studies, (pre)medicine, music, music education, pastoral counseling, physical education, psychology, religious education, religious studies, sacred music, secretarial science, theology.

WILLIAM TYNDALE COLLEGE
Biblical studies, business administration, early childhood education, English, history, liberal arts and studies, Middle Eastern studies, music, music (general performance), music (piano and organ performance), music (voice and choral/opera performance), pastoral counseling, psychology, religious education, sacred music, social sciences, theology.

Majors Index by Major

ACCOUNTING
Abilene Christian University, TX
Anderson University, IN
Asbury College, KY
Azusa Pacific University, CA
Bartlesville Wesleyan College, OK
Belhaven College, MS
Bethel College, IN
Bethel College, KS
Bethel College, MN
Biola University, CA
Bluffton College, OH
Calvin College, MI
Campbellsville University, KY
Campbell University, NC
Cedarville College, OH
College of the Ozarks, MO
Colorado Christian University, CO
Cornerstone College, MI
Dallas Baptist University, TX
Dordt College, IA
Eastern College, PA
Eastern Mennonite University, VA
Eastern Nazarene College, MA
East Texas Baptist University, TX
Erskine College, SC
Evangel University, MO
Fresno Pacific University, CA
Geneva College, PA
George Fox University, OR
Gordon College, MA
Goshen College, IN
Grace College, IN
Grand Canyon University, AZ
Greenville College, IL
Houghton College, NY
Huntington College, IN
Indiana Wesleyan University, IN
John Brown University, AR
Judson College, IL
King College, TN
Lee University, TN
LeTourneau University, TX
Malone College, OH
The Master's College and Seminary, CA
Messiah College, PA
MidAmerica Nazarene University, KS
Milligan College, TN
Montreat College, NC
Mount Vernon Nazarene College, OH
North Park University, IL
Northwestern College, IA
Northwestern College, MN
Northwest Nazarene College, ID
Nyack College, NY
Oklahoma Baptist University, OK

Oklahoma Christian University of Science and
 Arts, OK
Olivet Nazarene University, IL
Oral Roberts University, OK
Point Loma Nazarene University, CA
Redeemer College, ON
Roberts Wesleyan College, NY
Seattle Pacific University, WA
Simpson College and Graduate School, CA
Southern California College, CA
Southern Nazarene University, OK
Southern Wesleyan University, SC
Southwest Baptist University, MO
Spring Arbor College, MI
Sterling College, KS
Tabor College, KS
Taylor University, IN
Trevecca Nazarene University, TN
Trinity Christian College, IL
Trinity International University, IL
Union University, TN
University of Sioux Falls, SD
Warner Southern College, FL
Western Baptist College, OR
Whitworth College, WA

ACTUARIAL SCIENCE
The Master's College and Seminary, CA
Tabor College, KS

ADAPTED PHYSICAL EDUCATION
Messiah College, PA

ADULT/CONTINUING EDUCATION
Bethel College, MN
Biola University, CA
Colorado Christian University, CO
Cornerstone College, MI
Milligan College, TN
Southern Nazarene University, OK
Tabor College, KS

ADVERTISING
Abilene Christian University, TX
Campbell University, NC
Eastern Nazarene College, MA
Milligan College, TN
Oklahoma Baptist University, OK
Oklahoma Christian University of Science and
 Arts, OK

AEROSPACE ENGINEERING
Bethel College, IN
Eastern Nazarene College, MA

AGRIBUSINESS
Abilene Christian University, TX

AGRICULTURAL BUSINESS
College of the Ozarks, MO

Dordt College, IA
MidAmerica Nazarene University, KS
Tabor College, KS

AGRICULTURAL MECHANIZATION
College of the Ozarks, MO

AGRICULTURAL SCIENCES
Dordt College, IA
Eastern Mennonite University, VA

AGRONOMY/CROP SCIENCE
College of the Ozarks, MO

AIRCRAFT MECHANIC/AIRFRAME
College of the Ozarks, MO
LeTourneau University, TX

AIRCRAFT PILOT (PROFESSIONAL)
College of the Ozarks, MO
Cornerstone College, MI
LeTourneau University, TX

ALCOHOL/DRUG ABUSE
COUNSELING
Indiana Wesleyan University, IN

AMERICAN GOVERNMENT
The Master's College and Seminary, CA

AMERICAN STUDIES
Abilene Christian University, TX
Cedarville College, OH
Erskine College, SC
King College, TN
Montreat College, NC
Warner Pacific College, OR
Whitworth College, WA

ANIMAL SCIENCES
Abilene Christian University, TX
College of the Ozarks, MO
Dordt College, IA

ANTHROPOLOGY
Biola University, CA
Judson College, IL
North Park University, IL
Southern California College, CA
Wheaton College, IL

APPLIED ART
Azusa Pacific University, CA
Biola University, CA
Mount Vernon Nazarene College, OH
Oklahoma Baptist University, OK
University of Sioux Falls, SD

APPLIED MATHEMATICS
Asbury College, KY
Biola University, CA
California Baptist University, CA

Majors Index by Major

Oklahoma Baptist University, OK
Southern Nazarene University, OK
Taylor University, IN
Wheaton College, IL

BIBLICAL STUDIES

Abilene Christian University, TX
Anderson University, IN
Asbury College, KY
Azusa Pacific University, CA
Belhaven College, MS
Bethel College, IN
Bethel College, KS
Bethel College, MN
Biola University, CA
Bryan College, TN
California Baptist University, CA
Calvin College, MI
Campbellsville University, KY
Campbell University, NC
Cedarville College, OH
Colorado Christian University, CO
Cornerstone College, MI
Covenant College, GA
Dallas Baptist University, TX
Eastern College, PA
Eastern Mennonite University, VA
Erskine College, SC
Evangel University, MO
Fresno Pacific University, CA
Geneva College, PA
George Fox University, OR
Gordon College, MA
Goshen College, IN
Grace College, IN
Grand Canyon University, AZ
Hope International University, CA
Houghton College, NY
Huntington College, IN
Indiana Wesleyan University, IN
John Brown University, AR
Judson College, IL
King College, TN
Lee University, TN
LeTourneau University, TX
Malone College, OH
The Master's College and Seminary, CA
Messiah College, PA
Milligan College, TN
Montreat College, NC
Mount Vernon Nazarene College, OH
North Park University, IL
Northwest Christian College, OR
Northwest College, WA
Northwestern College, MN
Nyack College, NY
Oklahoma Baptist University, OK
Oklahoma Christian University of Science and
    Arts, OK
Olivet Nazarene University, IL
Oral Roberts University, OK
Point Loma Nazarene University, CA
Redeemer College, ON
Simpson College and Graduate School, CA
Southern California College, CA
Southern Nazarene University, OK
Tabor College, KS
Taylor University, IN
Trinity International University, IL

Trinity Western University, BC
Warner Pacific College, OR
Warner Southern College, FL
Western Baptist College, OR
Wheaton College, IL
William Tyndale College, MI

BILINGUAL/BICULTURAL EDUCATION

Biola University, CA
Calvin College, MI
Fresno Pacific University, CA
Goshen College, IN

BIOCHEMISTRY

Abilene Christian University, TX
Azusa Pacific University, CA
Bethel College, MN
Biola University, CA
Calvin College, MI
Campbell University, NC
Eastern College, PA
Eastern Mennonite University, VA
John Brown University, AR
Messiah College, PA
Mount Vernon Nazarene College, OH
Oklahoma Christian University of Science and
    Arts, OK
Olivet Nazarene University, IL
Oral Roberts University, OK
Point Loma Nazarene University, CA
Roberts Wesleyan College, NY
Spring Arbor College, MI

BIOENGINEERING

Eastern Nazarene College, MA
Oral Roberts University, OK

BIOLOGICAL AND PHYSICAL SCIENCES

Bartlesville Wesleyan College, OK
Bethel College, IN
Bethel College, KS
Calvin College, MI
Cedarville College, OH
Eastern Nazarene College, MA
Erskine College, SC
George Fox University, OR
Houghton College, NY
Huntington College, IN
Indiana Wesleyan University, IN
Judson College, IL
King College, TN
Lee University, TN
The Master's College and Seminary, CA
Milligan College, TN
Mount Vernon Nazarene College, OH
North Park University, IL
Northwest Nazarene College, ID
Oklahoma Baptist University, OK
Oklahoma Christian University of Science and
    Arts, OK
Olivet Nazarene University, IL
Redeemer College, ON
Roberts Wesleyan College, NY
Southern California College, CA
Southern Nazarene University, OK
Tabor College, KS
Trevecca Nazarene University, TN

Trinity Western University, BC
Union University, TN
Warner Pacific College, OR

BIOLOGY

Abilene Christian University, TX
Anderson University, IN
Asbury College, KY
Azusa Pacific University, CA
Bartlesville Wesleyan College, OK
Belhaven College, MS
Bethel College, IN
Bethel College, KS
Bethel College, MN
Biola University, CA
Bluffton College, OH
Bryan College, TN
California Baptist University, CA
Calvin College, MI
Campbellsville University, KY
Campbell University, NC
Cedarville College, OH
College of the Ozarks, MO
Colorado Christian University, CO
Cornerstone College, MI
Covenant College, GA
Dallas Baptist University, TX
Dordt College, IA
Eastern College, PA
Eastern Mennonite University, VA
Eastern Nazarene College, MA
East Texas Baptist University, TX
Erskine College, SC
Evangel University, MO
Fresno Pacific University, CA
Geneva College, PA
George Fox University, OR
Gordon College, MA
Goshen College, IN
Grace College, IN
Grand Canyon University, AZ
Greenville College, IL
Houghton College, NY
Huntington College, IN
Indiana Wesleyan University, IN
John Brown University, AR
Judson College, IL
King College, TN
The King's University College, AB
Lee University, TN
LeTourneau University, TX
Malone College, OH
The Master's College and Seminary, CA
Messiah College, PA
MidAmerica Nazarene University, KS
Milligan College, TN
Mount Vernon Nazarene College, OH
North Park University, IL
Northwestern College, IA
Northwestern College, MN
Northwest Nazarene College, ID
Oklahoma Baptist University, OK
Oklahoma Christian University of Science and
    Arts, OK
Olivet Nazarene University, IL
Oral Roberts University, OK
Palm Beach Atlantic College, FL
Point Loma Nazarene University, CA
Redeemer College, ON

Biology (continued)

Roberts Wesleyan College, NY
Seattle Pacific University, WA
Southern California College, CA
Southern Nazarene University, OK
Southern Wesleyan University, SC
Southwest Baptist University, MO
Spring Arbor College, MI
Sterling College, KS
Tabor College, KS
Taylor University, IN
Trevecca Nazarene University, TN
Trinity Christian College, IL
Trinity International University, IL
Trinity Western University, BC
Union University, TN
University of Sioux Falls, SD
Warner Pacific College, OR
Warner Southern College, FL
Westmont College, CA
Wheaton College, IL
Whitworth College, WA
Williams Baptist College, AR

BIOLOGY EDUCATION
Abilene Christian University, TX
East Texas Baptist University, TX
Greenville College, IL
King College, TN
Messiah College, PA
Northwest Nazarene College, ID
Oklahoma Baptist University, OK
Trevecca Nazarene University, TN
Trinity Christian College, IL

BIOMEDICAL SCIENCE
Oral Roberts University, OK

BIOMEDICAL TECHNOLOGY
Campbell University, NC

BRITISH LITERATURE
Point Loma Nazarene University, CA

BROADCAST JOURNALISM
Abilene Christian University, TX
Biola University, CA
Campbell University, NC
Cedarville College, OH
Colorado Christian University, CO
Cornerstone College, MI
Evangel University, MO
Geneva College, PA
Goshen College, IN
Huntington College, IN
John Brown University, AR
Malone College, OH
The Master's College and Seminary, CA
Milligan College, TN
Mount Vernon Nazarene College, OH
Oklahoma Baptist University, OK
Oklahoma Christian University of Science and
   Arts, OK
Olivet Nazarene University, IL
Oral Roberts University, OK
Trevecca Nazarene University, TN

BUSINESS
Anderson University, IN

Asbury College, KY
Colorado Christian University, CO
George Fox University, OR
King College, TN
Trinity Christian College, IL

BUSINESS ADMINISTRATION
Abilene Christian University, TX
Anderson University, IN
Azusa Pacific University, CA
Bartlesville Wesleyan College, OK
Belhaven College, MS
Bethel College, IN
Bethel College, KS
Bethel College, MN
Biola University, CA
Bluffton College, OH
Bryan College, TN
California Baptist University, CA
Calvin College, MI
Campbellsville University, KY
Campbell University, NC
Cedarville College, OH
College of the Ozarks, MO
Colorado Christian University, CO
Cornerstone College, MI
Covenant College, GA
Dallas Baptist University, TX
Dordt College, IA
Eastern College, PA
Eastern Mennonite University, VA
Eastern Nazarene College, MA
East Texas Baptist University, TX
Erskine College, SC
Evangel University, MO
Fresno Pacific University, CA
Geneva College, PA
George Fox University, OR
Gordon College, MA
Goshen College, IN
Grace College, IN
Grand Canyon University, AZ
Greenville College, IL
Hope International University, CA
Houghton College, NY
Huntington College, IN
Indiana Wesleyan University, IN
John Brown University, AR
Judson College, IL
King College, TN
The King's University College, AB
Lee University, TN
LeTourneau University, TX
Malone College, OH
The Master's College and Seminary, CA
Messiah College, PA
MidAmerica Nazarene University, KS
Milligan College, TN
Montreat College, NC
Mount Vernon Nazarene College, OH
North Park University, IL
Northwest Christian College, OR
Northwest College, WA
Northwestern College, IA
Northwestern College, MN
Northwest Nazarene College, ID
Nyack College, NY
Oklahoma Baptist University, OK

Oklahoma Christian University of Science and
   Arts, OK
Olivet Nazarene University, IL
Oral Roberts University, OK
Palm Beach Atlantic College, FL
Point Loma Nazarene University, CA
Redeemer College, ON
Roberts Wesleyan College, NY
Seattle Pacific University, WA
Simpson College and Graduate School, CA
Southern California College, CA
Southern Nazarene University, OK
Southern Wesleyan University, SC
Southwest Baptist University, MO
Spring Arbor College, MI
Sterling College, KS
Tabor College, KS
Taylor University, IN
Trevecca Nazarene University, TN
Trinity Christian College, IL
Trinity International University, IL
Trinity Western University, BC
Union University, TN
University of Sioux Falls, SD
Warner Pacific College, OR
Warner Southern College, FL
Western Baptist College, OR
Whitworth College, WA
Williams Baptist College, AR
William Tyndale College, MI

BUSINESS COMMUNICATIONS
Northwest Christian College, OR
Oklahoma Baptist University, OK
Point Loma Nazarene University, CA

BUSINESS COMPUTER PROGRAMMING
Oklahoma Baptist University, OK

BUSINESS ECONOMICS
Anderson University, IN
Biola University, CA
Bluffton College, OH
Calvin College, MI
Campbellsville University, KY
Campbell University, NC
Cedarville College, OH
Dallas Baptist University, TX
George Fox University, OR
Grand Canyon University, AZ
Huntington College, IN
King College, TN
Messiah College, PA
Milligan College, TN
Montreat College, NC
Olivet Nazarene University, IL
Seattle Pacific University, WA
Spring Arbor College, MI
Union University, TN
Westmont College, CA
Wheaton College, IL

BUSINESS EDUCATION
Abilene Christian University, TX
Bartlesville Wesleyan College, OK
Bethel College, IN
Bethel College, KS
Biola University, CA

Bluffton College, OH
Campbellsville University, KY
College of the Ozarks, MO
Cornerstone College, MI
Dordt College, IA
East Texas Baptist University, TX
Evangel University, MO
Fresno Pacific University, CA
Goshen College, IN
Grand Canyon University, AZ
Huntington College, IN
John Brown University, AR
Lee University, TN
MidAmerica Nazarene University, KS
Mount Vernon Nazarene College, OH
Northwestern College, IA
Oklahoma Baptist University, OK
Oklahoma Christian University of Science and
    Arts, OK
Oral Roberts University, OK
Southern Nazarene University, OK
Southwest Baptist University, MO
Tabor College, KS
Trinity Christian College, IL
Union University, TN

BUSINESS HOME ECONOMICS
Point Loma Nazarene University, CA

BUSINESS MACHINE REPAIR
Biola University, CA

BUSINESS MARKETING AND MARKETING MANAGEMENT
Abilene Christian University, TX
Anderson University, IN
Azusa Pacific University, CA
Biola University, CA
Campbellsville University, KY
Cedarville College, OH
College of the Ozarks, MO
Cornerstone College, MI
Dallas Baptist University, TX
Evangel University, MO
George Fox University, OR
Grand Canyon University, AZ
Greenville College, IL
Indiana Wesleyan University, IN
LeTourneau University, TX
Messiah College, PA
Montreat College, NC
Mount Vernon Nazarene College, OH
North Park University, IL
Northwest Christian College, OR
Northwestern College, MN
Northwest Nazarene College, ID
Oklahoma Baptist University, OK
Oklahoma Christian University of Science and
    Arts, OK
Olivet Nazarene University, IL
Oral Roberts University, OK
Palm Beach Atlantic College, FL
Southern California College, CA
Southern Nazarene University, OK
Tabor College, KS
Trevecca Nazarene University, TN
Trinity Christian College, IL
Trinity International University, IL

Union University, TN
University of Sioux Falls, SD

CARDIOVASCULAR TECHNOLOGY
Eastern College, PA

CERAMIC ARTS
Trinity Christian College, IL

CHEMICAL ENGINEERING
Bethel College, IN
Geneva College, PA
Oral Roberts University, OK

CHEMISTRY
Abilene Christian University, TX
Anderson University, IN
Asbury College, KY
Azusa Pacific University, CA
Bartlesville Wesleyan College, OK
Belhaven College, MS
Bethel College, IN
Bethel College, KS
Bethel College, MN
Biola University, CA
Bluffton College, OH
California Baptist University, CA
Calvin College, MI
Campbellsville University, KY
Campbell University, NC
Cedarville College, OH
College of the Ozarks, MO
Covenant College, GA
Dordt College, IA
Eastern College, PA
Eastern Mennonite University, VA
Eastern Nazarene College, MA
East Texas Baptist University, TX
Erskine College, SC
Evangel University, MO
Fresno Pacific University, CA
George Fox University, OR
Gordon College, MA
Goshen College, IN
Grand Canyon University, AZ
Greenville College, IL
Houghton College, NY
Huntington College, IN
Indiana Wesleyan University, IN
John Brown University, AR
Judson College, IL
King College, TN
The King's University College, AB
Lee University, TN
LeTourneau University, TX
Malone College, OH
Messiah College, PA
MidAmerica Nazarene University, KS
Milligan College, TN
Mount Vernon Nazarene College, OH
North Park University, IL
Northwestern College, IA
Northwest Nazarene College, ID
Oklahoma Baptist University, OK
Oklahoma Christian University of Science and
    Arts, OK
Olivet Nazarene University, IL
Oral Roberts University, OK
Point Loma Nazarene University, CA

Roberts Wesleyan College, NY
Seattle Pacific University, WA
Southern California College, CA
Southern Nazarene University, OK
Southern Wesleyan University, SC
Southwest Baptist University, MO
Spring Arbor College, MI
Tabor College, KS
Taylor University, IN
Trevecca Nazarene University, TN
Trinity Christian College, IL
Trinity International University, IL
Trinity Western University, BC
Union University, TN
University of Sioux Falls, SD
Westmont College, CA
Wheaton College, IL
Whitworth College, WA

CHEMISTRY EDUCATION
Abilene Christian University, TX
East Texas Baptist University, TX
Greenville College, IL
King College, TN
Messiah College, PA
Northwest Nazarene College, ID
Oklahoma Baptist University, OK
Trevecca Nazarene University, TN
Trinity Christian College, IL

CHILD CARE/DEVELOPMENT
Abilene Christian University, TX
Bethel College, MN
Bluffton College, OH
Campbell University, NC
College of the Ozarks, MO
Evangel University, MO
Goshen College, IN
Hope International University, CA
Montreat College, NC
Northwestern College, MN
Oklahoma Baptist University, OK
Oklahoma Christian University of Science and
    Arts, OK
Olivet Nazarene University, IL
Point Loma Nazarene University, CA
Southwest Baptist University, MO
Trevecca Nazarene University, TN

CHILD GUIDANCE
Oklahoma Baptist University, OK

CIVIL ENGINEERING
Bethel College, IN
Calvin College, MI
George Fox University, OR
Messiah College, PA

CLASSICS
Asbury College, KY
California Baptist University, CA
Calvin College, MI

CLINICAL PSYCHOLOGY
Eastern Nazarene College, MA
Redeemer College, ON

CLOTHING AND TEXTILES
Bluffton College, OH
Campbell University, NC
Olivet Nazarene University, IL

CLOTHING/APPAREL/TEXTILE STUDIES
Seattle Pacific University, WA

COGNITIVE PSYCHOLOGY AND PSYCHOLINGUISTICS
George Fox University, OR

COMMUNICATION DISORDERS
Northwest Christian College, OR

COMMUNICATIONS
Belhaven College, MS
Bethel College, KS
Colorado Christian University, CO
Eastern College, PA
Gordon College, MA
Indiana Wesleyan University, IN
Malone College, OH
Northwestern College, MN
Nyack College, NY
Point Loma Nazarene University, CA
Seattle Pacific University, WA
Simpson College and Graduate School, CA
Tabor College, KS
Trevecca Nazarene University, TN
Trinity Christian College, IL
Warner Southern College, FL
Westmont College, CA

COMMUNITY SERVICES
Eastern Mennonite University, VA
North Park University, IL
Oklahoma Christian University of Science and
    Arts, OK
Western Baptist College, OR

COMPUTER EDUCATION
Abilene Christian University, TX
East Texas Baptist University, TX

COMPUTER ENGINEERING
Eastern Nazarene College, MA
George Fox University, OR
LeTourneau University, TX
Oklahoma Christian University of Science and
    Arts, OK

COMPUTER ENGINEERING TECHNOLOGY
LeTourneau University, TX
Mount Vernon Nazarene College, OH

COMPUTER GRAPHICS
John Brown University, AR
Judson College, IL

COMPUTER/INFORMATION SCIENCES
Abilene Christian University, TX
Biola University, CA
Colorado Christian University, CO
Dallas Baptist University, TX
East Texas Baptist University, TX
Messiah College, PA
Northwestern College, MN
Oklahoma Baptist University, OK
Seattle Pacific University, WA

COMPUTER MANAGEMENT
Oklahoma Baptist University, OK

COMPUTER PROGRAMMING
Biola University, CA
Eastern Mennonite University, VA
Southern Nazarene University, OK
Taylor University, IN

COMPUTER SCIENCE
Abilene Christian University, TX
Anderson University, IN
Azusa Pacific University, CA
Belhaven College, MS
Bethel College, IN
Bethel College, KS
Bethel College, MN
Biola University, CA
Bluffton College, OH
Bryan College, TN
Calvin College, MI
Campbell University, NC
College of the Ozarks, MO
Covenant College, GA
Dallas Baptist University, TX
Dordt College, IA
Eastern Mennonite University, VA
Eastern Nazarene College, MA
Evangel University, MO
Geneva College, PA
George Fox University, OR
Gordon College, MA
Goshen College, IN
Greenville College, IL
Houghton College, NY
Huntington College, IN
Judson College, IL
LeTourneau University, TX
Malone College, OH
MidAmerica Nazarene University, KS
Milligan College, TN
Mount Vernon Nazarene College, OH
Northwestern College, IA
Northwest Nazarene College, ID
Oklahoma Baptist University, OK
Oklahoma Christian University of Science and
    Arts, OK
Olivet Nazarene University, IL
Oral Roberts University, OK
Point Loma Nazarene University, CA
Roberts Wesleyan College, NY
Southern Nazarene University, OK
Southwest Baptist University, MO
Spring Arbor College, MI
Sterling College, KS
Tabor College, KS
Taylor University, IN
Trinity Christian College, IL
Trinity International University, IL
Trinity Western University, BC
Union University, TN
University of Sioux Falls, SD
Western Baptist College, OR
Westmont College, CA
Wheaton College, IL
Whitworth College, WA

COMPUTER SYSTEMS ANALYSIS
Oklahoma Baptist University, OK

CONSTRUCTION ENGINEERING
John Brown University, AR

CONSTRUCTION MANAGEMENT
John Brown University, AR

CONSUMER SERVICES
College of the Ozarks, MO

CORRECTIONS
College of the Ozarks, MO

COUNSELING PSYCHOLOGY
Abilene Christian University, TX
Geneva College, PA

CREATIVE WRITING
Bethel College, MN
Eastern College, PA
Houghton College, NY
Indiana Wesleyan University, IN
Oklahoma Christian University of Science and
    Arts, OK
Taylor University, IN

CRIMINAL JUSTICE/LAW ENFORCEMENT ADMINISTRATION
Abilene Christian University, TX
Anderson University, IN
Bluffton College, OH
Calvin College, MI
Campbellsville University, KY
Campbell University, NC
Cedarville College, OH
College of the Ozarks, MO
Dallas Baptist University, TX
Dordt College, IA
Evangel University, MO
Grace College, IN
Grand Canyon University, AZ
MidAmerica Nazarene University, KS
Mount Vernon Nazarene College, OH
Olivet Nazarene University, IL
Roberts Wesleyan College, NY
Southern Nazarene University, OK
Southern Wesleyan University, SC

CRIMINAL JUSTICE STUDIES
Indiana Wesleyan University, IN
Judson College, IL
Northwestern College, MN

CRIMINOLOGY
College of the Ozarks, MO

CULTURAL STUDIES
Bethel College, MN

CURRICULUM AND INSTRUCTION
Indiana Wesleyan University, IN

DANCE
Belhaven College, MS

DATA PROCESSING TECHNOLOGY
Campbellsville University, KY
Campbell University, NC
Dordt College, IA
Eastern Mennonite University, VA
Mount Vernon Nazarene College, OH

DENTAL HYGIENE
Oral Roberts University, OK

(PRE)DENTISTRY
Abilene Christian University, TX

Anderson University, IN
Bartlesville Wesleyan College, OK
Belhaven College, MS
Bethel College, IN
Bethel College, KS
Bethel College, MN
California Baptist University, CA
Calvin College, MI
Campbellsville University, KY
Campbell University, NC
Cedarville College, OH
Cornerstone College, MI
Dordt College, IA
Eastern Mennonite University, VA
Eastern Nazarene College, MA
East Texas Baptist University, TX
Evangel University, MO
George Fox University, OR
Goshen College, IN
Grand Canyon University, AZ
Greenville College, IL
Houghton College, NY
Huntington College, IN
Indiana Wesleyan University, IN
King College, TN
LeTourneau University, TX
Messiah College, PA
Milligan College, TN
Montreat College, NC
Mount Vernon Nazarene College, OH
North Park University, IL
Northwest Nazarene College, ID
Oklahoma Baptist University, OK
Oklahoma Christian University of Science and
   Arts, OK
Olivet Nazarene University, IL
Oral Roberts University, OK
Redeemer College, ON
Roberts Wesleyan College, NY
Southern Nazarene University, OK
Tabor College, KS
Taylor University, IN
Trinity Christian College, IL
Trinity Western University, BC
Union University, TN
University of Sioux Falls, SD
Westmont College, CA
Whitworth College, WA
Williams Baptist College, AR

DEVELOPMENTAL/CHILD PSYCHOLOGY

Bluffton College, OH
Eastern Nazarene College, MA
Fresno Pacific University, CA
Oklahoma Baptist University, OK
Oklahoma Christian University of Science and
   Arts, OK
Olivet Nazarene University, IL
University of Sioux Falls, SD

DEVELOPMENT ECONOMICS

Eastern Mennonite University, VA

DIETETICS

Bluffton College, OH
College of the Ozarks, MO
Messiah College, PA

Olivet Nazarene University, IL
Point Loma Nazarene University, CA

DIVINITY/MINISTRY

Abilene Christian University, TX
Azusa Pacific University, CA
Bartlesville Wesleyan College, OK
Bethel College, IN
Bethel College, MN
Biola University, CA
Bluffton College, OH
Campbellsville University, KY
Campbell University, NC
Colorado Christian University, CO
Cornerstone College, MI
Eastern Mennonite University, VA
Eastern Nazarene College, MA
Fresno Pacific University, CA
George Fox University, OR
Gordon College, MA
Grace College, IN
Grand Canyon University, AZ
Greenville College, IL
Houghton College, NY
Huntington College, IN
Indiana Wesleyan University, IN
John Brown University, AR
LeTourneau University, TX
The Master's College and Seminary, CA
MidAmerica Nazarene University, KS
Milligan College, TN
North Park University, IL
Northwest College, WA
Northwest Nazarene College, ID
Oklahoma Baptist University, OK
Oklahoma Christian University of Science and
   Arts, OK
Oral Roberts University, OK
Roberts Wesleyan College, NY
Simpson College and Graduate School, CA
Southern Nazarene University, OK
Southern Wesleyan University, SC
Spring Arbor College, MI
Tabor College, KS
Trinity International University, IL
Warner Pacific College, OR
Western Baptist College, OR
Williams Baptist College, AR

DRAFTING

Abilene Christian University, TX
LeTourneau University, TX

DRAMA AND DANCE EDUCATION

Abilene Christian University, TX
East Texas Baptist University, TX
Greenville College, IL
Oklahoma Baptist University, OK

DRAMA THERAPY

Oral Roberts University, OK

DRAWING

Biola University, CA
Judson College, IL
Northwest Nazarene College, ID
Trinity Christian College, IL

EARLY CHILDHOOD EDUCATION

Bethel College, IN

Bethel College, KS
Bethel College, MN
Bluffton College, OH
Bryan College, TN
Cedarville College, OH
Cornerstone College, MI
Dallas Baptist University, TX
Eastern Mennonite University, VA
Eastern Nazarene College, MA
East Texas Baptist University, TX
Erskine College, SC
Evangel University, MO
Gordon College, MA
Goshen College, IN
Greenville College, IL
Hope International University, CA
John Brown University, AR
Judson College, IL
King College, TN
Malone College, OH
Messiah College, PA
MidAmerica Nazarene University, KS
Milligan College, TN
Mount Vernon Nazarene College, OH
North Park University, IL
Oklahoma Baptist University, OK
Oklahoma Christian University of Science and
   Arts, OK
Olivet Nazarene University, IL
Oral Roberts University, OK
Palm Beach Atlantic College, FL
Southern Nazarene University, OK
Southern Wesleyan University, SC
Southwest Baptist University, MO
Spring Arbor College, MI
Tabor College, KS
Taylor University, IN
Trevecca Nazarene University, TN
Union University, TN
University of Sioux Falls, SD
Warner Pacific College, OR
Williams Baptist College, AR
William Tyndale College, MI

EARTH SCIENCES

Olivet Nazarene University, IL

ECOLOGY

Montreat College, NC

ECONOMICS

Bethel College, IN
Bethel College, KS
Bethel College, MN
Biola University, CA
Bluffton College, OH
Calvin College, MI
Campbellsville University, KY
Campbell University, NC
Cedarville College, OH
Covenant College, GA
Eastern College, PA
Eastern Mennonite University, VA
George Fox University, OR
Gordon College, MA
Goshen College, IN
Grand Canyon University, AZ
Huntington College, IN
Indiana Wesleyan University, IN

Economic Hat *Economics (continued)*

King College, TN
Messiah College, PA
Montreat College, NC
North Park University, IL
Northwestern College, IA
Olivet Nazarene University, IL
Point Loma Nazarene University, CA
Southern Nazarene University, OK
Taylor University, IN
Trevecca Nazarene University, TN
Trinity International University, IL
Union University, TN
University of Sioux Falls, SD
Wheaton College, IL
Whitworth College, WA

EDUCATION
Anderson University, IN
Bartlesville Wesleyan College, OK
Bethel College, IN
Bethel College, KS
Bethel College, MN
Biola University, CA
Bluffton College, OH
Bryan College, TN
California Baptist University, CA
Calvin College, MI
Campbell University, NC
Cedarville College, OH
College of the Ozarks, MO
Cornerstone College, MI
Dallas Baptist University, TX
Dordt College, IA
Eastern Mennonite University, VA
Eastern Nazarene College, MA
Evangel University, MO
Fresno Pacific University, CA
George Fox University, OR
Gordon College, MA
Goshen College, IN
Greenville College, IL
Houghton College, NY
Huntington College, IN
Indiana Wesleyan University, IN
John Brown University, AR
Judson College, IL
King College, TN
The King's University College, AB
Lee University, TN
The Master's College and Seminary, CA
Milligan College, TN
Montreat College, NC
Mount Vernon Nazarene College, OH
North Park University, IL
Northwest College, WA
Northwestern College, IA
Oklahoma Baptist University, OK
Olivet Nazarene University, IL
Oral Roberts University, OK
Palm Beach Atlantic College, FL
Redeemer College, ON
Roberts Wesleyan College, NY
Simpson College and Graduate School, CA
Southern California College, CA
Southern Nazarene University, OK
Southern Wesleyan University, SC
Sterling College, KS

Tabor College, KS
Taylor University, IN
Trinity Christian College, IL
Trinity International University, IL
Trinity Western University, BC
Union University, TN
University of Sioux Falls, SD
Warner Pacific College, OR
Western Baptist College, OR
Williams Baptist College, AR

EDUCATION ADMINISTRATION
Campbell University, NC

EDUCATION (MULTIPLE LEVELS)
East Texas Baptist University, TX

EDUCATION OF THE EMOTIONALLY HANDICAPPED
Oklahoma Baptist University, OK
Trinity Christian College, IL

EDUCATION OF THE MENTALLY HANDICAPPED
Oklahoma Baptist University, OK
Trinity Christian College, IL

EDUCATION OF THE SPECIFIC LEARNING DISABLED
Malone College, OH
Oklahoma Baptist University, OK
Trinity Christian College, IL

ELECTRICAL/ELECTRONIC ENGINEERING TECHNOLOGY
LeTourneau University, TX

ELECTRICAL/ELECTRONICS ENGINEERING
Abilene Christian University, TX
Bethel College, IN
Calvin College, MI
Cedarville College, OH
Dordt College, IA
Eastern Nazarene College, MA
George Fox University, OR
John Brown University, AR
LeTourneau University, TX
Oklahoma Christian University of Science and
    Arts, OK
Oral Roberts University, OK
Seattle Pacific University, WA

ELEMENTARY EDUCATION
Abilene Christian University, TX
Anderson University, IN
Asbury College, KY
Bartlesville Wesleyan College, OK
Belhaven College, MS
Bethel College, IN
Bethel College, KS
Bethel College, MN
Biola University, CA
Bluffton College, OH
Bryan College, TN
California Baptist University, CA
Calvin College, MI
Campbellsville University, KY
Campbell University, NC
Cedarville College, OH

College of the Ozarks, MO
Colorado Christian University, CO
Cornerstone College, MI
Covenant College, GA
Dallas Baptist University, TX
Dordt College, IA
Eastern College, PA
Eastern Mennonite University, VA
Eastern Nazarene College, MA
East Texas Baptist University, TX
Erskine College, SC
Evangel University, MO
Fresno Pacific University, CA
Geneva College, PA
George Fox University, OR
Gordon College, MA
Goshen College, IN
Grace College, IN
Grand Canyon University, AZ
Greenville College, IL
Hope International University, CA
Houghton College, NY
Huntington College, IN
Indiana Wesleyan University, IN
John Brown University, AR
Judson College, IL
King College, TN
Lee University, TN
LeTourneau University, TX
Malone College, OH
The Master's College and Seminary, CA
Messiah College, PA
MidAmerica Nazarene University, KS
Milligan College, TN
Mount Vernon Nazarene College, OH
North Park University, IL
Northwest Christian College, OR
Northwest College, WA
Northwestern College, IA
Northwestern College, MN
Northwest Nazarene College, ID
Nyack College, NY
Oklahoma Baptist University, OK
Oklahoma Christian University of Science and
    Arts, OK
Olivet Nazarene University, IL
Oral Roberts University, OK
Palm Beach Atlantic College, FL
Redeemer College, ON
Roberts Wesleyan College, NY
Simpson College and Graduate School, CA
Southern Nazarene University, OK
Southern Wesleyan University, SC
Southwest Baptist University, MO
Spring Arbor College, MI
Sterling College, KS
Tabor College, KS
Taylor University, IN
Trevecca Nazarene University, TN
Trinity Christian College, IL
Trinity International University, IL
Trinity Western University, BC
Union University, TN
University of Sioux Falls, SD
Warner Pacific College, OR
Warner Southern College, FL
Western Baptist College, OR
Westmont College, CA

Wheaton College, IL
Whitworth College, WA
Williams Baptist College, AR

EMERGENCY MEDICAL TECHNOLOGY

Oklahoma Christian University of Science and Arts, OK
Southwest Baptist University, MO

ENGINEERING

Asbury College, KY
Calvin College, MI
Dordt College, IA
Geneva College, PA
George Fox University, OR
John Brown University, AR
LeTourneau University, TX
Messiah College, PA
Milligan College, TN
Oklahoma Christian University of Science and Arts, OK
Olivet Nazarene University, IL
Oral Roberts University, OK
Seattle Pacific University, WA
Southern Nazarene University, OK

(PRE)ENGINEERING

Anderson University, IN
Bethel College, MN
Campbell University, NC
Covenant College, GA
Eastern Mennonite University, VA
Montreat College, NC
Mount Vernon Nazarene College, OH
Tabor College, KS
University of Sioux Falls, SD

ENGINEERING DESIGN

LeTourneau University, TX

ENGINEERING/INDUSTRIAL MANAGEMENT

John Brown University, AR
Oral Roberts University, OK

ENGINEERING MECHANICS

Dordt College, IA

ENGINEERING PHYSICS

Abilene Christian University, TX
Eastern Nazarene College, MA
Northwest Nazarene College, ID
Oklahoma Christian University of Science and Arts, OK
Point Loma Nazarene University, CA
Taylor University, IN
Westmont College, CA

ENGINEERING SCIENCE

Abilene Christian University, TX
Belhaven College, MS
Bethel College, IN
George Fox University, OR
Oral Roberts University, OK

ENGINEERING TECHNOLOGY

John Brown University, AR
LeTourneau University, TX

ENGLISH

Abilene Christian University, TX

Anderson University, IN
Asbury College, KY
Azusa Pacific University, CA
Bartlesville Wesleyan College, OK
Belhaven College, MS
Bethel College, IN
Bethel College, KS
Bethel College, MN
Biola University, CA
Bluffton College, OH
Bryan College, TN
California Baptist University, CA
Calvin College, MI
Campbellsville University, KY
Campbell University, NC
Cedarville College, OH
College of the Ozarks, MO
Colorado Christian University, CO
Cornerstone College, MI
Covenant College, GA
Dallas Baptist University, TX
Dordt College, IA
Eastern College, PA
Eastern Mennonite University, VA
Eastern Nazarene College, MA
East Texas Baptist University, TX
Erskine College, SC
Evangel University, MO
Fresno Pacific University, CA
Geneva College, PA
George Fox University, OR
Gordon College, MA
Goshen College, IN
Grace College, IN
Grand Canyon University, AZ
Greenville College, IL
Houghton College, NY
Huntington College, IN
Indiana Wesleyan University, IN
John Brown University, AR
Judson College, IL
King College, TN
The King's University College, AB
Lee University, TN
LeTourneau University, TX
Malone College, OH
The Master's College and Seminary, CA
Messiah College, PA
MidAmerica Nazarene University, KS
Milligan College, TN
Montreat College, NC
Mount Vernon Nazarene College, OH
North Park University, IL
Northwest College, WA
Northwestern College, IA
Northwestern College, MN
Northwest Nazarene College, ID
Nyack College, NY
Oklahoma Baptist University, OK
Oklahoma Christian University of Science and Arts, OK
Olivet Nazarene University, IL
Oral Roberts University, OK
Palm Beach Atlantic College, FL
Redeemer College, ON
Roberts Wesleyan College, NY
Seattle Pacific University, WA
Simpson College and Graduate School, CA

Southern California College, CA
Southern Nazarene University, OK
Southern Wesleyan University, SC
Southwest Baptist University, MO
Spring Arbor College, MI
Sterling College, KS
Tabor College, KS
Taylor University, IN
Trevecca Nazarene University, TN
Trinity Christian College, IL
Trinity International University, IL
Trinity Western University, BC
Union University, TN
University of Sioux Falls, SD
Warner Pacific College, OR
Warner Southern College, FL
Western Baptist College, OR
Westmont College, CA
Whitworth College, WA
Williams Baptist College, AR
William Tyndale College, MI

ENGLISH COMPOSITION

Oklahoma Baptist University, OK

ENGLISH EDUCATION

Abilene Christian University, TX
Anderson University, IN
Colorado Christian University, CO
Eastern College, PA
East Texas Baptist University, TX
Greenville College, IL
Hope International University, CA
King College, TN
Messiah College, PA
Northwestern College, MN
Northwest Nazarene College, ID
Oklahoma Baptist University, OK
Seattle Pacific University, WA
Simpson College and Graduate School, CA
Trevecca Nazarene University, TN
Trinity Christian College, IL
Westmont College, CA

ENTREPRENEURSHIP

Trinity Christian College, IL

ENVIRONMENTAL BIOLOGY

Cedarville College, OH
Grand Canyon University, AZ
Greenville College, IL
The Master's College and Seminary, CA
Northwest College, WA
Tabor College, KS
Taylor University, IN
Trinity Western University, BC

ENVIRONMENTAL SCIENCE

Abilene Christian University, TX
Azusa Pacific University, CA
Bethel College, KS
Bethel College, MN
Calvin College, MI
Dordt College, IA
Eastern College, PA
Eastern Mennonite University, VA
Eastern Nazarene College, MA
John Brown University, AR
The King's University College, AB
Messiah College, PA

Environmental science (continued)

Montreat College, NC
Northwestern College, IA
Olivet Nazarene University, IL
Taylor University, IN
Wheaton College, IL

EUROPEAN STUDIES

Biola University, CA
Calvin College, MI
Seattle Pacific University, WA

EXERCISE SCIENCES

Abilene Christian University, TX
Bartlesville Wesleyan College, OK
Bluffton College, OH
Calvin College, MI
Campbell University, NC
Dordt College, IA
Gordon College, MA
Grand Canyon University, AZ
Huntington College, IN
Indiana Wesleyan University, IN
John Brown University, AR
Malone College, OH
Messiah College, PA
MidAmerica Nazarene University, KS
Milligan College, TN
North Park University, IL
Northwestern College, IA
Oklahoma Baptist University, OK
Oral Roberts University, OK
Redeemer College, ON
Seattle Pacific University, WA
Trevecca Nazarene University, TN
University of Sioux Falls, SD
Warner Pacific College, OR
Warner Southern College, FL
Westmont College, CA

EXPERIMENTAL PSYCHOLOGY

Redeemer College, ON

FAMILY/COMMUNITY STUDIES

Goshen College, IN
Messiah College, PA
Oklahoma Christian University of Science and
   Arts, OK
Olivet Nazarene University, IL

FAMILY/CONSUMER STUDIES

Abilene Christian University, TX
College of the Ozarks, MO

FAMILY STUDIES

Anderson University, IN
Point Loma Nazarene University, CA

FASHION DESIGN/ILLUSTRATION

Bluffton College, OH

FASHION MERCHANDISING

Abilene Christian University, TX
Bluffton College, OH
George Fox University, OR
Olivet Nazarene University, IL

FILM STUDIES

Biola University, CA

Calvin College, MI
Olivet Nazarene University, IL

FILM/VIDEO PRODUCTION

Southern California College, CA

FINANCE

Abilene Christian University, TX
Anderson University, IN
Bethel College, MN
Biola University, CA
Campbell University, NC
Cedarville College, OH
Dallas Baptist University, TX
Grand Canyon University, AZ
Indiana Wesleyan University, IN
The Master's College and Seminary, CA
North Park University, IL
Northwestern College, MN
Northwest Nazarene College, ID
Oklahoma Baptist University, OK
Olivet Nazarene University, IL
Oral Roberts University, OK
Palm Beach Atlantic College, FL
Southern California College, CA
Union University, TN
Western Baptist College, OR

FINANCIAL PLANNING

Trinity Christian College, IL

FINE/STUDIO ARTS

Abilene Christian University, TX
Anderson University, IN
Asbury College, KY
Bethel College, MN
Biola University, CA
Calvin College, MI
Campbell University, NC
College of the Ozarks, MO
Grand Canyon University, AZ
Indiana Wesleyan University, IN
Judson College, IL
King College, TN
North Park University, IL
Northwestern College, MN
Oklahoma Baptist University, OK
Oral Roberts University, OK
Roberts Wesleyan College, NY
Wheaton College, IL
Whitworth College, WA
Williams Baptist College, AR

FOOD PRODUCTS RETAILING

Campbell University, NC

FOOD SCIENCES

College of the Ozarks, MO
George Fox University, OR
Olivet Nazarene University, IL

FOREIGN LANGUAGES EDUCATION

Greenville College, IL

FOREIGN LANGUAGES/ LITERATURES

Gordon College, MA

FORENSIC TECHNOLOGY

College of the Ozarks, MO

FRENCH

Abilene Christian University, TX
Anderson University, IN
Asbury College, KY
Bethel College, IN
Calvin College, MI
Campbell University, NC
College of the Ozarks, MO
Eastern College, PA
Eastern Mennonite University, VA
Eastern Nazarene College, MA
Erskine College, SC
Gordon College, MA
Grace College, IN
Greenville College, IL
Houghton College, NY
King College, TN
Messiah College, PA
North Park University, IL
Northwestern College, IA
Oklahoma Baptist University, OK
Olivet Nazarene University, IL
Oral Roberts University, OK
Redeemer College, ON
Spring Arbor College, MI
Taylor University, IN
Union University, TN
Westmont College, CA
Wheaton College, IL
Whitworth College, WA

FRENCH LANGUAGE EDUCATION

Abilene Christian University, TX
Anderson University, IN
King College, TN
Messiah College, PA
Oklahoma Baptist University, OK

GENERAL STUDIES

Anderson University, IN
Hope International University, CA
Indiana Wesleyan University, IN
Northwest Christian College, OR
Nyack College, NY
Seattle Pacific University, WA
Simpson College and Graduate School, CA
Warner Southern College, FL

GEOGRAPHY

Calvin College, MI
Trinity Western University, BC

GEOLOGY

Abilene Christian University, TX
Calvin College, MI
Olivet Nazarene University, IL
Wheaton College, IL

GERMAN

Abilene Christian University, TX
Anderson University, IN
Bethel College, KS
Calvin College, MI
College of the Ozarks, MO
Dordt College, IA
Eastern Mennonite University, VA
Goshen College, IN
Grace College, IN
Messiah College, PA
Oklahoma Baptist University, OK

Oral Roberts University, OK
Wheaton College, IL

GERMAN LANGUAGE EDUCATION
Abilene Christian University, TX
Anderson University, IN
Oklahoma Baptist University, OK

GERONTOLOGY
Bethel College, IN
College of the Ozarks, MO

GRAPHIC DESIGN/COMMERCIAL ART/ILLUSTRATION
Abilene Christian University, TX
Anderson University, IN
Bethel College, IN
Biola University, CA
Bluffton College, OH
Campbell University, NC
College of the Ozarks, MO
Dordt College, IA
Grace College, IN
Grand Canyon University, AZ
Huntington College, IN
John Brown University, AR
Judson College, IL
Northwestern College, MN
Northwest Nazarene College, ID
Oklahoma Christian University of Science and Arts, OK
Olivet Nazarene University, IL
Oral Roberts University, OK
Point Loma Nazarene University, CA
Roberts Wesleyan College, NY
Southwest Baptist University, MO
Taylor University, IN
Trinity Christian College, IL
University of Sioux Falls, SD

GREEK (ANCIENT AND MEDIEVAL)
Asbury College, KY
Grace College, IN

GREEK (MODERN)
Abilene Christian University, TX
Calvin College, MI
Southern Wesleyan University, SC
Union University, TN

HEALTH EDUCATION
Abilene Christian University, TX
Anderson University, IN
Bethel College, IN
Bethel College, KS
Bethel College, MN
Bluffton College, OH
Campbellsville University, KY
Campbell University, NC
Cedarville College, OH
Eastern Mennonite University, VA
John Brown University, AR
Lee University, TN
MidAmerica Nazarene University, KS
Milligan College, TN
Oral Roberts University, OK
Southern Nazarene University, OK
Tabor College, KS
University of Sioux Falls, SD

HEALTH/PHYSICAL EDUCATION
Abilene Christian University, TX
Anderson University, IN
Eastern College, PA
Malone College, OH
Northwest Nazarene College, ID
Oklahoma Baptist University, OK
Point Loma Nazarene University, CA
Redeemer College, ON

HEALTH SCIENCE
Campbell University, NC
College of the Ozarks, MO
Covenant College, GA
Milligan College, TN
Mount Vernon Nazarene College, OH
Northwest College, WA
Southern Nazarene University, OK
Warner Pacific College, OR
Western Baptist College, OR

HEALTH SERVICES ADMINISTRATION
Dallas Baptist University, TX
Eastern College, PA
John Brown University, AR
Milligan College, TN
Oklahoma Baptist University, OK

HISPANIC-AMERICAN STUDIES
Goshen College, IN

HISTORY
Abilene Christian University, TX
Anderson University, IN
Asbury College, KY
Azusa Pacific University, CA
Bartlesville Wesleyan College, OK
Belhaven College, MS
Bethel College, IN
Bethel College, KS
Bethel College, MN
Biola University, CA
Bluffton College, OH
Bryan College, TN
California Baptist University, CA
Calvin College, MI
Campbellsville University, KY
Campbell University, NC
Cedarville College, OH
College of the Ozarks, MO
Colorado Christian University, CO
Cornerstone College, MI
Covenant College, GA
Dallas Baptist University, TX
Dordt College, IA
Eastern College, PA
Eastern Mennonite University, VA
Eastern Nazarene College, MA
East Texas Baptist University, TX
Erskine College, SC
Evangel University, MO
Fresno Pacific University, CA
Geneva College, PA
George Fox University, OR
Gordon College, MA
Goshen College, IN
Grand Canyon University, AZ
Greenville College, IL

Houghton College, NY
Huntington College, IN
Indiana Wesleyan University, IN
John Brown University, AR
Judson College, IL
King College, TN
The King's University College, AB
Lee University, TN
LeTourneau University, TX
Malone College, OH
The Master's College and Seminary, CA
Messiah College, PA
MidAmerica Nazarene University, KS
Milligan College, TN
Montreat College, NC
Mount Vernon Nazarene College, OH
North Park University, IL
Northwest Christian College, OR
Northwest College, WA
Northwestern College, IA
Northwestern College, MN
Northwest Nazarene College, ID
Nyack College, NY
Oklahoma Baptist University, OK
Oklahoma Christian University of Science and Arts, OK
Olivet Nazarene University, IL
Oral Roberts University, OK
Palm Beach Atlantic College, FL
Point Loma Nazarene University, CA
Redeemer College, ON
Roberts Wesleyan College, NY
Seattle Pacific University, WA
Simpson College and Graduate School, CA
Southern California College, CA
Southern Nazarene University, OK
Southern Wesleyan University, SC
Southwest Baptist University, MO
Spring Arbor College, MI
Sterling College, KS
Tabor College, KS
Taylor University, IN
Trevecca Nazarene University, TN
Trinity Christian College, IL
Trinity International University, IL
Trinity Western University, BC
Union University, TN
University of Sioux Falls, SD
Warner Pacific College, OR
Warner Southern College, FL
Westmont College, CA
Whitworth College, WA
Williams Baptist College, AR
William Tyndale College, MI

HISTORY EDUCATION
Abilene Christian University, TX
East Texas Baptist University, TX
King College, TN
Northwest Nazarene College, ID
Oklahoma Baptist University, OK
Trevecca Nazarene University, TN
Trinity Christian College, IL

HOME ECONOMICS
Abilene Christian University, TX
Bluffton College, OH
Campbell University, NC

Home economics (continued)

College of the Ozarks, MO
George Fox University, OR
The Master's College and Seminary, CA
Mount Vernon Nazarene College, OH
Olivet Nazarene University, IL
Point Loma Nazarene University, CA
Seattle Pacific University, WA

HOME ECONOMICS EDUCATION
Abilene Christian University, TX
Bluffton College, OH
Campbell University, NC
College of the Ozarks, MO
George Fox University, OR
Mount Vernon Nazarene College, OH
Olivet Nazarene University, IL

HORTICULTURE SCIENCE
College of the Ozarks, MO

HOTEL AND RESTAURANT MANAGEMENT
College of the Ozarks, MO

HUMAN ECOLOGY
Bethel College, KS

HUMANITIES
Belhaven College, MS
Biola University, CA
Bluffton College, OH
Calvin College, MI
Colorado Christian University, CO
Fresno Pacific University, CA
Houghton College, NY
Messiah College, PA
Milligan College, TN
Northwest Christian College, OR
Northwestern College, IA
Oklahoma Baptist University, OK
Oral Roberts University, OK
Redeemer College, ON
Roberts Wesleyan College, NY
Tabor College, KS
Trinity International University, IL
Trinity Western University, BC
University of Sioux Falls, SD
Western Baptist College, OR

HUMAN RESOURCES MANAGEMENT
Abilene Christian University, TX
Bethel College, IN
Colorado Christian University, CO
Fresno Pacific University, CA
Geneva College, PA
Grand Canyon University, AZ
Judson College, IL
Messiah College, PA
MidAmerica Nazarene University, KS
Northwestern College, MN
Oklahoma Baptist University, OK
Olivet Nazarene University, IL
Palm Beach Atlantic College, FL
Roberts Wesleyan College, NY
Simpson College and Graduate School, CA
Trinity Christian College, IL
Trinity International University, IL

HUMAN SERVICES
Judson College, IL
Milligan College, TN
Montreat College, NC
Mount Vernon Nazarene College, OH
Southwest Baptist University, MO
Trinity Western University, BC

INDIVIDUAL/FAMILY DEVELOPMENT
Abilene Christian University, TX
Hope International University, CA
Lee University, TN
Warner Pacific College, OR

INDUSTRIAL ARTS
College of the Ozarks, MO

INDUSTRIAL ARTS EDUCATION
Abilene Christian University, TX

INDUSTRIAL ENGINEERING
Eastern Nazarene College, MA

INDUSTRIAL RADIOLOGIC TECHNOLOGY
University of Sioux Falls, SD

INDUSTRIAL TECHNOLOGY
Abilene Christian University, TX

INFORMATION SCIENCES/ SYSTEMS
Bartlesville Wesleyan College, OK
Bethel College, IN
Biola University, CA
California Baptist University, CA
Campbellsville University, KY
Campbell University, NC
Cedarville College, OH
College of the Ozarks, MO
Colorado Christian University, CO
Cornerstone College, MI
Eastern Mennonite University, VA
George Fox University, OR
Goshen College, IN
Judson College, IL
Lee University, TN
Messiah College, PA
Oklahoma Baptist University, OK
Oklahoma Christian University of Science and Arts, OK
Olivet Nazarene University, IL
Palm Beach Atlantic College, FL
Southern Nazarene University, OK
Southwest Baptist University, MO
Taylor University, IN
Trevecca Nazarene University, TN
Trinity Christian College, IL
Trinity International University, IL
Union University, TN
University of Sioux Falls, SD

INTERDISCIPLINARY STUDIES
Abilene Christian University, TX
Bethel College, KS
Calvin College, MI
College of the Ozarks, MO
Cornerstone College, MI
Covenant College, GA
Dallas Baptist University, TX

George Fox University, OR
Hope International University, CA
John Brown University, AR
LeTourneau University, TX
Northwest Christian College, OR
Northwest College, WA
Nyack College, NY
Oklahoma Baptist University, OK
Olivet Nazarene University, IL
Southern California College, CA
Southwest Baptist University, MO
Tabor College, KS
Union University, TN
University of Sioux Falls, SD
Western Baptist College, OR
Wheaton College, IL

INTERIOR DESIGN
Abilene Christian University, TX
Bethel College, IN
George Fox University, OR
Oklahoma Christian University of Science and Arts, OK

INTERMEDIA
Eastern College, PA

INTERNATIONAL BUSINESS
Campbell University, NC
Cedarville College, OH
Eastern Mennonite University, VA
George Fox University, OR
Grand Canyon University, AZ
John Brown University, AR
Judson College, IL
King College, TN
Messiah College, PA
MidAmerica Nazarene University, KS
North Park University, IL
Northwestern College, MN
Northwest Nazarene College, ID
Oklahoma Baptist University, OK
Oral Roberts University, OK
Palm Beach Atlantic College, FL
Southern California College, CA
Taylor University, IN
Whitworth College, WA

INTERNATIONAL BUSINESS MARKETING
Oklahoma Baptist University, OK

INTERNATIONAL ECONOMICS
Cedarville College, OH
Taylor University, IN

INTERNATIONAL RELATIONS
Abilene Christian University, TX
Azusa Pacific University, CA
Bethel College, KS
Bethel College, MN
Biola University, CA
Campbell University, NC
Cedarville College, OH
George Fox University, OR
Gordon College, MA
Grand Canyon University, AZ
Houghton College, NY
John Brown University, AR
Lee University, TN

Malone College, OH
North Park University, IL
Northwest Nazarene College, ID
Southern Nazarene University, OK
Tabor College, KS
Taylor University, IN
Trinity Western University, BC
Whitworth College, WA

JAPANESE
Calvin College, MI

JOURNALISM
Abilene Christian University, TX
Asbury College, KY
Bethel College, IN
Biola University, CA
California Baptist University, CA
Calvin College, MI
Campbellsville University, KY
Campbell University, NC
College of the Ozarks, MO
Dordt College, IA
Eastern Nazarene College, MA
Evangel University, MO
Goshen College, IN
John Brown University, AR
Judson College, IL
Malone College, OH
Messiah College, PA
Milligan College, TN
Northwestern College, MN
Oklahoma Baptist University, OK
Oklahoma Christian University of Science and
    Arts, OK
Olivet Nazarene University, IL
Oral Roberts University, OK
Point Loma Nazarene University, CA
Southern Nazarene University, OK
Tabor College, KS
Union University, TN
Whitworth College, WA

LATIN (ANCIENT AND MEDIEVAL)
Asbury College, KY
Calvin College, MI

(PRE)LAW
Abilene Christian University, TX
Anderson University, IN
Azusa Pacific University, CA
Bartlesville Wesleyan College, OK
Belhaven College, MS
Bethel College, IN
Bethel College, KS
Bethel College, MN
Biola University, CA
Bluffton College, OH
Calvin College, MI
Campbellsville University, KY
Campbell University, NC
Cedarville College, OH
College of the Ozarks, MO
Cornerstone College, MI
Covenant College, GA
Eastern Nazarene College, MA
Evangel University, MO
Fresno Pacific University, CA
George Fox University, OR
Goshen College, IN

Grace College, IN
Grand Canyon University, AZ
Greenville College, IL
Houghton College, NY
Huntington College, IN
Indiana Wesleyan University, IN
John Brown University, AR
Judson College, IL
King College, TN
LeTourneau University, TX
Malone College, OH
Messiah College, PA
Montreat College, NC
Mount Vernon Nazarene College, OH
North Park University, IL
Northwest Nazarene College, ID
Oklahoma Baptist University, OK
Oklahoma Christian University of Science and
    Arts, OK
Olivet Nazarene University, IL
Oral Roberts University, OK
Palm Beach Atlantic College, FL
Redeemer College, ON
Southern Nazarene University, OK
Tabor College, KS
Taylor University, IN
Trinity Western University, BC
Union University, TN
University of Sioux Falls, SD
Warner Pacific College, OR
Western Baptist College, OR
Westmont College, CA
Whitworth College, WA
Williams Baptist College, AR

LAW AND LEGAL STUDIES
Milligan College, TN

LAW ENFORCEMENT/POLICE SCIENCE
College of the Ozarks, MO

LEGAL ADMINISTRATIVE ASSISTANT
Tabor College, KS

LIBERAL ARTS AND STUDIES
Abilene Christian University, TX
Azusa Pacific University, CA
Bartlesville Wesleyan College, OK
Bethel College, IN
Bethel College, MN
Biola University, CA
Bluffton College, OH
Bryan College, TN
California Baptist University, CA
Calvin College, MI
Campbell University, NC
Colorado Christian University, CO
Dallas Baptist University, TX
Eastern College, PA
Eastern Mennonite University, VA
Eastern Nazarene College, MA
East Texas Baptist University, TX
Fresno Pacific University, CA
George Fox University, OR
Goshen College, IN
Grand Canyon University, AZ
Greenville College, IL

John Brown University, AR
Malone College, OH
The Master's College and Seminary, CA
MidAmerica Nazarene University, KS
Milligan College, TN
Montreat College, NC
Mount Vernon Nazarene College, OH
Northwest College, WA
Northwestern College, MN
Northwest Nazarene College, ID
Nyack College, NY
Oklahoma Christian University of Science and
    Arts, OK
Olivet Nazarene University, IL
Oral Roberts University, OK
Point Loma Nazarene University, CA
Redeemer College, ON
Simpson College and Graduate School, CA
Southern Nazarene University, OK
Spring Arbor College, MI
Sterling College, KS
Trevecca Nazarene University, TN
Trinity International University, IL
Trinity Western University, BC
University of Sioux Falls, SD
Warner Pacific College, OR
Western Baptist College, OR
Westmont College, CA
Williams Baptist College, AR
William Tyndale College, MI

LINGUISTICS
Bartlesville Wesleyan College, OK
Calvin College, MI
Judson College, IL
Trinity Western University, BC

LITERATURE
Bethel College, MN
Biola University, CA
Bryan College, TN
Calvin College, MI
Eastern Nazarene College, MA
Fresno Pacific University, CA
George Fox University, OR
Grand Canyon University, AZ
Houghton College, NY
Judson College, IL
Montreat College, NC
Mount Vernon Nazarene College, OH
North Park University, IL
Olivet Nazarene University, IL
Oral Roberts University, OK
Southern Nazarene University, OK
Taylor University, IN
Wheaton College, IL

MANAGEMENT INFORMATION SYSTEMS/BUSINESS DATA PROCESSING
Anderson University, IN
Azusa Pacific University, CA
Bethel College, MN
Biola University, CA
Colorado Christian University, CO
Dallas Baptist University, TX
Dordt College, IA
George Fox University, OR
Grace College, IN

Management information systems/business data processing (continued)

Greenville College, IL
Judson College, IL
The Master's College and Seminary, CA
Montreat College, NC
Northwestern College, MN
Oklahoma Baptist University, OK
Oral Roberts University, OK
Point Loma Nazarene University, CA
Southern Nazarene University, OK
Taylor University, IN
Trinity Christian College, IL
University of Sioux Falls, SD

MARINE BIOLOGY
Oral Roberts University, OK
Union University, TN

MARRIAGE AND FAMILY COUNSELING
Oklahoma Baptist University, OK

MASS COMMUNICATIONS
Abilene Christian University, TX
Anderson University, IN
Azusa Pacific University, CA
Bartlesville Wesleyan College, OK
Bethel College, IN
Bethel College, KS
Bethel College, MN
Biola University, CA
Bluffton College, OH
Bryan College, TN
Calvin College, MI
Campbellsville University, KY
Campbell University, NC
Cedarville College, OH
College of the Ozarks, MO
Colorado Christian University, CO
Cornerstone College, MI
Dallas Baptist University, TX
Dordt College, IA
Eastern Nazarene College, MA
Evangel University, MO
Fresno Pacific University, CA
George Fox University, OR
Gordon College, MA
Goshen College, IN
Grace College, IN
Grand Canyon University, AZ
Greenville College, IL
Houghton College, NY
Huntington College, IN
Indiana Wesleyan University, IN
John Brown University, AR
Judson College, IL
Lee University, TN
The Master's College and Seminary, CA
MidAmerica Nazarene University, KS
Milligan College, TN
Montreat College, NC
Mount Vernon Nazarene College, OH
North Park University, IL
Northwest Christian College, OR
Northwestern College, IA
Oklahoma Baptist University, OK

Oklahoma Christian University of Science and Arts, OK
Olivet Nazarene University, IL
Oral Roberts University, OK
Point Loma Nazarene University, CA
Roberts Wesleyan College, NY
Southern California College, CA
Southern Nazarene University, OK
Southwest Baptist University, MO
Spring Arbor College, MI
Tabor College, KS
Taylor University, IN
Trevecca Nazarene University, TN
Trinity International University, IL
Trinity Western University, BC
Union University, TN
University of Sioux Falls, SD
Wheaton College, IL
Whitworth College, WA

MATHEMATICS
Abilene Christian University, TX
Anderson University, IN
Asbury College, KY
Azusa Pacific University, CA
Bartlesville Wesleyan College, OK
Belhaven College, MS
Bethel College, IN
Bethel College, KS
Bethel College, MN
Biola University, CA
Bluffton College, OH
Bryan College, TN
California Baptist University, CA
Calvin College, MI
Campbellsville University, KY
Campbell University, NC
Cedarville College, OH
College of the Ozarks, MO
Colorado Christian University, CO
Cornerstone College, MI
Dallas Baptist University, TX
Dordt College, IA
Eastern College, PA
Eastern Mennonite University, VA
Eastern Nazarene College, MA
East Texas Baptist University, TX
Erskine College, SC
Evangel University, MO
Fresno Pacific University, CA
George Fox University, OR
Gordon College, MA
Goshen College, IN
Grace College, IN
Grand Canyon University, AZ
Greenville College, IL
Houghton College, NY
Huntington College, IN
Indiana Wesleyan University, IN
John Brown University, AR
Judson College, IL
King College, TN
Lee University, TN
LeTourneau University, TX
Malone College, OH
The Master's College and Seminary, CA
Messiah College, PA
MidAmerica Nazarene University, KS
Milligan College, TN

Montreat College, NC
Mount Vernon Nazarene College, OH
North Park University, IL
Northwestern College, IA
Northwestern College, MN
Northwest Nazarene College, ID
Oklahoma Baptist University, OK
Oklahoma Christian University of Science and Arts, OK
Olivet Nazarene University, IL
Oral Roberts University, OK
Palm Beach Atlantic College, FL
Point Loma Nazarene University, CA
Redeemer College, ON
Roberts Wesleyan College, NY
Seattle Pacific University, WA
Simpson College and Graduate School, CA
Southern California College, CA
Southern Nazarene University, OK
Southern Wesleyan University, SC
Southwest Baptist University, MO
Spring Arbor College, MI
Sterling College, KS
Tabor College, KS
Taylor University, IN
Trevecca Nazarene University, TN
Trinity Christian College, IL
Trinity International University, IL
Trinity Western University, BC
Union University, TN
University of Sioux Falls, SD
Warner Pacific College, OR
Western Baptist College, OR
Westmont College, CA
Wheaton College, IL
Whitworth College, WA

MATHEMATICS/COMPUTER SCIENCE
Anderson University, IN
King College, TN

MATHEMATICS EDUCATION
Abilene Christian University, TX
Anderson University, IN
Bethel College, IN
Colorado Christian University, CO
East Texas Baptist University, TX
Geneva College, PA
Greenville College, IL
King College, TN
Messiah College, PA
Northwestern College, MN
Northwest Nazarene College, ID
Oklahoma Baptist University, OK
Seattle Pacific University, WA
Trevecca Nazarene University, TN
Trinity Christian College, IL
Westmont College, CA

MECHANICAL DESIGN TECHNOLOGY
LeTourneau University, TX

MECHANICAL ENGINEERING
Bethel College, IN
Calvin College, MI
Cedarville College, OH
Eastern Nazarene College, MA

John Brown University, AR
LeTourneau University, TX
Oklahoma Christian University of Science and Arts, OK
Oral Roberts University, OK

MECHANICAL ENGINEERING TECHNOLOGY
LeTourneau University, TX

MEDICAL ADMINISTRATIVE ASSISTANT
Tabor College, KS

MEDICAL LABORATORY TECHNICIAN
Milligan College, TN

MEDICAL LABORATORY TECHNOLOGIES
Evangel University, MO

MEDICAL TECHNOLOGY
Anderson University, IN
Asbury College, KY
Bluffton College, OH
Calvin College, MI
Campbellsville University, KY
Campbell University, NC
Cedarville College, OH
College of the Ozarks, MO
Dordt College, IA
Eastern Mennonite University, VA
East Texas Baptist University, TX
Erskine College, SC
Evangel University, MO
Houghton College, NY
Indiana Wesleyan University, IN
John Brown University, AR
King College, TN
Lee University, TN
Malone College, OH
Messiah College, PA
Mount Vernon Nazarene College, OH
North Park University, IL
Northwestern College, IA
Oklahoma Christian University of Science and Arts, OK
Olivet Nazarene University, IL
Oral Roberts University, OK
Roberts Wesleyan College, NY
Southern Wesleyan University, SC
Southwest Baptist University, MO
Tabor College, KS
Taylor University, IN
Trevecca Nazarene University, TN
Union University, TN
University of Sioux Falls, SD

(PRE)MEDICINE
Abilene Christian University, TX
Anderson University, IN
Bartlesville Wesleyan College, OK
Belhaven College, MS
Bethel College, IN
Bethel College, KS
Bethel College, MN
Biola University, CA
Bluffton College, OH
Bryan College, TN

Calvin College, MI
Campbellsville University, KY
Campbell University, NC
Cedarville College, OH
College of the Ozarks, MO
Cornerstone College, MI
Covenant College, GA
Dordt College, IA
Eastern Mennonite University, VA
Eastern Nazarene College, MA
East Texas Baptist University, TX
Evangel University, MO
Fresno Pacific University, CA
George Fox University, OR
Goshen College, IN
Grace College, IN
Grand Canyon University, AZ
Greenville College, IL
Houghton College, NY
Huntington College, IN
Indiana Wesleyan University, IN
John Brown University, AR
Judson College, IL
King College, TN
LeTourneau University, TX
The Master's College and Seminary, CA
Messiah College, PA
Milligan College, TN
Montreat College, NC
Mount Vernon Nazarene College, OH
North Park University, IL
Northwest Christian College, OR
Northwest Nazarene College, ID
Oklahoma Baptist University, OK
Oklahoma Christian University of Science and Arts, OK
Olivet Nazarene University, IL
Oral Roberts University, OK
Palm Beach Atlantic College, FL
Redeemer College, ON
Southern Nazarene University, OK
Tabor College, KS
Taylor University, IN
Trinity Christian College, IL
Trinity International University, IL
Trinity Western University, BC
Union University, TN
University of Sioux Falls, SD
Warner Pacific College, OR
Westmont College, CA
Whitworth College, WA
Williams Baptist College, AR

MENTAL HEALTH/ REHABILITATION
Evangel University, MO

METALLURGICAL ENGINEERING
Bethel College, IN

MIDDLE EASTERN STUDIES
William Tyndale College, MI

MIDDLE SCHOOL EDUCATION
Asbury College, KY
Biola University, CA
Bryan College, TN
Campbell University, NC
College of the Ozarks, MO

Eastern Mennonite University, VA
Eastern Nazarene College, MA
Gordon College, MA
Indiana Wesleyan University, IN
John Brown University, AR
King College, TN
The Master's College and Seminary, CA
MidAmerica Nazarene University, KS
Northwest College, WA
Oklahoma Christian University of Science and Arts, OK
Southwest Baptist University, MO
Taylor University, IN
Trinity Christian College, IL
University of Sioux Falls, SD
Warner Pacific College, OR

MISSIONARY STUDIES
Abilene Christian University, TX
Asbury College, KY
Hope International University, CA
Northwest Christian College, OR
Northwestern College, MN
Northwest Nazarene College, ID
Nyack College, NY
Oklahoma Baptist University, OK
Simpson College and Graduate School, CA

MODERN LANGUAGES
Biola University, CA
Gordon College, MA
Greenville College, IL
King College, TN
Lee University, TN
MidAmerica Nazarene University, KS
Mount Vernon Nazarene College, OH
North Park University, IL
Northwest Christian College, OR
Olivet Nazarene University, IL
Oral Roberts University, OK
Redeemer College, ON
Southern Nazarene University, OK
Westmont College, CA

MOLECULAR BIOLOGY
Bethel College, MN

MORTUARY SCIENCE
Milligan College, TN

MUSIC
Abilene Christian University, TX
Asbury College, KY
Azusa Pacific University, CA
Bartlesville Wesleyan College, OK
Belhaven College, MS
Bethel College, IN
Bethel College, KS
Bethel College, MN
Biola University, CA
Bluffton College, OH
Bryan College, TN
California Baptist University, CA
Calvin College, MI
Campbellsville University, KY
Campbell University, NC
Cedarville College, OH
College of the Ozarks, MO
Colorado Christian University, CO
Cornerstone College, MI

Music (continued)

Covenant College, GA
Dallas Baptist University, TX
Dordt College, IA
Eastern College, PA
Eastern Mennonite University, VA
Eastern Nazarene College, MA
East Texas Baptist University, TX
Erskine College, SC
Evangel University, MO
Fresno Pacific University, CA
Geneva College, PA
George Fox University, OR
Gordon College, MA
Goshen College, IN
Grace College, IN
Grand Canyon University, AZ
Greenville College, IL
Houghton College, NY
Huntington College, IN
Indiana Wesleyan University, IN
John Brown University, AR
Judson College, IL
King College, TN
The King's University College, AB
Lee University, TN
Malone College, OH
The Master's College and Seminary, CA
Messiah College, PA
MidAmerica Nazarene University, KS
Milligan College, TN
Montreat College, NC
Mount Vernon Nazarene College, OH
North Park University, IL
Northwest Christian College, OR
Northwest College, WA
Northwestern College, IA
Northwest Nazarene College, ID
Nyack College, NY
Oklahoma Baptist University, OK
Oklahoma Christian University of Science and
    Arts, OK
Olivet Nazarene University, IL
Oral Roberts University, OK
Palm Beach Atlantic College, FL
Point Loma Nazarene University, CA
Redeemer College, ON
Roberts Wesleyan College, NY
Seattle Pacific University, WA
Simpson College and Graduate School, CA
Southern California College, CA
Southern Nazarene University, OK
Southern Wesleyan University, SC
Southwest Baptist University, MO
Spring Arbor College, MI
Sterling College, KS
Tabor College, KS
Taylor University, IN
Trevecca Nazarene University, TN
Trinity Christian College, IL
Trinity International University, IL
Trinity Western University, BC
Union University, TN
University of Sioux Falls, SD
Warner Pacific College, OR
Western Baptist College, OR
Westmont College, CA

Wheaton College, IL
Whitworth College, WA
Williams Baptist College, AR
William Tyndale College, MI

MUSICAL INSTRUMENT TECHNOLOGY
Malone College, OH

MUSIC BUSINESS MANAGEMENT AND MERCHANDISING
Anderson University, IN
Bryan College, TN
Erskine College, SC
Geneva College, PA
Grand Canyon University, AZ
The Master's College and Seminary, CA
Montreat College, NC
North Park University, IL
Point Loma Nazarene University, CA
Southern Nazarene University, OK
Tabor College, KS
Taylor University, IN
Trevecca Nazarene University, TN
University of Sioux Falls, SD
Warner Pacific College, OR
Wheaton College, IL

MUSIC EDUCATION
Abilene Christian University, TX
Anderson University, IN
Asbury College, KY
Bethel College, IN
Bethel College, KS
Bethel College, MN
Biola University, CA
Bluffton College, OH
Bryan College, TN
Calvin College, MI
Campbellsville University, KY
Campbell University, NC
Cedarville College, OH
College of the Ozarks, MO
Colorado Christian University, CO
Cornerstone College, MI
Dallas Baptist University, TX
Dordt College, IA
Eastern Mennonite University, VA
Eastern Nazarene College, MA
East Texas Baptist University, TX
Erskine College, SC
Evangel University, MO
Fresno Pacific University, CA
Geneva College, PA
George Fox University, OR
Gordon College, MA
Goshen College, IN
Grace College, IN
Grand Canyon University, AZ
Greenville College, IL
Hope International University, CA
Houghton College, NY
Huntington College, IN
Indiana Wesleyan University, IN
John Brown University, AR
Judson College, IL
Lee University, TN
Malone College, OH
The Master's College and Seminary, CA

Messiah College, PA
MidAmerica Nazarene University, KS
Milligan College, TN
Montreat College, NC
Mount Vernon Nazarene College, OH
North Park University, IL
Northwest College, WA
Northwestern College, IA
Northwestern College, MN
Northwest Nazarene College, ID
Nyack College, NY
Oklahoma Baptist University, OK
Oklahoma Christian University of Science and
    Arts, OK
Olivet Nazarene University, IL
Oral Roberts University, OK
Palm Beach Atlantic College, FL
Roberts Wesleyan College, NY
Seattle Pacific University, WA
Simpson College and Graduate School, CA
Southern Nazarene University, OK
Southern Wesleyan University, SC
Southwest Baptist University, MO
Sterling College, KS
Tabor College, KS
Taylor University, IN
Trevecca Nazarene University, TN
Trinity Christian College, IL
Trinity International University, IL
Union University, TN
University of Sioux Falls, SD
Warner Pacific College, OR
Warner Southern College, FL
Western Baptist College, OR
Westmont College, CA
Wheaton College, IL
Whitworth College, WA
Williams Baptist College, AR

MUSIC (GENERAL PERFORMANCE)
Anderson University, IN
Bartlesville Wesleyan College, OK
Colorado Christian University, CO
Geneva College, PA
Gordon College, MA
Northwestern College, MN
Northwest Nazarene College, ID
Trinity Christian College, IL
William Tyndale College, MI

MUSIC HISTORY
Calvin College, MI
Wheaton College, IL

MUSIC (PIANO AND ORGAN PERFORMANCE)
Abilene Christian University, TX
Bethel College, IN
Biola University, CA
Bryan College, TN
Campbellsville University, KY
Campbell University, NC
Cedarville College, OH
Dallas Baptist University, TX
Erskine College, SC
Grace College, IN
Grand Canyon University, AZ
Houghton College, NY
Huntington College, IN

John Brown University, AR
Lee University, TN
The Master's College and Seminary, CA
Milligan College, TN
Montreat College, NC
Mount Vernon Nazarene College, OH
Northwest College, WA
Nyack College, NY
Oklahoma Baptist University, OK
Olivet Nazarene University, IL
Oral Roberts University, OK
Roberts Wesleyan College, NY
Southern Nazarene University, OK
Tabor College, KS
Taylor University, IN
Trinity Christian College, IL
Union University, TN
University of Sioux Falls, SD
Wheaton College, IL
Whitworth College, WA
William Tyndale College, MI

MUSIC THEORY AND COMPOSITION

Northwest Nazarene College, ID
Nyack College, NY
Oklahoma Baptist University, OK

MUSIC (VOICE AND CHORAL/ OPERA PERFORMANCE)

Abilene Christian University, TX
Bethel College, IN
Biola University, CA
Bryan College, TN
Calvin College, MI
Campbellsville University, KY
Campbell University, NC
Cedarville College, OH
Colorado Christian University, CO
Dallas Baptist University, TX
East Texas Baptist University, TX
Erskine College, SC
Grand Canyon University, AZ
Houghton College, NY
Huntington College, IN
John Brown University, AR
Judson College, IL
Lee University, TN
The Master's College and Seminary, CA
MidAmerica Nazarene University, KS
Milligan College, TN
Montreat College, NC
Mount Vernon Nazarene College, OH
North Park University, IL
Northwest College, WA
Nyack College, NY
Oklahoma Baptist University, OK
Oklahoma Christian University of Science and Arts, OK
Olivet Nazarene University, IL
Oral Roberts University, OK
Palm Beach Atlantic College, FL
Roberts Wesleyan College, NY
Southern Nazarene University, OK
Tabor College, KS
Taylor University, IN
Trinity Christian College, IL
Union University, TN
University of Sioux Falls, SD

Wheaton College, IL
Whitworth College, WA
William Tyndale College, MI

NATURAL RESOURCES MANAGEMENT

Huntington College, IN
Mount Vernon Nazarene College, OH

NATURAL SCIENCES

Bartlesville Wesleyan College, OK
Bethel College, KS
Calvin College, MI
Campbell University, NC
Covenant College, GA
Dordt College, IA
Erskine College, SC
Fresno Pacific University, CA
Goshen College, IN
Houghton College, NY
Lee University, TN
LeTourneau University, TX
The Master's College and Seminary, CA
North Park University, IL
Oklahoma Baptist University, OK
Olivet Nazarene University, IL
Oral Roberts University, OK
Redeemer College, ON
Roberts Wesleyan College, NY
Southern Nazarene University, OK
Sterling College, KS
Tabor College, KS
Taylor University, IN
Trinity Western University, BC
Westmont College, CA

NONPROFIT/PUBLIC MANAGEMENT

Nyack College, NY

NURSING

Abilene Christian University, TX
Anderson University, IN
Asbury College, KY
Azusa Pacific University, CA
Bartlesville Wesleyan College, OK
Bethel College, IN
Bethel College, KS
Bethel College, MN
Biola University, CA
Cedarville College, OH
College of the Ozarks, MO
Covenant College, GA
Eastern College, PA
Eastern Mennonite University, VA
East Texas Baptist University, TX
Goshen College, IN
Grand Canyon University, AZ
Indiana Wesleyan University, IN
Judson College, IL
Messiah College, PA
MidAmerica Nazarene University, KS
Milligan College, TN
Mount Vernon Nazarene College, OH
North Park University, IL
Oklahoma Baptist University, OK
Olivet Nazarene University, IL
Oral Roberts University, OK
Point Loma Nazarene University, CA

Roberts Wesleyan College, NY
Seattle Pacific University, WA
Southern Nazarene University, OK
Southern Wesleyan University, SC
Southwest Baptist University, MO
Trinity Christian College, IL
Trinity Western University, BC
Union University, TN
Warner Pacific College, OR
Whitworth College, WA

NUTRITION SCIENCE

Abilene Christian University, TX
Bluffton College, OH
College of the Ozarks, MO
The Master's College and Seminary, CA

NUTRITION STUDIES

Seattle Pacific University, WA

OCCUPATIONAL THERAPY

Calvin College, MI

OFFICE MANAGEMENT

Northwestern College, MN

OPHTHALMIC/OPTOMETRIC SERVICES

Oral Roberts University, OK

ORGANIZATIONAL BEHAVIOR

Northwestern College, MN

ORGANIZATIONAL PSYCHOLOGY

Abilene Christian University, TX
Point Loma Nazarene University, CA

PAINTING

Trinity Christian College, IL

PARALEGAL/LEGAL ASSISTANT

East Texas Baptist University, TX
Milligan College, TN

PASTORAL COUNSELING

Bethel College, IN
Biola University, CA
Campbellsville University, KY
Campbell University, NC
Cedarville College, OH
Colorado Christian University, CO
Cornerstone College, MI
Dallas Baptist University, TX
Eastern Mennonite University, VA
Eastern Nazarene College, MA
East Texas Baptist University, TX
Fresno Pacific University, CA
Greenville College, IL
Houghton College, NY
Indiana Wesleyan University, IN
John Brown University, AR
Lee University, TN
Malone College, OH
The Master's College and Seminary, CA
Milligan College, TN
Northwest Christian College, OR
Northwest College, WA
Northwestern College, MN
Northwest Nazarene College, ID
Nyack College, NY
Oklahoma Baptist University, OK

Pastoral counseling (continued)

Oklahoma Christian University of Science and
    Arts, OK
Oral Roberts University, OK
Redeemer College, ON
Simpson College and Graduate School, CA
Southern California College, CA
Southern Nazarene University, OK
Tabor College, KS
University of Sioux Falls, SD
Warner Pacific College, OR
Western Baptist College, OR
Williams Baptist College, AR
William Tyndale College, MI

PEACE AND CONFLICT STUDIES
Bethel College, KS
Bluffton College, OH
Whitworth College, WA

PHARMACY
Campbell University, NC
College of the Ozarks, MO
Eastern Nazarene College, MA

(PRE)PHARMACY STUDIES
Abilene Christian University, TX
King College, TN
Oklahoma Baptist University, OK

PHILOSOPHY
Anderson University, IN
Asbury College, KY
Azusa Pacific University, CA
Belhaven College, MS
Bethel College, IN
Bethel College, MN
Biola University, CA
Bluffton College, OH
California Baptist University, CA
Calvin College, MI
Campbell University, NC
Cedarville College, OH
College of the Ozarks, MO
Covenant College, GA
Dallas Baptist University, TX
Dordt College, IA
Eastern College, PA
Geneva College, PA
Gordon College, MA
Greenville College, IL
Houghton College, NY
Huntington College, IN
Indiana Wesleyan University, IN
Judson College, IL
The King's University College, AB
Messiah College, PA
Mount Vernon Nazarene College, OH
North Park University, IL
Northwest College, WA
Northwestern College, IA
Northwest Nazarene College, ID
Nyack College, NY
Oklahoma Baptist University, OK
Olivet Nazarene University, IL
Palm Beach Atlantic College, FL
Point Loma Nazarene University, CA
Redeemer College, ON
Seattle Pacific University, WA

Southern Nazarene University, OK
Spring Arbor College, MI
Sterling College, KS
Tabor College, KS
Taylor University, IN
Trinity Christian College, IL
Trinity International University, IL
Trinity Western University, BC
Union University, TN
University of Sioux Falls, SD
Westmont College, CA
Wheaton College, IL
Whitworth College, WA

PHOTOGRAPHY
Trinity Christian College, IL

PHYSICAL EDUCATION
Abilene Christian University, TX
Anderson University, IN
Asbury College, KY
Azusa Pacific University, CA
Bartlesville Wesleyan College, OK
Bethel College, IN
Bethel College, KS
Bethel College, MN
Biola University, CA
Bluffton College, OH
Bryan College, TN
California Baptist University, CA
Campbellsville University, KY
Campbell University, NC
Cedarville College, OH
College of the Ozarks, MO
Cornerstone College, MI
Dallas Baptist University, TX
Dordt College, IA
Eastern Mennonite University, VA
Eastern Nazarene College, MA
East Texas Baptist University, TX
Erskine College, SC
Evangel University, MO
Fresno Pacific University, CA
George Fox University, OR
Goshen College, IN
Grace College, IN
Grand Canyon University, AZ
Greenville College, IL
Houghton College, NY
Huntington College, IN
Indiana Wesleyan University, IN
John Brown University, AR
Judson College, IL
Lee University, TN
LeTourneau University, TX
Malone College, OH
The Master's College and Seminary, CA
Messiah College, PA
MidAmerica Nazarene University, KS
Milligan College, TN
Montreat College, NC
Mount Vernon Nazarene College, OH
North Park University, IL
Northwestern College, IA
Northwestern College, MN
Northwest Nazarene College, ID
Oklahoma Baptist University, OK

Oklahoma Christian University of Science and
    Arts, OK
Olivet Nazarene University, IL
Oral Roberts University, OK
Palm Beach Atlantic College, FL
Seattle Pacific University, WA
Southern California College, CA
Southern Nazarene University, OK
Southern Wesleyan University, SC
Southwest Baptist University, MO
Spring Arbor College, MI
Sterling College, KS
Tabor College, KS
Taylor University, IN
Trevecca Nazarene University, TN
Trinity Christian College, IL
Trinity International University, IL
Trinity Western University, BC
Union University, TN
University of Sioux Falls, SD
Warner Pacific College, OR
Warner Southern College, FL
Westmont College, CA
Wheaton College, IL
Whitworth College, WA
Williams Baptist College, AR

PHYSICAL SCIENCES
Asbury College, KY
Biola University, CA
California Baptist University, CA
Calvin College, MI
Goshen College, IN
Grand Canyon University, AZ
Houghton College, NY
Judson College, IL
The Master's College and Seminary, CA
Oklahoma Baptist University, OK
Olivet Nazarene University, IL
Roberts Wesleyan College, NY
Warner Pacific College, OR

PHYSICAL THERAPY
Bartlesville Wesleyan College, OK
Campbell University, NC
Eastern Nazarene College, MA
Hope International University, CA
Northwest Nazarene College, ID
Oral Roberts University, OK
Southern California College, CA

PHYSICIAN ASSISTANT
Campbell University, NC
Trevecca Nazarene University, TN

PHYSICS
Abilene Christian University, TX
Anderson University, IN
Azusa Pacific University, CA
Bethel College, KS
Bethel College, MN
Biola University, CA
Bluffton College, OH
California Baptist University, CA
Calvin College, MI
Campbellsville University, KY
Dordt College, IA
Eastern Nazarene College, MA
Erskine College, SC
Geneva College, PA

Gordon College, MA
Goshen College, IN
Greenville College, IL
Houghton College, NY
LeTourneau University, TX
Messiah College, PA
MidAmerica Nazarene University, KS
North Park University, IL
Northwest Nazarene College, ID
Oklahoma Baptist University, OK
Oral Roberts University, OK
Point Loma Nazarene University, CA
Roberts Wesleyan College, NY
Seattle Pacific University, WA
Southern Nazarene University, OK
Spring Arbor College, MI
Taylor University, IN
Trevecca Nazarene University, TN
Westmont College, CA
Wheaton College, IL
Whitworth College, WA

PHYSICS EDUCATION
Abilene Christian University, TX
Bethel College, IN
Greenville College, IL
King College, TN

PHYSIOLOGICAL PSYCHOLOGY/ PSYCHOBIOLOGY
Hope International University, CA

POLITICAL SCIENCE
Abilene Christian University, TX
Anderson University, IN
Azusa Pacific University, CA
Bartlesville Wesleyan College, OK
Bethel College, MN
Bluffton College, OH
California Baptist University, CA
Calvin College, MI
Campbellsville University, KY
Campbell University, NC
Cedarville College, OH
College of the Ozarks, MO
Colorado Christian University, CO
Dallas Baptist University, TX
Dordt College, IA
Eastern College, PA
Evangel University, MO
Fresno Pacific University, CA
Geneva College, PA
Gordon College, MA
Goshen College, IN
Grand Canyon University, AZ
Greenville College, IL
Houghton College, NY
Indiana Wesleyan University, IN
King College, TN
The Master's College and Seminary, CA
Messiah College, PA
North Park University, IL
Northwestern College, IA
Northwest Nazarene College, ID
Oklahoma Baptist University, OK
Oral Roberts University, OK
Palm Beach Atlantic College, FL
Point Loma Nazarene University, CA

Redeemer College, ON
Seattle Pacific University, WA
Southern California College, CA
Southern Nazarene University, OK
Southwest Baptist University, MO
Sterling College, KS
Taylor University, IN
Trinity Western University, BC
University of Sioux Falls, SD
Westmont College, CA
Wheaton College, IL
Whitworth College, WA

POULTRY SCIENCE
College of the Ozarks, MO

PRINTMAKING
Trinity Christian College, IL

PSYCHOLOGY
Abilene Christian University, TX
Anderson University, IN
Asbury College, KY
Azusa Pacific University, CA
Belhaven College, MS
Bethel College, IN
Bethel College, KS
Bethel College, MN
Biola University, CA
Bluffton College, OH
Bryan College, TN
California Baptist University, CA
Calvin College, MI
Campbellsville University, KY
Campbell University, NC
Cedarville College, OH
College of the Ozarks, MO
Colorado Christian University, CO
Cornerstone College, MI
Covenant College, GA
Dallas Baptist University, TX
Dordt College, IA
Eastern College, PA
Eastern Mennonite University, VA
Eastern Nazarene College, MA
East Texas Baptist University, TX
Erskine College, SC
Evangel University, MO
Fresno Pacific University, CA
Geneva College, PA
George Fox University, OR
Gordon College, MA
Goshen College, IN
Grace College, IN
Grand Canyon University, AZ
Greenville College, IL
Hope International University, CA
Houghton College, NY
Huntington College, IN
Indiana Wesleyan University, IN
John Brown University, AR
Judson College, IL
King College, TN
The King's University College, AB
Lee University, TN
LeTourneau University, TX
Malone College, OH
Messiah College, PA
MidAmerica Nazarene University, KS

Milligan College, TN
Mount Vernon Nazarene College, OH
North Park University, IL
Northwest Christian College, OR
Northwest College, WA
Northwestern College, IA
Northwestern College, MN
Northwest Nazarene College, ID
Nyack College, NY
Oklahoma Baptist University, OK
Oklahoma Christian University of Science and
    Arts, OK
Olivet Nazarene University, IL
Oral Roberts University, OK
Palm Beach Atlantic College, FL
Point Loma Nazarene University, CA
Redeemer College, ON
Roberts Wesleyan College, NY
Seattle Pacific University, WA
Simpson College and Graduate School, CA
Southern California College, CA
Southern Nazarene University, OK
Southern Wesleyan University, SC
Southwest Baptist University, MO
Spring Arbor College, MI
Tabor College, KS
Taylor University, IN
Trevecca Nazarene University, TN
Trinity Christian College, IL
Trinity International University, IL
Trinity Western University, BC
Union University, TN
University of Sioux Falls, SD
Warner Pacific College, OR
Warner Southern College, FL
Western Baptist College, OR
Westmont College, CA
Wheaton College, IL
Whitworth College, WA
Williams Baptist College, AR
William Tyndale College, MI

PUBLIC ADMINISTRATION
Abilene Christian University, TX
Campbell University, NC
Cedarville College, OH
Evangel University, MO
LeTourneau University, TX

PUBLIC RELATIONS
Abilene Christian University, TX
Biola University, CA
Campbell University, NC
College of the Ozarks, MO
Greenville College, IL
John Brown University, AR
The Master's College and Seminary, CA
MidAmerica Nazarene University, KS
Milligan College, TN
Oklahoma Baptist University, OK
Oklahoma Christian University of Science and
    Arts, OK
University of Sioux Falls, SD

RADIO/TELEVISION BROADCASTING
Abilene Christian University, TX
Biola University, CA
Campbell University, NC

Radio/television broadcasting (continued)

Cedarville College, OH
Eastern Nazarene College, MA
Evangel University, MO
Geneva College, PA
John Brown University, AR
The Master's College and Seminary, CA
Messiah College, PA
Milligan College, TN
Northwestern College, MN
Oklahoma Baptist University, OK
Oklahoma Christian University of Science and
   Arts, OK
Olivet Nazarene University, IL
Oral Roberts University, OK
Southern California College, CA
Union University, TN
University of Sioux Falls, SD

RADIO/TELEVISION BROADCASTING TECHNOLOGY
Asbury College, KY

RANGE MANAGEMENT
Abilene Christian University, TX

READING EDUCATION
Abilene Christian University, TX
Southern Nazarene University, OK

RECREATION AND LEISURE STUDIES
Bethel College, IN
Bluffton College, OH
Calvin College, MI
Campbellsville University, KY
Dordt College, IA
Eastern Mennonite University, VA
Evangel University, MO
Gordon College, MA
Greenville College, IL
Houghton College, NY
Huntington College, IN
Messiah College, PA
Northwest Nazarene College, ID
Oklahoma Baptist University, OK
Oral Roberts University, OK
Redeemer College, ON
Southern Wesleyan University, SC
Southwest Baptist University, MO
Taylor University, IN
Trinity Western University, BC
Warner Southern College, FL

RECREATION/LEISURE FACILITIES MANAGEMENT
Asbury College, KY
College of the Ozarks, MO
Indiana Wesleyan University, IN
John Brown University, AR

RELIGIOUS EDUCATION
Asbury College, KY
Biola University, CA
Bryan College, TN
Calvin College, MI
Campbellsville University, KY
Campbell University, NC
Cornerstone College, MI

Dallas Baptist University, TX
East Texas Baptist University, TX
Erskine College, SC
Gordon College, MA
Houghton College, NY
Indiana Wesleyan University, IN
John Brown University, AR
Lee University, TN
The Master's College and Seminary, CA
Messiah College, PA
MidAmerica Nazarene University, KS
Milligan College, TN
Mount Vernon Nazarene College, OH
Northwest College, WA
Northwestern College, IA
Northwestern College, MN
Northwest Nazarene College, ID
Nyack College, NY
Oklahoma Baptist University, OK
Oklahoma Christian University of Science and
   Arts, OK
Olivet Nazarene University, IL
Oral Roberts University, OK
Seattle Pacific University, WA
Simpson College and Graduate School, CA
Southern California College, CA
Southern Nazarene University, OK
Southwest Baptist University, MO
Sterling College, KS
Taylor University, IN
Trinity Christian College, IL
Warner Pacific College, OR
Western Baptist College, OR
Wheaton College, IL
Williams Baptist College, AR
William Tyndale College, MI

RELIGIOUS STUDIES
Abilene Christian University, TX
Anderson University, IN
Azusa Pacific University, CA
Bartlesville Wesleyan College, OK
Bethel College, IN
Bethel College, KS
Biola University, CA
Bluffton College, OH
Calvin College, MI
Campbellsville University, KY
College of the Ozarks, MO
Cornerstone College, MI
Dordt College, IA
Eastern Mennonite University, VA
Eastern Nazarene College, MA
East Texas Baptist University, TX
Erskine College, SC
Fresno Pacific University, CA
George Fox University, OR
Goshen College, IN
Grand Canyon University, AZ
Greenville College, IL
Houghton College, NY
Huntington College, IN
John Brown University, AR
Judson College, IL
King College, TN
LeTourneau University, TX
The Master's College and Seminary, CA
Messiah College, PA
MidAmerica Nazarene University, KS

Milligan College, TN
Montreat College, NC
Mount Vernon Nazarene College, OH
North Park University, IL
Northwest College, WA
Northwestern College, IA
Northwest Nazarene College, ID
Nyack College, NY
Oklahoma Baptist University, OK
Oklahoma Christian University of Science and
   Arts, OK
Olivet Nazarene University, IL
Palm Beach Atlantic College, FL
Redeemer College, ON
Roberts Wesleyan College, NY
Seattle Pacific University, WA
Southern California College, CA
Southern Nazarene University, OK
Southern Wesleyan University, SC
Southwest Baptist University, MO
Spring Arbor College, MI
Sterling College, KS
Tabor College, KS
Taylor University, IN
Trevecca Nazarene University, TN
Trinity Christian College, IL
Trinity Western University, BC
Union University, TN
University of Sioux Falls, SD
Warner Pacific College, OR
Western Baptist College, OR
Westmont College, CA
Wheaton College, IL
Whitworth College, WA
Williams Baptist College, AR

RESPIRATORY THERAPY
Lee University, TN

RETAIL MANAGEMENT
Bluffton College, OH

ROMANCE LANGUAGES
Olivet Nazarene University, IL
Point Loma Nazarene University, CA
Redeemer College, ON

SACRED MUSIC
Anderson University, IN
Bethel College, IN
Bethel College, MN
Bryan College, TN
Calvin College, MI
Campbellsville University, KY
Cedarville College, OH
Colorado Christian University, CO
Dallas Baptist University, TX
Eastern Nazarene College, MA
East Texas Baptist University, TX
Erskine College, SC
Evangel University, MO
Fresno Pacific University, CA
Grand Canyon University, AZ
Greenville College, IL
Hope International University, CA
Houghton College, NY
Indiana Wesleyan University, IN
Malone College, OH
The Master's College and Seminary, CA
MidAmerica Nazarene University, KS

Milligan College, TN
Mount Vernon Nazarene College, OH
North Park University, IL
Northwest College, WA
Northwest Nazarene College, ID
Nyack College, NY
Oklahoma Baptist University, OK
Olivet Nazarene University, IL
Oral Roberts University, OK
Palm Beach Atlantic College, FL
Point Loma Nazarene University, CA
Simpson College and Graduate School, CA
Southern Nazarene University, OK
Taylor University, IN
Trevecca Nazarene University, TN
Trinity International University, IL
Union University, TN
Warner Southern College, FL
Williams Baptist College, AR
William Tyndale College, MI

SALES OPERATIONS
Trevecca Nazarene University, TN

SCANDINAVIAN LANGUAGES
North Park University, IL

SCIENCE EDUCATION
Abilene Christian University, TX
Anderson University, IN
Bartlesville Wesleyan College, OK
Bethel College, IN
Bethel College, KS
Bethel College, MN
Biola University, CA
Bryan College, TN
Calvin College, MI
Campbellsville University, KY
Campbell University, NC
Cedarville College, OH
College of the Ozarks, MO
Colorado Christian University, CO
Cornerstone College, MI
Dallas Baptist University, TX
Eastern Mennonite University, VA
East Texas Baptist University, TX
Evangel University, MO
Fresno Pacific University, CA
George Fox University, OR
Goshen College, IN
Grace College, IN
Grand Canyon University, AZ
Greenville College, IL
Houghton College, NY
Huntington College, IN
Indiana Wesleyan University, IN
Judson College, IL
Malone College, OH
The Master's College and Seminary, CA
MidAmerica Nazarene University, KS
Milligan College, TN
Mount Vernon Nazarene College, OH
Oklahoma Baptist University, OK
Oklahoma Christian University of Science and
    Arts, OK
Olivet Nazarene University, IL
Oral Roberts University, OK
Seattle Pacific University, WA
Southern Nazarene University, OK

Tabor College, KS
Taylor University, IN
Trinity Christian College, IL
Union University, TN
University of Sioux Falls, SD
Warner Pacific College, OR
Warner Southern College, FL

SCULPTURE
Trinity Christian College, IL

SECONDARY EDUCATION
Abilene Christian University, TX
Bartlesville Wesleyan College, OK
Bethel College, IN
Bethel College, KS
Bethel College, MN
Biola University, CA
Bluffton College, OH
Bryan College, TN
California Baptist University, CA
Calvin College, MI
Campbellsville University, KY
Campbell University, NC
Cedarville College, OH
College of the Ozarks, MO
Colorado Christian University, CO
Cornerstone College, MI
Dallas Baptist University, TX
Dordt College, IA
Eastern College, PA
Eastern Mennonite University, VA
Eastern Nazarene College, MA
East Texas Baptist University, TX
Evangel University, MO
Fresno Pacific University, CA
Geneva College, PA
George Fox University, OR
Goshen College, IN
Grand Canyon University, AZ
Greenville College, IL
Houghton College, NY
Huntington College, IN
Indiana Wesleyan University, IN
John Brown University, AR
Judson College, IL
King College, TN
Lee University, TN
LeTourneau University, TX
The Master's College and Seminary, CA
MidAmerica Nazarene University, KS
Milligan College, TN
Montreat College, NC
Mount Vernon Nazarene College, OH
North Park University, IL
Northwest College, WA
Northwestern College, IA
Northwest Nazarene College, ID
Nyack College, NY
Oklahoma Baptist University, OK
Oklahoma Christian University of Science and
    Arts, OK
Olivet Nazarene University, IL
Oral Roberts University, OK
Palm Beach Atlantic College, FL
Redeemer College, ON
Roberts Wesleyan College, NY
Simpson College and Graduate School, CA
Southern California College, CA

Southern Nazarene University, OK
Southwest Baptist University, MO
Spring Arbor College, MI
Tabor College, KS
Taylor University, IN
Trevecca Nazarene University, TN
Trinity Christian College, IL
Trinity International University, IL
Trinity Western University, BC
Union University, TN
University of Sioux Falls, SD
Warner Pacific College, OR
Western Baptist College, OR
Westmont College, CA
Whitworth College, WA

SECRETARIAL SCIENCE
Bartlesville Wesleyan College, OK
Bethel College, IN
Campbellsville University, KY
Cedarville College, OH
Dordt College, IA
Evangel University, MO
Grace College, IN
Lee University, TN
Mount Vernon Nazarene College, OH
Northwestern College, IA
Northwestern College, MN
Southwest Baptist University, MO
Tabor College, KS
University of Sioux Falls, SD
Williams Baptist College, AR

SIGN LANGUAGE
INTERPRETATION
Bethel College, IN

SOCIAL SCIENCE EDUCATION
Abilene Christian University, TX
Hope International University, CA
Northwest Nazarene College, ID
Oklahoma Baptist University, OK
Seattle Pacific University, WA
Simpson College and Graduate School, CA
Warner Southern College, FL
Westmont College, CA

SOCIAL SCIENCES
Asbury College, KY
Azusa Pacific University, CA
Bartlesville Wesleyan College, OK
Bethel College, IN
Bethel College, KS
Biola University, CA
Bluffton College, OH
California Baptist University, CA
Calvin College, MI
Campbellsville University, KY
Campbell University, NC
Cedarville College, OH
Dordt College, IA
Eastern Nazarene College, MA
Evangel University, MO
Fresno Pacific University, CA
Grand Canyon University, AZ
Hope International University, CA
Houghton College, NY
Indiana Wesleyan University, IN
John Brown University, AR

Social sciences (continued)

Judson College, IL
The King's University College, AB
Lee University, TN
Malone College, OH
Montreat College, NC
Mount Vernon Nazarene College, OH
North Park University, IL
Northwest Christian College, OR
Northwest College, WA
Northwestern College, MN
Northwest Nazarene College, ID
Nyack College, NY
Oklahoma Baptist University, OK
Olivet Nazarene University, IL
Oral Roberts University, OK
Point Loma Nazarene University, CA
Roberts Wesleyan College, NY
Simpson College and Graduate School, CA
Southern California College, CA
Southern Nazarene University, OK
Southern Wesleyan University, SC
Southwest Baptist University, MO
Spring Arbor College, MI
Tabor College, KS
Taylor University, IN
Trevecca Nazarene University, TN
Trinity International University, IL
Trinity Western University, BC
University of Sioux Falls, SD
Warner Pacific College, OR
Warner Southern College, FL
Western Baptist College, OR
Westmont College, CA
William Tyndale College, MI

SOCIAL STUDIES EDUCATION
Abilene Christian University, TX
Anderson University, IN
Colorado Christian University, CO
East Texas Baptist University, TX
Erskine College, SC
Greenville College, IL
Malone College, OH
Messiah College, PA
Northwestern College, MN
Oklahoma Baptist University, OK

SOCIAL WORK
Abilene Christian University, TX
Anderson University, IN
Asbury College, KY
Azusa Pacific University, CA
Bethel College, KS
Bethel College, MN
Bluffton College, OH
Calvin College, MI
Campbellsville University, KY
Campbell University, NC
Cedarville College, OH
College of the Ozarks, MO
Cornerstone College, MI
Dordt College, IA
Eastern College, PA
Eastern Mennonite University, VA
Eastern Nazarene College, MA
Evangel University, MO
Fresno Pacific University, CA

George Fox University, OR
Gordon College, MA
Goshen College, IN
Greenville College, IL
Hope International University, CA
Indiana Wesleyan University, IN
Malone College, OH
Messiah College, PA
Milligan College, TN
Mount Vernon Nazarene College, OH
Northwestern College, IA
Northwest Nazarene College, ID
Oklahoma Baptist University, OK
Oral Roberts University, OK
Point Loma Nazarene University, CA
Roberts Wesleyan College, NY
Spring Arbor College, MI
Taylor University, IN
Trevecca Nazarene University, TN
Union University, TN
University of Sioux Falls, SD
Warner Pacific College, OR
Warner Southern College, FL

SOCIOLOGY
Abilene Christian University, TX
Anderson University, IN
Asbury College, KY
Azusa Pacific University, CA
Bethel College, IN
Bethel College, KS
Biola University, CA
Bluffton College, OH
California Baptist University, CA
Calvin College, MI
Campbellsville University, KY
Cedarville College, OH
College of the Ozarks, MO
Cornerstone College, MI
Covenant College, GA
Dallas Baptist University, TX
Dordt College, IA
Eastern College, PA
Eastern Mennonite University, VA
Eastern Nazarene College, MA
East Texas Baptist University, TX
Evangel University, MO
Fresno Pacific University, CA
Geneva College, PA
George Fox University, OR
Gordon College, MA
Goshen College, IN
Grace College, IN
Grand Canyon University, AZ
Greenville College, IL
Houghton College, NY
Huntington College, IN
Indiana Wesleyan University, IN
Judson College, IL
The King's University College, AB
Lee University, TN
Messiah College, PA
MidAmerica Nazarene University, KS
Milligan College, TN
Mount Vernon Nazarene College, OH
North Park University, IL
Northwestern College, IA
Oklahoma Baptist University, OK
Oral Roberts University, OK

Point Loma Nazarene University, CA
Redeemer College, ON
Roberts Wesleyan College, NY
Seattle Pacific University, WA
Southern California College, CA
Southern Nazarene University, OK
Southwest Baptist University, MO
Spring Arbor College, MI
Tabor College, KS
Taylor University, IN
Trinity Christian College, IL
Trinity International University, IL
Union University, TN
University of Sioux Falls, SD
Westmont College, CA
Wheaton College, IL
Whitworth College, WA

SPANISH
Abilene Christian University, TX
Anderson University, IN
Asbury College, KY
Azusa Pacific University, CA
Bethel College, IN
Bethel College, KS
Bethel College, MN
Bluffton College, OH
California Baptist University, CA
Calvin College, MI
Campbell University, NC
Cedarville College, OH
College of the Ozarks, MO
Cornerstone College, MI
Dordt College, IA
Eastern College, PA
Eastern Mennonite University, VA
Eastern Nazarene College, MA
East Texas Baptist University, TX
Erskine College, SC
Evangel University, MO
Fresno Pacific University, CA
Geneva College, PA
George Fox University, OR
Gordon College, MA
Goshen College, IN
Grace College, IN
Greenville College, IL
Houghton College, NY
Indiana Wesleyan University, IN
King College, TN
Malone College, OH
Messiah College, PA
MidAmerica Nazarene University, KS
Montreat College, NC
Mount Vernon Nazarene College, OH
North Park University, IL
Northwestern College, IA
Northwestern College, MN
Oklahoma Baptist University, OK
Oklahoma Christian University of Science and
    Arts, OK
Olivet Nazarene University, IL
Oral Roberts University, OK
Point Loma Nazarene University, CA
Southern California College, CA
Southern Nazarene University, OK
Southwest Baptist University, MO
Spring Arbor College, MI
Taylor University, IN

Union University, TN
Westmont College, CA
Wheaton College, IL
Whitworth College, WA

SPANISH LANGUAGE EDUCATION

Abilene Christian University, TX
Anderson University, IN
East Texas Baptist University, TX
Greenville College, IL
King College, TN
Messiah College, PA
Oklahoma Baptist University, OK

SPECIAL EDUCATION

Abilene Christian University, TX
Bethel College, KS
Bluffton College, OH
Calvin College, MI
Cedarville College, OH
Eastern Mennonite University, VA
Eastern Nazarene College, MA
Erskine College, SC
Evangel University, MO
Gordon College, MA
Grand Canyon University, AZ
Greenville College, IL
Huntington College, IN
Indiana Wesleyan University, IN
John Brown University, AR
Lee University, TN
The Master's College and Seminary, CA
Milligan College, TN
Mount Vernon Nazarene College, OH
Northwest Nazarene College, ID
Oklahoma Baptist University, OK
Oklahoma Christian University of Science and
    Arts, OK
Seattle Pacific University, WA
Southern Wesleyan University, SC
Tabor College, KS
Trinity Christian College, IL
Union University, TN
Warner Southern College, FL
Whitworth College, WA

SPEECH EDUCATION

Abilene Christian University, TX
Anderson University, IN
East Texas Baptist University, TX
Greenville College, IL
Malone College, OH
Northwest Nazarene College, ID
Oklahoma Baptist University, OK

SPEECH-LANGUAGE PATHOLOGY/AUDIOLOGY

Abilene Christian University, TX
Biola University, CA
Calvin College, MI
Geneva College, PA
Northwest Nazarene College, ID

SPEECH/RHETORICAL STUDIES

Abilene Christian University, TX
Asbury College, KY
Bethel College, KS
Bethel College, MN
Bluffton College, OH
Calvin College, MI

Cedarville College, OH
Cornerstone College, MI
East Texas Baptist University, TX
Evangel University, MO
Geneva College, PA
Grand Canyon University, AZ
Greenville College, IL
Judson College, IL
The Master's College and Seminary, CA
North Park University, IL
Northwest Christian College, OR
Northwest Nazarene College, ID
Oklahoma Baptist University, OK
Oklahoma Christian University of Science and
    Arts, OK
Olivet Nazarene University, IL
Point Loma Nazarene University, CA
Southern California College, CA
Southern Nazarene University, OK
Spring Arbor College, MI
Sterling College, KS
Trevecca Nazarene University, TN
University of Sioux Falls, SD
Wheaton College, IL
Whitworth College, WA

SPEECH THERAPY

Biola University, CA

SPORT/FITNESS ADMINISTRATION

Belhaven College, MS
Bluffton College, OH
Campbell University, NC
Cornerstone College, MI
Erskine College, SC
Fresno Pacific University, CA
Indiana Wesleyan University, IN
Judson College, IL
LeTourneau University, TX
Montreat College, NC
Mount Vernon Nazarene College, OH
Northwestern College, MN
Southern Nazarene University, OK
Southwest Baptist University, MO
Taylor University, IN
Warner Southern College, FL
Western Baptist College, OR

STRINGED INSTRUMENTS

Houghton College, NY
Oklahoma Baptist University, OK
Olivet Nazarene University, IL
Palm Beach Atlantic College, FL
Wheaton College, IL

SYSTEMS ENGINEERING

Eastern Nazarene College, MA

TEACHER ASSISTANT/AIDE

Dordt College, IA
Eastern Mennonite University, VA

TEACHING ENGLISH AS A SECOND LANGUAGE

Bartlesville Wesleyan College, OK
Biola University, CA
Goshen College, IN
John Brown University, AR
Northwest College, WA

Northwestern College, MN
Nyack College, NY
Oklahoma Christian University of Science and
    Arts, OK
Oral Roberts University, OK

TECHNICAL WRITING

Cedarville College, OH

TELECOMMUNICATIONS

Calvin College, MI
George Fox University, OR
Oklahoma Baptist University, OK
Oral Roberts University, OK
Union University, TN

THEATER ARTS/DRAMA

Abilene Christian University, TX
Anderson University, IN
Belhaven College, MS
Bethel College, IN
Bethel College, KS
Bethel College, MN
Biola University, CA
California Baptist University, CA
Calvin College, MI
Campbell University, NC
Cedarville College, OH
College of the Ozarks, MO
Colorado Christian University, CO
Dordt College, IA
Eastern Nazarene College, MA
East Texas Baptist University, TX
Goshen College, IN
Grand Canyon University, AZ
Greenville College, IL
Huntington College, IN
Judson College, IL
King College, TN
Malone College, OH
Messiah College, PA
Milligan College, TN
Mount Vernon Nazarene College, OH
North Park University, IL
Northwestern College, IA
Northwestern College, MN
Oklahoma Baptist University, OK
Oklahoma Christian University of Science and
    Arts, OK
Oral Roberts University, OK
Palm Beach Atlantic College, FL
Point Loma Nazarene University, CA
Redeemer College, ON
Seattle Pacific University, WA
Southern California College, CA
Southwest Baptist University, MO
Sterling College, KS
Taylor University, IN
Trevecca Nazarene University, TN
Trinity Western University, BC
Union University, TN
University of Sioux Falls, SD
Westmont College, CA
Wheaton College, IL
Whitworth College, WA

THEATER DESIGN

Tabor College, KS

THEOLOGY

Anderson University, IN
Azusa Pacific University, CA
Bartlesville Wesleyan College, OK
Bethel College, KS
Bethel College, MN
Biola University, CA
Calvin College, MI
Campbell University, NC
Cedarville College, OH
Colorado Christian University, CO
Dordt College, IA
Eastern College, PA
Eastern Mennonite University, VA
Grand Canyon University, AZ
Greenville College, IL
Huntington College, IN
Indiana Wesleyan University, IN
John Brown University, AR
Lee University, TN
The Master's College and Seminary, CA
Milligan College, TN
Mount Vernon Nazarene College, OH
North Park University, IL
Northwest College, WA
Northwestern College, IA
Northwestern College, MN
Northwest Nazarene College, ID
Nyack College, NY
Oklahoma Baptist University, OK
Olivet Nazarene University, IL
Oral Roberts University, OK
Point Loma Nazarene University, CA
Redeemer College, ON
Southern Nazarene University, OK
Southwest Baptist University, MO
Taylor University, IN
Trinity Christian College, IL
Union University, TN
Warner Pacific College, OR
Western Baptist College, OR
Williams Baptist College, AR
William Tyndale College, MI

(PRE)THEOLOGY

Geneva College, PA

George Fox University, OR
Messiah College, PA
Northwest Christian College, OR
Northwestern College, MN
Redeemer College, ON
Trinity Christian College, IL
Warner Southern College, FL

TRADE AND INDUSTRIAL EDUCATION

College of the Ozarks, MO

URBAN STUDIES

Eastern College, PA
Malone College, OH
North Park University, IL

(PRE)VETERINARY STUDIES

Abilene Christian University, TX
Anderson University, IN
Bartlesville Wesleyan College, OK
Bethel College, MN
Calvin College, MI
Campbellsville University, KY
Campbell University, NC
Cedarville College, OH
College of the Ozarks, MO
Cornerstone College, MI
Dordt College, IA
Eastern Mennonite University, VA
Eastern Nazarene College, MA
Evangel University, MO
George Fox University, OR
Goshen College, IN
Grace College, IN
Grand Canyon University, AZ
Greenville College, IL
Houghton College, NY
Huntington College, IN
Indiana Wesleyan University, IN
John Brown University, AR
King College, TN
LeTourneau University, TX
Messiah College, PA
Milligan College, TN
Mount Vernon Nazarene College, OH

North Park University, IL
Northwest Nazarene College, ID
Oklahoma Baptist University, OK
Oklahoma Christian University of Science and
    Arts, OK
Olivet Nazarene University, IL
Oral Roberts University, OK
Redeemer College, ON
Southern Nazarene University, OK
Tabor College, KS
Taylor University, IN
Trinity Christian College, IL
Trinity Western University, BC
Union University, TN
University of Sioux Falls, SD
Warner Pacific College, OR
Westmont College, CA
Whitworth College, WA

VISUAL/PERFORMING ARTS

Seattle Pacific University, WA

WELDING TECHNOLOGY

LeTourneau University, TX

WILDLIFE BIOLOGY

Grand Canyon University, AZ

WIND AND PERCUSSION INSTRUMENTS

Bryan College, TN
Grand Canyon University, AZ
Houghton College, NY
Mount Vernon Nazarene College, OH
Oklahoma Baptist University, OK
Oklahoma Christian University of Science and
    Arts, OK
Olivet Nazarene University, IL
Palm Beach Atlantic College, FL
University of Sioux Falls, SD
Wheaton College, IL

ZOOLOGY

Olivet Nazarene University, IL
Tabor College, KS

Athletic Index

BADMINTON

Redeemer College, ON	M, W
Wheaton College, IL	M, W

BASEBALL

Abilene Christian University, TX	M(s)
Anderson University, IN	M
Asbury College, KY	M
Azusa Pacific University, CA	M(s)
Bartlesville Wesleyan College, OK	M(s)
Belhaven College, MS	M(s)
Bethel College, IN	M(s)
Bethel College, KS	M
Bethel College, MN	M
Biola University, CA	M(s)
Bluffton College, OH	M
California Baptist University, CA	M(s)
Calvin College, MI	M
Campbellsville University, KY	M(s)
Campbell University, NC	M(s)
Cedarville College, OH	M(s)
College of the Ozarks, MO	M(s)
Cornerstone College, MI	M(s)
Dallas Baptist University, TX	M(s)
Eastern College, PA	M
Eastern Mennonite University, VA	M
Eastern Nazarene College, MA	M
East Texas Baptist University, TX	M(s)
Erskine College, SC	M(s)
Evangel University, MO	M(s)
Geneva College, PA	M(s)
George Fox University, OR	M
Gordon College, MA	M
Goshen College, IN	M(s)
Grace College, IN	M(s)
Grand Canyon University, AZ	M(s)
Huntington College, IN	M(s)
Indiana Wesleyan University, IN	M(s)
Judson College, IL	M(s)
King College, TN	M(s)
LeTourneau University, TX	M(s)
Malone College, OH	M(s)
The Master's College and Seminary, CA	M(s)
Messiah College, PA	M
MidAmerica Nazarene University, KS	M(s)
Milligan College, TN	M
Montreat College, NC	M(s)
Mount Vernon Nazarene College, OH	M(s)
North Park University, IL	M
Northwestern College, IA	M(s)
Northwestern College, MN	M
Northwest Nazarene College, ID	M(s)
Nyack College, NY	M
Oklahoma Baptist University, OK	M(s)
Oklahoma Christian University of Science and Arts, OK	M(s)
Olivet Nazarene University, IL	M(s)
Oral Roberts University, OK	M(s), W

Palm Beach Atlantic College, FL	M(s)
Point Loma Nazarene University, CA	M(s)
Southern California College, CA	M(s)
Southern Nazarene University, OK	M
Southern Wesleyan University, SC	M(s)
Southwest Baptist University, MO	M(s)
Spring Arbor College, MI	M(s)
Sterling College, KS	M(s)
Tabor College, KS	M(s)
Taylor University, IN	M(s)
Trevecca Nazarene University, TN	M(s)
Trinity Christian College, IL	M(s)
Trinity International University, IL	M
Union University, TN	M(s)
University of Sioux Falls, SD	M
Warner Southern College, FL	M(s)
Westmont College, CA	M(s)
Wheaton College, IL	M
Whitworth College, WA	M
Williams Baptist College, AR	M(s)

BASKETBALL

Abilene Christian University, TX	M(s), W(s)
Anderson University, IN	M, W
Asbury College, KY	M, W
Azusa Pacific University, CA	M(s), W(s)
Bartlesville Wesleyan College, OK	M(s), W(s)
Belhaven College, MS	M(s), W(s)
Bethel College, IN	M(s), W(s)
Bethel College, KS	M(s), W(s)
Bethel College, MN	M, W
Biola University, CA	M(s), W(s)
Bluffton College, OH	M, W
Bryan College, TN	M(s), W(s)
California Baptist University, CA	M(s), W(s)
Calvin College, MI	M, W
Campbellsville University, KY	M(s), W(s)
Campbell University, NC	M(s), W(s)
Cedarville College, OH	M(s), W(s)
College of the Ozarks, MO	M(s), W(s)
Colorado Christian University, CO	M(s), W(s)
Cornerstone College, MI	M(s), W(s)
Covenant College, GA	M(s), W(s)
Dordt College, IA	M(s), W(s)
Eastern College, PA	M, W
Eastern Mennonite University, VA	M, W
Eastern Nazarene College, MA	M, W
East Texas Baptist University, TX	M(s), W(s)
Erskine College, SC	M(s), W(s)
Evangel University, MO	M(s), W(s)
Fresno Pacific University, CA	M(s), W(s)
Geneva College, PA	M(s), W(s)
George Fox University, OR	M, W
Gordon College, MA	M, W
Goshen College, IN	M(s), W(s)
Grace College, IN	M(s), W(s)
Grand Canyon University, AZ	M(s), W(s)
Greenville College, IL	M, W

Hope International University, CA	M(s), W(s)
Houghton College, NY	M(s), W(s)
Huntington College, IN	M(s), W(s)
Indiana Wesleyan University, IN	M(s), W(s)
John Brown University, AR	M(s), W(s)
Judson College, IL	M(s), W(s)
King College, TN	M(s), W(s)
The King's University College, AB	M(s), W(s)
Lee University, TN	M(s), W(s)
LeTourneau University, TX	M(s), W(s)
Malone College, OH	M(s), W(s)
The Master's College and Seminary, CA	M(s), W(s)
Messiah College, PA	M, W
MidAmerica Nazarene University, KS	M(s), W(s)
Milligan College, TN	M(s), W(s)
Montreat College, NC	M(s), W(s)
Mount Vernon Nazarene College, OH	M(s), W(s)
North Park University, IL	M, W
Northwest Christian College, OR	M(s)
Northwest College, WA	M(s), W(s)
Northwestern College, IA	M(s), W(s)
Northwestern College, MN	M, W
Northwest Nazarene College, ID	M(s), W(s)
Nyack College, NY	M(s), W(s)
Oklahoma Baptist University, OK	M(s), W(s)
Oklahoma Christian University of Science and Arts, OK	M(s), W(s)
Olivet Nazarene University, IL	M(s), W(s)
Oral Roberts University, OK	M(s), W(s)
Palm Beach Atlantic College, FL	M(s)
Point Loma Nazarene University, CA	M(s), W(s)
Redeemer College, ON	M, W
Roberts Wesleyan College, NY	M(s), W(s)
Seattle Pacific University, WA	M(s), W(s)
Simpson College and Graduate School, CA	M, W
Southern California College, CA	M, W
Southern Nazarene University, OK	M(s), W(s)
Southern Wesleyan University, SC	M(s), W(s)
Southwest Baptist University, MO	M(s), W(s)
Spring Arbor College, MI	M(s), W(s)
Sterling College, KS	M(s), W(s)
Tabor College, KS	M(s), W(s)
Taylor University, IN	M(s), W(s)
Trevecca Nazarene University, TN	M(s), W(s)
Trinity Christian College, IL	M(s), W(s)
Trinity International University, IL	M(s), W(s)
Trinity Western University, BC	M, W
Union University, TN	M(s), W(s)
University of Sioux Falls, SD	M(s), W(s)
Warner Pacific College, OR	M
Warner Southern College, FL	M(s), W(s)
Western Baptist College, OR	M(s), W(s)
Westmont College, CA	M(s), W(s)
Wheaton College, IL	M, W

Basketball (continued)

Whitworth College, WA	M, W
Williams Baptist College, AR	M(s), W(s)

CREW

Seattle Pacific University, WA	M, W
Wheaton College, IL	M, W

CROSS-COUNTRY RUNNING

Abilene Christian University, TX	M(s), W(s)
Anderson University, IN	M, W
Asbury College, KY	M, W
Azusa Pacific University, CA	M(s), W(s)
Belhaven College, MS	M(s), W(s)
Bethel College, IN	M(s), W(s)
Bethel College, MN	M, W
Biola University, CA	M(s), W(s)
Bluffton College, OH	M, W
California Baptist University, CA	M(s), W(s)
Calvin College, MI	M, W
Campbellsville University, KY	M(s), W(s)
Campbell University, NC	M(s), W(s)
Cedarville College, OH	M(s), W(s)
Colorado Christian University, CO	M, W
Cornerstone College, MI	M(s), W(s)
Covenant College, GA	M(s), W(s)
Dallas Baptist University, TX	M, W
Dordt College, IA	M(s), W(s)
Eastern College, PA	W
Eastern Mennonite University, VA	M, W
Eastern Nazarene College, MA	M, W
Erskine College, SC	M(s), W(s)
Evangel University, MO	M(s), W(s)
Fresno Pacific University, CA	M(s), W(s)
Geneva College, PA	M(s), W(s)
George Fox University, OR	M, W
Gordon College, MA	M, W
Goshen College, IN	M(s), W(s)
Grace College, IN	M(s), W(s)
Grand Canyon University, AZ	M(s), W(s)
Greenville College, IL	M, W
Houghton College, NY	M(s), W(s)
Huntington College, IN	M(s), W(s)
Indiana Wesleyan University, IN	M(s), W(s)
Judson College, IL	M(s), W(s)
Lee University, TN	M(s), W(s)
LeTourneau University, TX	M, W
Malone College, OH	M(s), W(s)
The Master's College and Seminary, CA	M(s), W(s)
Messiah College, PA	M, W
MidAmerica Nazarene University, KS	M(s), W(s)
Montreat College, NC	M, W
North Park University, IL	M, W
Northwest Christian College, OR	W(s)
Northwest College, WA	M(s), W(s)
Northwestern College, IA	M(s), W(s)
Northwestern College, MN	M, W
Nyack College, NY	M, W
Oklahoma Baptist University, OK	M(s), W(s)
Oklahoma Christian University of Science and Arts, OK	M(s), W(s)
Olivet Nazarene University, IL	M(s), W(s)
Oral Roberts University, OK	M(s), W(s)
Palm Beach Atlantic College, FL	M, W
Point Loma Nazarene University, CA	M(s), W(s)

Redeemer College, ON	M, W
Roberts Wesleyan College, NY	M(s), W(s)
Seattle Pacific University, WA	M(s), W(s)
Southern California College, CA	M(s), W(s)
Southern Nazarene University, OK	M, W
Southern Wesleyan University, SC	M(s), W(s)
Southwest Baptist University, MO	M(s), W(s)
Spring Arbor College, MI	M(s), W(s)
Sterling College, KS	M(s), W(s)
Tabor College, KS	M(s), W(s)
Taylor University, IN	M(s), W(s)
Trinity International University, IL	M, W
University of Sioux Falls, SD	M(s), W(s)
Warner Southern College, FL	M(s), W(s)
Westmont College, CA	M(s), W(s)
Wheaton College, IL	M, W
Whitworth College, WA	M, W
Williams Baptist College, AR	M, W

EQUESTRIAN SPORTS

Erskine College, SC	M, W
Taylor University, IN	M, W
Wheaton College, IL	W

FIELD HOCKEY

Eastern College, PA	W
Eastern Mennonite University, VA	W
Gordon College, MA	W
Houghton College, NY	W(s)
Messiah College, PA	W

FOOTBALL

Abilene Christian University, TX	M(s)
Anderson University, IN	M
Azusa Pacific University, CA	M(s)
Belhaven College, MS	M(s)
Bethel College, KS	M(s)
Bethel College, MN	M
Bluffton College, OH	M
Campbellsville University, KY	M(s)
Evangel University, MO	M(s)
Geneva College, PA	M(s)
Greenville College, IL	M
Malone College, OH	M(s)
MidAmerica Nazarene University, KS	M(s)
North Park University, IL	M
Northwestern College, IA	M(s)
Northwestern College, MN	M
Olivet Nazarene University, IL	M(s)
Southwest Baptist University, MO	M(s)
Sterling College, KS	M(s)
Tabor College, KS	M(s)
Taylor University, IN	M(s)
Trinity International University, IL	M(s)
University of Sioux Falls, SD	M(s)
Wheaton College, IL	M
Whitworth College, WA	M

GOLF

Abilene Christian University, TX	M(s)
Anderson University, IN	M, W
Azusa Pacific University, CA	M(s)
Bartlesville Wesleyan College, OK	M(s)
Belhaven College, MS	M(s), W(s)
Bethel College, IN	M(s)
Bethel College, MN	M
Bluffton College, OH	M
California Baptist University, CA	M(s)
Calvin College, MI	M, W

Campbellsville University, KY	M(s), W(s)
Campbell University, NC	M(s), W(s)
Cedarville College, OH	M(s)
Colorado Christian University, CO	M(s)
Cornerstone College, MI	M(s)
Dordt College, IA	M(s)
Eastern College, PA	M, W
Evangel University, MO	W(s)
Goshen College, IN	M(s)
Grace College, IN	M(s)
Grand Canyon University, AZ	M(s)
Greenville College, IL	M
Huntington College, IN	M(s), W(s)
Indiana Wesleyan University, IN	M(s)
King College, TN	M(s)
Lee University, TN	M(s)
Malone College, OH	M(s)
Messiah College, PA	M
Milligan College, TN	M(s)
Montreat College, NC	M
North Park University, IL	M
Northwestern College, IA	M(s), W(s)
Northwestern College, MN	M
Oklahoma Baptist University, OK	M(s), W(s)
Olivet Nazarene University, IL	M(s)
Oral Roberts University, OK	M(s), W(s)
Palm Beach Atlantic College, FL	M, W
Point Loma Nazarene University, CA	M(s)
Southern Nazarene University, OK	M(s)
Southern Wesleyan University, SC	M(s)
Southwest Baptist University, MO	M(s)
Spring Arbor College, MI	M(s)
Tabor College, KS	M(s), W
Taylor University, IN	M(s)
Trinity International University, IL	M(s)
Union University, TN	M(s)
University of Sioux Falls, SD	M(s), W(s)
Wheaton College, IL	M
Whitworth College, WA	M

GYMNASTICS

Seattle Pacific University, WA	W(s)

ICE HOCKEY

Bethel College, MN	M
Calvin College, MI	M
Dordt College, IA	M
Wheaton College, IL	M

LACROSSE

Calvin College, MI	M
Eastern College, PA	M, W
Eastern Nazarene College, MA	M
Gordon College, MA	M, W
Messiah College, PA	M, W
Westmont College, CA	W
Wheaton College, IL	M, W

RUGBY

Trinity Western University, BC	M, W
Westmont College, CA	M

SOCCER

Abilene Christian University, TX	M, W
Anderson University, IN	M, W
Asbury College, KY	M
Azusa Pacific University, CA	M(s), W(s)
Bartlesville Wesleyan College, OK	M(s), W(s)
Belhaven College, MS	M(s), W(s)

Bethel College, IN	M(s), W(s)
Bethel College, KS	M(s), W(s)
Bethel College, MN	M, W
Biola University, CA	M(s), W(s)
Bluffton College, OH	M, W
Bryan College, TN	M(s), W(s)
California Baptist University, CA	M(s), W(s)
Calvin College, MI	M, W
Campbellsville University, KY	M(s), W(s)
Campbell University, NC	M(s), W(s)
Cedarville College, OH	M(s), W(s)
Colorado Christian University, CO	M(s), W(s)
Cornerstone College, MI	M(s), W(s)
Covenant College, GA	M(s), W(s)
Dallas Baptist University, TX	M, W(s)
Dordt College, IA	M(s), W(s)
Eastern College, PA	M, W
Eastern Mennonite University, VA	M
Eastern Nazarene College, MA	M, W
East Texas Baptist University, TX	M(s), W
Erskine College, SC	M(s), W(s)
Fresno Pacific University, CA	M(s)
Geneva College, PA	M(s), W(s)
George Fox University, OR	M, W
Gordon College, MA	M, W
Goshen College, IN	M(s), W(s)
Grace College, IN	M(s), W(s)
Grand Canyon University, AZ	M(s), W(s)
Greenville College, IL	M, W
Hope International University, CA	M(s), W(s)
Houghton College, NY	M(s), W(s)
Huntington College, IN	M(s)
Indiana Wesleyan University, IN	M(s), W(s)
John Brown University, AR	M(s)
Judson College, IL	M(s), W(s)
King College, TN	M(s), W(s)
The King's University College, AB	M, W
Lee University, TN	M(s), W(s)
LeTourneau University, TX	M(s)
Malone College, OH	M(s), W(s)
The Master's College and Seminary, CA	M(s), W(s)
Messiah College, PA	M, W
Milligan College, TN	M(s), W(s)
Montreat College, NC	M(s), W(s)
Mount Vernon Nazarene College, OH	M(s)
North Park University, IL	M, W
Northwest College, WA	M(s)
Northwestern College, IA	M(s), W(s)
Northwestern College, MN	M, W
Northwest Nazarene College, ID	M(s), W(s)
Nyack College, NY	M(s), W(s)
Oklahoma Christian University of Science and Arts, OK	M(s), W(s)
Olivet Nazarene University, IL	M(s), W(s)
Oral Roberts University, OK	M(s), W(s)
Palm Beach Atlantic College, FL	M(s), W
Point Loma Nazarene University, CA	M(s)
Redeemer College, ON	M, W
Roberts Wesleyan College, NY	M(s), W(s)
Seattle Pacific University, WA	M(s), W
Simpson College and Graduate School, CA	M, W
Southern California College, CA	M(s), W(s)
Southern Nazarene University, OK	M(s), W(s)
Southern Wesleyan University, SC	M(s), W(s)
Southwest Baptist University, MO	M(s), W(s)
Spring Arbor College, MI	M(s), W(s)

Sterling College, KS	M(s), W(s)
Tabor College, KS	M(s), W
Taylor University, IN	M(s), W(s)
Trinity Christian College, IL	M(s), W(s)
Trinity International University, IL	M(s), W(s)
Trinity Western University, BC	M, W
Union University, TN	M(s)
University of Sioux Falls, SD	M(s), W(s)
Western Baptist College, OR	M(s), W(s)
Westmont College, CA	M(s), W(s)
Wheaton College, IL	M, W
Whitworth College, WA	M, W
Williams Baptist College, AR	M
William Tyndale College, MI	M

SOFTBALL

Abilene Christian University, TX	W(s)
Anderson University, IN	W
Asbury College, KY	W
Azusa Pacific University, CA	W(s)
Bartlesville Wesleyan College, OK	W(s)
Belhaven College, MS	W(s)
Bethel College, IN	W(s)
Bethel College, MN	W
Bluffton College, OH	W
California Baptist University, CA	W(s)
Calvin College, MI	W
Campbellsville University, KY	W(s)
Campbell University, NC	W(s)
Cedarville College, OH	W(s)
Cornerstone College, MI	W(s)
Dordt College, IA	W(s)
Eastern College, PA	W
Eastern Mennonite University, VA	W
Eastern Nazarene College, MA	W
East Texas Baptist University, TX	W(s)
Erskine College, SC	W(s)
Evangel University, MO	W(s)
Geneva College, PA	W(s)
George Fox University, OR	W
Gordon College, MA	W
Goshen College, IN	W(s)
Grace College, IN	W(s)
Hope International University, CA	W(s)
Huntington College, IN	W(s)
Indiana Wesleyan University, IN	W(s)
Judson College, IL	W(s)
Lee University, TN	W(s)
Malone College, OH	W(s)
Messiah College, PA	W
Milligan College, TN	W
Montreat College, NC	W(s)
Mount Vernon Nazarene College, OH	W(s)
North Park University, IL	W
Northwest Christian College, OR	W(s)
Northwestern College, IA	W(s)
Northwestern College, MN	W
Nyack College, NY	W
Oklahoma Baptist University, OK	W(s)
Oklahoma Christian University of Science and Arts, OK	W(s)
Olivet Nazarene University, IL	W(s)
Point Loma Nazarene University, CA	W(s)
Simpson College and Graduate School, CA	W
Southern California College, CA	W(s)
Southern Nazarene University, OK	W(s)
Southern Wesleyan University, SC	W(s)

Southwest Baptist University, MO	W(s)
Spring Arbor College, MI	W(s)
Sterling College, KS	W(s)
Tabor College, KS	W(s)
Taylor University, IN	W(s)
Trevecca Nazarene University, TN	W(s)
Trinity Christian College, IL	W(s)
Trinity International University, IL	W(s)
Union University, TN	W(s)
University of Sioux Falls, SD	W(s)
Wheaton College, IL	W
Williams Baptist College, AR	W

SWIMMING AND DIVING

Asbury College, KY	M, W
Biola University, CA	M, W
Calvin College, MI	M, W
Campbellsville University, KY	M(s), W(s)
Gordon College, MA	M, W
John Brown University, AR	M, W
Wheaton College, IL	M, W
Whitworth College, WA	M, W

TENNIS

Abilene Christian University, TX	M(s), W(s)
Anderson University, IN	M, W
Asbury College, KY	M, W
Azusa Pacific University, CA	M(s)
Belhaven College, MS	M(s), W(s)
Bethel College, IN	M(s), W(s)
Bethel College, KS	M(s), W(s)
Bethel College, MN	M, W
Biola University, CA	M(s), W(s)
Bluffton College, OH	M, W
Bryan College, TN	M, W
California Baptist University, CA	M(s), W(s)
Calvin College, MI	M, W
Campbellsville University, KY	M(s), W(s)
Campbell University, NC	M(s), W(s)
Cedarville College, OH	M(s), W(s)
Colorado Christian University, CO	M(s), W(s)
Cornerstone College, MI	M(s)
Dallas Baptist University, TX	M, W
Dordt College, IA	M(s), W(s)
Eastern College, PA	M, W
Eastern Mennonite University, VA	M, W
Eastern Nazarene College, MA	M, W
East Texas Baptist University, TX	W(s)
Erskine College, SC	M(s), W(s)
Geneva College, PA	M(s), W(s)
George Fox University, OR	M, W
Gordon College, MA	M, W
Goshen College, IN	M(s), W(s)
Grace College, IN	M(s), W(s)
Grand Canyon University, AZ	W(s)
Greenville College, IL	M, W
Hope International University, CA	M(s), W(s)
Huntington College, IN	M(s), W(s)
Indiana Wesleyan University, IN	M(s), W(s)
John Brown University, AR	M(s), W(s)
Judson College, IL	M(s), W(s)
King College, TN	M(s), W(s)
Lee University, TN	M(s), W(s)
Malone College, OH	M(s), W(s)
Messiah College, PA	M, W
Milligan College, TN	M(s), W(s)
Montreat College, NC	M(s), W(s)
North Park University, IL	W

Tennis (continued)

Northwestern College, IA	M(s), W(s)
Northwestern College, MN	M, W
Northwest Nazarene College, ID	W(s)
Oklahoma Baptist University, OK	M(s), W(s)
Oklahoma Christian University of Science and Arts, OK	M(s)
Olivet Nazarene University, IL	M(s), W(s)
Oral Roberts University, OK	M(s), W(s)
Palm Beach Atlantic College, FL	M, W
Point Loma Nazarene University, CA	M(s), W(s)
Southern California College, CA	M(s), W(s)
Southern Nazarene University, OK	M(s), W(s)
Southwest Baptist University, MO	M(s), W(s)
Spring Arbor College, MI	M(s), W(s)
Sterling College, KS	M(s), W(s)
Tabor College, KS	M(s), W(s)
Taylor University, IN	M(s), W(s)
Trinity International University, IL	M(s), W(s)
Union University, TN	M(s), W(s)
University of Sioux Falls, SD	M(s), W(s)
Westmont College, CA	M(s), W(s)
Wheaton College, IL	M, W
Whitworth College, WA	M, W

TRACK AND FIELD

Abilene Christian University, TX	M(s), W(s)
Anderson University, IN	M, W
Azusa Pacific University, CA	M(s), W(s)
Bethel College, IN	M(s), W(s)
Bethel College, KS	M(s), W(s)
Bethel College, MN	M, W
Biola University, CA	M(s), W(s)
Bluffton College, OH	M, W
California Baptist University, CA	M(s), W(s)
Calvin College, MI	M, W
Campbell University, NC	M(s), W(s)
Cedarville College, OH	M(s), W(s)
Dordt College, IA	M(s), W(s)
Eastern Mennonite University, VA	M, W
Evangel University, MO	M(s), W(s)
Fresno Pacific University, CA	M(s), W(s)
Geneva College, PA	M(s), W(s)
George Fox University, OR	M, W
Goshen College, IN	M(s), W(s)
Grace College, IN	M(s), W(s)
Greenville College, IL	M, W
Houghton College, NY	M(s), W(s)
Huntington College, IN	M(s), W(s)
Indiana Wesleyan University, IN	M(s), W(s)
Malone College, OH	M(s), W(s)
Messiah College, PA	M, W
MidAmerica Nazarene University, KS	M(s), W(s)
North Park University, IL	M, W
Northwest College, WA	M(s), W(s)
Northwestern College, IA	M(s), W(s)
Northwestern College, MN	M, W

Oklahoma Baptist University, OK	M(s), W(s)
Oklahoma Christian University of Science and Arts, OK	M(s), W(s)
Olivet Nazarene University, IL	M(s), W(s)
Oral Roberts University, OK	M(s), W(s)
Point Loma Nazarene University, CA	M(s), W(s)
Roberts Wesleyan College, NY	M(s), W(s)
Seattle Pacific University, WA	M(s), W(s)
Southern California College, CA	M(s), W(s)
Southern Nazarene University, OK	M, W
Southwest Baptist University, MO	M, W
Spring Arbor College, MI	M(s), W(s)
Sterling College, KS	M(s), W(s)
Tabor College, KS	M(s), W(s)
Taylor University, IN	M(s), W(s)
Trinity Christian College, IL	M, W
Trinity International University, IL	M, W
University of Sioux Falls, SD	M(s), W(s)
Westmont College, CA	M(s), W(s)
Wheaton College, IL	M, W
Whitworth College, WA	M, W

VOLLEYBALL

Abilene Christian University, TX	W(s)
Anderson University, IN	W
Asbury College, KY	W
Azusa Pacific University, CA	M, W(s)
Bartlesville Wesleyan College, OK	W(s)
Belhaven College, MS	W(s)
Bethel College, IN	W(s)
Bethel College, KS	W(s)
Bethel College, MN	W
Biola University, CA	W(s)
Bluffton College, OH	W
Bryan College, TN	W(s)
California Baptist University, CA	M(s), W(s)
Calvin College, MI	M, W
Campbellsville University, KY	W(s)
Campbell University, NC	W(s)
Cedarville College, OH	W(s)
College of the Ozarks, MO	W(s)
Colorado Christian University, CO	W(s)
Cornerstone College, MI	W(s)
Covenant College, GA	W(s)
Dallas Baptist University, TX	W(s)
Dordt College, IA	W(s)
Eastern College, PA	M, W
Eastern Mennonite University, VA	M, W
Eastern Nazarene College, MA	M, W
East Texas Baptist University, TX	W(s)
Evangel University, MO	W(s)
Fresno Pacific University, CA	W(s)
Geneva College, PA	M, W(s)
George Fox University, OR	W
Gordon College, MA	M, W
Goshen College, IN	W(s)
Grace College, IN	W(s)
Grand Canyon University, AZ	W(s)
Greenville College, IL	W

Hope International University, CA	M(s), W(s)
Houghton College, NY	W(s)
Huntington College, IN	W(s)
Indiana Wesleyan University, IN	W(s)
John Brown University, AR	W(s)
Judson College, IL	W(s)
King College, TN	W(s)
The King's University College, AB	M(s), W(s)
Lee University, TN	W(s)
LeTourneau University, TX	W(s)
Malone College, OH	W(s)
The Master's College and Seminary, CA	W(s)
Messiah College, PA	W
MidAmerica Nazarene University, KS	W(s)
Milligan College, TN	W(s)
Montreat College, NC	W(s)
Mount Vernon Nazarene College, OH	W(s)
North Park University, IL	M, W
Northwest College, WA	W(s)
Northwestern College, IA	W(s)
Northwestern College, MN	W
Northwest Nazarene College, ID	W(s)
Nyack College, NY	M, W(s)
Olivet Nazarene University, IL	M, W(s)
Oral Roberts University, OK	W(s)
Palm Beach Atlantic College, FL	W(s)
Point Loma Nazarene University, CA	W(s)
Redeemer College, ON	M, W
Roberts Wesleyan College, NY	W(s)
Seattle Pacific University, WA	W(s)
Simpson College and Graduate School, CA	M, W
Southern California College, CA	W(s)
Southern Nazarene University, OK	W(s)
Southern Wesleyan University, SC	W(s)
Southwest Baptist University, MO	W(s)
Spring Arbor College, MI	W(s)
Sterling College, KS	W(s)
Tabor College, KS	W(s)
Taylor University, IN	M, W(s)
Trevecca Nazarene University, TN	W(s)
Trinity Christian College, IL	M, W(s)
Trinity International University, IL	M, W(s)
Trinity Western University, BC	M, W
Union University, TN	W(s)
University of Sioux Falls, SD	W(s)
Warner Pacific College, OR	W
Warner Southern College, FL	W(s)
Western Baptist College, OR	W(s)
Westmont College, CA	M, W(s)
Wheaton College, IL	M, W
Whitworth College, WA	W
Williams Baptist College, AR	W(s)

WRESTLING

Campbell University, NC	M(s)
Messiah College, PA	M
Northwestern College, IA	M(s)
Wheaton College, IL	M

Graduate Majors Index

ACCOUNTING
Abilene Christian University	M
Dallas Baptist University	M
Eastern College	M
Oral Roberts University	M
Southwest Baptist University	M

ADVANCED PRACTICE NURSING
Seattle Pacific University	M

AMERICAN STUDIES
Wheaton College (IL)	M†

BIOETHICS
Trinity International University	M

BUSINESS ADMINISTRATION AND MANAGEMENT
Abilene Christian University	M
Azusa Pacific University	M†
Belhaven College	M
Bethel College (IN)	M
California Baptist University	M
Campbell University	M
Southern Wesleyan University	M
Colorado Christian University	M
Dallas Baptist University	M
Eastern College	M
Eastern Mennonite University	M
East Texas Baptist University	M
Fresno Pacific University	M
George Fox University	M
Grand Canyon University	M
Indiana Wesleyan University	M
LeTourneau University	M
Malone College	M
MidAmerica Nazarene University	M
Montreat College	M
North Park University	M
Northwest Nazarene College	M
Olivet Nazarene University	M
Oral Roberts University	M
Hope International University	M
Palm Beach Atlantic College	M
Roberts Wesleyan College	M
Seattle Pacific University	M*
University of Sioux Falls	M
Southern Nazarene University	M
Southwest Baptist University	M
Spring Arbor College	M
Union University	M
Whitworth College	M

CHILD AND FAMILY STUDIES
Abilene Christian University	M
Roberts Wesleyan College	M

CLINICAL PSYCHOLOGY
Abilene Christian University	M
Azusa Pacific University	M,D†
George Fox University	M,D*
Seattle Pacific University	D
Wheaton College (IL)	M,D†

COMMUNICATION
Abilene Christian University	M
Bethel College (MN)	M
Wheaton College (IL)	M,O†

COMPUTER SCIENCE
Azusa Pacific University	M,O*†

CONFLICT RESOLUTION AND MEDIATION/PEACE STUDIES
Dallas Baptist University	M
Eastern Mennonite University	M
Fresno Pacific University	M

COUNSELING PSYCHOLOGY
Abilene Christian University	M
Eastern College	M*
Eastern Nazarene College	M
Lee University (TN)	M
Palm Beach Atlantic College	M
Southern Nazarene University	M
Trevecca Nazarene University	M
Trinity International University	M
Trinity Western University	M

COUNSELOR EDUCATION
Abilene Christian University	M
Campbell University	M
Dallas Baptist University	M
Eastern College	M
Fresno Pacific University	M
Indiana Wesleyan University	M
John Brown University	M
Malone College	M
Northwest Nazarene College	M
Palm Beach Atlantic College	M
Seattle Pacific University	M
Trevecca Nazarene University	M
Whitworth College	M

CURRICULUM AND INSTRUCTION
Azusa Pacific University	M†
California Baptist University	M
Calvin College	M
Colorado Christian University	M
Fresno Pacific University	M
Indiana Wesleyan University	M
Malone College	M
MidAmerica Nazarene University	M
Northwest Nazarene College	M
Olivet Nazarene University	M

Oral Roberts University	M
Seattle Pacific University	M
Simpson College and Graduate School (CA)	M
Trevecca Nazarene University	M

EARLY CHILDHOOD EDUCATION
Dallas Baptist University	M
Eastern Nazarene College	M,O
Malone College	M
Oral Roberts University	M

ECONOMICS
Eastern College	M

EDUCATION
Abilene Christian University	M
Azusa Pacific University	M,D†
Bethel College (MN)	M
Biola University	M
Bluffton College	M
California Baptist University	M
Calvin College	M
Campbellsville University	M
Campbell University	M
Covenant College	M*
Dallas Baptist University	M
Dordt College	M
Eastern College	M,O*
Eastern Mennonite University	M
Eastern Nazarene College	M,O
Fresno Pacific University	M
Geneva College	M
George Fox University	M
Gordon College (MA)	M*
Grand Canyon University	M
Indiana Wesleyan University	M
Lee University (TN)	M
Malone College	M
MidAmerica Nazarene University	M
Milligan College	M
Mount Vernon Nazarene College	M
North Park University	M
Northwest Nazarene College	M
Olivet Nazarene University	M
Oral Roberts University	M
Hope International University	M
Palm Beach Atlantic College	M
Point Loma Nazarene University	M,D,O
Roberts Wesleyan College	M
Seattle Pacific University	M,D
University of Sioux Falls	M
Southern California College	M*
Southern Nazarene University	M
Southwest Baptist University	M
Spring Arbor College	M
Trevecca Nazarene University	M
Union University	M
Wheaton College (IL)	M†

Education (continued)

Whitworth College   M

EDUCATIONAL ADMINISTRATION
Abilene Christian University   M
Azusa Pacific University   M,D†
California Baptist University   M
Calvin College   M
Campbell University   M
Dallas Baptist University   M
Eastern Nazarene College   M,O
Fresno Pacific University   M
Malone College   M
Northwest Nazarene College   M
Oral Roberts University   M
Seattle Pacific University   M,D
University of Sioux Falls   M
Southwest Baptist University   M
Trevecca Nazarene University   M
Whitworth College   M

EDUCATIONAL MEASUREMENT AND EVALUATION
Abilene Christian University   M

EDUCATIONAL MEDIA/ INSTRUCTIONAL TECHNOLOGY
Azusa Pacific University   M†
Fresno Pacific University   M
Malone College   M
University of Sioux Falls   M

EDUCATIONAL PSYCHOLOGY
Eastern College   M

EDUCATION OF THE GIFTED
Whitworth College   M

EDUCATION OF THE MULTIPLY HANDICAPPED
Fresno Pacific University   M

ELEMENTARY EDUCATION
Abilene Christian University   M
Campbell University   M
Dallas Baptist University   M
Eastern Nazarene College   M,O
Grand Canyon University   M
Olivet Nazarene University   M
Palm Beach Atlantic College   M
Trevecca Nazarene University   M

ENGLISH
Abilene Christian University   M

ENGLISH AS A SECOND LANGUAGE
Azusa Pacific University   M,O†
Biola University   M,O
Eastern College   O
Eastern Nazarene College   M,O
Fresno Pacific University   M
Grand Canyon University   M
Oral Roberts University   M
Seattle Pacific University   M
Wheaton College (IL)   O†
Whitworth College   M

ENGLISH EDUCATION
California Baptist University   M
Campbell University   M

EXERCISE AND SPORTS SCIENCE
California Baptist University   M
Malone College   M

FINANCE AND BANKING
Dallas Baptist University   M
Eastern College   M
Oral Roberts University   M

GERONTOLOGY
Abilene Christian University   M

HEALTH EDUCATION
Eastern College   M

HEALTH SERVICES MANAGEMENT AND HOSPITAL ADMINISTRATION
Southwest Baptist University   M

HIGHER EDUCATION
Azusa Pacific University   M†
Dallas Baptist University   M
Geneva College   M*

HISTORY
Abilene Christian University   M

HUMAN RESOURCES DEVELOPMENT
Abilene Christian University   M
Azusa Pacific University   M†
Palm Beach Atlantic College   M

HUMAN RESOURCES MANAGEMENT
Dallas Baptist University   M

HUMAN SERVICES
Abilene Christian University   M
Roberts Wesleyan College   M

INTERDISCIPLINARY STUDIES
Fresno Pacific University   M
Trinity International University   M
Wheaton College (IL)   M†

INTERNATIONAL BUSINESS
Azusa Pacific University   M†
Dallas Baptist University   M
Oral Roberts University   M
Hope International University   M
Whitworth College   M

JOURNALISM
Abilene Christian University   M
Wheaton College (IL)   M†

LAW
Campbell University   P
Trinity International University   P

LIBERAL STUDIES
Abilene Christian University   M
Dallas Baptist University   M
Lee University (TN)   M

LINGUISTICS
Biola University   M

MANAGEMENT INFORMATION SYSTEMS
Dallas Baptist University   M
Seattle Pacific University   M*

MANAGEMENT STRATEGY AND POLICY
Azusa Pacific University   M†

MARKETING
Dallas Baptist University   M
Eastern College   M
Oral Roberts University   M

MARRIAGE AND FAMILY THERAPY
Abilene Christian University   M
California Baptist University   M
Eastern Nazarene College   M
George Fox University   M
John Brown University   M
Northwest Christian College   M,O*
Oklahoma Baptist University   M
Palm Beach Atlantic College   M
Seattle Pacific University   M
Southern California College   M*
Trevecca Nazarene University   M

MASS COMMUNICATION
Abilene Christian University   M

MATHEMATICS EDUCATION
Campbell University   M
Fresno Pacific University   M

MEDIA STUDIES
Wheaton College (IL)   M†

MIDDLE SCHOOL EDUCATION
Campbell University   M
Eastern Nazarene College   M,O
Malone College   M

MISSIONS AND MISSIOLOGY
Abilene Christian University   M
Biola University   D
Nyack College   M
Oral Roberts University   M
Hope International University   M
Simpson College and Graduate School (CA)   M
Trinity International University   M
Wheaton College (IL)   M,O†

MULTILINGUAL AND MULTICULTURAL EDUCATION
Azusa Pacific University   M†
California Baptist University   M
Eastern College   M
Eastern Nazarene College   M,O
Fresno Pacific University   M

MUSIC
Azusa Pacific University   M†
Lee University (TN)   M
Hope International University   M

MUSIC EDUCATION
Azusa Pacific University	M†
Campbellsville University	M
Eastern Nazarene College	M,O

NONPROFIT MANAGEMENT
Eastern College	M
Hope International University	M

NURSING
Abilene Christian University	M
Azusa Pacific University	M†
Bethel College (MN)	M
Indiana Wesleyan University	M
North Park University	M
Seattle Pacific University	M

NURSING EDUCATION
Indiana Wesleyan University	M

OCCUPATIONAL THERAPY
Milligan College	M

ORGANIZATIONAL BEHAVIOR
Bethel College (MN)	M
Dallas Baptist University	M
Geneva College	M
Trevecca Nazarene University	M

PASTORAL MINISTRY AND COUNSELING
Abilene Christian University	M,D
Azusa Pacific University	M†
Bethel College (IN)	M
Southern Wesleyan University	M
Eastern Mennonite University	M
George Fox University	M
Huntington College	M*
Malone College	M
Nyack College	P,M
Oklahoma Christian University of Science and Arts	M
Olivet Nazarene University	M
Oral Roberts University	M
Hope International University	M
Trinity International University	M,D

PHARMACY
Campbell University	P

PHYSICAL EDUCATION
Azusa Pacific University	M†
Campbell University	M
Eastern Nazarene College	M,O
Malone College	M
Whitworth College	M

PHYSICAL THERAPY
Azusa Pacific University	M†
Southwest Baptist University	M

PHYSICIAN ASSISTANT STUDIES
Trevecca Nazarene University	M

PSYCHOLOGY
Abilene Christian University	M
Bethel College (MN)	M
Biola University	D
Geneva College	M*
George Fox University	M,D*
Grace College	M
Southern Nazarene University	M
Wheaton College (IL)	M,D†

PUBLIC HEALTH NURSING
Indiana Wesleyan University	M

READING EDUCATION
Abilene Christian University	M
California Baptist University	M
Calvin College	M
Dallas Baptist University	M
Eastern Nazarene College	M,O
Fresno Pacific University	M
Grand Canyon University	M
Malone College	M
Seattle Pacific University	M
University of Sioux Falls	M
Whitworth College	M

RELIGION
Abilene Christian University	M
Azusa Pacific University	M†
Biola University	M
Colorado Christian University	M
Eastern Mennonite University	M
Northwest Nazarene College	M
Olivet Nazarene University	M
Point Loma Nazarene University	M
Southern California College	M*
Southern Nazarene University	M
Trevecca Nazarene University	M
Trinity International University	M
Trinity Western University	M
Warner Pacific College	M
Wheaton College (IL)	M†

RELIGIOUS EDUCATION
Abilene Christian University	M
Biola University	M,D
Campbell University	M
George Fox University	M
Huntington College	M
Nyack College	P
Oral Roberts University	M
Trinity International University	M,D
Wheaton College (IL)	M†

SCHOOL PSYCHOLOGY
Abilene Christian University	M
Fresno Pacific University	M

SCIENCE EDUCATION
Fresno Pacific University	M

SECONDARY EDUCATION
Abilene Christian University	M
Campbell University	M

Eastern Nazarene College	M,O
Grand Canyon University	M
Olivet Nazarene University	M
Seattle Pacific University	M
Wheaton College (IL)	M†

SOCIAL SCIENCES EDUCATION
Campbell University	M

SOCIAL WORK
Roberts Wesleyan College	M

SOFTWARE ENGINEERING
Azusa Pacific University	M,O*†

SPECIAL EDUCATION
Azusa Pacific University	M†
California Baptist University	M
Calvin College	M
Eastern Nazarene College	M,O
Fresno Pacific University	M
Malone College	M
Whitworth College	M

SPEECH AND INTERPERSONAL COMMUNICATION
Abilene Christian University	M

SPORTS ADMINISTRATION
Whitworth College	M

TELECOMMUNICATIONS
Azusa Pacific University	M,O*†

THEOLOGY
Abilene Christian University	P,M
Anderson University	P,M,D
Azusa Pacific University	P,M,D†
Biola University	P,M,D
Campbell University	P,M
Eastern Mennonite University	P,M
George Fox University	P,M
Indiana Wesleyan University	M
The Master's College and Seminary	P,M
Mount Vernon Nazarene College	M
Nyack College	P,M
Oklahoma Christian University of Science and Arts	M
Olivet Nazarene University	M
Oral Roberts University	P,M,D
Hope International University	M
Palm Beach Atlantic College	M
Simpson College and Graduate School (CA)	M
Southern California College	M*
Southern Nazarene University	M
Trinity International University	P,M,D,O
Trinity Western University	P,M,D
Wheaton College (IL)	M,O†

VOCATIONAL AND TECHNICAL EDUCATION
California Baptist University	M

WRITING
Abilene Christian University	M

Study Abroad Index

ALBANIA
Eastern Mennonite University, VA

AMSTERDAM
Eastern Mennonite University, VA

ARGENTINA
Grace College, IN

AUSTRALIA
George Fox University, OR
Northwest Nazarene College, ID

AUSTRIA
Abilene Christian University, TX
Belhaven College, MS
Bethel College, KS
MidAmerica Nazarene University, KS
Oklahoma Christian University, OK
Oral Roberts University, OK

BELGIUM
Abilene Christian University, TX
Oral Roberts University, OK

BELIZE
Eastern Nazarene College, MA
George Fox University, OR
The King's University College, AB CANADA
Mount Vernon Nazarene College, OH
Trinity Western University, BC CANADA

BRAZIL
Grand Canyon University, AZ
Oklahoma Baptist University, OK
Oklahoma Christian University, OK

CANADA
Gordon College, MA

CHINA
Bethel College, IN
Biola University, CA
Californian Baptist University, CA
Eastern Mennonite University, VA
Geneva College, PA
Goshen College, IN
Grand Canyon University, AZ
Judson College, IL
Lee University, TN
Messiah College, PA
Northwest Nazarene College, ID
Northwestern College, MN
Oklahoma Baptist University, OK
Roberts Wesleyan College, NY
Southwest Baptist University, MO
Tabor College, KS
Taylor University, IN
Union University, TN
Wheaton College, IL
Whitworth College, WA

COLOMBIA
Eastern Mennonite University, VA

COMMONWEALTH OF INDEPENDENT STATES
Grand Canyon University, AZ

COSTA RICA
Asbury College, KY
Azusa Pacific University, CA
Bethel College, KS

Biola University, CA
Bluffton College, OH
Bryan College, TN
Calvin College, MI
Cedarville College, OH
Dordt College, IA
East Texas Baptist University, TX
Geneva College, PA
George Fox University, OR
Gordon College, MA
Goshen College, IN
Indiana Wesleyan University, IN
King College, TN
The King's University College, AB CANADA
Malone College, OH
The Master's College, CA
MidAmerica Nazarene University, KS
Mount Vernon Nazarene College, OH
North Park University, IL
Northwest Christian College, OR
Northwest College, WA
Northwestern College, IA
Northwestern College, MN
Northwest Nazarene College, ID
Nyack College, NY
Olivet Nazarene University, IL
Roberts Wesleyan College, NY
Seattle Pacific University, WA
Southern California College, CA
Southern Nazarene University, OK
Southern Wesleyan University, SC
Southwest Baptist University, MO
Tabor College, KS
Taylor University, IN
Trinity International University, IL
Trinity Western University, BC CANADA
Warner Pacific College, OR
Whitworth College, WA

CZECH REPUBLIC
Abilene Christian University, TX
Covenant College, GA

DOMINICAN REPUBLIC
Goshen College, IN

ECUADOR
Azusa Pacific University, CA
Bethel College, IN
Bethel College, KS
Californian Baptist University, CA
Messiah College, PA

EGYPT
Asbury College, KY
Biola University, CA
Bethel College, KS
Calvin College, MI
Geneva College, PA
George Fox University, OR
Gordon College, MA
King College, TN
The King's University College, AB CANADA
The Master's College, CA
Northwest Christian College, OR
Northwest College, WA
Northwestern College, MN
Nyack College, NY
Olivet Nazarene University, IL
Roberts Wesleyan College, NY
Simpson College, CA
Southern California College, CA
Southern Wesleyan University, SC
Southwest Baptist University, MO
Tabor College, KS
Taylor University, IN
Trinity International University, IL
Warner Pacific College, OR
Westmont College, CA

EL SALVADOR
MidAmerica Nazarene University, KS

ENGLAND
Abilene Christian University, TX
Asbury College, KY
Belhaven College, MS
Bethel College, KS
Bethel College, MN
Biola University, CA
Bryan College, TN
Calvin College, MI
Campbellsville University, KY
Dallas Baptist University, TX
East Texas Baptist University, TX
Eastern Mennonite University, VA
Eastern Nazarene College, MA
Erskine College, SC
Geneva College, PA
Gordon College, MA
Indiana Wesleyan University, IN
Judson College, IL
King College, TN
The King's University College, AB CANADA
Lee University, TN
The Master's College, CA
Messiah College, PA
Milligan College, TN
Northwest Christian College, OR
Northwestern College, MN
Northwest Nazarene College, ID
Nyack College, NY
Olivet Nazarene University, IL
Palm Beach Atlantic College, FL
Roberts Wesleyan College, NY
Seattle Pacific University, WA
Southern Nazarene University, OK
Southern Wesleyan University, SC
Southwest Baptist University, MO
Tabor College, KS

Taylor University, IN
Trinity International University, IL
Trinity Western University, BC CANADA
Warner Pacific College, OR
Westmont College, CA
Wheaton College, IL
Whitworth College, WA
Williams Baptist College, AR

FINLAND
Belhaven College, MS

FRANCE
Abilene Christian University, TX
Belhaven College, MS
Bethel College, KS
Campbellsville University, KY
Campbell University, NC
Eastern Mennonite University, VA
Eastern Nazarene College, MA
Erskine College, SC
Gordon College, MA
Grace College, IN
Grand Canyon University, AZ
King College, TN
Messiah College, PA
Northwestern College, IA
Olivet Nazarene University, IL
Oral Roberts University, OK
Redeemer College, ON CANADA
Seattle Pacific University, WA
Taylor University, IN
Westmont College, CA
Wheaton College, IL
Whitworth College, WA

GERMANY
Abilene Christian University, TX
Belhaven College, MS
Bethel College, KS
Bethel College, MN

Calvin College, MI
Dordt College, IA
Eastern Mennonite University, VA
Eastern Nazarene College, MA
George Fox University, OR
Gordon College, MA
Goshen College, IN
Grace College, IN
Grand Canyon University, AZ
King College, TN
Lee University, TN
Messiah College, PA
MidAmerica Nazarene University, KS
Oral Roberts University, OK
Seattle Pacific University, WA
Wheaton College, IL
Whitworth College, WA

GHANA
Eastern Mennonite University, VA

GREECE
Bethel College, KS
George Fox University, OR
Messiah College, PA
Oral Roberts University, OK

GUATEMALA
Abilene Christian University, TX
Bluffton College, OH
Eastern Mennonite University, VA
Malone College, OH
MidAmerica Nazarene University, KS
Warner Pacific College, OR
Whitworth College, WA

HONDURAS
Calvin College, MI
MidAmerica Nazarene University, KS
Warner Pacific College, OR

Westmont College, CA
Whitworth College, WA

HUNGARY
Calvin College, MI
Grand Canyon University, AZ
Oklahoma Baptist University, OK

INDIA
Bethel College, KS

INDONESIA
Goshen College, IN
Roberts Wesleyan College, NY

IRELAND
Bluffton College, OH
Trinity Western University, BC CANADA

ISRAEL
Abilene Christian University, TX
Asbury College, KY
Azusa Pacific University, CA
Bethel College, IN
Bethel College, MN
Biola University, CA
Bryan College, TN
Campbellsville University, KY
Cedarville College, OH
Eastern Mennonite University, VA
Geneva College, PA
George Fox University, OR
Gordon College, MA
Indiana Wesleyan University, IN
King College, TN
The King's University College, AB CANADA
Mount Vernon Nazarene College, OH
Northwestern College, MN
Nyack College, NY
Simpson College, CA
Southern California College, CA
Taylor University, IN

Peterson's Christian Colleges & Universities

Trinity International University, IL
Trinity Western University, BC CANADA
Westmont College, CA
Wheaton College, IL
Whitworth College, WA

ITALY

Gordon College, MA
Indiana Wesleyan University, IN
MidAmerica Nazarene University, KS
Oral Roberts University, OK

IVORY COAST

Eastern Mennonite University, VA
Goshen College, IN

JAMAICA

Eastern Mennonite University, VA

JAPAN

Abilene Christian University, TX
Azusa Pacific University, CA
Biola University, CA
Eastern Mennonite University, VA
Messiah College, PA
North Park University, IL
Northwestern College, MN
Oklahoma Baptist University, OK
Oklahoma Christian University, OK
University of Sioux Falls, SD
Wheaton College, IL

JORDAN

Eastern Mennonite University, VA

KENYA

Bethel College, MN
George Fox University, OR
Gordon College, MA
Seattle Pacific University, WA
Taylor University, IN

KOREA

Biola University, CA
Eastern Mennonite University, VA
Whitworth College, WA

LIECHTENSTEIN

MidAmerica Nazarene University, KS

LITHUANIA

Grand Canyon University, AZ
Taylor University, IN

MEXICO

Abilene Christian University, TX
Azusa Pacific University, CA
Bluffton College, OH
Campbell University, NC
Dordt College, IA
Eastern Mennonite University, VA
Grand Canyon University, AZ
King College, TN
MidAmerica Nazarene University, KS
North Park University, IL
Wheaton College, IL
Whitworth College, WA

THE NETHERLANDS

Belhaven College, MS
Calvin College, MI
College of the Ozarks, MO
Dordt College, IA
King College, TN
The King's University College, AB CANADA
Northwestern College, IA
Oral Roberts University, OK
Trinity Christian College, IL

NEW ZEALAND

George Fox University, OR

NICARAGUA

Bluffton College, OH
Eastern Mennonite University, VA
Whitworth College, WA

NORWAY
North Park University, IL

PANAMA
MidAmerica Nazarene University, KS

POLAND
Bluffton College, OH

ROMANIA
Eastern Nazarene College, MA

RUSSIA
Abilene Christian University, TX
Asbury College, KY
Belhaven College, MS
Biola University, CA
Bryan College, TN
Californian Baptist University, CA
Calvin College, MI
Dordt College, IA
East Texas Baptist University, TX
Geneva College, PA
George Fox University, OR
Gordon College, MA
Grace College, IN
Indiana Wesleyan University, IN
King College, TN
The King's University College, AB CANADA
The Master's College, CA
North Park University, IL
Northwest Christian College, OR
Northwest College, WA
Northwestern College, MN
Northwest Nazarene College, ID
Nyack College, NY
Oklahoma Baptist University, OK
Olivet Nazarene University, IL
Roberts Wesleyan College, NY
Seattle Pacific University, WA
Southern California College, CA

Southern Wesleyan University, SC
Southwest Baptist University, MO
Tabor College, KS
Taylor University, IN
Trinity International University, IL
Trinity Western University, BC CANADA
Union University, TN
Warner Pacific College, OR
Wheaton College, IL

SCOTLAND
Erskine College, SC

SOUTH AFRICA
Westmont College, CA

SOUTH KOREA
King College, TN
Montreat College, NC
Wheaton College, IL

SPAIN
Abilene Christian University, TX
Bethel College, KS
Calvin College, MI
Eastern Nazarene College, MA
Erskine College, SC
Grand Canyon University, AZ
King College, TN
The Master's College, CA
Messiah College, PA
Northwestern College, IA
Oklahoma Baptist University, OK
Olivet Nazarene University, IL
Oral Roberts University, OK
Seattle Pacific University, WA
Southwest Baptist University, MO
Taylor University, IN
Trinity Christian College, IL
Union University, TN

Westmont College, CA
Wheaton College, IL

SWEDEN
Bethel College, MN
North Park University, IL
Taylor University, IN

SWITZERLAND
Belhaven College, MS
Eastern Nazarene College, MA
MidAmerica Nazarene University, KS
Oral Roberts University, OK

TAIWAN
Azusa Pacific University, CA
Seattle Pacific University, WA

TANZANIA
Houghton College, NY

UKRAINE
Lee University, TN

UNITED KINGDOM
Houghton College, NY

UNITED STATES
The King's University College, AB CANADA
Redeemer College, ON CANADA
Trinity International University, IL
Trinity Western University, BC CANADA

URUGUAY
Oklahoma Christian University, OK